SOCIAL REALITY AND THE EARLY CHRISTIANS

GERD THEISSEN

SOCIAL REALITY
and the
EARLY CHRISTIANS

◆

Theology, Ethics, and the World of the New Testament

Translated by
Margaret Kohl

FORTRESS PRESS
MINNEAPOLIS

SOCIAL REALITY AND THE EARLY CHRISTIANS
Theology, Ethics, and the World of the New Testament

First English-language edition published 1992 by Fortress Press.
Translated from the German by Margaret Kohl.

Chapters 1, 2, 3, 4, 6, and 8 were published in *Studien zur Soziologie des Urchristentums*, by Gerd Theissen. Copyright 1979, 1983 by Gerd Theissen/J. C. B. Mohr (Paul Siebeck), Tübingen, Germany. Chapter 5 was published in the German language in *Kerygma und Dogma* 20 (1974), 282–304. Translated by permission of Vandenhoeck & Ruprecht, Göttingen, Germany. The introduction and chapters 7 and 9 are published here for the first time.

Cover design: Lecy Design
Cover art: Alinari/Art Resource, NY: Brogi9598 Interior of a material shop. Uffizi, Florence
Interior design: The HK Scriptorium, Inc.

Library of Congress Cataloging-in-Publication Data

Theissen, Gerd.
   [Studien zur Soziologie des Urchristentums. English]
   Social reality and the early Christians : Theology, ethics, and the world of the New Testament / Gerd Theissen ; translated by Margaret Kohl.
      p.   cm.
   Translation of: Studien zur Soziologie des Urchristentums.
   Includes bibliographical references and index.
   ISBN 0-8006-2560-9 (alk. paper)
   1. Sociology, Christian — History — Early church, ca. 30–600.
I. Title
BR166.T4813   1992
270.1 — dc20   92-8495
                                         CIP

Manufactured in the U.S.A.   1-2560

96   95   94   93   92   1   2   3   4   5   6   7   8   9   10

Contents

◆

17.67

v

86122

PART II
STUDIES ON PAULINE THEOLOGY
AND THE SOCIAL REALITY OF THE FIRST CENTURY

PART III
STUDIES ON EARLY CHRISTIANITY
AND THE SOCIAL REALITY OF THE FIRST CENTURY

Preface

———————◆———————

Are there correlations between the theological and ethical convictions of the first Christians and the social realities of the world in which they lived? This is the question prompting the essays gathered together in this volume. It is a question for the sociology of knowledge. It takes up form criticism's inquiry about the *Sitz im Leben* of the early Christian texts — their real-life situation — but it expands that inquiry, so as to ask about the significance of early Christian convictions in society as a whole.

The introductory chapter, "Sociological Research into the New Testament: Some Ideas Offered by the Sociology of Knowledge for a New Exegetical Approach," surveys sociological research into the New Testament up to the present day. Its purpose is to show that research during the last hundred years into the social reality of early Christianity has always been to some degree determined by the social reality of the interpreters themselves — the part they played in society, scholarship, and the church. Here the sociological method is applied to sociological research itself.

The other essays investigate the center of the New Testament itself: the relationship to Jesus. In the writings that have come down to us, this relationship assumes two different forms: discipleship of the earthly Jesus and faith in the kerygmatic Christ. The discipleship of Jesus is described in the Synoptic Gospels, where it is linked with a radical ethic of homelessness, hostility to family ties, and contempt for possessions. Faith in the crucified and risen Christ, on the other hand, is to be found preeminently in Paul. This faith is linked with a radical concept of redemption — the conviction that a person is transformed from a sinner into a new being (although the ethic of the Pauline epistles is more moderate than that of the Synoptics). The purpose of these studies is to show that these different forms of relationship to Jesus are molded by social conditions, so that there is in fact a correlation between social life and discipleship, or faith.

In spite of all these differences between the Synoptics and Paul, sociologically they have one common denominator. The relationship to Jesus, or to the kerygmatic Christ as the case may be, is always linked with mobility in real social life. But this mobility varies in character.

In the Synoptics we find the mobility of "wandering charismatics": the radical ethic of the Synoptic tradition is the ethic of people who have left house and home. That is the thesis of the first study, "The Wandering Radicals." The homeless existence of these first followers of Jesus was partly conditioned by a widespread crisis in first-century Palestine. This is considered in the second essay, "'We have left everything . . .' (Mark 10:28)." In this crisis, tensions between the city of Jerusalem and its hinterland made themselves felt, and these are investigated in "Jesus' Temple Prophecy." Jesus and the Jesus movement confront all these tensions and conflicts with the command to love our enemies. This has undoubtedly a general reference, but it was originally related to specific social conflicts and tensions in the Palestine of the time. This is shown in the study "Nonviolence and Love of Our Enemies (Matt. 5:38-48; Luke 6:27-38."

In Paul, the relation to Christ was marked by different forms of human mobility. Our starting point here is the observation that his images of redemption are drawn partly from social experience and partly from the natural world. The study "Soteriological Symbolism in the Pauline Writings" shows that there is a hidden logic in these images. They describe the transformation of men and women in "sociomorphic" images, as liberation, justification, and reconciliation, and in "physiomorphic" images as change of form, dying with Jesus, and union with him. The essay that follows, "Christology and Social Experience," explores the social dynamic behind these images. Compared with the societies that preceded it, Roman-Hellenistic civilization offered more opportunities for social rise and decline. In the real world of that society, loyalty to an earthly master was the normal way up the social ladder — though certainly for only a few. In contrast, through the bond with the one Lord "Jesus Christ," early Christianity offered everyone opportunities for a change for the better and made these opportunities experienceable for everyone in the congregation.

Apart from the dynamic of social rise and decline (in which the frontier dividing "above" from "below" was crossed), we see a second form of social mobility in Paul too; for in Paul early Christianity throws itself open to Gentiles. It is therefore seized by a dynamic that crosses the

frontiers of in-group and out-group; and the most important instrument in this transition is faith — the personal, charismatic relation to
Christ. Paul makes this "faith" the principle of the new religion, setting
it over against the Jewish mother religion, which he thinks is characterized by "works." The essay "Judaism and Christianity in Paul" purposes
to show how through this antithesis between faith and works two
religions with different authority structures develop in Paul, the one
structure being charismatic, the other legalistic. And the charismatic
structure of early Christianity offered particularly favorable opportunities for overcoming social disadvantage.

If correlations are probable for the center of the early Christian
religion (the relation to Jesus Christ), then this suggests that a comprehensive sociological theory should be developed for early Christianity
as a whole. The last two essays have this purpose. The first, "Sociological
Theories of Religion and the Analysis of Early Christianity," outlines
the program for a comprehensive interpretation of this kind and pleads
for a pluralism of theoretical approaches. The final essay, "Some Ideas
about a Sociological Theory of Early Christianity," pursues the program.
Early Christianity is interpreted from three theoretical angles: from the
perspectives of phenomenology, integration theory, and the theory of
conflict. It appears as an innovatory movement that is determined by
a new experience of the holy — with radical consequences for the conduct of the first Christians and for their social relationships. The new
religion spread in corners of Roman-Hellenistic society where integration was insufficient, and here it stood in latent rivalry to the upper
class. Christianity represented a deviating minority, which especially
stressed its *conformity* with the world around at points where it shared
the ethical standards of that world. There was even a tendency to outbid this consensus: the Christian minority did not merely want to be
good; it wanted to be better — to be exemplary. In this way, both through
deviation and through excellence, the first Christians displayed an
aristocratic turn of mind without being people of aristocratic origin.
As outsiders claiming to be "the light of the world," they were rejected
by the world around them and were exposed to pressure and persecution.

The essays collected in the present volume therefore have to do first
of all with the center of the early Christian faith: the relationship to
Jesus. Their second focus is early Christianity as a whole. They start
from the awareness that research into early Christianity does not take
place in a vacuum. It is part of the social self-knowledge of the
investigating scholars themselves.

For that very reason, the essays have an ethical and a practical concern.
If the social dimension of Christian faith and action emerges of itself

from the biblical texts (if they are read without prejudice) and if this reading, as a consistent extension of historical-critical concern with the Bible, conforms to the rigorous standards of modern research, then the social responsibility of Christians will be firmly rooted in the center of the Christian faith: in the Bible. More important, therefore, than any given sociological hypothesis about the biblical texts is the awareness that the basic texts of the Christian faith do at all events have a social dimension. We can sometimes discern this dimension clearly, sometimes less well; but it is always present. The essays presented here hope to make a contribution along these lines, so that Christians can perceive their social responsibility more clearly in the light of biblical texts.

All the studies were written during the last twenty years. Some of them gave rise to intensive discussion. For that reason they are printed here in the form in which they made their original impact on research.

I should like to express particular thanks to Margaret Kohl for her meticulous translation into English, and to the staff of Fortress Press for their care in preparing this and other work for publication.

Gerd Theissen
Heidelberg, March 1991

Translator's Note

Biblical quotations have been taken from the Revised Standard Version of the Bible, except where changes of wording were required in order to bring out the precise nuance of the German text. Where English translations of books referred to exist, references to these have been given as far as possible, but in many cases quotations have been translated directly from the German. The absence in the relevant note of a page reference to the English translation will make this clear.

I should like to express my thanks to Professor Theissen for his patient help in answering questions and elucidating difficulties.

Margaret Kohl

Abbreviations

———◆———

Angelos	*Angelos.* Archiv für neutestamentliche Zeitgeschichte und Kulturkunde, Leipzig, 1925–32
ANRW	*Aufstieg und Niedergang der römischen Welt,* ed. H. Temporini, Berlin and New York, 1972– (polyglott: German, English and French)
ASNU	Acta Seminarii Neotestamentici Upsaliensis, Uppsala
ASTI	*Annual of the Swedish Theological Institute* (in Jerusalem), Leiden
AV	Authorized Version of the Bible (1611: King James Version)
BHTh	Beiträge zur historischen Theologie, Tübingen
Bibl	*Biblica,* Rome
BiLe	*Bibel und Leben,* Düsseldorf
BZ	*Biblische Zeitschrift,* Paderborn
BZNW	Beihefte zur Zeitschrift für die neutestamentliche Wissenschaft, Berlin, etc.
CB.NT	Coniectanea biblica — New Testament series, Lund
CBQ	*Catholic Biblical Quarterly,* Washington D.C.
CD	Damascus Document
CIJ	*Corpus inscriptionum Judaicarum,* Vatican City, 1936–52
CPJ	*Corpus papyrorum Judaicarum,* Cambridge, Mass., 1957ff.
CRINT	Compendia Rerum Iudaicarum ad Novum Testamentum, Assen and Minneapolis (previously Philadelphia)
DLZ	*Deutsche Literaturzeitung,* Berlin

EphLov	*Ephemerides theologicae Lovanienses,*Louvain, 1924–
FRLANT	Forschungen zur Religion und Literatur des Alten und Neuen Testaments, Göttingen
FThL	Forum Theologiae Linguisticae, Bonn
GGA	*Göttingische gelehrte Anzeigen,* Göttingen
Gymnasium	*Gymnasium, Zeitschrift für Kultur der Antike und humanistische Bildung,* Heidelberg
Hermes	*Hermes. Zeitschrift für klassische Philologie,* Wiesbaden
HNT	Handbuch zum Neuen Testament, Tübingen
HNT Erg.-Bd.	Handbuch zum Neuen Testament, Tübingen, Ergänzungsband
HThK	Herders theologischer Kommentar zum Neuen Testament, Freiburg, 1953–
HThR	*Harvard Theological Review*
HZ	*Historische Zeitschrift,* Munich
IEJ	*Israel Exploration Journal,* Jerusalem
IG	*Inscriptiones Graecae,* Berlin 1873ff.
IJRS	*Internationales Jahrbuch für Religionssoziologie,* Cologne
Interpretation	*Interpretation. A Journal of Bible and Theology,* Richmond, Virginia
JAC	*Jahrbuch für Antike und Christentum,* Münster
JBL	*Journal of Biblical Literature,* Atlanta
JESHO	*Journal of the Economic and Social History of the Orient,* Leiden
JR	*Journal of Religion,* Chicago
JRH	*Journal of Religious History,* Sydney
JRS	*Journal of Roman Studies,* London
JSJ	*Journal of the Study of Judaism in the Persian, Hellenistic and Roman Period,* Leiden
JThS	*Journal of Theological Studies,* Oxford
Kairos	*Kairos: Zeitschrift für Religionswissenschaft und Theologie,* Salzburg
KEK	Kritisch-exegetischer Kommentar über das Neue Testament, Göttingen
Klio	*Klio: Beiträge zur alten Geschichte,* Leipzig, etc.
KZSS	*Kölner Zeitschrift für Soziologie,* Sonderheft, Cologne
MS.SNT	Monograph Series, Society for New Testament Studies, Cambridge
NF	Neue Folge
NovTest	*Novum Testamentum,* Leiden
NTA	Neutestamentliche Abhandlungen, Münster

NTS	*New Testament Studies*
Numen	*Numen: International Review for the History of Religions,* Leiden
NZSysThR	*Neue Zeitschrift für systematische Theologie und Religionsphilosophie,* Berlin
OGIS	*Orientis Graeci Inscriptiones selectae,* ed. W. Dittenberger, 2 vols., 1903–05
PEQ	*Palestine Exploration Quarterly,* London
PL	*Patrologia cursus completus,* ed. J. P. Migne, Series Latina, Paris, 1941ff.
PW	*Real-Encyclopädie der classischen Altertumswissenschaft,* ed. A. F. von Pauly, rev. G. Wissowa et al., 33 vols., Stuttgart, 1893–1972 (Pauly-Wissowa)
4QFlor	Florilegium; Sammlung Eschatologischer Midraschim, in E. Lohse, *Die Texte aus Qumran* (Darmstadt, 1964) 269–75
1QM	The Scroll of the War of the Sons of Light against the Sons of Darkness (*War Scroll*)
1QMyst	Livre des Mystères, in D. Barthélemy and J. T. Milik, *Discoveries in the Judaean Desert I* (Oxford, 1955), 102–7
1QpHab	Habakkuk Commentary
4QpPs37	Midrasch zu Psalm 37, in E. Lohse, *Die Texte aus Qumran* (Darmstadt, 1964) 269–75
1QS	*Manual of Discipline*
1QSa	Rule of the Whole Congregation of Israel at the End of Days (second part of Rule Scroll)
1QSb	Benedictions (third part of Rule Scroll)
RAC	*Reallexikon für Antike und Christentum,* ed. T. Klauser, Stuttgart, 1950ff.
Saeculum	*Saeculum: Jahrbuch für Universalgeschichte,* Munich
SBS	Stuttgarter Bibelstudien, Stuttgart
Semeia	*Semeia: An Experimental Journal for Biblical Criticism,* Atlanta
StTh	*Studia Theologica,* Lund, etc.
StUNT	Studien zur Umwelt des Neuen Testaments, Göttingen
Suppl NovTest	*Novum Testamentum,* supplement, Leiden
TB	Theologische Bücherei, Munich
TDNT	*Theological Dictionary of the New Testament* (trans. of *ThWNT* by G. W. Bromiley), Grand Rapids and London, 1964–76.

ThBl	*Theologische Blätter,* Leipzig
ThEx	Theologische Existenz heute, Munich
ThHNT	Theologischer Handkommentar zum Neuen Testament, Leipzig, Berlin, 1928ff.
ThLZ	*Theologische Literaturzeitung,* Leipzig
ThStKr	*Theologische Studien und Kritiken,* Hamburg, etc.
ThW	Theologische Wissenschaft, Suttgart, etc.
ThWNT	*Theologisches Wörterbuch zum Neuen Testament,* ed. G. Kittel et al., Stuttgart, 1933–79
ThZ	*Theologische Zeitschrift,* Basel
TS	*Theological Studies,* Baltimore
TU	Texte und Untersuchungen, Berlin, etc.
WdF	Wege der Forschung, Darmstadt
WMANT	Wissenschaftliche Monographien zum Alten und Neuen Testament, Neukirchen-Vluyn
WUNT	Wissenschaftliche Untersuchungen zum Neuen Testament, Tübingen
ZDPV	*Zeitschrift des deutschen Palästina-Vereins,* Wiesbaden
ZNW	*Zeitschrift für die neutestamentliche Wissenschaft,* Berlin
ZThK	*Zeitschrift für Theologie und Kirche,* Tübingen
ZWTh	*Zeitschrift für wissenschaftliche Theologie,* Jena, etc.

Sociological Research into the New Testament

◆

Some Ideas Offered by the Sociology of Knowledge for a New Exegetical Approach

W HEN WE CONSIDER the social history of the early Christian communities, the *object* of our research is a tiny religious subculture in the ancient world of the first and second centuries. The determining *subjects* of this kind of research, however — the people who pursue it — belong to a tiny "exegetical subculture"in modern society. We might therefore describe sociological exegesis as a specific form of encounter between two subcultures that are very different from each other in their social structure. On the one hand, we have a movement deeply rooted in the lower classes of society; on the other, men and women who may be described as middle or upper class. On the one hand, we see a religious minority, deviating from the general religious consensus; on the other, representatives of a religion that — in spite of an advanced secularization — our society acknowledges to be the common origin from which it springs. Here we have a charismatic movement; there (in Germany at least) civil servants* who are the intellectual administrators of the Christian faith rather than the inspiring source of new ideas about that faith.

Yet in spite of all these differences, there is a profound link between the two subcultures. For the writings of that ancient Christian subculture are not merely the object of research for our modern exegetical subculture: they also provide its fundamental legitimation. More indeed, they enjoy legitimating force in the church and even in society as a whole. If sociological research applies its own methods to itself, it will have

---

* [Translator's note: Universities in Germany are state financed.]

to presume from the very outset that there will prove to be an intimate connection between the history of the modern exegetical subculture itself and the rise and development of sociohistorical exegesis. In what I am about to say I should like to make readers at least aware of this connection. I shall be unable to clarify it completely, for no one can ever fully survey the stream in which he himself is swimming. But as long as he still keeps his head above water, he will go on trying to discover how the river flows and where its dangers lie. To abandon the metaphor: knowledge is always an interplay between the knower and the object of knowledge. This means among other things that knowledge never merely reflects the social world of the investigators and is never exclusively the "objective" reproduction of the object they desire to know. It is worthwhile creating a greater open-mindedness toward the object by thinking about one's own cognitive situation. For we are quite well able to arrive at insights that run counter to the trends of our own social world.

The exegetical subculture of the last hundred years has assigned three different roles and social contexts to the people belonging to it. And this means that those concerned have often been exposed to contradictory expectations.

In the first place, as university teachers they are members of the bourgeoisie, the middle class; and the social developments of the last hundred years have confronted this class with a great many challenges. In Germany, one of the greatest of these challenges was the fascist attack on liberal forms of rule. This plunged bourgeois culture into a profound crisis and permanently changed society. This change was bound up with problems that are still unsolved today: the challenge to economic rule through the labor movement; the sweeping-aside of imperialist domination by the nations of "the Third World"; and the breakdown of patriarchal rule in the family. It is probable on the face of it that we shall find the history of the middle classes, and the deadlocks in which they are involved, reflected in the history of sociological exegesis.

Second, in their function as scholars, the expounders of texts are members of the universities. The scientific or scholarly methods that are also applied to the investigation of social history are forms of socialization in scientific or scholarly institutions. They are the rules of dialogue for a rational handling of problems, rules that are based on long experience and which help to decide about the themes to be preferred, and about permissible arguments and plausible interpretations. So the general methodological development is an important factor in the history of sociological interpretation; and this is especially true in the relationship between the study of history and sociology.

Third, and not least: the interpreters are theologians. They form a leading group in the modern churches, with whose history their own history is closely linked. In a scientific society, they are also among the members of the church who have a decisive responsibility for the church's communication with society as a whole. Changes in the relationship between society and the church, as well as trends within the churches themselves, will play an important part in the development of a socio-logical exegesis.

We might therefore say that the exegetical subculture has three roles. The people belonging to it are at once members of the civic commu-nity, scholars, and theologians. As a rule, even today, these people are men, and men belonging to the industrial countries of the West, though this will no doubt change in the future. How, then, did this modern subculture come to investigate the life and writings of an ancient sub-culture as a social phenomenon? This is by no means a matter of course. On the contrary, three phases can clearly be distinguished in the history of sociological exegesis. This kind of interpretation grew up in the heyday of liberal theology (ca. 1870–1920), faded into the background almost entirely in Germany in the era of dialectical theology (ca. 1920–1970) and has had a renaissance in the last fifteen years, under new presup-positions. A history of sociological exegesis has to interpret these three successive phases, as well as the fact that outside Germany things developed differently.

I should like to put forward here a few preliminary reflections for a history of this kind. They will concentrate on the course of events in the German-speaking world and will show how, in recent times, these have become increasingly interwoven with international and ecumenical developments in the church, in theology, and in society.

A. THE GROWTH OF SOCIOLOGICAL EXEGESIS
IN THE ERA OF THEOLOGICAL LIBERALISM, 1870–1920

Whenever the history of society is considered worth studying scien-tifically (and not only the history of kings and countries), this is a sign that a society is aware that it has a value of its own, which is independent of governmental direction or manipulation. Research into social history is therefore almost always linked with an actively critical attitude toward the traditional authorities of the state (and the church). This kind of research grew up at a time when a liberal middle class was investigating the history of past societies, in order to satisfy itself of its independent identity, over against state and church.

These critical impulses are evident also in the rise of sociological exegesis at the end of the last century.[1] In the nineteenth century, the

---

1. I may mention two books on church history in modern times that take into account

new independent stance of society over against the old authorities made itself felt in the struggle for new constitutions in state and church— although in Germany liberalism was unable to prevail at that time, in either the political or the ecclesiastical sphere. The new independent attitude also emerged in the burgeoning of clubs and associations, in which people could pursue their personal, self-appointed goals. Finally, it showed itself in an increased scope for dissent, both political and religious. How far were these three developments important for the history of exegesis?

The historical-critical method of exegesis was undoubtedly one way through which the liberal middle classes achieved freedom from the tutelage of dogma. It was out of this tradition that, at the end of the century, Hermann Gunkel (1862–1932) developed "form criticism." This method was able to show that biblical texts do not merely express theological concepts and are not simply the utterances of authoritative individuals; they reflect the faith of simple men and women, and their common life. The situation, the *Sitz im Leben*, from which the Bible springs is the life of the people. The Bible can be read "from below."

What theological liberalism strove for in the exegetical field, by anchoring the texts in "the life of the people," it tried to achieve in church politics by pressing for a "popular" church (a *Volkskirche* as they called it) to replace the state church controlled from above. Attempts to strengthen the presbyterial or synodal element in the constitutions of the German churches and the attention paid to social context in the exegesis of biblical texts are two aspects of the same intention. On November 14, 1918, after the collapse of the old authorities in the First World War, Martin Rade called for "popular church councils" to be set up, and he was supported by Martin Dibelius, who was the founder of New Testament form criticism.[2] Anyone who was accustomed to see the New Testament as the literature of little unimportant people—people belonging to the lower middle classes—could assent with the utmost conviction to a church that was neither guided nor supported from above.

The struggle for new constitutions in church and state is only one expression of liberal strivings in the nineteenth century. Parallel to these was the blossoming of clubs and associations. The structures of the national church were not equal to the new tasks facing it in charitable

---

the connection between society, church, and theology: H. W. Krumwiede, *Geschichte des Christentums, III: Neuzeit: 17. bis 20. Jahrhundert* (Stuttgart, 1977); and M. Greschat, *Das Zeitalter der Industriellen Revolution, Christentum und Gesellschaft* (Stuttgart, 1980).

2. See Krumwiede, *Geschichte*, 192.

work and missionary activity. Associations grew up in which civic and Christian initiatives could develop more freely. These were not always in harmony with the traditional churches. It is not by chance that one of the first studies in social history was devoted to the question whether the early Christian congregations were organized in the form of "associations" (G. Heinrici).[3] If the early church itself was a society or an association, then this form of contemporary church activity was not merely legitimate; it was actually more in accordance with the essence of Christianity than the state church. Rudolph Sohm's plea for "spirit" as against "law," and for the charismatically organized congregations of the early years instead of the legally constituted Catholicism of the patristic period,[4] also had liberal criticism of the church as its premise. The reconstruction of the constitutional history of the early church was one way by which the contemporary church arrived at an understanding of its own identity.

Last but not least, liberalism meant a plea for the liberty to dissent, in religious matters. It was therefore among other things the expression of an increasing secularization, which for the first time gave more and more groups of people a real opportunity to decide openly against the Christian faith. It is true that at the end of the nineteenth century society still viewed itself as Christian. To dissolve one's ties with the church could still be seen as a deviation from the norm. But it was impossible to ignore the fact that Christianity had to compete with other convictions embodied in different systems. People were nevertheless confident of Christianity's persuasive, radiating power, provided that it was rightly interpreted. Adolf von Harnack's book *The Mission and Expansion of Christianity* (1902; Eng. trans. by James Moffatt, 1904–1905) was a work of fundamental importance for the social history of the early Christian communities, but it can also be read as a historical verification of that conviction: if in its early days the Christian faith spread without any compulsion, simply because of its intrinsic superiority, why should this not be possible at the present day as well?

But work on social history was not limited to the context of the progressive liberal purposes I have described. The same liberal middle class that was so critical toward the authorities of state and church changed from the offensive to the defensive where the labor movement was concerned. The Bible was still one of the legitimating foundations of society.

---

3. G. Heinrici, "Die Christengemeinde Korinths und die religiösen Genossenschaften der Griechen," *ZWTh* 19 (1876): 465–562.

4. R. Sohm, *Kirchenrecht* (Munich and Leipzig, 1892); see also his *Wesen und Ursprung des Katholizismus* (Leipzig, 1909).

Biblical exegesis could become the arena for a legitimation conflict about the proper form society ought to take. And this was especially the case when biblical exegesis drew on social history.

Marxist philosophy had given the labor movement a legitimation basis that was independent of religion. It was only occasionally that the movement appealed to the Bible. When it did so, it was in order to show that the Scriptures could not be used to legitimate bourgeois society. This intention is evident in Friedrich Engels's article "On the History of Primitive Christianity" ("Zur Geschichte des Urchristentums," 1894–95), in which early Christianity and the communist movement are presented as parallels: both were proletarian movements and both were persecuted; and the two are intrinsically related. The message is plain: the road from the New Testament leads to socialism. Karl Kautsky spread this message further in *Foundations of Christianity* (1908; Eng. trans. 1925). The labor movement, not the Christian "bourgeoisie," appeared to be the legitimate heir of primitive Christianity.

Theological attempts to find a social ethic based on the Bible have an apologetic character in comparison. Their aim is to show that present-day social questions can be solved in the framework of a biblical ethic — that is to say, within the bounds of a socially accepted paradigm. These social questions are not a compelling reason for abandoning this time-tested paradigm in favor of new Marxist and social-democratic answers. Gerhard Uhlhorn's book *Christian Charity in the Ancient Church* (1882; Eng. trans. 1883) can be read in this sense. Uhlhorn's thesis is that in ancient times Christianity brought love into a loveless world and that it is capable of solving present-day social questions in the same way. In his book we find social history as the background music for the Innere Mission — the charitable organization that was the German Protestant churches' response to early industrialism in the first half of the nineteenth century.

Concern about social questions took on new form in the Evangelisch-Sozialer Kongress (from 1890 on), which may be interpreted as the churches' answer to the second phase of industrialization, which followed at the end of the century.[5] Here people tried to arrive at a sociological analysis of contemporary problems. Historical work was really marginal. But it is worth mentioning that one of the lastingly influential contributions to the social history of the early church was first expounded at the Evangelisch-Sozialer Kongress in Dessau in 1908. This was Adolf Deissmann's "Das Urchristentum und die unteren Schichten" ("Primitive

---

5. See G. Kretschmar, *Der Evangelisch-Soziale Kongress* (Stuttgart, 1972). He gives an account of all the members (pp. 115ff.), which include A. von Harnack, A. Deissmann, A. von Soden, G. Troeltsch, and M. Weber, and also lists the subjects treated.

Christianity and the Lower Classes"). Here a New Testament scholar showed that the early congregations came from the very sections of society that were now threatening to drift away from the church altogether. Implicitly, the lecture has an unambiguous message: commitment to the problems of the lower classes is completely in line with the original intention and history of Christianity in its earliest form.

It should now have become clear that when biblical scholars began to ask these questions about social history they were doing so as members of their own society and as theologians of their own church. But they also raised these questions as historians. Developments in the field of scholarship itself had allowed a climate to develop that favored a social-history approach.[6] At that time, many disciplines viewed themselves as historical, or were deeply influenced by "historical schools." This was true of law and economics, but it also applied to linguistic and religious studies and to theology. Cultural and social life as a whole was subjected to a historical viewpoint. The demand for a comprehensive study of history was in the air. Karl Lamprecht formulated this demand around the turn of the century in the form of a sharp attack on the traditional approach, which concentrated on political history and biography.[7] He had visions of a cultural history that would include economic and social affairs, as well as factors of social psychology. In Germany, the debate that he provoked ended in an almost unanimous rejection of this program by professional historians. They continued to cling to the primacy of (foreign) policy and to concentrate on great statesmen. In my view, this concentration reflects a disheartening aspect of German life. Liberal members of the middle classes waived any extension of democracy in the sphere of home affairs in favor of a strong national policy based on a powerful state. And people were prepared to let this policy be worked out by authoritarian exponents of *Realpolitik*.

It was therefore not so much the professional historians who pushed forward social history in Germany. It was rather scholars belonging to other fields, who were pursuing their disciplines historically but were guided in the process by systematic questions. Interdisciplinary collaboration developed among these experts, the cooperation between Max Weber and Ernst Troeltsch being of fundamental importance. The two men lived in Heidelberg, in the same house, and they influenced each other mutually. The crown of the social history written by liberal

---

6. On the development of social history in the framework of historical studies in general, see H. U. Wehler, *Geschichte als historische Sozialwissenschaft* (Frankfurt, 1973); J. Kocka, *Sozialgeschichte* (Göttingen, 1977); also P. Burke, *Sociology and History* (London and Boston: Allen & Unwin, 1980).

7. See K. Lamprecht, *Alte und neue Richtungen in der Geschichtswissenschaft* (Berlin, 1896).

theologians was Troeltsch's *Die Soziallehren der christlichen Kirchen und Gruppen* (1912; Eng. trans. *The Social Teaching of the Christian Churches,* 1931).[8] This book was profoundly influenced by the practical concerns of a Christian middle class that was deeply concerned about the question: Can the social teachings of Christianity provide the foundation for a modern social ethic? But the question did not preempt the answer, for the answer was on the whole skeptical. Here scholarly work emancipated itself from the practical need that prompted it. For that very reason Troeltsch's work is illuminating even today. It drives home the lesson that Christians have to accept responsibility for their own answers to social questions.

The beginning of research into the social history of early Christianity therefore reflects the social situation of its interpreters in a number of different ways. We can see a close link with liberal Protestantism's critical attitude toward the authorities of church and state. But at the same time we detect an apologetic tendency in the dispute with the labor movement and Marxism. But for all that, the beginnings are not solely an expression of this social situation. There was a tendency for the various scholarly disciplines to view all cultural and social phenomena from a historical perspective. And this led to scholarly achievements of lasting value.

All in all, it must be stressed that social history was a subsidiary theme. The primary concerns of theological liberalism were different and were concentrated on the religious personality, the conscience, and the relationship to God.[9] Social responsibility was a matter for the conscience too. But the social and political upheavals which convulsed Europe after 1914 certainly made the limitations of that social conscience evident.

B. THE DECLINING INTEREST IN SOCIAL HISTORY DURING THE ERA OF DIALECTICAL THEOLOGY, 1920–1970

The First World War led to a European crisis, and one of its results was that research into the social history of the early church petered out

---

8. E. Troeltsch wished to supplement the "ideological" view of Christianity carried through in the history of dogma by a "sociological" way of looking at things. But he restricted himself to the social doctrines of the churches and sects, writing: "Research into real, practical conditions is so extensive a task that it was beyond my powers" (*Meine Bücher* in *Gesammelte Schriften 4* [Tübingen, 1925], 12).

9. W. Bousset may count as paradigm in liberal biblical research. He combined a reverence for great men (in which he was influenced by Thomas Carlyle) with a neo-Kaubian philosophy of religion. Social responsibility is a subsidiary theme; see K. Berger's account in *Exegese und Philosophie,* SBS 123/4 (Stuttgart, 1986), 85–126.

almost completely. We might actually have expected that in this crisis of society the need for sociological enlightenment about present and past would have been all the more pressing. But the opposite happened, and it is important to understand why.

The theological answer to the crisis was dialectical theology—a return to the transcendent origin of the Christian faith. The question about God became so central that the question about society paled into insignificance. Listening to what the New Testament texts have to say in substance took over so intensively that the social context of those texts seemed to be of minor importance. This reversion to the beginnings was essential historically, if theology and the church were to be made aware of their independent character over against a questionable and transitory society. But it was substantially necessary too, since religion is much more than its social function.

Yet the pointer to dialectical theology does not in itself explain the marked decline of interest in social history. For after all, vehement criticism of culture and society is an intrinsic feature of this theology. God's Word was understood as a radical criticism of every society. The Word had its origin beyond human will and human acts, and forced all willing, and all acting, into a crisis. Why did this impulse toward criticism of society fail to evoke any practical interest in a sociological clarification of theology and the church? Why was it neutralized? To illustrate the point from an individual's biographical development: Why did Karl Barth, one of the main exponents of the new theology, turn away almost demonstratively from his beginnings as a religious socialist?[10]

We have to see the development of form criticism in exegesis as a parallel to dialectical theology's neutralization of the impulse toward social criticism. This new way of looking at things also had sociological implications. Texts were now to be understood in the light of their social context. Yet here too the sociological impulses were neutralized. The requirements of the early congregations molded the New Testament texts: that was the postulate. But of all these many congregational requirements, only the religious ones were perceived; and the only part of the social context to which scholars paid any attention was congregational life.

---

10. This was the impression given by Barth's Tambach address "Der Christ in der Gesellschaft" ("The Christian in Society") given in September 1919. A. Lindt stresses: "The result of the profound impression made by Barth's Tambach address, however, was largely that many of the people who were prepared to listen to what he had to say devoted all their energies solely to the new theological ideas. They hardly committed themselves politically or socially at all any more" (*Das Zeitalter des Totalitarismus,* Christentum und Gesellschaft 13 [Stuttgart, 1981], 89). This was not Barth's intention. But the political implications of his theology did not make any impact at that time.

The congregation's *Sitz im Leben* — its situation in life — was tacitly confined to its *Sitz im Glauben* — its situation in faith.[11] Total social structures and interactions were hardly investigated at all.

This parallel development in theology and exegesis led to the momentous alliance between form criticism and kerygma theology.[12] Form criticism showed that the New Testament texts had always served a preaching which proclaimed the imminent end of the world. What they preached pointed beyond the world. They did not fit into the literary concepts of antiquity, and this was true down to the special characteristics that could be observed with the methods of form criticism. "Kerygma" theology (another name for "dialectical" theology) viewed the insights contributed by form criticism as the legitimation for making New Testament texts — at the present day too — the foundation for a proclamation that preached to every society God's judgment and his grace. Form-critical exegesis had once taught people to read biblical texts "from below"; but in this way it now became the legitimating basis for a theological interpretation "from above." In this interpretation, the impulse toward social criticism was *aufgehoben*, in the double sense of that German word: it was both negated, and gathered into and preserved in something else. A total abrogation of society makes any specific criticism superfluous.

The "neutralization" of existing impulses toward social criticism in kerygma theology, then, was paralleled by the neutralization of sociological implications in exegesis. And this parallel development is comprehensible only in the light of the social situation of the theological and exegetical "subculture" after the collapse of the old conditions in Germany in 1918. Theology and the church had been closely bound up with the earlier society — indeed, as the war went on this link was strengthened and endorsed. The clergy were not prepared for the new conditions. About 80 percent of them were against the new republic.[13] A theology that relativized society as provisional, open to criticism and

---

11. Although form criticism was the decisive new methodological approach in twentieth-century exegesis, we look in vain for the heading "Sociology" or "Social History" in W. G. Kümmel's excellent survey of research *Das Neue Testament im 20. Jahrhundert*, SBS 50 (Stuttgart, 1970). No better illustration could be given of the neutralization of the sociological theme, which actually belongs intrinsically to form criticism.

12. See here my article "Die 'Formgeschichte des Evangeliums' von Martin Dibelius und ihre gegenwärtige Bedeutung," in *Lesezeichen: Festschrift für A. Findeiss*, Beihefte zu den Dilheimer Blättern zum Alten Testament 3 (Heidelberg, 1984), 143–58.

13. Krumwiede, *Geschichte*, 195. The New Testament scholar Erik Peterson wrote to A. von Harnack in 1928: "Sociologically the [German] Protestant church corresponds roughly to the mental and sociological status of the deutsch-nationale Volkspartei [the German National People's Party]" (quoted in Lindt, *Totalitarismus*, 83).

transitory, was in line with their deepest convictions. A theology critical of society which favored social and democratic development would have been for them unendurable. Karl Barth was a democrat. He pleaded for a democratic socialism. But the dialectical theology he maintained only had a chance if this critical attitude toward existing society moved out of the center onto the periphery. Many of Barth's German supporters in any case viewed this social aspect as the Swiss theologian's private affair. When Barth moved away from his beginnings as a religious socialist, this confirmed their view. That is how it came about that after the First World War Barth was able to work together theologically with Friedrich Gogarten,[14] although the two men embodied diametrically opposite political attitudes. Gogarten was an exponent of a reactionary, authoritarian social criticism, which in 1933 welcomed Germany's "national renewal." Barth was a social democrat who was dismissed from his post by the National Socialist regime in 1935. But in the years after 1918 the two men were able to combine, the necessary presupposition being that the dialectical theology which they both maintained presented itself as criticism of *every* society—even the society for which democratic forces were striving. The social criticism that dialectical theology implied was bound to remain abstract. Any practical form it might have taken would have shown that society was being criticized from diametrically opposite directions.[15]

Where theology remains abstract in its social criticism, exegesis cannot be concrete about social history either. The few sociohistorical contributions after 1918 were made by scholars who still cherished the traditions of a liberal Protestantism. The changed theological situation becomes plain when we see that those concerned now had to prove apologetically that a concern about social history was legitimate. The "history-of-religions" school had brought out the eschatological character of early Christianity; and—if only to do justice to this recognition—it was only after the *unworldly* character of the gospel had been worked out that any attempt was made to fit it into this world. For example,

14. See the illuminating section "Dialektische Theologie und antiliberale Zeitstimmung" ("antidialectical theology and the antiliberal mood of the time") in Lindt, *Totalitarismus*, 90f.

15. Compared with other theological trends, "dialectical theology" was a step forward, in spite of its links with an antiliberal attitude. It helped many people to free themselves from "the old society" which had come to an end—even if this meant cutting Christianity off from every society and from all politics. As time went on, the progressive elements in Barth's thinking increasingly came to the fore (especially in reaction to fascism), so that under his influence many people moved away from a nationalist, conservative stance to one that was "democratic and critical." In this respect Barth exercised a salutary influence.

in his little book on social questions in early Christianity (*Soziale Fragen im Urchristentum,* 1921), Ernst Lohmeyer invokes the "remoteness from the world" of Jesus' inner nature, the complete "detachment of his external life from every earthly tie, whether it take the form of possessions or education, family or marriage, social position or country" (p. 67). Only after that does he venture to concede a certain importance to earthly conditions. Martin Dibelius retained his interest in social history all his life. He was one of the few German university teachers who assented to the republic out of conviction. Being a Christian was for him inseparable from social responsibility. But in his book on the social theme in the New Testament (*Das soziale Motiv im Neuen Testament,* 1933) he too was forced to offer proofs, contrary to the prevailing trend, to show that there are motifs in the New Testament which — as imminent expectation of the parousia declines — enjoin a reshaping of social life.[16]

But it was Rudolph Bultmann, not Martin Dibelius, who was responsible for the neutralization of the social history impulse in form criticism. In his "constructive" procedure, Dibelius first of all painted a picture of early Christianity as a whole, fitting in the New Testament texts and genres. One constitutive element in this overall view was the recognition that the early Christian congregations were drawn from the *petit bourgeoisie,* the lower middle classes, and that their literature was the literature of little unimportant people. Large parts of the Jesus tradition were understood as parenesis, rules of behavior, the history of which Dibelius traced back to late New Testament times. In Bultmann this interest in the living context of the texts recedes into the background. His strength is the analysis of structures and forms. He fits these into early Christianity by assigning them to the Palestinian or the early Hellenistic congregations. Theological interest is directed not so much to the life behind the texts as to the unworldly message contained in the Pauline and Johannine writings: Christian faith means "withdrawal" from the world and has little to do with society in its concrete form. There is no such thing as a specifically New Testament ethic. Bultmann's

---

16. M. Dibelius was strongly influenced by the social-liberal theologian and politician F. Naumann. He belonged to the German Democratic Party and was an active supporter of the republic. Through him, or by way of his pupils, the old social and sociohistorical concerns of liberal theology were preserved: E. Lohmeyer wrote his professorial thesis under him in Heidelberg in 1918. One of his pupils, H. D. Wendland, taught both New Testament and social ethics. Another, H. Greeven, wrote *Das Hauptproblem der Sozialethik in der neueren Stoa und im Urchristentum* (1935). My own teacher, P. Vielhauer, was also a pupil of Dibelius. His reaction to my first essays in the field of social history was favorable and encouraging — very different from the dismissive attitude of many adherents of the so-called Bultmann school. In this respect we can trace a line from Dibelius down to the present day.

views had been shaped by dialectical theology, and it was he who exerted the decisive influence on the development of exegesis. Dibelius was overshadowed by him.

Although interest in social history was suspended at the time when dialectical theology was flourishing, dialectical theology is for all that one of the historical preconditions for the interest in social history that has come alive again in the last fifteen years. In dialectical theology, Christianity (or, to be more precise, German Protestantism) freed itself for the first time after a long period from its ties with existing society. Indeed, in the struggles of the Confessing Church it experienced that society as manifestly anti-Christian — and particularly so at the very point where people such as the pro-Nazi "German Christians" appealed to new forms of religious thought and experience, which were allegedly more suited to the changed modern situation. The result was a double detachment: a detachment from society and a detachment from "religion"— that is to say, from religious forms of experience and behavior insofar as these are an expression of human life. But detachment always means a chance for perception. The theologians of the next generations, who were at the universities during the 1950s and 1960s, discovered this chance for new recognitions drawn from historical experience — a readiness to analyze society and religion critically too.

In retrospect, we may ask why this chance for perception was not used by the theologians and textual scholars who were still marked by the struggles of the Confessing Church and by dialectical theology. They had experienced a profound conflict between Christianity and society. They had shouldered social responsibility when a new society was built up after 1945. Why did the social awareness that was suspended (though still latent) in dialectical theology and form criticism remain dormant for so long? Why did none of the theologians and textual scholars of the postwar period develop this awareness in historical and exegetical work?

In order to make this comprehensible, let me first draw attention to an almost traumatic hindrance to perception among many dialectical theologians, which frequently neutralized their preparedness for the critical analysis of religion and society I have talked about. The search for connections between society and religion reminded many of them of disastrous links between "folk" or "nation" and religion. Attempts to clarify the social function of religion scientifically were therefore now and then associated with the kind of German theology in which religion was seen as a function of folk consciousness. So although people might quite readily assent to a limited "sociology of the church" (which would enable the church's administrative organs to inform themselves more thoroughly about the preconditions of what they were doing) there was no interest in a comprehensive sociology of religion—and certainly not in its application to the Holy of Holies of every Christian theology: the New Testament.

To this we may add a development in the science of sociology itself. Around the turn of the century, liberal theologians discovered that sociologists who were working and thinking historically could be discussion partners. The historical method was common to both sides. But since that time sociology had changed. On the one hand it had turned to empirical methods, with which it investigated contemporary society. On the other it had adopted functionalist theories for interpreting its empirical findings. Functionalism abstracts from the origin and history of a social phenomenon. For the explanation functionalism offers, it is enough to show the phenomenon's function in the present social context. Functionalist theories and empirical methods correspond. And both turn away from the older sociology, which had proceeded historically.[17]

This meant that the text interpreter had no compelling reason, either as a theologian or as an exact scholar, for turning to the investigation of social history. In Germany at the end of the war (that is, after 1945) there was still another hindrance to perception which affected the scholar as a member of society: he had to wrestle with the problem of Germany's past; and this was sometimes linked with conflicts about a sociological approach in the discipline of history as a whole. In a sociological view of history, the unimaginable political and moral catastrophes of the years 1933 to 1945 can no longer be explained as nothing more than the outcome of contingent and unfortunate constellations. Sociology raises the question whether these events were not already "preprogrammed," built into the very structures of German society. The same may be said of German Protestantism's wrestlings with its own history. As a history of ideas, this is often a fascinating chapter in the history of the critical mind; as social history, it is sometimes a depressing chapter in the history of reactionary aberrations.

To sum up: The theology of crisis was a new recollection of the transcendent origin of the message that was beyond society. It was a new recognition that the kerygma stands in contradiction to society. But the impulses for social criticism implicit in this theology were suspended, just as were the implications of form-critical methods for social history. Right down to the 1950s and 1960s, theologians and textual scholars felt that it was in harmony with their social situation for

---

17. See the account in Burke, *Sociology and History*, esp. 21ff.

them to keep the Christian faith free from any intimate ties with society. This was part of a conscious, deliberate divergence from "religious socialism" (which in any case had very few exponents in Germany), and it also reflected an emphatic abandonment of theological liberalism.

In the United States, in contrast, "the Chicago school" was able to go on pursuing the concern of a liberal and social Christianity that the methods of sociological investigation be used to throw light on the Bible and the early Christian communities.[18] Consequently, even today socio-historical research is more readily accepted in America. It is not by chance that most of the recent contributions to the social history of the early church have been provided by American scholars.

C. THE RENEWAL OF SOCIOLOGICAL EXEGESIS IN THE 1970S

If the suspension of sociological concern in exegesis was the expression of a particular social situation, the same may be said of its renewal in recent years.[19] The determining factors in this development can be classified according to the three roles that text interpreters play: they are "citizens" of their society, members of the academic world, and theologians of their churches.

In the last forty years society has undergone a great transformation. Technological progress has enabled working productivity to increase to an incredible degree. The world in which human beings live has changed in a relatively short while. This is not yet enough to explain the newly awakened interest in social history. Social change had been felt for a long time. But what was special about this social change was that, to an extent never previously known, it also increased the chance that this change would be consciously thought about by many groups of people. The increase in productivity led to an expansion of the social spheres in which men and women can inquire with greater insistence

---

18. S. J. Case, *The Evolution of Early Christianity* (Chicago: University of Chicago Press, 1914); idem, *The Social Triumph of the Ancient Church* (New York: Harper & Bros.; London: Allen & Unwin, 1934); S. Mathews, *The Social Teaching of Jesus: An Essay in Christian Sociology* (New York and London: Macmillan, 1897); idem, *The Atonement and the Social Process* (New York: Macmillan, 1930). Another important book that must be named is F. C. Grant, *The Economic Background of the Gospels* (London: Humphrey Milford, 1926).

19. For an account of the research here see, among other contributions, D. Harrington, "Social Concepts in the Early Church: A Decade of Research," *TS* 41 (1980): 181–90; R. Scroggs, "The Sociological Interpretation of the New Testament: The Present State of Research," *NTS* 26 (1980): 164–79. Two fairly recent books give a good overall view: D. Tidball, *An Introduction to the Sociology of the New Testament* (Exeter: Paternoster Press, 1983); and C. Osiek, *What Are They Saying About the Social Setting of the New Testament?* (New York: Paulist Press, 1984).

about meaning and values. Education lasted longer. More opportunities for education were available (particularly higher education), and leisure increased. There were more posts for teachers, consultants, and the purveyors of opinion—people who count as the custodians of values and social life. The expansion of this sector created a wide public sensitive to social questions. And this also meant a potential for reflection and protest that had hitherto never existed to this degree in a relatively stable society. The student revolts of the late 1960s and the "green" alternative movement of the 1980s have their *Sitz im Leben* here: this is the situation from which they spring. They are one result of technological progress. For technological progress lightens labor and at the same time increases expectations that life can have significance. At the same time it sharpens a sensitivity for the unsolved problems of human society which is actually necessary for our survival: sensitivity for underdevelopment, the danger of war, the destruction of the environment, minorities, and the inhumanity of authoritarian traditions and institutions.

The expansion of the sector that has to do with significance in life and with social values was more than a merely quantitative expansion of the traditional educated classes by new groups. It is symptomatic that in this process the quality of what we call "education" changed. The traditional educational canon was based on philosophy and the literary disciplines. This was now supplemented, and sometimes even replaced, by competence in the communication of a popularized social science. In the first half of this century, educated men and women still expressed the way they saw themselves in philosophical terms—generally with the help of existential philosophy and the "philosophy of life." Nowadays they use a sociological and psychological "koine," a lingua franca in which the fundamental questions of life can be discussed everywhere. Earlier, people used words like "authenticity" and "nonauthenticity," "care" and "thrownness." Nowadays they talk about identity and identity conflicts, aggression and frustration, communication and consensus. This expansion of the educational canon by a canon of terms drawn from the social sciences is in itself an expression of a social process. It expresses the heightened claim of the sector concerned with significance and social values, which in its new power aims to influence not merely individuals in society but the very structures of society itself. Because "education" is intended to be socially effective, education now uses the language of the social sciences. In other words, the expanded educated class which social change has brought into being is demanding an influence on society as a whole. And in fact it is succeeding in influencing public discussion in many spheres—for example, in questions about upbringing and education, or environmental problems. In especially problematic

situations, the group concerned with significance and social values undoubtedly has a chance to influence the whole of society—even if this
group is notoriously inclined to overestimate the possibilities open to it.

The effects of this development on theology must not be underestimated. When the educational canon based on literature and philosophy lost ground, the interpretation of the New Testament based on
existential philosophy lost plausibility, especially since the existential
interpretation of the Christian message (which appeals to the individual)
does not fit groups which demand influence on society as a whole. If
the groups concerned with questions of meaning and value now develop
a common social-science parlance, a shared koine, the theologians (who
are society's oldest custodians of significance and social values) have
to ask themselves whether they are not prepared to express their concerns in this language too. Attempts in this direction are certainly not
as numerous as the many warnings against them—warnings that have
run far ahead of the development itself. Of course, we have to assume
from the outset that all the problems involved in any "translation" would
apply here too. A change of language could mean loss of content. It
may also quite justly be pointed out that the addressees of an attempted
translation of this kind are by no means "modern men and women";
they are at most what Schleiermacher called "the cultured despisers"
of religion, among whom the chances of success are in any case slight.

Nevertheless, if we were to pinpoint a trend in present-day exegesis
that picks up and develops the concern of the existential interpretation with the help of sociological exegesis, this trend is what I should
like to call "socio-kerygmatic exegesis." Its concern is convincingly brought
out in a book published in 1978 by Luise Schottroff and Wolfgang Stegemann, *Jesus von Nazareth—Hoffnung der Armen* (Eng. trans. *Jesus and the
Hope of the Poor,* 1986). The book aims to extract a social message from
the New Testament texts. Its hermeneutical canon is "the gospel for the
poor," God's option for the oppressed and the suffering, to which the
Bible testifies. Largely speaking, this socio-kerygmatic exegesis uses the
proved traditional methods. It dispenses with sociological terminology.
Indeed, it is notable for its general comprehensibility.[20] What is known
as "materialist exegesis" is very different in this respect. This kind of
interpretation was widely adopted in the Latin countries especially. It
links a complicated, structuralist textual theory with a Marxist theory

---

20. See also the collection by W. Schottroff and W. Stegemann, *Der Gott der kleinen
Leute: Sozialgeschichtliche Auslegungen,* 2 vols. (Munich and Gelnhausen, 1979); and N.
Gottwald, ed., *The Bible and Liberation: Political and Social Hermeneutics* (Maryknoll, N.Y.:
Orbis Books, 1983).

of society.[21] Here we really do find an attempt to express the message of the New Testament in the social-science language of our time.

Up to now no comprehensive socio-kerygmatic hermeneutic has been developed. But this is undoubtedly due to developments in theology itself rather than to the anxious warnings against any such attempt. For scholars are not merely (educated) members of their society; they are also members of the academic world. The exegetical subculture is closely bound up with the fate of universities, colleges, and seminaries. And here a whole new sector has come to the fore — the social sciences. Work in this field has profoundly influenced the traditional disciplines. Ever since the 1960s, historical and literary studies have been unthinkable without it. In the 1970s, exegesis caught up with what had already developed elsewhere. True, the expansion and influence of the social sciences ran parallel to the spread of a social-science koine in the everyday cultural world of educated men and women. But this expansion and influence must be distinguished from the general cultural process. At a general, nonscientific level, men and women used the theories of the social sciences as a help in finding bearings and significance in life. Yet the social scientists themselves were conscious that the function which their studies were thereby being assigned was a highly problematic one. An intensive discussion about the nature of these studies was carried on, and in the course of it uninhibited, nonscientific assertions and claims evaporated — either because of the development of strict empirical methods (and the recognition of their limitations); or because the social sciences adoped a strictly critical, historical analysis of the sources; or because of hermeneutical reflection about the vital human concerns invested in social-science research.

This self-reflection was of great importance for the influence that radiated from the social sciences to other disciplines. The methods of the social sciences can be permanently integrated in other disciplines only if openness for the questions asked does not mean taking over particular political options, whether these be Marxist, liberal, or conservative. The result has to be increased knowledge for everyone, irrespective of any particular standpoint. It is only then, too, that this field of knowledge can serve life in the way it is pledged to do, that is, by rational enlightenment. And this is all the more necessary the more life adopts for itself fragments from the social sciences as a way of understanding questions of meaning and value. In short: the social sciences have, if

---

21. F. Belo, *Lecture Materialiste de l'Evangile de Marc* (Paris, 1974), 376; M. Clévenot, *Approches materialiste de la Bible* (Paris, 1976). This exegesis is "materialist" in its "anti-idealistic trend" especially: the texts are not to be read only as an expression of theological ideas.

anything, come to be increasingly cautious, in a countermovement to trends in the sector that has to do with significance and social values.

The same caution marks work in the field of social history, which draws on sociological models as a way of interpreting the social data extracted from the ancient sources. Whereas sociokerygmatic exegesis often aims to speak directly to the present-day reader, attempts at a "socio-historical historiography"[22] of this kind are characterized by the attempt to avoid any over-hasty modernization of conditions in the ancient world. There are three different methods of proceeding, depending on the provenance of the sociological models used.

1. The models may be taken from the ancient world itself. History (as an account of the past) is analyzed by way of historical types. For it was characteristic of the ancient world of Greece and Rome to interpret itself in theoretical categories. We find there reflections about the *polis,* or political community, "the house" and its administration, and about the relationship between rich and poor. E. A. Judge pleads that social history should in principle be pursued mainly by way of the categories of the ancient world itself—though at the same time he is acutely aware that the primitive church cannot be fitted into these categories.[23] In his analysis of the Pauline congregations, Judge himself drew on "the school" as historical "type." Judge's influence is to be seen in the work of Peter Marshall, who has interpreted Paul's relations with the congregation in Corinth in the categories of friendship, as this was known in the ancient world.[24] Dieter Lührmann has drawn on ancient reflections about the *oikos* ("house") for an analysis of the duty codes, or *Haustafeln.*[25] More examples could be cited. Every historian would assent to the requirement that an era be understood in its own categories. This is a bar to any over-hasty modernization.

2. Another method is to draw on ethnological models. The societies which the enthnologists investigate are in many respects closer to the ancient world than they are to us. But they have the advantage of being

---

22. W. Stegemann used the term "soziohistorische Geschichtsschreibung" in discussion, and I am taking over the term here.

23. E. A. Judge's programmatic essay in this context is "The Social Identity of the First Christians: A Question of Method in Religious History," *JRH* 11 (1980): 201–17. He already pursued this program in his very first publication on early Christian social history, *The Social Pattern of Christian Groups in the First Century* (London: Tyndale Press, 1960). This little book deserves a place of honor in the history of modern sociological exegesis.

24. P. Marshall, *Enmity in Corinth: Social Conventions in Paul's Relations with the Corinthians,* WUNT 2/23 (Tübingen, 1987).

25. D. Lührmann, "Neutestamentliche Haustafeln und antike Ökonomie," *NTS* 27 (1981): 83–97.

accessible to direct observation, by way of field studies. The intercultural comparison of these groups with biblical societies and forms of community has proved a fruitful approach.[26] In the Old Testament, the period of the Judges was analyzed by Frank Crüsemann as a "segmentary society," so that—after the erosion of the classic amphictyony theory—a comprehensive interpretation again became possible for the first time.[27] In the New Testament, the Jesus movement and early Christianity were investigated as a "millenaristic" or "chiliastic" movement (J. G. Gager).[28] B. J. Malina raised this ethnological or socioanthropological procedure to the status of a methodic program or principle.[29] He emphasizes that in the ancient world we cannot yet reckon with the "monadic" human being of modern times. Here we have to do with a "dyadic" type of personality, by which he means someone who "perceives himself and forms his self-image in terms of what others perceive and feed back to him" (p.55)—which in my view is also to some extent true of people today.

3. The scholarly tradition of social history provides a third source of models. Many terms and concepts are drawn from sociologically oriented historical studies. A classic example is the term "charisma." Max Weber developed this New Testament concept into a general sociological category. It has proved so useful in connection with so many phenomena that we cannot now get along without it.[30] Other categories that have meanwhile proved their worth are role and status, class and mobility,

---

26. For the Old Testament, see B. Lang, "Spione im gelobten Land: Ethnologen als Leser des Alten Testaments," *KZSS* 26 (1984): 158–77.

27. F. Crüsemann, *Der Widerstand gegen das Königtum: Die antiköniglichen Texte des Alten Testaments und der Kampf um den frühen israelitischen Staat* (Neukirchen, 1978).

28. J. G. Gager, *Kingdom and Community: The Social World of Early Christianity* (Englewood Cliffs, N.J.: Prentice-Hall, 1975).

29. B. J. Malina, *The New Testament World: Insights from Cultural Anthropology* (Atlanta: John Knox Press, 1981). *Social-Scientific Criticism of the New Testament and its Social World,* ed. J. H. Elliott (*Semeia* 35 [1986]) contains a series of further studies: J. L. White, "Grid and Group in Matthew's Community: The Righteousness/Honor Code in the Sermon on the Mount" (pp. 61–90); J. H. Neyrey, "The Idea of Purity in Mark's Gospel" (pp. 91–128) and "Body Language in 1 Corinthians: The Use of Anthropological Models for Understanding Paul and his Opponents" (pp. 129–70). See also Malina's more recent book, *Christian Origins and Cultural Anthropology: Practical Models for Biblical Interpretation* (Atlanta: John Knox Press, 1986).

30. See J. H. Schütz, *Paul and the Anatomy of Apostolic Authority,* MS.SNT 26 (London and New York: Cambridge University Press, 1975); and B. Holmberg, *Paul and Power: The Structure of Authority in the Primitive Church as Reflected in the Pauline Epistles,* CB.NT 11 (Lund, 1978). Also R. Bendix, "Umbildungen des persönlichen Charismas. Eine Anwendung von Max Webers Charismabegriff auf das Frühchristentum" in *Max Webers Sicht des antiken Christentums,* ed. W. Schluchter (Frankfurt, 1985), 404–43; see here esp. the editor's introduction: "Max Webers Analyse des antiken Christentums: Grundzüge eines unvollendeten Projekts."

ideology and legitimation, church and sect. Let me mention only one example drawn from recent research. W. A. Meeks has introduced into New Testament scholarship the highly illuminating concept of "status inconsistency" or "status dissonance." He uses these terms to describe the incontrovertible phenomenon that people's status varies according to the yardstick applied.[31] He has been able to make use of this term in New Testament research with all the more justification because it had already proved useful in the social history of the ancient world. It covers the phenomenon that slaves and freedmen could be inferior where their legal rights were concerned, but could still in certain circumstances enjoy a high status socially and economically.[32]

Anyone who raises the stereotyped reproach that sociological exegesis violates the ancient texts by subjecting them to modern categories fails in my view to recognize the methodological caution with which models are applied in this type of research. Here the interpreters observe the rules of the academic world to which they belong.

Changes in society and in science and scholarship have undoubtedly strongly influenced the "exegetical subculture." But a third factor is also of central importance for the renewal of sociohistorical research: the church. The interpreters of the texts are theologians. If the new approach in sociological exegesis looks different today from what it once did, at its beginnings during the era of liberal theology, this is due to the different position of the churches in society. Here three trends have come to be important.

1. Secularization. Churches have turned into special, particularist cultures within their societies, and Christians are now a cognitive minority. In what were once Christian societies, Christianity has become a now-faded framework for the convictions of the majority.

2. Decolonization. Today the churches are involved in a web of ecumenical relationships that also embraces the young churches in the countries of the Third World.

3. Society's legitimation crisis. The validity of traditional authorities has become problematic, and this includes the norms based on the Bible.

Let us look briefly at these three trends.

---

31. W. A. Meeks, *The First Urban Christians: The Social World of the Apostle Paul* (New Haven and London: Yale University Press, 1983). Up to now this is the most mature summing up of the social history of early Christianity. An account of "status dissonance," the new aspect expounded in this book, may be found in W. A. Meeks, "The Social Context of Pauline Theology," *Interpretation* 36 (1982): 266–77.

32. P. R. C. Weaver, "Social Mobility in the Early Roman Empire: The Evidence of the Imperial Freedmen and Slaves," *Past and Present* 37 (1967): 3–20.

1. Secularization and Its Result:
The "People's Church" Has Become a Minority Church.

In the era of theological liberalism, biblical exegesis was pursued within the framework of a "Christian" society. This is no longer true. The Bible has ceased to be the legitimating mainstay for society as a whole. Consequently social history has been freed from the burden of defending a social order that cannot be defended with the help of biblical texts. But then what social function does it have? In order to answer this question we have to look at the church's tasks in a now-secularized society. We can see three forms of reaction, which may be summed up under the headings "defensive," "communicative," and "oppositionist" church.

Once the church shrinks into a minority, its concern to survive is vitally affected. In the face of this development it will take on a defensive character, so as to retain as far as possible all the groups that (still) find a home in it. The unspoken motto is this: On no account do anything that could cause annoyance and drive anyone out of the church! The aim is to stabilize a domestic ecclesiastical culture.

But if the church wants to maintain relations with society as a whole, two possibilities are open to it. It can put all its energies into promoting its ability to communicate with society outside the church. The church is to be capable of dialogue with everyone—and above all with "outsiders." It must try to take their perspectives into account too, in its shaping of life and faith.

The other possibility is to see the opportunity that is open to a minority, as an opposition to dominant trends in society. The more the church settles for a place on the fringe of society, the readier and more open it will be for options presenting an alternative to society as it exists.

In this situation theologians can take over two roles, provided that they do not confine themselves to stabilizing a domestic ecclesiastical culture in little groups. One is the role of the opposition prophet, who puts into words the religious and ethical alternatives that have been repressed and in this very way "serves" a society that otherwise pays little attention to him. The other is the role of the person who as representative formulates the timeless questions of human life, even for people in whom these questions have become mute.

Sociological exegesis can be valuable from both these perspectives. It can be pursued from below as an "opposition exegesis," which reads the Bible from the viewpoint of groups that are on the periphery of society, not at its center. Socio-kerygmatic exegesis undoubtedly possesses this oppositional prophetic character. It reminds the church of the people who know life only from its dark side—and not least of the great majority who have to live out their lives in circumstances devoid of any kind of human dignity.

But sociological exegesis can also be prompted by the wish to convey the outward and inward perspectives or viewpoints of the biblical texts. The intention is to make new communication of the biblical tradition possible by applying the alien—even alienating—methods of sociological analysis. The aim of this exegesis is not to find biblical justification for particular value judgments. Its purpose is to awaken sensibility for the values of the social impulses the Bible contains—a sensibility that many people have lost because for them the Bible has become enshrouded in an ecclesiastical aura. This sensibility also includes an awareness that in the biblical texts God is on the side of the poor.

The two possibilities open to sociological exegesis are closely connected with the church's contemporary situation. More even: there seems to be a kind of elective affinity between favored theories about the sociology of religion and the way theologians appear to themselves. Do they see themselves as prophets or as representatives? Men and women who assign themselves an opposition role will be inclined to adopt conflict theories in the sociology of religion and will see religion as being woven into the historical struggle about the distribution of opportunities in life. These people will probably be open-minded about Marxist approaches.[33] Conversely, a theologian who sees himself as "representative" will tend to hold integration theories in the sociology of religion. Religion is then seen as the attempt to build up a symbolic world of meaning in which everybody can live, a commonwealth of which everyone can be a loyal citizen. Religion offers a common language in which people can communicate about the fundamental questions of existence.

To say that there are elective affinities between our roles and our convictions does not mean that these things are predetermined: we are not nailed down to a particular theoretical perspective because of our social situation. On the contrary, the phrase "elective" affinity indicates that in fact we have a limited freedom. The recognition that there are elective affinities should not merely confirm us in our choice. It should increase our opportunities for choosing whether we continue, quite

---

33. For a very important analysis of early Palestinian Judaism inspired by conflict theory, see H. G. Kippenberg, *Religion und Klassenbildung im antiken Judäa: Eine religions-soziologische Studie zum Verhältnis von Tradition und gesellschaftlicher Entwicklung* (Göttingen, 1978; 2nd ed. 1982).

deliberately, to maintain our own viewpoint, as a choice made from among a number of possible perspectives, or whether we combine our own stance with other opinions. It would in fact be helpful for studies in social history if every inquirer could adopt a number of different theoretical standpoints. For different perspectives are both an expression of our complex social situation and an adaptation to a complex subject, which cannot be sufficiently elucidated from any single angle.[34]

But criticism of sociological research is equally an expression of our situation. For the objections are always the same: the texts, we are told, are read "from below," in a one-sided way, so that what emerges is not social history at all but "left-wing socio-hagiography." Or—another criticism—the texts are analyzed "from outside," with such detachment that their theological content does not make its proper impact. One reason for the uneasiness about social history is that here biblical texts are being seen from the perspective of groups who are hardly represented at all in the church today. The "outsiders" stay away in any case, and the lower classes too for the most part. So when the Bible is read "from below" or "from outside," the social groups that dominate theology and the church are bound to feel that an attempt is being made to snatch their own Holy Scripture away from them, in order to give it to other people.

The secularization process and the church's development into a minority body are undoubtedly reflected in sociohistorical exegesis. During the era of theological liberalism, exegesis of this kind expressed a transition from state church to "people's" church. It now stands at the point of transition from a people's church, embedded in society as a whole, to the church of a minority.

2. The Intensification of Ecumenical Communication as a Result of Global Communication and Decolonization

At the very time when attachment to the church was declining in society as a whole, theology and the church experienced an upsurge

---

34. My essay in the present book "Sociological Theories of Religion and the Analysis of Early Christianity: Some Reflections" is an attempt to link up as many different perspectives as possible—both integration and conflict theories. In a society that is disinclined to accept (Marxist-inspired) conflict theories, the essay is a distinct plea that these perspectives be adopted as indispensable, because conflicts are necessary for the further development of society. In "Social-Scientific Criticism of the New Testament and Its Social World" (*Semeia* 35 [1986]: 1-34), J. H. Elliott has fundamentally misunderstood my intention when he reduces my work to the common denominator of a functionalism concerned for social stability and the reduction of conflict; see my comments at the end of the above-mentioned essay in the present volume.

of new opportunities. Today modern means of travel and communication make it possible for ecumenical ties to be realized in quite practical terms. After the catastrophes caused by nationalism and racism, to develop ecumenical relationships became a theological and ethical duty. After 1945, theology and exegesis became more ecumenical than ever before — even if we are still more deeply rooted in our own particular traditions than we like to think.

What significance does this have for exegesis? Scholars are experiencing in their own world what they had otherwise come across mainly as the subject of their analysis: the exchange between different cultures and societies. One of the major themes of New Testament research has always been the dispute between Judaism and Hellenism. This was taken up again in a new way. Now the Hellenization of Judaism was no longer analyzed merely in the context of the history of ideas; it was considered in the framework of social history too. Hellenism was no longer seen only as an intellectual and spiritual world; it was understood as a supreme military, economic, and social power. As far as Palestine is concerned, we are indebted to Martin Hengel for a comprehensive exposition of this sociological process. His seminal work *Judaism and Hellenism* appeared in 1969 (2nd ed. 1973; Eng. trans. 1974).[35] Anyone who read it at the beginning of the 1970s could perceive a direct contemporary analogy: the conflict between European culture and the indigenous cultures of the developing countries. In the ancient world, civilizing Hellenistic culture threatened to assimilate the little indigenous culture of Judaism and came up against violent resistance. And in the same way, another "superior" civilization in the form of European culture was threatening to spread all over the world. For a long time people viewed this process as a matter of course, but this naïveté disintegrated in the postcolonial era. It was the resistance of little Asiatic and African peoples that proved to be superior. Many people in Western societies looked on with sympathy as former colonial countries struggled to assert their own identity — just as the reader of *Judaism and Hellenism* finds that his sympathies are on the side of Judaism in its efforts to stand its ground.

It is not by chance that the first attempt at a comprehensive sociological interpretation of early Christianity should have defined and conceptualized the connections and relationships I have outlined. In *Kingdom and Community* (1975), J. G. Gager interpreted Christianity in its earliest form as a millenarian movement. He therefore placed it among a whole

---

35. For a further summing up, see M. Hengel, *Jews, Greeks and Barbarians: Aspects of the Hellenization of Judaism in the Pre-Christian Period,* trans. J. Bowden (London: SCM Press; Philadelphia: Fortress Press, 1980).

series of renewal movements in indigenous cultures, movements that we can find again and again today, as reactions against an advancing, "superior" foreign culture. But above all his book presents a fundamental change of perspective. Christianity is generally identified with European culture, in all its crushing force. But here Christianity in its earliest form appears as the exponent of a threatened oriental culture which is struggling for independent existence but which, in the form of a religious movement, overmasters the superior European culture from within. And this suggests a question: Are new religious movements in the former colonies, and are the young churches, perhaps closer to the New Testament church than European Christianity?[36]

But it is not only because of individual results of this kind that research into social history is important for the ecumenical dialogue between the "young" churches and the "old" ones. It is also important as method. We have to realize quite clearly that social change is experienced in different ways in the countries of the First World and the countries of the Third. We are often frightened by change; for when people's needs and wants are sated, change can mean a change for the worse. Elsewhere change is something to hope for, because to stick with the status quo would be unendurable. There is no doubt that a positive attitude to social change is a strong motive for thinking about social history. Western theology could in my view make an important contribution to an intercultural theology if it were to offer a soundly based social history of Israel, early Christianity, and the church. Whether this could be of any help in the situation of the young churches today, their own theologians must decide.

3. The Revision of Traditional Patterns of Behavior Following the Legitimation Crisis of Traditional Forms of Living

Social change always means that traditional patterns of behavior are called in question. As recently as a hundred years ago, readers of the Bible in Germany and elsewhere could find in it many aspects of the world in which they lived. They were living in a monarchy. There were laborers and maidservants ("handmaids") on all the farms. In the family, patriarchal patterns of living enjoyed unquestioned validity. Today every reader senses that when he opens the Bible he is entering a different social world. Patterns of behavior that were once unquestioned and that

---

36. Perhaps I may point out here that these questions were in my mind when I wrote my study "Lokal- und Sozialkolorit in der Geschichte von der syrophönikischen Frau (Mk 7, 24-30)," *ZNW* 75 (1984): 202–25: an exorcist from the backwoods encounters a "gentlewoman" belonging to Hellenistic urban culture.

took their legitimation from the Bible have become problematic. In this situation people rightly expect research into social history to provide information about the development and function of traditional behavior patterns in politics, economic life, and the family. Social history can make these things comprehensible in their historical framework, and in this way it can explain the conflict between our ethical values and judgments and the behavior patterns we find in the Bible.

It is impossible to mention here all the sectors in which sociological research is being pursued at the present time in the context of "ethical revisions." Research into historical aspects of patriarchalism, anti-Semitism, and militarism is especially intensive. Often these contributions confine themselves to an analysis of ideas about women, Jews, and war. Analyses of this kind can only properly be termed sociological if they fit these ideas into the whole of life as it was lived.

Intensified research into the role of women in the Bible does not merely have as background the general dissolution of patriarchal rule in society. It is also connected with changes in the composition of the theological world. The last fifteen years have seen an enormous rise in the number of women theological students. (In Heidelberg the proportion rose from about 10 percent to 40 percent.) The role of pastor was one of the first positions open to women where leadership was a publicly evident function. This induced many independent women to study theology. And it was precisely these women who came up against restrictive Christian traditions. It was out of that tension that feminist theology developed. This is not a passing fashion; it is closely linked with structural changes in the church and society. In the feminist reading of the Bible, one of the methodological problems of all social history crops up again in intensified form: the lack of symmetry in sources and interpretations. By that I mean that the upper classes have a greater chance of leaving behind a portrait of themselves than the lower classes. This lack of symmetry in the sources is intensified by the lack of symmetry in the interpretations: the interpreters too generally belong to the upper or upper-middle classes, and their attention is concentrated on the groups to which they feel closest. The same applies to the relation between men and women. Most of the sources derive from men and are generally interpreted by men. This is changing only very slowly, but today some important contributions to the social history of early Christianity have already been made by women. Elisabeth Schüssler Fiorenza has presented a comprehensive account of the social history of the early Christian congregations from a feminist viewpoint, and she brings out very clearly the problems I have mentioned. Among other contributions I should like to mention especially the work of Bernadette Brooten and Luise Schottroff.[37]

The numerous studies on anti-Judaism in the Christian church have also to be seen in the context of a fundamental "ethical revision": anti-Judaism has been a fateful constant in the history of Christendom. It was only after the Holocaust that there came to be a growing insight that the relationship to Judaism has to undergo a fundamental renewal — and this insight is still by no means accepted everywhere. New Testament scholars have a special function here,[38] for they have the task of investigating historically the period when the paths of Jews and Christians diverged. A comprehensive social history of early Christianity must make "the schism between Jews and Christians" comprehensible. But theologically too New Testament exegesis is confronted with a great challenge at this point. Coming to terms with that challenge will involve decisions as to whether Christian identity can be defined in such a way that it does not imply a negative definition of Judaism, but recognizes Judaism's enduring theological right to existence.

Finally, let me mention the link between social history and the discussion about peace. Up to a few generations ago, the values and behavior of an enthnocentric militarism enjoyed unbroken prestige. It was considered inevitable that countries should maintain their interests by means of war. Courage and valor in battle were generally extolled. Here too attitudes that prevailed for centuries are being revised — and in this revision appeal is quite rightly made to the New Testament. Of course, not every analysis of New Testament ideas about peace is social history. The term can be applied only to those analyses which investigate the structural conditions of war and peace in the ancient world, and which examine the attitudes of the early church to war in the context of the real social situation of the first Christians. Klaus Wengst has published a book on this subject which deserves attention.[39]

---

37. E. Schüssler Fiorenza, *In Memory of Her: A Feminist Theological Reconstruction of Christian Origins* (New York: Crossroad; London: SCM Press, 1983); B. Brooten, *Women Leaders in the Ancient Synagogue,* Brown Judaic Studies 36 (Chico, Calif.: Scholars Press, 1982); L. Schottroff, "Frauen in der Nachfolge Jesu in neutestamentlicher Zeit," in *Traditionen der Befreiung,* vol. 2: *Frauen in der Bibel,* ed. W. Schottroff and W. Stegemann (Munich, 1980): 91–133.

38. Here let me draw attention to just two comprehensive accounts written by two New Testament scholars: F. Mussner, *Tractate on the Jews* (Eng. trans. Philadelphia: Fortress Press, 1984); and P. von der Osten-Sacken, *Christian-Jewish Dialogue: Theological Foundations,* trans. Margaret Kohl (Philadelphia: Fortress Press, 1986).

39. K. Wengst, *Pax Romana: Anspruch und Wirklichkeit. Erfahrungen und Wahrnehmungen des Friedens bei Jesus und im Urchristentum* (Munich, 1986).

We have come to the end of our attempt to shed some light on the progress of sociological research into early Christianity with the help of the methods of social history. Science and scholarship must never forget that they are the work of men and women and that they are sustained by tiny subcultures in our society. The exegetical subculture is closely interwoven with general trends in society, scholarship, and the church. What the text interpreters do will be determined by their roles as citizens, scholars, and theologians, and by the expectations that are linked with those roles. For that very reason we are in duty bound to think about these expectations and to decide what they are, so that we do not unconsciously conform to them at points where we ought to be following our own values and criteria—values and criteria that we generally become aware of only when they conflict with what other people expect. Text interpreters too are continually required to make decisons of conscience which are related to their social environment and yet must not be determined by that. Here sociological exegesis can be a help. What is more important here than any individual results in this branch of scholarship is the fundamental recognition that all biblical texts belong within a total social context. And this is the case even when the texts themselves are intending to controvert that context. Sometimes we can recognize clearly what the context is; sometimes it evades us; but it always exists. The fundamental convictions that are at work in the biblical religions belong within a social structure from the very outset; and even when religious groups and institutions deliberately separate themselves from "the world" (as we can see them doing in the early years of Christianity) this is a social process of differentiation and detachment.

Sociological exegesis aims to establish sensibility for the social dimension of our religious convictions once and for all. Then the social consciences of theologians will no longer be roused only when they are confronted by the social problems of the present day; for those consciences will be continually schooled afresh at the very center of their theological work: in their wrestlings with the Bible.

PART I

STUDIES ON THE JESUS TRADITION
AND THE SOCIAL REALITY
OF THE FIRST CENTURY

1

The Wandering Radicals

---◆---

Light Shed by the Sociology of Literature on the Early Transmission of Jesus Sayings[1]

THE SOCIOLOGY of literature investigates the relations between written texts and human behavior. It studies the social behavior of the people who make the texts, pass them on, interpret them, and adopt them.[2] And it analyzes this behavior under two aspects: first, as typical behavior; second, as contingent behavior—behavior conditioned by outside circumstances.[3]

It was form criticism that introduced the first of these aspects into biblical studies.[4] Typical features of the texts led the critics to conclusions about equally typical features in the social conduct of the people

---

1. Lecture held in the university of Bonn on November 25, 1972. Some of its main ideas arose out of discussion with my colleague the Rev. H. Frost. I should like to thank him here for his stimulating suggestions.

2. See H. N. Fügen, *Die Hauptrichtungen der Literatursoziologie,* 4th ed. (Bonn, 1970), 14: the sociology of literature "has to do with the actions of the people who are involved in literature; its subject is the interactions of these people." The actions concerned must be typical ways of behavior (p. 29). It is less convincing when Fügen distinguishes a socio-literary inquiry (which investigates the contingency of literature in the framework of historical causality) from the questions raised in the sociology of literature.

3. Max Scheler, for example, describes sociological inquiry under these two aspects; see *Die Wissensformen und die Gesellschaft,* 2nd ed. (Leipzig, 1960), 17.

4. The questions asked by the sociology of literature have been part of historical-critical research from the beginning. In his *Tractatus Theologico Politicus* of 1670 (Eng. trans. by R. Willis, London, 1862), Spinoza demanded a historical interpretation of the Bible, meaning by this: (1) research into the language; (2) the interpretation of biblical books in the light of their own presuppositions; (3) the question about the author, the situation in which the books came into being, and their reception, as well as the practices and customs of their own environment (see chapter 2 below, pp. 89ff., esp. 91f.). This last question undoubtedly includes questions belonging to the sociology of literature.

33

concerned. That is to say, they argued back to a *Sitz im Leben* — a real-life situation, in which a text was continually used, and where this use actually shaped the text itself. We may think of instruction, for example, or perhaps mission, or worship.

The second aspect was the question about the circumstances determining the behavior that has made the text what it is. This question goes a little way beyond form criticism. Form criticism is primarily concerned with the intentions of the transmitters of a text and of its addressees. In the case of the biblical texts, these intentions are largely religious. So explaining a text in the light of its place in early Christian congregational life was generally interpreted to mean showing how it developed out of the faith of that congregation. But of course the life of early Christian communities included aspects that were not religious at all. One of these aspects was the problem of making a living, in the quite down-to-earth, commonplace sense. Another was the different social conditions in which a Galilean farmer lived, compared with a man or woman living in the great cosmopolitan city of Corinth. Surely we should expect life in this wider sense too to have influenced the New Testament texts?

To investigate the New Testament in the light of the sociology of literature therefore means asking about the intentions and conditions determining the typical social behavior of the authors, transmitters, and addressees of the New Testament texts. Now, we can ponder long enough about how to see the relationship between spiritual intentions and their less spiritual conditions.[5] According to Max Scheler, for example, the essential content of a mental or spiritual insight can never be derived from historical and social factors; but the spread and acceptance of that insight may very well be influenced by these things.[6] And here our subject

---

5. We may name only a few possible models: (1) Determination models. Intellectual or spiritual traditions are retrospectively explained, in a process of hindsight, by way of (material) factors of cause and effect or by teleological intentions (history's plan, etc.). (2) Reflection models. In intellectual and spiritual traditions, natural processes of growth arrive at an awareness of themselves. (3) Action models. Traditions are attempts to respond to historical social situations. On the one hand, the traditions are confronted by these situations. On the other hand, the conditions also have their effect on human intentions.

6. Scheler, *Wissensformen*, 21: "The mind . . . determines solely and exclusively the make-up of possible cultural factors — why they are as they are and not otherwise. But the mind as such does not originally and essentially possess the least trace of 'power' or 'efficacy' by which to bring these factors into existence. It is certainly a 'determining' factor, but not an 'implementing' one in the genesis of the potential culture." This model is undoubtedly somewhat dogmatic. That is to say, it is influenced by the desire to rescue, a priori, at least one sector from the grasp of sociological investigation. In my view, the genesis of a religious tradition cannot be understood apart from factors of social history; nor can the prevailing power of such a tradition be put down exclusively to these factors. What is true is that we always find the emergence of something new more mysterious than its later history.

is not the *birth* of a spiritual tradition. We are discussing its spread, its transmission, and its preservation. It must surely be admitted that this is a sociological problem, even if one believes that the importance of sociological research for illuminating intellectual and spiritual traditions can be as clearly limited as Max Scheler maintains.

The transmission of Jesus sayings in the early Christian community is a sociological problem particularly because Jesus gave no fixed, written form to what he said. A written tradition can survive for a time even when it has no bearing on the behavior of men and women, or even if the tradition's intention runs counter to that behavior.[7] But oral tradition is at the mercy of the interests and concerns of the people who pass it on and to whom it is addressed. Its survival is dependent on specific social conditions.[8] To mention only one of these: the people who pass the tradition on must in some way or other identify with that tradition. It is improbable that ethical precepts will be passed on for long if no one takes them seriously, and if no one makes at least an attempt to practice them. Given this premise, if we ask about the *Sitz im Leben* of Jesus' ethical teachings — the real-life situation to which they belong — we soon find ourselves in difficulty. Form criticism postulates that these teachings had their situation in congregational life. But — to take one example — what about the saying in Luke 14:26: "If any one comes to me and does not hate his own father and mother and wife and children and brothers and sisters, yes, and even his own life, he cannot be my disciple"? We should be inclined to call in question the

---

7. See here the important essay by P. G. Bogatyrev and R. Jakobson, "Die Folklore als eine besondere Form des Schaffens" in *Donum Natalicium Schrijnen* (Nijmwegen and Utrecht, 1929), 900–913.

8. Social conditions for the oral traditions about Jesus may be designated as follows: (1) The Jesus tradition was rooted in recurrent, typical behavior toward other people on the part of the transmitters. This was relatively independent of individual preference or caprice. If mental or spiritual attitudes are to survive, they must be anchored in the permanent necessities of life and in the constant characteristics of a particular life-style. (2) An interest on the part of the people addressed, who are the passive preservers of tradition (see C. W. von Sydow, "On the Spread of Tradition" in *Selected Papers on Folklore* [Copenhagen, 1948], 11–43, esp. 15–18). Traditions continue to be passed on only as long as they find listeners. Whatever runs counter to the concerns and attitudes of these listeners will be eliminated or modified. It will fall victim to what Bogatyrev and Jakobson call "the preventive censorship of the community" (see "Folklore," 903). We need only think of the adaptation to congregational conditions which we can observe in the different variants of the Jesus sayings. (3) A sociological continuity between Jesus and the people who passed on his sayings. Scandinavian scholars quite properly tried to show that this continuity existed, their aim in so doing being to overcome the skepticism of the form critics about the authenticity of Jesus' sayings (see H. Riesenfeld, *The Gospel Tradition and Its Beginnings* [London: Mowbray, 1957], 43–56; B. Gerhardsson, *Memory and Manuscript*, ASNU 22 [Uppsala, 1964]). In my view, however, the attempt is a failure.

whole postulate about a situation in congregational life, rather than to assume that a saying like this could ever have provided the basis for the shared life of men and women. Their ethical radicalism makes Jesus' sayings absolutely impracticable as a regulative for everyday behavior. So we are faced all the more inescapably with the question: Who passed on sayings like these by word of mouth over a period of thirty years and more? Who took them seriously? This is the problem on which we shall be concentrating here.

Are there any criteria that can help us to find an answer to the question? We might start off skeptically. All we have at our disposal are texts. We have no direct knowlege about the social behavior which is involved, and which they reflect. It can only be deduced. Form criticism had three ways of making this deduction:[9]

(1) *analytical deduction* from the form and content of a tradition to its situation (or *Sitz im Leben*);
(2) *constructive deduction* from direct statements about the situation presumed to the traditions that were anchored there;
(3) *deduction by analogy* from contemporary parallels that are similar in content.

In the course of our discussion I shall use all three methods of deduction.

The sayings tradition offers a particular wealth of material for analytical deduction. The sayings enjoin particular behavior. This is translated into reflective form in general maxims and is pictorially presented in parables and apophthegmatic scenes which illustrate the maxim in question. Of course the behavior that is commanded, thought about, and illustrated, on the one hand does not simply coincide with actual behavior on the other. But if the divergences are typical ones, they can be allowed for in our deductions: as we know, commandments are radical at points where real life inclines toward compromise.[10] Prohibitions often allow us to deduce that the forbidden behavior actually exists.[11] But in general we may assume heuristically, or as a working hypothesis, that

---

9. See R. Bultmann, *Die Geschichte der synoptischen Tradition*, 5th ed. (Göttingen, 1961), 5f., 7f. (Eng. trans. *The History of the Synoptic Tradition*, trans. John Marsh [Oxford: Blackwell; New York, Harper & Row, 1963]).

10. For example, it was one of Paul's maxims not to allow himself to be kept by his congregations. This did not prevent him from gratefully accepting support from the congregation in Philippi (Phil. 4:10ff.), although elsewhere he almost makes his salvation depend on his making no use of an apostle's usual privileges (1 Cor. 9:13-18).

11. The staff forbidden in Matt. 10:10 is conceded to the early Christian missionaries in Mark 6:8. The mission to the Gentiles is forbidden in Matt. 10:5f.; yet, as we know, it took place.

the sayings of Jesus were practiced in some form or other. If they had been notoriously disregarded, they would hardly have survived over a period of one or two generations. It seems more likely (and there is evidence of the fact here and there) that they were *adapted* to actual behavior—so that the analytical inference, or induction, from the sayings to this behavior suggests itself even more. There should be no doubt about the fact that the sayings of Jesus are meant seriously and literally. We must not assume that the early congregations already harbored the kind of text interpreters who assure us that none of it was intended to be taken so seriously—interpreters who maintain that this saying was added later, that the other was conditioned by the time, that the third was symbolic, the fourth contradictory, and that the fifth can be relativized by other New Testament statements. On the contrary, we must assume that Jesus' sayings were consistently taken seriously and were practiced. We should not forget that one of these sayings asks: "Why do you call me 'Lord, Lord,' and not do what I tell you?" (Luke 6:46).

Let us now consider why Jesus sayings were passed on, looking also at the conditions of the transmission. We shall draw on the help of the criteria I have suggested and shall proceed in two stages. First, we must start from the way the transmitters saw themselves, as this emerges from the form and content of the logia, or sayings. Our aim here is to discover the behavior that is behind them. Our findings will have to be tested by the methods of constructive deduction and analogy. In a second stage we can then go on to ask about the conditions that determined this behavior, even when the transmitters were not consciously aware of the fact.

I. THE SELF-UNDERSTANDING OF THE TRANSMITTERS AND THEIR CONDUCT

The sayings tradition is characterized by an ethical radicalism that is shown most noticeably in the renunciation of a home, family, and possessions. From the precepts that have to do with these things, we can arrive analytically at some conclusions about the life-style that was characteristic of the people who passed on the texts.

Jesus' sayings preach an ethic that is based on homelessness. The call to discipleship means renouncing any permanent abode. The people who are called leave their boats and their fields, their customshouse and their home. Jesus tells one of his disciples: "Foxes have holes, and birds of the air have nests; but the Son of man has nowhere to lay his head" (Matt. 8:20). Homelessness belonged to the discipleship of Jesus, and not merely during his lifetime. The *Didache,* for example, is familiar with itinerant Christian charismatics and says that they practice τρόπους κυρίου, the Lord's way of living (*Did.* 11.8).

The ethic of the sayings excludes family ties as well. Giving up a fixed place of abode means breaking with family relationships. To hate father and mother, wife and children, brother and sister is one of the conditions for discipleship (Luke 14:26). According to Mark 10:29, the disciples left their homes, their fields, and their families. They violated even the minimum requirements of family piety. One disciple wants to bury his father, who has just died. But he is told: "Leave the dead to bury their own dead" (Matt. 8:22).[12] To have children oneself is undesirable: one saying talks about people who have deprived themselves of their procreative power for the kingdom's sake (Matt. 19:12).[13] What someone with an average ethical attitude to the family thought about the early Christian wandering charismatics requires no very extensive discussion. Understandably enough, the early Christian prophet did not count for much in his hometown and in his own family (Mark 6:4).[14] We could hardly expect the abandoned families to have reverenced him as a hero. It was in fact difficult to justify his behavior. There are sayings that postulate the disintegration of the family as a necessary manifestation of the end time (Luke 12:52f.).[15] Others remodel the concept of the family:

---

12. See M. Hengel, "Nachfolge und Charisma," BZNW 34 (Berlin, 1968). H. G. Klemm rightly objects to interpretations that tone down the "offensive" sayings of Jesus ("Das Wort von der Selbstbestattung der Toten," *NTS* 16 [1969–70]: 60–75).

13. It is hard to say how far the logion should be taken literally. J. Blinzler believes that it is intended to defend the disciples against the insulting term "eunuch" ("Εἰσὶν εὐνοῦχοι: Zur Auslegung von Mt 19, 12," *ZNW* 48 [1957]: 254–70). H. Greeven thinks that this is a pictorial way of talking about the people who are leading a sexually ascetic life ("Ehe nach dem Neuen Testament," *NTS* 15 [1968–69]: 365–88). Q. Quesnell even claims that what is under discussion is the sexual asceticism of someone whose wife has been unfaithful, who—although he casts the woman off for adultery—abstains from a new marriage out of faithfulness to the old one ("Made Themselves Eunuchs for the Kingdom of Heaven," *CBQ* 30 [1968]: 335–58).

14. In Mark 6:4, relatives and members of the family (οἰκία) are explicitly mentioned, although these are missing in *POxy.* 1.5 and *Gospel of Thomas* 31. Either Mark 6:4 has modified a general adage (Bultmann's view in *Geschichte,* German ed., 31f.), or *POxy.* 1.5 and *Gospel of Thomas* 31 are secondary developments of Mark 6:4. This is the view taken by W. Schrage, "Das Verhältnis des Thomasevangeliums zur synoptischen Tradition und zu den koptischen Evangelienübersetzungen," BZNW 29 (1964): 75, 77; see also E. Grässer, "Jesus in Nazareth," *NTS* 16 (1969–70): 1–23. The saying probably once existed on its own, out of context (see E. Haenchen, *Der Weg Jesu* [Berlin, 1966], 220). In this form it would then certainly, like Matt. 5:11f., have referred to early Christian prophets.

15. This actualized a prophetic, apocalyptic tradition: Mic. 7:6; Zech. 13:3; *1 Enoch* 100:2; 99:5; *Jub.* 23:16; *Syr. Bar.* 70:6; 2 Esd. 6:24. It is interesting that Matthew should take up this saying in the sending of the Twelve (Matt. 10:21); that is, that he lets it be

one's brothers, sisters, and parents are the people who do God's will (Mark 3:35). On the other hand, the breach with the family was probably hardly ever put into practice consistently. For example, many men took their wives with them on their wanderings (see 1 Cor. 9:5).

A third characteristic of the sayings tradition is criticism of wealth and possessions.[16] As the story of the rich young ruler shows, renunciation of possessions was considered essential for full discipleship (Mark 10:17ff.). Treasure should be gathered in heaven, not on earth (Matt. 6:19-21).[17] It is easier for a camel to go through the eye of a needle than for a rich man[18] to enter the kingdom of God (Mark 10:25). A person who renounces possessions is renouncing the usual way of saving himself from anxiety. That is why the saying passed down to us says:

> Do not be anxious about your life, what you shall eat or what you shall drink, nor about your body, what you shall put on. Is not life more than food, and the body more than clothing? Look at the birds of the air: they neither sow nor reap nor gather into barns, and yet your heavenly Father feeds them. Are you not of more value than they? . . . And why are you anxious about clothing? Consider the lilies of the field, how they grow, they neither toil nor spin. . . . (Matt. 6:25ff.)

We should not read into this saying the mood of a Sunday afternoon stroll with the family. It has nothing to do with delight in birds and

---

addressed to wandering charismatics especially. On Luke 12:51-53, see S. Schulz, *Q: Die Spruchquelle der Evangelisten* (Zurich, 1972), 258-60.

16. On this problem, see H. J. Degenhardt, "Besitz und Besitzverzicht in den Lukanischen Schriften" (diss., Würzburg, 1963); on the rich young ruler, see pp. 136-49.

17. In Luke the command not to gather treasure on earth is missing. It has been transformed into a positive exhortation: he should use his wealth in order to give alms. According to W. Pesch, Luke is modifying the tradition here, formulating a "message to the Christian congregations in the Hellenistic world, with their socially difficult class structures" ("Zur Exegese von Mt 6, 19-21 und Lk 12, 33-34," *Bibl* 41 [1960]: 356-78; quotation from p. 375). I believe that this interpretation is correct. According to Degenhardt, however, it is the version in Matthew that is secondary ("Besitz," 88-93). Yet another view is taken by H. T. Wrege, *Die Überlieferungsgeschichte der Bergpredigt*, WUNT 9 (Tübingen, 1968), 109-13. H. Riesenfeld would like to prove that this parenetic Synoptic tradition is presupposed in the epistles too ("Vom Schätzesammeln und Sorgen — ein Thema urchristlicher Paränese," in *Neotestamentica et Patristica: Festschrift für O. Cullmann*, Suppl. NovTest 6 [Leiden, 1962], 47-58). But I myself doubt this.

18. There is in my view no reason for assuming that the original reading was "man" (ἄνθρωπος) instead of the present "rich man." This is S. Legasse's view in "Jésus a-t-il annoncé la Conversion Finale d'Israel (A propos de Marc X, 23-27)," *NTS* 10 (1963-64): 480-87. Similarly N. Walter, "Zur Analyse von Mc 10, 17-31," *ZNW* 53 (1962): 206-18. He maintains that the saying is not asserting "that a human being could perhaps enter the kingdom of God by casting away earthly possessions or through other ascetic endeavors" (p. 210). This is sound Protestant dogmatics, but hardly in line with early Christian radicalism.

flowers and green fields. On the contrary: what this saying is talking about is the whole rigor of the life led by the wandering charismatics, outlawed, without any home and without protection, people who made their way through the countryside without any possessions and without any work.[19]

We can now formulate our thesis:[20] the ethical radicalism of the sayings transmitted to us is the radicalism of itinerants. It can be practiced and passed on only under extreme living conditions. It is only the person who has severed his everyday ties with the world—the person who has left home and possessions, wife and child, who lets the dead bury their dead, and takes the birds and the lilies of the field as his model—it is only a person like this who can consistently preach renunciation of a settled home, a family, possessions, the protection of the law, and his own defense. It is only in this context that the ethical precepts which match this way of life can be passed on without being unconvincing. This ethic only has a chance on the fringes of society; this is the only real-life situation it can have. Or to be more exact: it does not have a situation *in* real life at all. It has to put up with an existence *on the fringes* of normal life, an existence that from the outsider's point of view is undoubtedly questionable. It is only here that Jesus' words were saved from being reduced to allegory, from reinterpretation, from softening or repression—simply because they were taken seriously and put into practice. And that was possible only for homeless charismatics.

We can check the soundness of this thesis in a second process of thought, by means of a constructive deduction from the evidence. In the charge with which the disciples are sent out in the Synoptics[21] and

---

19. In my opinion P. Hoffmann is correct here; see his *Studien zur Theologie der Logienquelle*, NTA NF 8 (Münster, 1972), 327f. For a different view, see Schulz, *Q,* 149–57.

20. This thesis is a development of G. Kretschmar's ideas in "Ein Beitrag zur Frage nach dem Ursprung frühchristlicher Askese," *ZThK* 61 (1964): 27–67. Hoffmann takes these ideas further in a similar direction (*Logienquelle*, 312–34). The theory I am maintaining here grew out of a conversation with the Rev. H. Frost, who drew my attention particularly to the significance of the charge with which the disciples are sent forth, and what it tells us about the people who passed on the Jesus tradition.

21. For modern analyses of the sending discourse, see F. Hahn, *Das Verständnis der Mission im Neuen Testament*, WMANT 13, 2nd ed. (Neukirchen-Vluyn, 1965), 33–36 (Eng. trans. *Mission in the New Testament*, trans. F. Clarke, Studies in Biblical Theology 47 [London: SCM Press; Naperville, Ill.: Allenson, 1965]); H. Schürmann, *Das Lukasevangelium*, HThK III/1 (Freiburg, 1969), 504f.; Hoffmann, *Logienquelle*, 236–334; Schulz, *Q,* 404–19. The interpretation I am putting forward here is especially close to Hoffmann's, but I have not tried to follow up his attempt to localize the logia traditions in the history of the time—that is, in the context of the disputes between "the hawks" and "the doves" before the Jewish War.

in the *Didache* too,[22] direct statements about the early Christian itinerant charismatics have been preserved for us. In the Synoptics we are told the rules given to the first Christian missionaries. The *Didache* gives the rules for dealing with these people. We now have to show that to some extent these directives point to the very behavior which we have discovered was characteristic of the people who passed on the sayings.

The obligation to dispense with home and one's familiar country is included in the charge to the disciples. In the *Didache*, the point is made even more forcibly: an apostle is to remain no more than one day, or at most two, in the same place. If he remains three days, he is a false prophet (*Did.* 11.5).

Poverty is an equally clear obligation. The missionaries are to take no money with them, no purse, only one garment, neither shoes nor staff (Matt. 10:10). According to the *Didache*, the apostles should be given bread for only a single day, and never money. If anyone asks for money he is a false prophet (*Did.* 11.6).

The nonfamily character of this wandering life does not emerge so strongly. A puzzling passage in the *Didache* says that the wandering prophets practice the μυστήριον τῆς ἐκκλησίας, "the mystery of the church."[23] They are not to be condemned for this. Judgment is to be left to God—provided that these prophets do not teach other people to behave in the same way (*Did.* 11.11). This is probably an allusion to women who accompanied the wandering prophets, and whose relations with them were not unequivocal. Sexual abstinence was no doubt an official requirement. However, the passage is still a μυστήριον for us too.

The conduct enjoined in the transmitted sayings was therefore practiced by at least *one* group of early Christians: the itinerant charismatics, the apostles, prophets, and missionaries. That does not necessarily prove that these people were also the transmitters of the sayings themselves. But this is probable, especially since there are some clues that point in this direction.

---

22. On the rules in the *Didache* about the treatment and condemnation of the itinerant Christian charismatics, see A. von Harnack, *Lehre der Zwölf Apostel nebst Untersuchungen zur ältesten Geschichte der Kirchenverfassung und des Kirchenrechts*, TU 2, 1-2 (Leipzig, 1884), esp. 88ff.; J. P. Audet, *La Didachè: Instructions des apôtres* (Paris, 1958), 435–57; Kretschmar, "Beitrag," 36f. Kretschmar points to some illuminating links with Syrian itinerant ascetics.

23. Audet gives a survey of exegetical opinion (*Didachè*, 451f.). He himself argues against a sexual interpretation. But it is quite possible that what is being thought of is the practice of adoptive or spiritual brotherhood or sisterhood—that is, living together with the obligation to abstain from sexual relations. This is R. Knopf's view in *Die Lehre der zwölf Apostel*, HNT suppl. vol. 1 (Tübingen, 1920), 32f. The woman's pregnancy will often have made the problematical character of this undertaking apparent, as Irenaeus makes plain when he is talking about this practice among the Valentinians (*Adv. haer.* 1.6.3).

In the passage about the sending of the Twelve in the Gospel of Matthew there is an explicit mention of the "words" of the wandering charismatics: "If any one will not receive you or listen to your words. . ." (Matt. 10:14). Now, these do not have to have been Jesus' own words. But the only saying that Matthew quotes directly as having been proclaimed by these wandering charismatics is a saying of Jesus: "The rule of God is at hand" (Matt. 10:7; Luke 10:9). Their sayings were therefore at least partly identical with Jesus' own sayings.

The missionary charge in Luke goes even further: "He who hears you hears me, and he who rejects you rejects me" (Luke 10:16; cf. Matt. 10:40). Jesus himself is present in the words of the itinerant missionaries. This presence should not be viewed as a mystical identity. The wandering missionary is Jesus' voice because he passes on Jesus' words—because he is Jesus' messenger. This is confirmed by the form of the logia. Some of them are in the first person.[24] In some of them the Amen formula shows that they are meant as a revealed truth taken over by the speaker.[25] The two groups complement each other. For example, the person who in the first person utters the "But I say to you" of the Sermon on the Mount becomes Jesus' representative through what he says: "He who hears you hears me." This applied particularly to wandering charismatics, as a variant of this saying shows: "He who receives you receives me, and he who receives me receives him who sent me" (Matt. 10:40). This saying is a recommendation to the congregations to take the wandering charismatics in.[26]

---

24. In Mark 13:6 early Christian prophets are characterized by the first-person style of their discourses. These people will hardly have been purporting to be the returning Messiah, for anyone who "comes in Jesus' name" (Mark 13:6) will hardly claim identity with him. The ἐγώ εἰμι ("I am") is rather to be viewed as a stylistic device of prophetic speech. Luke's polemic at this point against early Christian itinerant prophets is even more unambiguous. Their proclamation that ὁ καιρὸς ἤγγικεν, "the time is at hand" (Luke 21:8), corresponds precisely to the charge in the missionary discourse (Luke 10:9; Matt. 10:7).

25. See K. Berger, *Die Amen-Worte Jesu*, BZNW 29 (Berlin, 1970). He is probably right here, contrary to V. Hasler, *Amen* (Zurich and Stuttgart, 1969).

26. E. Käsemann already put forward this view in "Die Anfänge christlicher Theologie," *ZThK* 57 (1960): 162–85 (Eng. trans. "The Beginnings of Christian Theology," in *New Testament Questions of Today*, trans. W. J. Montague et al. [London: SCM Press; Philadelphia: Fortress Press, 1969], 82ff.). Cf. also the *Didache*'s instruction that wandering charismatics are to be received as if they were the Lord (*Did.* 11.2). The wandering charismatics' awareness that they were Jesus' representatives is to be found in other logia as well. In my view it explains the change from the first person to the third in Mark 8:38, which has always been felt to be a puzzle: "Whoever is ashamed of me and of my words . . . of him will the Son of man also be ashamed. . . ." The saying has given rise to an extensive debate. Here I may mention only P. Vielhauer, "Gottesreich und Menschensohn in der Verkündigung Jesu," in *Aufsätze zum Neuen Testament* (Munich, 1965), 55–91; esp. too

In my view, these rules for the early Christian itinerant charismatics allow us to make a constructive deduction: these people were practicing an ethic that corresponded to the logia tradition; the tradition's eschatological theme was part of their proclamation; and they saw themselves as people who were in line with Jesus' sayings. They were the transmitters of Jesus' words, even after the Gospels had taken form. In the second century, Papias was still culling Jesus traditions from the itinerant disciples of the Lord who passed by.[27]

Finally, we can underpin our thesis by a conclusion from analogy. All wandering charismatics were not Christians. In the first and second centuries there were numerous itinerant Cynic philosophers and preachers as well. They too existed on the fringes of society.[28] They were in opposition to the emperors Vespasian and Domitian, and the emperors in their turn joined battle with them. Other people thought

---

101-7; also the most recent discussion in Schulz, *Q,* 66–76. As the transmitter of Jesus' sayings, the early Christian wandering prophet could identify himself with Jesus and speak in the first person ("Whoever is ashamed of me and of my words . . ."). But he was very well able to distinguish between himself and the future judge. The closest analogy to this is to be found in the sending of the Twelve, where we read "If any one will not receive you or listen to your words . . ." (Matt. 10:14). Corresponding to this is the other saying: "Whoever is ashamed of me and of my words . . ." — "my words" meaning the words of Jesus passed on by the wandering charismatics, which could be distinguished from the person of Jesus because of this transmission through other people. A similar awareness that they were representatives comes out in the saying about the sin against the Holy Spirit, that is, against the Spirit of the early Christian prophets (Mark 3:28f. par.). We already find this "prophet" interpretation in *Did.* 11.7. See Berger, *Amen-Worte,* 36–41. Wrege rightly sees this saying as "an expression of the foundation of the Synoptic logia tradition also" (*Überlieferungsgeschichte,* 169): behavior before Easter is relativized and Jesus' words again become the touchstone of judgment. R. Scroggs traces the saying back to an enthusiastic trend in Syro-Palestinian Christianity which he believes is being attacked in Matt. 7:22f. ("The Exaltation of the Spirit by Some Early Christians," *JBL* 84 [1965]: 359–73). In my view it is a particular sociological type of Christian faith that finds expression here — that is, the radicalism of the early Christian itinerants. Perhaps the sense of being representatives, which was cherished by the early Christian wandering charismatics, is also present in Matt. 25:31-46; see J. R. Michaelis, "Apostolic Hardships and Righteous Gentiles," *JBL* 84 (1965): 27–37. Michaelis identifies "the least of the brethren" with the apostles. This interpretation would in fact be in line with logia which make God's attitude to men and women at the judgment dependent on their behavior toward Jesus' messengers (Luke 10:16; Matt. 10:40ff.). Nevertheless, the command to be hospitable is no doubt intended to apply to everyone. See also L. Cope, "Matthew XXV, 31-46 'The Sheep and the Goats' Reinterpreted," *NovTest* 11 (1969): 32–44.

27. Eusebius *Ecclesiastical History* 3.39.4: "But when anyone came who was a disciple of the elders, I asked them about the elders' words."

28. See L. Friedlaender, *Darstellungen aus der Sittengeschichte Roms in der Zeit von August bis zum Ausgang der Antonine,* 8th ed. (Leipzig, 1910), 4:315f., 346–53 (reprint, Hildesheim, 1967); D. R. Dudley, *A History of Cynicism* (London: Methuen, 1937; reprint 1967), esp. 125ff.

that the finest of these men were patterns of human living—the philosopher Epictetus, for example. Talking about the Cynics, Epictetus asks: "How is it possible to live happily without worldly possessions, naked and without house or home, without any care for the body, without a servant and without a country?" And he replies:

> Behold, God has sent you the man who can prove through his deeds that it is possible. I have none of these things. I sleep upon the ground. I have neither wife nor children, no little palace, nothing but earth and heaven and a single great cloak. And yet what do I lack? Am I not free of anxiety? Being without fear, am I not free? (*Discourses* 20.46–48)

The ethic of the early Christian sayings that have come down to us and the ethic of Cynic philosophy resemble each other in their three most important features: they are ethics based on the renunciation of home and country, family ties, and possessions. Since the ethic of the Cynics was spread by itinerant philosophers, it will be permissible to conclude, by analogy, that the people who passed on the Jesus tradition belonged to a comparable sociological group. This conclusion by analogy is based on structural similarities, not on historical links between the two movements. All the same, links are not entirely lacking.[29] In Gadara, in east Jordan, Menippus, Meleager, and Oinomaos are evidence that Cynic ideas existed for a period of five hundred years.[30] Even more significant is the fact that in the second century, Peregrinus—the target of Lucian of Samosata's mockery—was at first an itinerant Christian charismatic who was then converted to Cynicism and continued his wandering life under different colors.[31] Itinerant Cynic philosophers and early Christian wandering charismatics alike stepped outside normal life. But of course their inward, spiritual reason for doing so differed. The philosophers detached themselves from existing conventions and customs by way of an intellectual process in which they set φύσις ("nature") over against νόμος ("law") as antitheses. The early Christian wandering preachers did the same in mythical images in which the old world, doomed to destruction, was contrasted with a new one.

If the sayings of Jesus were passed on by wandering charismatics, what

---

29. H. Hommel draws attention to points of intersection between the logia tradition and philosophical motifs belonging to the Socratic tradition ("Herrenworte im Lichte sokratischer Überlieferung," *ZNW* 57 [1966]: 1-23). He sees a link especially in the theme about the priority of spiritual relationships over family ones, which is particularly relevant for the logia tradition. On the theme that the wise man accepts no money, see H. D. Betz, *Der Apostel Paulus und die sokratische Tradition,* BHTh 45 (Tübingen, 1972), 100–117.

30. On these cynically influenced writers or philosophers, see the relevant articles in PW and in *Lexikon der alten Welt,* ed. K. Bartels and L. Huber (Zurich and Stuttgart, 1965).

31. J. Bernays, *Lucian und die Kyniker* (Berlin, 1879).

does this tell us about their authenticity? The skepticism of the form critics is based on the recognition that the Jesus sayings were shaped by the institutions and needs of the congregations that grew up after Easter. These institutions and needs were neither established by Jesus nor envisaged by him. For, as Alfred Loisy said: "Jesus proclaimed the kingdom of God, and what happened was the church."[32] If by the church we understand local congregations and their institutions, then there is no sociological continuity between Jesus and Christianity in its early form.[33] But it was different in the case of the wandering charismatics. Here Jesus' social situation and the social situation of one branch of early Christianity are comparable: Jesus was the first wandering charismatic. The people who passed on his sayings took over "the Lord's way of life," the τρόπους κυρίου (*Did.* 11.8); thus, sayings that show the impress of their life-style are by no means necessarily "nongenuine." The radicalism of their wandering life goes back to Jesus himself. It is authentic. Probably more of the sayings must be "suspected" of being genuine than many a modern skeptic would like to think.

But the Jesus tradition is authentic in a different, transferred sense as well. It is *existentially* authentic. It was practiced. Here both modernist and conservative interpreters are often equally blind. Thus an exponent of existential interpretation and the "new hermeneutics" sees the demand to the rich young ruler to give away his possessions as a call to accept Jesus' word.[34] The hearer must hear. In this encounter, we are told, the call to discipleship must "no longer be interpreted ethically or sociologically"; what is being said is "religious in the most genuine sense."[35] Now, the new hermeneutic aims to interpret bygone texts for the present—in this case, no doubt, for a present in which it is quite coolly taken for granted that Jesus' words are not practiced. The aim itself is no cause for reproach. But no one should make it a reason for letting himself be seduced into using hermeneutical profundity as a

---

32. See A. Loisy, *L'Évangile et l'Église,* 3rd ed. (Bellevue, 1904), 155. On the interpretation of his famous dictum, see D. Hoffmann-Axthelm, "Loisys 'L'Évangile et l'Église': Besichtigung eines zeitgenössischen Schlachtfeldes," *ZThK* 65 (1968): 291–328.

33. S. Schulz's extensive work *Q: Die Spruchquelle der Evangelisten* (see n. 15 above) is an attempt to localize the tradition of the sayings of Jesus in a Q congregation. Because of the radical ethics of the sayings, these congregations must be made highly "unworldly" ("enthusiastic"), this being put down largely to the imminent expectation of the parousia. Skepticism about the authenticity of the Jesus sayings is inevitably intensified.

34. E. Fuchs, *Jesus, Wort und Tat* (Tübingen, 1971), 10–20: "Here we must not too hastily lose ourselves in sociological questions, for 'sell' has a dialectical sense: discipleship consists in the acceptance of his Word" (p. 18).

35. Ibid., 19. Even the tentative sociological approaches made by classic form criticism are rejected: "We should not now draw on sociological categories, as is the inevitable practice in the form criticism of Bultmann and, especially, American theology" (p. 82).

way of setting aside the clear meaning of Jesus' sayings. This should be avoided, if only out of respect for the people who once took these sayings seriously. And even today it is worth remembering and thinking about the fact that once upon a time there were men and women who, when they passed on Jesus' sayings, could assure their listeners without the suspicion of a jarring note that "heaven and earth will pass away, but my words will not pass away" (Mark 13:31).

II. THE CONDUCT OF THE TRANSMITTERS
AND THE CONDITIONS THAT SHAPED IT

We started by considering the intentions behind the sayings tradition. The premise for the inference we made about practical behavior was that mental and spiritual intentions are something to be taken seriously; that is to say, they have practical consequences for "earthly" behavior. We shall now, in a second stage, proceed to reverse this heuristic assumption. We may also assume that entirely "earthly" conditions can have practical consequences for mental and spiritual intentions. The different factors that go to make up these earthly conditions may be divided into three groups, and we shall consider certain aspects of them, one after another: (1) socioeconomic factors, such as the question of how to make a living, a person's occupation, and the social class to which he or she belongs; (2) socioecological factors, such as urban or rural milieu; (3) sociocultural factors, such as the language, norms and values of particular groups of people. Since religious traditions deal only very shamefacedly with their not-so-religious preconditions (or do not deal with them at all), it is, in the nature of things, very difficult to arrive at soundly based assertions here. Methodologically justified skepticism is undoubtedly called for. But there are no grounds for the opportunistic skepticism which maintains that it is methodologically impossible to know anything about this sector—the real reason being that at bottom the skeptics have no desire to know anything about it. Generally these skeptics know astonishingly well in their heart of hearts that the factors I have named have at least a subordinate importance.

One very simple socioeconomic question is treated in the sayings tradition as clearly as we could wish. That is the question of livelihood, or means of support. The missionary charge to the disciples contains one negative and one positive utterance here. The negative instruction is as follows: "Take nothing for your journey, no staff, nor bag, nor bread, nor money; and do not have two tunics" (Luke 9:3); "salute no one on the road" (10:4). What interests us particularly is the renunciation of bag, staff,[36] bread, and money. Cloak, bag, and staff were the characteristic "uniform" of the itinerant Cynic philosophers,[37] the "mendicant friars of antiquity," as they have been called. The prohibition of bag[38] and staff was probably intended to avoid the least shadow of an impression that the Christian missionaries were these beggars, or were like them. They were probably forbidden to greet any one on the way for the same reason.[39] Anyone who demonstratively displays his poverty and accosts another person on the road could easily be misunderstood. The command not to move from house to house in the same village or town (Mark 6:10; Luke 10:7) has a similar point.[40] It might all too easily have suggested an attempt to exploit materially a village's readiness to receive the wanderers. It is clear that the early Christian itinerant charismatics were forbidden to employ the usual beggar's practices.[41] But they were also forbidden to make any planned provision for the future.

This gives even more force to the question: What did these people live from?[42] We have a positive instruction on this point:

---

36. To renounce the staff meant renouncing the most modest means of self-defense (see Hoffmann, *Logienquelle,* 313ff.). Anyone who wandered through the country in this way had no choice other than to abide by Jesus' saying "if any one strikes you on the right cheek, turn to him the other also . . . and if any one forces you to go one mile, go with him two miles" (Matt. 5:39-41). The logion could be directly related to the situation of the wandering charismatics. For someone who is in any case on the move, it is a matter of indifference whether he is forced to render any particular service for one mile or for five or three.

37. Diogenes Laertius 6.13. Here cloak, bag, and staff, appendages that later counted as signs of a Cynic philosopher, are probably being attributed to Antisthenes (see Dudley, *Cynicism,* 6). On traveling equipment in the ancient world in general, see Hoffmann, *Logienquelle,* 313ff.

38. The Cynic Crates wrote a play called Πήρα ("bag"). A. Deissmann (*Licht vom Osten,* 4th ed. [Tübingen, 1923], 86–88) accepts the meaning "beggar's sack" and refers to *Bulletin de Correspondance Hellénique* 21 (1897): 60 (Eng. trans. *Light from the Ancient East,* trans. L. R. M. Strachan [London: Hodder & Stoughton, 1910]). W. Michaelis takes a different view ("Πήρα," *ThWNT* 6:119–21). He writes: "Jesus will hardly have come across the type of the itinerant 'religious' or philosopher with the beggar's sack, such as were to be found in the cults of Asia Minor and among the Cynics" (p. 121 n. 13; see *TDNT* 6).

39. W. Grundmann, for example, takes a different view, maintaining that this was a warning against wasting time; see *Das Evangelium nach Lukas,* ThHNT 3 (Berlin, 1969), 209. Similarly Schulz, *Q,* 416.

40. Haenchen puts this prohibition down to experience: jealousy and quarrels arose when different families in turn received the missionaries (*Weg Jesu,* 230).

41. Haenchen also believes that the demonstrative poverty of the itinerant missionaries was intended to guard against the suspicion that they wanted to line their pockets (*Weg Jesu,* 222).

42. Although Schulz shows marked concern for the revolutionizing of material conditions in contemporary society, where the interpretation of texts is concerned (*Q,* 172ff., 487ff.), questions about the material conditions of their transmission do not seem to interest him. With regard to our problem he writes quite simply: "We must be careful

Whatever house you enter, first say, "Peace be to this house!" And if a son of peace is there, your peace shall rest upon him; but if not, it shall return to you. And remain in the same house, eating and drinking what they provide, for the laborer deserves his wages. Do not go from house to house. (Luke 10:5-7)

It was therefore evidently expected that there would always be people who would freely provide the necessary support. Here the appeal was not to a charitable turn of mind but to what was just and right: labor deserves its wage. What kind of labor? The charge to the disciples names two things: healings and eschatological proclamation — healings for the present, proclamation for the future. And the proclamation was not merely a matter of powerless words; it offered support at the last judgment. This emerges from the salutation of peace.[43] The greeting is conditional. If the wandering preachers are rejected, the greeting reverts to them like some magical power. But the hostile place will suffer a worse fate at the impending judgment than Sodom and Gomorrah (Matt. 10:15; Luke 10:12). We may conclude from this that if the wandering preachers were received, the eschatological judgment would pass the receptive houses and villages by. Healings in the present and eschatological protection — this was "the work performed" by the wandering preachers, and it was to be given without payment "You received without paying, give without pay" (Matt. 10:8). Nevertheless, the work performed was worthy of its proper wage. That it should be paid for in food, drink, and shelter was really a matter of course.[44] This is certainly not begging in the normal sense. It is an elevated kind of begging, charismatic begging, for which the problem of livelihood is only marginal, since "the beggar" is confident that this problem will solve itself, so to speak, according to the motto: "Seek first the kingdom of God and his righteousness, and all these things shall be yours as well" (Matt. 6:33). It is not just by chance that among the Jesus sayings we find what is really a piece of beggar's lore: "Ask, and it will be given you; seek, and you will find; knock, and it will be opened to you" (Luke 11:9ff. par).

Of course conditions in the real world will have seen to it that these

---

not to read more into this instruction than is actually said: the apocalyptic laborers in the harvest are real workers who have a claim to food and drink" (p. 417).

43. On the background of "the peace" in the history of religion, see Hoffmann, *Logien-quelle,* 296–302. On pp. 310ff. he interprets the salutation against the background of the time: "the sons of peace" are gathered together in their conflict with the zealots of the resistance movements. But does the salutation not have a very general connotation?

44. S. Krauss, "Die Instruktion Jesu an die Apostel," *Angelos* 1 (1925): 96–102: "Jesus apparently requires his disciples to live from the hospitality of the people to whom they happen to come and in whose towns or villages they preach."

things did *not* always take care of themselves. The story about the plucking of the ears of corn makes this clear. Form-critical analysis assumed that this incident transformed conditions in the early Christian congregations into an ideal scene.[45] But this prompted the objection that it can hardly have been a recurrent custom in these congregations to wander hungry through the fields on the Sabbath.[46] It is quite true that this could scarcely have happened in a local congregation of respectable working Christians. But for itinerant preachers, without money and without bread, it may well have been a typical situation. In the story, the breaking of the Sabbath is justified by the circumstance that in Old Testament times the priests had a right to the sacred bread. But the explanation is not logical. The priest was not breaking the Sabbath when he gave the offerings to unauthorized persons. But the logical flaw has been introduced for a practical reason, which emerges when we realize that the story has been molded by the problems of wandering charismatics; for their claim to material support was justified by Paul (1 Cor. 9:13) and in the *Didache* (13.3) by the very same right to the sacrificial offerings that was conferred on the priest in the Old Testament.[47] On this occasion theological logic (or the lack of it) has been adapted to very human needs.

The wandering charismatics will often have gone hungry because no one would take them in. They were often hunted away like vagabonds without any rights. A consoling saying which many scholars have puzzled

---

45. See Bultmann, *Geschichte*, German ed., 14.

46. See Haenchen, *Weg Jesu*, 118–23. He writes: "The Christians certainly did not have any particular preference for walking through the fields on the Sabbath, eating ears of corn" (p. 122). But F. W. Beare rightly points out that conflicts about the Sabbath could spring up even about minor matters, and that plucking ears of corn was perhaps merely an example of disputes of this kind ("The Sabbath was made for Man?" *JBL* 79 [1960]: 130–36). The original *Sitz im Leben* will probably have been similar to that described in a passage at the beginning of Part 4 of *Anton Reiser,* the autobiographical novel written by Goethe's friend K. P. Moritz. Anton Reiser is wandering through the countryside around Duderstadt with very little money. He goes through a cornfield "and he remembered Christ's disciples, who ate ears of corn on Sunday. He even tried to strip a handful of grains from the ears" (*Anton Reiser;* 1785–90; trans. P. E. Matheson [London and New York: Humphrey Milford, 1926]).

47. As far as I am aware, it was J. Roloff who first pointed out this connection (*Das Kerygma und der irdische Jesus* [Göttingen, 1970], 52–62, 71–73): "1 Cor. 9:14 therefore gives good grounds for considering that this logion [i.e., Mark 2:25f.] was also drawn upon in the post-Easter situation, as a way of justifying the claim to material support of those who proclaimed the gospel" (p. 72). I myself consider it most improbable that the *Sitz im Leben* was a eucharistic one (A. J. Grassi's view in "The Five Loaves of the High Priest," *NovTest* 7 [1964–65] 119–22). According to H. W. Kuhn, vv. 25f. were added only by Mark (see his *Ältere Sammlungen im Markusevangelium,* StUNT 8 [Göttingen, 1971], 72–81); but this can hardly be proved.

over is meant for this situation:[48] "When they persecute you in one town, flee to the next; for truly, I say to you, you will not have gone through all the towns of Israel, before the Son of man comes" (Matt. 10:23). If the people addressed here were merely single-minded missionaries, the saying could have been of little comfort; for the missionary must have despaired at not being able to reach all the different towns before the end. But for the charismatic mendicant it was consoling. Until the end of the world, he would continually find places in which he could manage to exist by preaching and healings, even if he was often driven away.

From all this it must surely be clear that the early Christian wandering charismatics were outsiders. They will have had some sympathizers in the various towns and villages. But it is not difficult to imagine what the majority thought about them — men without a home or a proper job, who upset other people by preaching the imminent end of the world, and who in their mind's eye already saw the places where they were rejected and found no support go up in flames. The general opinion will not have been very different from Karl Kautsky's view; he talked in plain unvarnished terms about "scroungers and conspirators," and ascribed to them arsonist fantasies — though it was the Messiah who was going to kindle the blaze for them.[49] In this judgment we do not merely hear the austere tones of the (early) socialist work ethic. It surely also reflects a very generally widespread rejection of outsiders of this kind. The wandering charismatics will have been held in similar contempt in their own time. A saying of Jesus consoles them: "Blessed are

---

48. See the historical survey of research on the subject in M. Künzi, *Das Naherwartungs-Logion Mt 10,23* (Tübingen, 1970). E. Bammel disputes that missionary motifs are to be found here at all ("Matthäus 10,23," *StTh* 15 [1961]: 79–92). H. Schürmann believes that the logion was applied to the missionary situation only at a later point ("Zur Traditions- und Redaktionsgeschichte von Mt 10,23," *BZ* NF 3 [1959]: 82–88). Hasler denies both missionary and consolation themes (*Amen*, 84–86). It is in my view correct that the saying can hardly be interpreted as reflecting the viewpoint of a single-minded missionary, but this does not mean calling in question all the missionary motifs. There were various forms of early Christian mission.

49. K. Kautsky, *Der Ursprung des Christentums. Eine historische Untersuchung*, 11th ed. (Stuttgart, 1921), 404f.: "and numerous scroungers without possessions or family or home wandered incessantly from place to place. . . . The final threat which the evangelist puts into Jesus' mouth is typical of the beggar's revengeful spirit, when his expectations of alms are disappointed. He would like in return to see the whole town go up in flames as a result — but the Messiah is to play arsonist for him" (Eng. trans. *Foundations of Christianity*, trans. J. W. Hartmann [London: Allen & Unwin, 1925; reprint, London: Orbach & Chambers, 1973]). As far as the revengeful spirit is concerned, this is correct enough. But on the other hand it is just this revengeful spirit that is resisted, as Luke 9:51-56 shows. Kautsky's summing up is as follows: "It was itinerant 'scroungers and conspirators' like this who, thinking themselves full of the Holy Spirit, brought . . . the fundamental principles of the new proletarian organization, the 'joyful message,' the gospel" (p. 405).

you when men revile you and persecute you and utter all kinds of evil against you falsely on my account. Rejoice and be glad, for your reward is great in heaven, for so men persecuted the prophets who were before you" (Matt. 5:11f.).

We may perhaps ask whether all the abuse was groundless? Were the wandering charismatics not to all intents and purposes indistinguishable from other vagabonds of dubious reputation? The *Didache* indicates that this was in fact the case. It warns people against traveling χριστέμποροι— people who hawk Christ round the doors. Lucian, probably unjustly, is able to jeer at one of these Christian prophets, meaning to unmask his would-be religious conduct as the behavior of a parasite. What subjectively seemed to be religiously justified freedom from the basic social ties could from outside look like work-shy vagrancy.

As outsiders, the early Christian wandering charismatics will have found their chief support among the people who were themselves living on the fringes of society: the weary and heavy-laden, the poor and the hungry, the men and women whom in their sayings they call blessed.[50] The Jesus tradition was characterized by commitment to the people who were socially and religiously the down-and-outs, the tax collectors and the prostitutes.[51] If this remained an essential element, it was no doubt because the people who passed on Jesus' sayings belonged to the lower levels of society themselves. It is not by chance that among these sayings we find aphorisms which are definitely and specifically suited to a particular social class: for example, "To everyone who has will more be given; but from him who has not, even what he has will be taken away"[52]

---

50. This is also Hoffmann's view in *Logienquelle*, 326.

51. G. Bouwman puts forward a view that is worth consideration ("La pécheresse hospitalière (Lc VII, 36-50)," *EphLov* 45 [1969]: 172–79). He supposes that the Christian preachers were occasionally hospitably received by people whose previous life was criticized by Pharisaic Christians (one may perhaps ask here whether it was only their *previous* life). He sees the *Sitz im Leben* of Luke 7:36ff. in this problematical situation. E. Laland also sees the *Sitz im Leben* of Luke 10:38ff. in the problems of itinerant missionaries ("Die Martha-Maria-Perikope Lukas 10, 38-42: Ihre kerygmatische Aktualität für das Leben der Urgemeinde," *StTh* 13 [1959]: 70–85). "The women of the house are immediately so much claimed by the need to minister to the guest's external wants that it is impossible for them to listen to the Lord's word" (p. 82). The houses visited by the itinerant missionaries were certainly not homes with a large staff of servants. And the saying "Few things are needful" (Luke 10:42; RSV alternative reading) is perhaps intended to stress the modesty of the itinerant charismatics: they will not be a burden on their hosts materially.

52. See J. D. M. Derrett, "Law in the New Testament: The Parable of the Talents and Two Logia," *ZNW* 56 (1965): 184–95, esp. 194f., where the saying is interpreted as describing the relationship between capital and profit "If a merchant possessing capital shows a profit, people eagerly offer him further capital, the trader who reports no profit loses the capital entrusted to him. From him that has not (profit to show) is taken (withdrawn)

(Matt. 25:29). Nobody who is one of the "haves" talks like this.[53] The Synoptic tradition is undoubtedly one of the few traditions in the ancient world where even groups that were otherwise dumb find a voice. History is written by the rulers, largely speaking; but here we see the world from a different perspective — "from below." What form criticism has shown to be the singularity of the Synoptic tradition is no doubt connected with this fact.

In my view, the sayings tradition can be better understood if we take into account the expressly social and economic factors — that is, the necessity of finding material support and justifying the claim to it, the outsider role of the people who passed the tradition on, and the "class" character of the tradition itself. To these social and economic factors must be added the socioecological ones. The tradition suggests a rural context. We need only think of the images in the parables. The characters in these stories are small-holders, day laborers and tenant farmers, shepherds and vineyard owners. We hear about seedtime and harvest, farmland and weeds, herds and fish.[54]

We have to take this rural background of the early Christian wandering charismatics into account if we want to understand their claim to the support of other people. Anyone who had once made a living as a farmer or fisherman gave up his chances of gainful employment when he renounced a settled place to live. Craftsmen were in a different position here, because tools could be carried, unlike fields and lakes.[55] Consequently the *Didache* sees few difficulties for itinerant artisans who want to settle down in a local community.[56] But in the case of the Christian incomer who does not happen to be an artisan, we find the revealing exhortation that the congregation should see to it "that no idle

---

even that (capital) which he still has." Perhaps this is somewhat too narrow an interpretation. The fact that the rich always become richer and the poor poorer is a very general experience, however conducive to pessimism it may be.

53. We may also remember the pessimistic picture of the law, for example, in the exhortation to reconciliation: the petty debtor is thrown into prison anyway, whatever the legal position may be (Matt. 5:25-26).

54. The rural character of the Synoptic tradition is stressed in Deissmann, *Licht vom Osten*, German ed., 210f.; M. Rostovtzeff, *Gesellschaft und Wirtschaft im Römischen Kaiserreich 2* (Leipzig, 1929), 10. (Eng. trans. *The Social and Economic History of the Roman Empire*, vol. 2. [Oxford: Clarendon Press, 1926; rev. ed. 1957]); E. A. Judge, *The Social Pattern of Christian Groups in the First Century* (London: Tyndale Press, 1960).

55. On the preconditions for the local mobility of artisans, see W. Bienert, *Die Arbeit nach der Lehre der Bibel: Eine Grundlegung evangelischer Sozialethik* (Stuttgart, 1954), 299–313. He points out that their job alone made it impossible for the Galilean fishermen to combine work with leadership of the Jerusalem congregation (p. 304).

56. For a different view, see Knopf, *Lehre*, 34. In his view the artisan was especially in need of help, whereas the seller of merchandise could help himself.

Christian lives among you" (*Did.* 12.4). A craftsman could move freely from place to place and earn his keep by working. If he produced "for the market," his geographical mobility was actually a help. What he did not sell in one place, he sold in the next. The bigger the market the better. The itinerant craftsman would therefore seek out the towns and cities. So is it just by chance that Paul, the craftsman, was able to renounce his right to material support when he and Barnabas began the mission to the great Hellenistic cities, whereas Peter, the fisherman, insisted on it (see 1 Cor. 9:5f.)?[57]

The wandering radicals are associated with a rural milieu for a second reason too. Urban congregations, because of their size, had to develop separate ministries and forms of organization quite early on. But itinerant charismatics could preserve their authority only where the local congregations did not confront them with unduly strong ministries or leadership forms.[58] The sayings tradition assumes that congregations will be small: "Where two or three are gathered in my name, there am I in the midst of them" (Matt. 18:20). For where two or three are gathered together, no particular authority structures are needed, but, as a tiny minority, the group is all the more dependent on the encouragement

---

57. G. Dautzenberg rightly sees that the renunciation of material support "must be seen in the context of the situation of the early Christian itinerant missionaries in Palestine-Syria, and was pre-Matthew" ("Der Verzicht auf das apostolische Unterhaltsrecht: Eine exegetische Untersuchung zu 1Kor 9," *Bibl* 50 [1969]: 212–32, quotation from p. 216). He takes sociological factors into account in explaining the generalized version of the claim to this support in 1 Corinthians 9. The background is the "transition of mission to the Hellenistic settlements of the Mediterranean world, which were no longer so firmly structured by family and kinship" (p. 217). In my view we should also bear in mind the recurrent theme of philosophical tradition: the sage takes no payment for his wisdom — a theme presupposing the widespread education and semi-education of urban society. See Betz, *Apostel Paulus,* 100–117. Dautzenberg also makes the urban milieu accountable for the renunciation of the claim to support: Paul and Barnabas "had deliberately left the interior of Syria-Palestine and had turned to the Hellenistic population of the great cities" (p. 218). It is true that Paul justifies his renunciation as something divinely imposed and tailored to him personally (see E. Käsemann, "Eine paulinische Variation des 'Amor fati,'" *ZThK* 56 [1959]: 138–54 [Eng. trans. "A Pauline Version of the 'Amor Fati'" in *New Testament Questions,* 217ff.]). But his interpretation must be somewhat relativized, for Barnabas also renounced his right to material support. It was more than merely a personal decision on Paul's part.

58. Käsemann ("The Beginnings of Christian Theology," in *New Testament Questions,* 82ff.) localizes the prophets whom he assumes passed on the logia in "little congregations along the borders of Palestine-Syria, where the small number of members meant that leadership by a charismatic was the only possible form of organization. An itinerant prophet may even have looked after a whole group of congregations of this kind" (trans. directly from the German text in *Exegetische Versuche und Besinnungen 2* [Göttingen, 1968], 91).

of supraregional authorities — that is, the prophets and apostles who moved about from place to place.

Finally, we must remember that villages and small towns were closer together than the cities. If, as the *Didache* says (11.6), a person was only permitted to take provisions for a single day's journey, this was hardly enough if the great distances separating the cities had to be covered.[59] This practice presupposes a rural mileu. If Paul really wanted to extend his mission to the cities of the whole world, he was well advised to dispense with the missionary's right to material support. No charismatic mendicant could have carried through a project of this scope; it required a planner and an organizer.

It is interesting that the logia tradition should have been originally rooted in a rural environment, because the Christianity of the ancient world was in fact largely an urban phenomenon. The countryman was *paganus,* a heathen. There are only two pieces of direct evidence for early rural Christianity.[60] The Bythinian governor Pliny reports to the emperor Trajan that "the plague of the new superstition" (he means Christianity) has spread "not merely throughout the cities but *also* in the villages and the countryside" (*Epistola* 10.96) — which confirms the mainly urban character of Christianity in its early days. The second piece of evidence is to be found in *1 Clement* (42.4). According to this, the apostles had proclaimed the βασιλεία τοῦ θεοῦ ("the kingdom of God") in country districts and cities. Now, the βασιλεία is one of the themes of the sayings tradition, and the apostles are wandering charismatics. The fact that the writer should mention the country areas first of all when he is considering their influence is a point at least worth bearing in mind.

If we ask why early Christianity was a largely urban phenomenon, we come across a sociocultural factor, among other things; and that is the language. I should like to look at this briefly now. In the cities the common, everyday language was *koine* Greek, whereas in the country areas the original vernaculars survived[61] — in Asia Minor until well into

---

59. According to Knopf, the assumption is "that the Christian congregations [i.e., those presupposed in the Didache] were not too widely scattered — at most a day's journey on foot from one another" (*Lehre,* 31). Conditions of this kind are more easily conceivable in the country than in the towns.

60. See R. Knopf, "Über die soziale Zusammensetzung der ältesten heiden-christlichen Gemeinden," *ZThK* 10 (1900): 325–47, esp. 326.

61. For example, when Irenaeus was in Lyons he tried to learn Celtic, so that he could preach to the country people (*Against the Heresies,* 1.10.2; 3.4.1f.). On the language problem, see W. Schneemelcher, "Das Problem der Sprache in der Alten Kirche," in *Das Problem der Sprache in Theologie und Kirche: Referate vom Deutschen Ev. Theologentag 27.-31. Mai in Berlin* (1959), 55–67; C. Andresen, *Die Kirchen der alten Christenheit,* Die Religionen der Menschheit 29, 1/2 (Stuttgart, 1971), 20f.

the sixth century.[62] But in the Syro-Palestinian area, from the very beginning, the language of Christianity was Aramaic, which was the dialect of the country people; and it is Aramaic that clearly underlies the sayings tradition. One of Jesus' sayings points to this area: "Go nowhere among the Gentiles, and enter no town of the Samaritans, but go rather to the lost sheep of the house of Israel" (Matt. 10:5).[63] If something is forbidden it is generally because it is being practiced; so we shall probably not go far wrong if we deduce that the wandering radicals had made their way from Palestine into other areas as well. But Palestine was no doubt the center.[64]

The economic, ecological, and cultural factors I have described were the social conditions under which the sayings were passed on. Without these conditions, they would neither have come down to us, nor would they have been transmitted in the form in which we now have them. Of course this does not mean that the tradition is *derived* from these conditions in any way. There are no sufficient grounds for any such postulate. The sources merely allow us to establish a connection, an interdependence between a religious tradition and particular social conditions. Anyone who maintains any more than that must believe that it is possible to make assertions about reality regardless of the data at

---

62. K. Holl, "Das Fortleben der Volkssprachen in Kleinasien in nachchristlicher Zeit," *Hermes* 43 (1908): 240–54 = *Gesammelte Aufsätze zur Kirchengeschichte,* vol. 2, *Der Osten* (Tübingen, 1928), 238–48.

63. H. Kasting believes that the saying is an editorial addition of Matthew's (*Die Anfänge urchristlicher Mission* [Munich, 1969], 110–14). It certainly fits in with Matthew's redactional concept, though only in the form given to it in Matt. 15:24, where it applies solely to Jesus. In 15:24 Matthew has probably altered the traditional logion of Matt. 10:5 during his editing process.

64. This localization of the movement also explains the Jewish-Christian character of the logia tradition. It presupposes Christian congregations belonging within the group of Jewish synagogues and subject to their jurisdiction (Matt. 10:17). The rabbis are recognized as authority (Matt. 23:2f.), but at the same time the scribes and Pharisees are sharply criticized. This ambivalence could be explained as follows. The local congregations distributed throughout the countryside did in fact belong to Judaism. But the main sustainers of the traditions separating Christianity from Judaism were itinerant charismatics, who did not belong to any organization. Here criticism of Judaism, and of the scribes and Pharisees, could remain very much alive, whereas their settled local sympathizers were inevitably inclined to make more or less considerable compromises. If it had not been for itinerant outsiders, Christianity would soon have lost its independent character. See Kretschmar, "Beitrag," 47: "In the historical situation of Palestinian Christianity before it dissolved its ties with the ethnic Jewish community, it is not surprising that we should hear nothing about any offices or ministries, apart from charismatics — that is, prophets, teachers, 'saints'. . . . Here these charismatics will have been the only representatives of the Christian message who made any distinct impression on the outside world."

our disposal—assertions that would be more than the necessary theoretical constructions without which it is impossible to uncover, investigate, or understand data at all. To make assertions of that kind would be to depart from the realm of critical scholarship. But even within these limits there is still enough that has to be investigated, interpreted, and comprehended. Let me in closing therefore mention some hypotheses about the transmission of the sayings in early Christianity which may take us a little further.

1. We come across very few Jesus sayings in the early Christian letters. There will be a sociological reason for this, among other things. These letters come mainly from the urban, Hellenistic congregations.[65] These congregations included people from different social classes. In Corinth and Rome (where we know most about conditions) this led to conflict.[66] The congregations that had this kind of structure were characterized by a family-like "love patriarchalism"[67] which preserved, mitigated, and softened the social differences. The early Christian "duty codes" (*Haustafeln*) are characteristic examples of this ethic. Here the nonfamily ethic of the early Christian wandering radicals had no place—simply because it was impracticable. Even if Jesus' sayings were known, it was still impossible to live accordingly. But any part of an oral tradition which a society is unable to accept will be jettisoned by way of the "preventive censorship" enforced by that society. A sociological transmission threshold hindered Jesus' sayings from gaining access to these congregations. Here the Son of man of the Synoptics was replaced by the cosmic Christ.

2. The logia tradition was able to gain ground beyond its original social setting in places where it changed its character. Where people

---

65. See Deissmann, *Licht vom Osten*, German ed., 210f.

66. On the congregation in Rome, see especially H. Gülzow's analyses in *Christentum und Sklaverei in den ersten drei Jahrhunderten* (Bonn, 1969). These culminate in the analysis of the schism between Callistus and Hippolytus, and its social background. I hope to be able to show elsewhere that social factors also played a part in the congregational conflicts in Corinth.

67. The concept of "love patriarchalism" derives in substance from E. Troeltsch, *Die Soziallehren der christlichen Kirchen und Gruppen, Gesammelte Schriften 1* (Tübingen, 1912), 67–83. Troeltsch characterizes Paul's fundamental ethical attitude as follows: "It was the type of Christian patriarchalism which was based on both a religious recognition of earthly inequalities and a religious transcending of them. This was already prepared for in late Judaism, but it acquired a special coloring through the warmth of the Christian idea of love—through the union of all in the body of Christ" (p. 67). Troeltsch talks about "the fundamental idea that the given inequalities should be accepted and made fruitful for the ethical values of the relationship between one person and another" (p. 68). (Eng. trans. *The Social Teaching of the Christian Churches and Sects,* trans. O. Wyon, 2 vols. [London: Allen & Unwin; New York: Macmillan, 1931]. The above passage has been translated directly from the German text.)

were unable to practice its ethical radicalism, they could transform it into gnostic radicalism. So radical action became a radicalism of perception, which does not necessarily have to have any practical consequences. We find a tradition that has been modified in this direction in the *Gospel of Thomas*,[68] a collection of Jesus sayings. Relatively homogeneous groups in the church probably provided the social setting for this gnostically modified radicalism. These groups were probably often made up of men and women who were fairly prosperous.[69] A radicalism of perception without any practical consequences was not unduly costly, even for these people.

3. The fact that the original spirit of these sayings has been more or less preserved for us is due to the written form they were given in the logia source and the Gospels. It is interesting in this connection that they should have come down to us only in the framework of the Gospel form — that is, embedded in accounts of Jesus' life. These look back without exception to a past era and already view the ethical radicalism of the transmitted sayings from a historical distance.

This distance is especially evident in Luke. He sensed so great a tension between the original social world of the Jesus tradition and the world of the people he was addressing that he appended to his Gospel a history of "the acts of the apostles." In Acts he shows how Christianity, starting in Galilee (or, to be more precise, in the renowned city of Jerusalem),

---

68. We must, of course, remember that in the *Gospel of Thomas* we find not only a modified logia tradition but also a tempered Gnosticism. But the concrete demands have lost their edge and have been translated into the realm of the speculative — and that is the important point here. This modification is not simply part of the tradition itself. This is J. M. Robinson's view in "ΛΟΓΟΙ ΣΟΦΩΝ: Zur Gattung der Spruchquelle Q," in *Zeit und Geschichte: Festgabe für R. Bultmann* (Tübingen, 1964), 77–96. He sees an immanent tendency to Gnosticism in the "sayings" collection, simply as genre. But here we must surely presuppose that the people who have passed the tradition on have changed themselves. They now came from a different social milieu, in which the words of Jesus in their plain and manifest sense were no longer practicable.

69. See Andresen's judgment about the Gnostics in *Kirchen der alten Christenheit*, 103: "These people came from social classes that did not generally find their way into the early Catholic congregations. The testimonies of Valentinian and Basilidian Gnosticism are imbued with the atmosphere of a certain liberalism which bursts apart the narrow bounds of a congregational piety concerned to preserve its own tradition." The problem is discussed in detail by H. G. Kippenberg, "Versuch einer soziologischen Verortung des antiken Gnostizismus," *Numen* 17 (1970): 211–31. He writes "Sociologically, I would localize Gnosticism in the intellectual Hellenistic class of the countries on the eastern fringe of the Roman empire, which had come under the heel of the Roman legions in the second and first centuries B.C." (p. 225). In "The Problem of 'Die soziologische Verortung des antiken Gnostizismus,'" *Numen* 19 (1972): 41–51, P. Munz criticizes Kippenberg's view. But in my opinion this criticism does not detract from Kippenberg's perception of the specifically class character of Gnosticism in the ancient world.

made its way into the great cities of the Hellenistic world.[70] Luke, even more clearly than the other evangelists, stresses that the period when Jesus was alive was a special era, in which special, different ethical rules applied. Because of this, he is able, on the one hand, to preserve Jesus' words most faithfully of all. Yet, on the other, he unmistakably dissociates himself from the radicalism of the early Christian itinerants. In the farewell discourse according to Luke, Jesus expressly revokes his commandments for wandering charismatics. From now on, the charge to go out without purse, bag, and shoes is no longer to apply. Now the disciples are to take with them money, bag, and even a sword. For times have changed (Luke 22:35f.). In his own era Luke was fighting the successors of the first wandering charismatics. For him they were false prophets. There were in any case only twelve legitimate apostles. These were the great itinerant missionaries of the early period. And even in this period it is not so much they who provide the pattern for Christianity in its model form; the model is rather the congregation in Jerusalem, of which Luke presents a highly idealized picture. Here, he tells us, everyone put his possessions at the disposal of the whole community. Significantly enough, however, the only evidence Luke can adduce for this is Barnabas — an apostle and an itinerant charismatic. And so he too involuntarily betrays what is in any case the historical probability: consistent discipleship was to be found only among the homeless, roving charismatic mendicants.

If we trace the transmission of Jesus' sayings in early Christianity, we discover that in those days the Christian faith assumed three social forms: the radicalism of the itinerant charismatics, love patriarchalism, and gnostic radicalism. Here we find the lines laid down for the three types whose annals Troeltsch traced throughout Christian history: sects, institutionalized church, and what he calls "spiritualism."[71] The ethic of the wandering radicals has continually sprung up afresh in sectarian movements — among the Montanists, the Syrian wandering ascetics, the medieval mendicant friars, and on the left wing of the Reformation. Gnostic radicalism has again and again found expression in individualistic and mystically disposed conventicles, inside and outside the church. But it is Christian love patriarchalism to which we owe the surviving institutions of the church. Quite successfully, and not without wisdom, this love patriarchalism tempered early Christian radicalism to a degree that made it possible for the Christian faith to become a practicable

---

70. The "town" or "city" already has considerable importance in the Gospel: Luke makes Jesus start his ministry in an urban milieu. See Hoffmann, *Logienquelle*, 278–80.

71. See Troeltsch, *Social Teachings*.

form of living for men and women in general. In the disputes of the second century this love patriarchalism prevailed over other social forms of early Christian faith such as Montanism and Gnosticism. It defined what was orthodox, what was canonical, and what was exegetically legitimate. But it did not completely suppress the other traditions, so that again and again it has provided nourishment for "heterodox" trends. This love patriarchalism has continually found a way of assimilating or excluding radical movements. As we know, the exclusion was effected with more patriarchalism than love—to put it more bluntly, through the application of physical force. This would have compromised Christianity irrevocably had it not been that the call to repentance continually made itself heard out of the traditions of early Christian radicalism.

2

''We Have Left Everything . . .''
(Mark 10:28)

◆

Discipleship and Social Uprooting
in the Jewish-Palestinian Society
of the First Century

A T THE BEGINNING, discipleship was a highly practical affair.
The disciples left their homes and families, their possessions
and their occupations. Peter said it for them all: "Lo, we have
left everything and followed you." We can view this life of discipleship[1]
under two aspects. Religiously it is the result of an encounter with
holiness. Sociologically it is a variant of social uprooting, the extent
of which points to a crisis in Jewish-Palestinian society. The texts make
the first of these aspects clear. The second aspect has to be laboriously
deduced. Since the New Testament texts offer very little information,
we are largely dependent on conclusions drawn from analogy. All the
manifestations of social uprooting in Jewish-Palestinian society may
count as analogous here. In this context social uprooting is understood
to mean that people leave their accustomed homes and surroundings;
but it also means the greater or lesser breach with familiar norms which
goes with that. The concept has two different aspects, one of them local,
one of them social. The local one is the abandonment of the settled
place of abode; the social one is the change in ways of behavior, in the
direction of conduct deviating from the rules of normal life. The term
embraces (wholly or in part) emigrants, new settlers, the Qumran people,
robbers and brigands, freedom fighters, vagrants, and prophetic

---

1. See M. Hengel, "Nachfolge und Charisma," BZNW 34 (Berlin, 1968), 60: "Discipleship
therefore means primarily something quite concrete: following him on his wanderings
and sharing with him his insecure, indeed endangered destiny." This also requires a
"breach with law and custom" (pp. 9ff.).

movements. In analyzing the fact of social uprooting three points are of interest to us.

1. *The extent of the phenomena.* Here we are following the theoretical premise that the more widespread a social phenomenon is, the more it requires a sociological explanation. Social uprooting can be found everywhere. It is only when it quite noticeably increases in a society that it is probably connected with specific structural problems in the society itself. Methodologically, proof that a phenomenon was widespread can take the form of quantitative information in the sources and a wide dissemination in time, space, and quality. What appears in a number of different forms often appears frequently too.

2. *The conditions of the phenomena.* Here the underlying theoretical premise is that socially there is no demonstrable "first cause" that explains everything else. Instead, different interlocking and mutually influential factors can be discovered — factors that may be economic, ecological, political, or cultural. Proof of certain factors can be provided methodologically by way of statements in the sources about the reason for certain types of behavior, by factual correlation between behavior and social data, and by chronological correlation between historical events and particular behavior patterns.

3. *The kinship between the different phenomena.* Here the theoretical premise is that the closer the kinship between two phenomena, the greater the likelihood that the one can be deduced from the other. This means that, apart from the fundamental common factor (which is the social uprooting), we have to inquire about additional comparable features in the Jesus movement and the other phenomena we are investigating in the world around — that is, comparable situations, modes of behavior, traditions, and intentions.[2]

Our study is divided into three parts. First we shall look at all the statements about social uprooting in the Jesus movement. In the second part we shall draw on analogous phenomena in the world around, as a way of interpreting these statements. In the third part we shall attempt to arrive at a general interpretation of social uprooting as "anomic" behavior (for this term see n. 63 below) and shall analyze links between early Christian discipleship as a way of life and the crisis of society.

---

2. On other fundamental problems, see my reflections in "Theoretische Probleme religionssoziologischer Forschung und die Analyse des Urchristentums," *NZSysThR* 16 (1974): 35–60; and "Die soziologische Auswertung religiöser Überlieferungen," *Kairos* 17 (1975): 284–99.

I. SOCIAL UPROOTING IN THE JESUS MOVEMENT

1. *Its dissemination.* "Call" stories (Mark 1:16ff.; 2:15ff.), sayings about discipleship (Matt. 8:19ff.; Mark 10:28ff.), and missionary instructions (Matt. 10:5ff.) all show that members of the Jesus movement left home and possessions in order to share the homeless life of itinerant charismatics. According to the definition we have given, these people were socially uprooted. How far was this behavior widespread in the Jesus movement? Let us start with the twelve apostles.[3] According to Luke, they were the leaders of the local congregation in Jerusalem (Acts 1:12ff.). Here Luke is probably painting his ideal picture of a collegial leadership. For at Paul's first visit to Jerusalem, of the supposed "leaders" he finds only Peter (Gal. 1:18),[4] and on his second visit only the three "pillars" (Gal. 2:9). The others were probably on their way through the countryside, missionizing and healing; for that is what they had been commissioned to do (Mark 3:13ff.), not to lead congregations. Even Peter was not always in Jerusalem. We find him in Samaria, for example (Acts 8:14), in Lydda and Joppa (9:32ff.), Caesarea (10:1ff.), Antioch (Gal. 2:11ff.) — perhaps also in Corinth (1 Cor. 1:12) and Rome too (1 Clem. 5.4). He also is a wandering charismatic. The group of the Twelve who were linked with him soon disappears. They probably scattered in all directions, since they saw their task as having to do with all the twelve tribes of Israel (Matt. 19:28).

But the early Christian itinerant charismatics were not confined to the Twelve or to the apostles. Paul, Barnabas (Acts 14:4, 14), Andronicus, and Junias (Rom. 16:7) were apostles too. The *Didache* calls everyone an apostle who, when he was moving about, modeled his behavior on "the teaching of the gospel" (*Did.* 11.3f.). When the title is limited to the Twelve (for example, in Luke 6:13; Rev. 21:14), it is probably meant to exclude the all-too-many "apostles" who were wandering around like vagrants, preaching in the name of Jesus (see Luke 21:8; Rev. 2:2). Itinerant charismatics were called "disciples of the Lord" as well as

---

3. See G. Klein, *Die Zwölf Apostel,* FRLANT 77 (Göttingen, 1961); J. Roloff, *Apostolat — Verkündigung — Kirche* (Gütersloh, 1965).

4. He also meets James, the Lord's brother, who does not, however, belong to the Twelve. Nor does he appear as an itinerant charismatic. He is the spokesman for the Jerusalem congregation (Acts 12:17; 15:13; 21:18; Gal. 2:9ff; Josephus *Antiquities of the Jews* 10.200; Eusebius *Ecclesiastical History* 2.23.4ff.). His conflict with Peter was perhaps conditioned by their different roles: local congregations were bound to be more concerned for harmony with their environment than itinerant charismatics.

apostles. We find this title in Papias. These disciples had successors — again itinerant Christians (frag. 2.4).[5] In Matt. 8:21 and 10:42 the term "disciple" can also refer to wandering charismatics. The same is true of the descriptions "prophet" (Matt. 10:41; *Did.* 11.3ff.; Acts 11:27), "righteous man" (Matt. 10:41), and "teacher" (Acts 13:1; *Did.* 13.2). The variation in the title indicates how widespread the underlying itinerant charismatic movement was. Luke especially knows that this movement was not restricted to the twelve apostles. In 10:1ff. he tells about the sending forth of seventy missionaries who were supposed to observe the same standards of behavior as the twelve who had been sent out before them (9:1ff.). He also talks about a group of prophets who wandered from Palestine to Antioch (Acts 11:27ff.). Among them is the itinerant charismatic Agabus, whom we later meet in Caesarea, after he had arrived there from Judea (Acts 21:10).

These wandering charismatics apart from the Twelve were not scattered individuals or lone wolves. We can detect groups that belonged together. The group of seven around Stephen,[6] who were allegedly chosen to distribute food, acted as independent missionaries (Acts 8:4; 11:19ff.). Luke explains this with their expulsion from Jerusalem. But Stephen had already been engaged in missionary activity earlier (Acts 6:8ff.). Local mobility went further back too: Nicolaus came from Antioch (Acts 6:5). In Antioch there was a group of five, largely made up of people from other places (Acts 13:1ff.): Barnabas came from Cyprus (4:36), Paul from Tarsus (22:3), Lucius from Cyrenaica, Menahem (Manaen) had been brought up with Herod Antipas, either in Jerusalem or Rome.[7] It is only Simeon about whom we know nothing. Two of the group of five, Barnabas and Paul, were manifestly itinerant preachers. They were "set apart" for mission. Basically, this was probably open to all of them (Acts 13:2). Another circle of itinerant charismatics was grouped around the

---

5. Three arguments speak in favor of the postulate that Papias's "disciples of the Lord" and "presbyters" were itinerant charismatics: (1) Since the five apostles named were itinerant charismatics and are called "disciples of the Lord," we may deduce from this that the same may be said of the two other disciples of the Lord, Aristion and John. (2) They have "followers." The term suggests a "wandering" existence. (3) These followers called on Papias: εἰ . . . παρηκολουθηκώς τις . . . ἔλθοι — that is, they themselves belonged to itinerant groups. It must also be pointed out that the term *presbyteros* in 3 John is probably the designation for an itinerant Christian (see below).

6. See M. Hengel, "Zwischen Jesus und Paulus," *ZThK* 72 (1975): 151–206.

7. According to Josephus *Ant.* 7.20, Antipas was brought up in Rome (τροφὰς εἶχον). Probably Menahem (Manaen) was there with him as σύντροφος. H. W. Hoehner, on the other hand, presumes on the basis of Acts 13:1 that Antipas was brought up in Palestine (*Herod Antipas* [Cambridge: Cambridge University Press, 1972], 14). But almost all the Christians named in Acts 13:1 come from the Diaspora, Menahem probably too. He would then be the first Christian known to us who had a connection with Rome.

presbyter of 3 John. The author of the letter indicates that he himself traveled (v. 14). He sends messengers with letters of recommendation (v. 12) and defends the conditions under which the early Christian wandering charismatics lived, which involved their reception and support by local Christians (vv. 5ff.).[8]

Other wandering charismatics must be looked for among Paul's opponents. Some of them came from Palestine and therefore called themselves "Hebrews" (2 Cor. 11:22), like the diaspora Jew Alypsios who came from Tiberias, and Makedonis, who came from Caesarea (*CIJ* 502, 370).[9] We find a record of other wandering ascetics in the pseudo-Clementine letters *Ad virgines*.[10] In addition, Lucian of Samosata made an early Christian itinerant charismatic the target of his mockery (*On the Death of Peregrinus* 16). So the wandering charismatics were a widespread phenomenon in early Christianity. As far as numbers go, the local congregations were certainly much stronger. But the practical importance of the wandering charismatics emerges from the fact that in my view they passed on and molded the radical ethic of the renunciation of home, family, possessions, and protection.[11]

2. *The conditions determining social uprooting in the Jesus movement.* The reasons for setting out into an existence of discipleship without the familiar surroundings of home were largely religious. The most important presupposition was Jesus' call. But the texts suggest that social conditions played a part as well. The "rich young ruler" also experienced the call to discipleship, but his riches prevented him from obeying it (Mark 10:22). Jesus' call "come here" (δεῦτε) was not only directed to the disciples (Mark 1:17); it was addressed to the "weary and heavy-laden" too (Matt. 11:28). Of course there are differences between the δεῦτε ὀπίσω μου ("come follow me") in the one place and the δεῦτε πρός με ("come to me") in the other. But the imagery of the call in Matt. 11:28 — the image of the yoke of the draught beasts and their rest after their labors — implies local movement.[12] No one can exclude the possibility that this

8. On the interpretation that these were itinerant missionaries, see A. von Harnack, *Über den dritten Johannes-Brief,* TU 15 (Berlin, 1897); R. Bultmann, *Die drei Johannesbriefe,* KEK 14 (Göttingen, 1967), 99.

9. J. B. Frey in *CIJ.* On the meaning of "Hebrews," see especially M. Hengel, "Zwischen Jesus und Paulus," 169ff.

10. See G. Kretschmar, "Ein Beitrag zur Frage nach dem Ursprung frühchristlicher Askese," *ZThK* 61 (1964): 27–67.

11. See chapter 1 above, "The Wandering Radicals"; also my essay "Legitimation und Lebensunterhalt," *NTS* 21 (1974): 192–221.

12. On the picture character, see J. B. Bauer, "Das milde Joch und die Ruhe, Matth. 11, 28-30," *ThZ* 17 (1961): 99–106. The image could even be derived from Jesus' own occupation. According to Justin (*Dialogue* 88), a carpenter made ἄροτρα καὶ ζυγά, "ploughs and yokes."

also meant a call to discipleship. At all events Jesus had followers among "the weary and heavy-laden" — for example, the beggar Bartimaeus (Mark 10:52) or the man from Gadara who was possessed. It is true that this man's wish to follow Jesus was rejected; but he then proclaims what has happened in the Decapolis, which was an area as big as Judea and Idumea put together. The story seems to suggest that there were wandering preachers in this region (Mark 5:18ff.).

Social motives shine through the story about the miraculous draft. After a night of unsuccessful fishing, Peter is called to discipleship (Luke 5:1ff.). Frustration with his occupation and a break with the familiar surroundings of home are connected to some extent here, even if the story itself intends to say something different.[13] At the same time, fishermen did not belong to the lowest classes. The Zebedees left their father with "the hired servants" (Mark 1:20). The family was able to pay outside workers. But the *Gospel of the Nazarenes* makes Zebedee "a poor fisherman" (frag. 33).[14] And we know from Josephus that "sailors and people who had nothing" raised a revolt at the beginning of the Jewish War (*Life* 66). The alliance with the poor shows that the situation of anyone who had to do with boats — fishermen no doubt among them — could be a critical one.[15]

Jesus himself is said to have been a carpenter (Mark 6:3). He can hardly have identified himself very deeply with his trade. We scarcely ever meet it as a source of images in the parables, where pictures from farming and the land predominate. In the family there were small-holders. When relatives of Jesus had to declare before Domitian what their property consisted of, they declared that "together they possessed only nine thousand denars, each of them half, and, they explained, not in the form of money but as the value of land amounting to no more than about thirty acres; they cultivated this with their own hands, in order to pay their taxes and to make enough to live on" (Hegesippus in Eusebius *Eccl.*

---

13. H. Kreissig, *Die sozialen Zusammenhänge des judäischen Krieges* (Berlin, 1970), 47: "Even the vision of the plentiful draft of fish, which is always specially cherished by the poor and which we come across in Peter's draft, shows that not a great deal could be earned by fishing." In the *Life of Pythagoras* (Porphyry *Vita Pyth.* 25), which is upper-class literature, emphasis in the story of a miraculous draft is no longer laid on the quantity of fish; the main point is now the precise prediction of the number.

14. The *Gospel of the Nazarenes* presupposes the existence of the Synoptic Gospels. Did the author see no contradiction between the employment of day laborers and poverty? Otherwise he stresses social aspects as well; see frags. 10 and 16. See P. Vielhauer in *Neutestamentliche Apokryphen*, ed. E. Hennecke and W. Schneemelcher, 3rd ed. (Tübingen, 1959), 1:93.

15. For a different view, see S. W. Baron, *A Social and Religious History of the Jews* I, 2nd rev. ed. (New York: Columbia University Press, 1952), 255: Fishermen had a "reputable if not high social standing."

His. 3.20.2). These were little, unimportant people, *petit bourgeoisie* (3.20.5), small-holders in modest, almost needy circumstances. But they too did not belong to the lowest classes;[16] for small-holders and fishermen possessed the means of production, unlike the lowest classes, who had no property at all — lease holders, farm hands, day laborers, and slaves. It is clear, however, that the Jesus movement did not recruit its members from the upper classes. It is true that there were a few upper-class sympathizers with settled homes — for example, Joanna, Chuza's wife (Luke 8:3), and Joseph of Arimathea (Mark 15:43). But it is significant that Jesus' homeless followers included the minor tax collector Levi, not the rich, chief tax official Zacchaeus (Luke 19:1ff.), and the sons of Zebedee, not the "rich young ruler." What we hear about the early Christian itinerant charismatics points to a social class halfway down the scale, whose situation was probably not very secure. Polemic against the rich (Luke 6:24ff. and frequently), commitment to "the weary and heavy-laden" (Matt. 11:28), the acceptance of poor beggars (Mark 10:46ff.), and occupational frustration (Luke 5:1ff.) all speak against any kind of *petit bourgeoisie* idyll.

II. SOCIAL UPROOTING IN THE PALESTINIAN WORLD OF THE JESUS MOVEMENT

In order to interpret the sparse information available to us from early Christian sources, we have to draw on analogous phenomena from the world around. We may initially classify the different groups according to the reasons that drew the people concerned together. On the one hand, there were internal Jewish revival or renewal movements — the Qumran community, freedom fighters, prophetic movements; on the other hand, we find the outcrop of a general disintegration which can be found everywhere — emigrants, thieves, and vagrants. Between the two groups there are again practical links: emigrants *and* Essenes leave the places where they have grown up in order to settle somewhere new. Among these people *evasive* modes of behavior are dominant; in the case of the thieves or brigands and the freedom fighters, the behavior is *aggressive*. Beggars and prophetic movements are alike in hoping for the help of others — alms from human beings or divine intervention.

---

16. Kreissig (*Zusammenhänge*, 55) rightly distinguishes between people owning property and the means of production (big land owners, small farmers) and people without property (lease holders, day laborers, slaves). But in my view what essentially determines assignment to the upper or the lower classes is not just the possession of the means of production but the power of disposal over other people which is based on that.

Life of this kind, based on hope for human or divine help, may be given the name *"subsiditive."* Neither evasive nor aggressive, it forms a third category.

This gives us the following diagram, although the distinctions are theoretically typified: the reality was more complex.

	Dominance of evasive behavior	Dominance of aggressive behavior	Dominance of subsiditive behavior
Phenomena of general disintegration	emigrants; new settlers	thieves; brigands	beggars; vagrants
Internal Jewish renewal movements	Qumran community	freedom fighters	prophetic movements

1. Evasive Behavior: Emigrants and New Settlers

We shall consider emigrants and new settlers together. Emigrants are new settlers in regions abroad; new settlers are "emigrants" who remain in their own country.

1.1 *Dissemination.* There were Jews all over the then-known world (Philo *Ad Gaium* 281f.; 1 Macc. 15:15ff.; Acts 2:5, 9; Strabo in Josephus *Ant.* 14.115). All numerical estimates agree that there were more Jews in the Diaspora than in Palestine.[17] Their numbers certainly increased through birth and conversion, but undoubtedly also because of considerable emigration. It is true that inscriptions record for us the names of only a few emigrants — emigrants from Sepphoris (*CIJ* 362), Caesarea (*CIJ* 370, 715), Tiberias (*CIJ* 502; *IG* V, 1, No. 1256) and Jerusalem (*CIJ* 556, 749; *IG²* II, No. 8934);[18] but the existence of a συναγωγὴ Ἑβραίων (a synagogue of the Hebrews) in Rome (*CIJ* 291, 317, 510, 535) and Corinth (*CIJ* 718), as well as Claudius's prohibition of Jewish immigration to Alexandria (*CPJ* 153, 96f.), testifies to considerable waves of emigration.

---

17. See the survey in Baron, *History,* 1:170; and M. Stern, "The Jewish Diaspora," in *CRINT* I, 1 (Assen, 1974), 119ff.

18. In addition there were many returning emigrants. In J. B. Frey's *Corpus,* inscriptions record six emigrants over against sixteen who returned home: from Egypt (*CIJ* 897, 918, 920, 928, 930, 934, 1256), North Africa (950, 1227), Asia Minor (910, 925, 931, 1414), Italy (1284), Sicily (? 1399), and Babylon (902). The tombs at Beth-she'arim record places of origin in Syria-Phoenicia especially; see M. Schwabe and B. Lifshitz, *Beth She'arim,* II: *The Greek Inscriptions* (Jerusalem, 1967), ix–xi. That explains why there were not more returnees. Inscriptions in other countries will not have mentioned unknown Jewish places. It is significant that the surviving inscriptions should mention three main cities.

If there had been only scattered, individual emigrants, no emigrant congregations would have been founded, nor would there have been any government intervention.[19] We know more about the extent of the new settlements. Herod and his sons founded numerous new towns between about 25 B.C.E. and 20 C.E. Already existing towns or villages were often expanded by the resettlement of new groups. In Sebaste there are supposed to have been six thousand new citizens (Josephus *Jewish War* 1.403). Without this influx of new citizens, it is inconceivable that there could have been new foundations of the order of Caesarea (Josephus *Ant.* 15.331ff.; *J.W.* 1.408ff.), Phasaelis (*J.W.* 1.418; *Ant.* 16.145), Bathrya and its surroundings (*Ant.* 17.23ff.), Archelais (*Ant.* 17.340), Antipatris (*J.W.* 1.417; *Ant.* 16.142f.), Tiberias (*Ant.* 18.37), and so on. Around about the turn of the era there must have been a large potential of men and women for whom existence in a new land was a more attractive prospect than remaining in their hometowns.

1.2 *Reasons and conditions.*   There were four reasons for emigration and new settlement. Jews ended up abroad as mercenaries, enslaved prisoners of war, or political refugees; or they were attracted by the prospect of better conditions.

1.2.1 *Mercenaries.*   The oldest Jewish military colony known to us is Elephantine. It already existed in the Persian period, but most of the records about mercenaries derive from the Hellenistic era.[20] In the Roman period, this type of "emigration" would hardly have existed. Even if the Jews were not in general dispensed from military service,[21] there would have been few Jewish soldiers in the Roman army, if only because of the emperor cult (but cf. the widow of a Jewish soldier in Italy [*CIJ* 640] and the tomb of a centurion in Jaffa [*CIJ* 920]). The settlement of mercenaries in Palestine itself was more important. Herod settled veterans in Sebaste (Josephus *Ant.* 15.296), Gaba (*J.W.* 3.36; *Ant.* 15.294), and Heshbon (*Ant.* 15.294). On the one hand, by so doing he prevented unrest—after his death, dissatisfied demobilized mercenaries took part

---

19. For the interpretation of the "synagogue of the Hebrews" as a reference to emigrants, see J. B. Frey, *CIJ*, lxxvii. He supposes that the synagogue of the *vernaculi* (meaning urban Romans) dissociated itself from the synagogue of the Hebrews in about the first century B.C.E., in reaction to an influx of immigrants.

20. The Ptolemaens, for example, settled deported Jews in Egyptian fortresses (Aristides 12.f.; *CPJ*, ed. V. A. Tcherikover and A. Fuks, vol. 2 [Cambridge, Mass., 1960], nos. 18–32). The Seleucids set up Jewish military settlements in Asia Minor (Josephus *Ant.* 12.147ff.; *Against Apion* 1.176ff.). For a detailed account of Jewish mercenaries, see M. Hengel, *Judentum und Hellenismus*, WUNT 10 (Tübingen, 1969), 27ff. (Eng. trans. *Judaism and Hellenism*, trans. J. Bowden [London: SCM Press; Philadelphia: Fortress Press, 1974]).

21. See S. Applebaum in *CRINT* I, 1, 458ff.

in revolts (*Ant.* 17.270); on the other hand, in this way he demonstrated his military presence in newly acquired areas, which had to be protected against "robbers" (*Ant.* 16.285; 17.23ff.).

1.2.2 *Slaves.* Many Jews were sold abroad as slaves.[22] Herod also tried to get rid of opponents by this means (*Ant.* 16.1), although the law forbade the sale of Jews to Gentiles. For that reason most of the slaves were prisoners of war taken by foreign powers—by Pompey (*Ant.* 14.71; *J.W.* 1.154), Gabinius (*J.W.* 1.163), Cassius (*J.W.* 1.180), Sosius,[23] and Varus. Varus had the inhabitants of Sepphoris sold as slaves because they had joined the revolt of Judas the Galilean (*Ant.* 17.289; *J.W.* 2.68). Up to the Jewish War, which gave a new impetus to the slave market (*J.W.* 3.304f., 540, 6.418ff., 420, 7.208), Josephus has nothing more to tell us about prisoners of war. But an inscription in Naples dating from the period of Claudius or Nero provides evidence that they existed in the intervening period (*CIJ* 556).[24] Where new settlements in Palestine are concerned, slaves are mentioned in only one passage: Herod Antipas also brought "riffraff" with him to Tiberias, and it was not always known whether these people were free or not (*Ant.* 18.37).[25]

1.2.3 *Refugees.* Many emigrants escaped abroad from internal tensions. According to Hekataios, many people escaped διὰ τὴν ἐν Συρίᾳ στάσιν to Egypt and Pheonicia (Josephus *Ag. Ap.* 1.194). Onias IV fled to Egypt with many followers (Jerome *In Daniel* 2.13f.; *PL* 25:562). Later on, as allies of the Hasmoneans, the Romans demanded the extradition of political refugees from Egypt and other Mediterranean countries (1 Macc. 15:16-23). There was a wave of emigration in the first century c.e., during the confusion that preceded the death of Caligula (40 c.e.). An edict of Claudius, issued in Alexandria in November 41, forbids the

---

22. See Hengel, *Judentum und Hellenismus,* German ed., 79f.

23. See the coins minted by Sosius in E. A. Sydenham, *The Coinage of the Roman Republic,* rev. ed. by G. C. Haines (London: Spink & Sons, 1952), 199 no. 1272: "Military trophy; at base two captives seated (Judaea and Antigonos)." Rather differently E. M. Smallwood, *Philonis Alexandrini Legatio ad Gaium,* 2nd ed. (Leiden, 1970), 236.

24. *CIJ* 556: "(Cl)audia Aster (H)ierosolymitana (ca)ptiva curam egit. (Tiberius) Claudius Aug(usti) liberus (Mas)culus. Rogo vos fac(ite prae)ter legem ne quis (mi)hi titulum deiciat cu(ra)m agatis. Vixit anni XXV." The fear of pagan inscriptions and motifs is reminiscent of the rejection of heathen images and emblems, for example, at the time of Pilate (*Ant.* 18.55ff.; Philo *Ad Gaium* 276ff.). According to Philo's testimony, a large proportion of Roman Jews were freed slaves (*Ad Gaium* 155). Perhaps there is connection here with the συναγωγὴ βερνακλησίων (*CIJ* 318, 383, 398, 494).

25. M. Avi-Yonah assumes that the slaves were freed specially in order to settle Tiberias ("The Foundation of Tiberias," *IEJ* 1 [1950–51]: 163). But then there could have been no doubt about their legal status. Perhaps some of these people were escaped slaves who made some kind of living as day laborers and vagrants.

Alexandrian Jews ἐπάγεσθαι ἢ προσείσθαι ἀπὸ Συρίας ἢ ᾿Αιγύπτου καταπλέοντας ᾿Ιουδαίους (*CPJ* 153, 96f.).[26] These emigrants probably upheld the aggressive attitude of the Jewish lower classes in the anti-Semitic conflicts in Alexandria, thus cutting across the harmonizing policy of the aristocracy, which Philo supported. They probably belonged to the lower classes, just as did the rebellious Sicarii, who at the end of the Jewish War made their way to Egypt (*J.W.* 7.410ff.) and Cyrene (*J.W.* 7.437). One of them was a weaver. Perhaps the "zealot" Jonios, who as we know was in Rome (*CIJ* 362), was a political refugee.[27] It is at least significant that Matthew can depict Joseph as being a political refugee who fled into Egypt (Matt. 2:13ff.). Other refugees were members of the upper classes. They had escaped shortly before the outbreak of the Jewish rising, in some cases fleeing from the attacks of the Roman procurator (*J.W.* 2.279), in other cases from the looting of the rebels (*Ant.* 20.256). There is no record of refugees in the resettlements in Palestine itself. After Herod's death the land was divided. It is therefore conceivable that some people escaped persecution by moving into a different territory (cf. Luke 13:31ff.).[28]

1.2.4 *The destitute.*   The prospects of better material conditions certainly impelled many people to emigrate. *Antiquities* 12.9 testifies to this with regard to Egypt. Otherwise, economic reasons are hardly mentioned. In the case of the new Palestinian settlements economic motives clearly existed. New settlers were favored materially. In Bathyra and its surroundings, they did not have to pay any taxes during Herod's lifetime (*Ant.* 17.27). In Tiberias they were freed of many obligations and were given land and houses (*Ant.* 18.38). In Sebaste they were assigned fertile land (*J.W.* 1.403). It seems reasonable to assume that there were comparable concessions elsewhere too.[29] We may therefore presume with A. Schalit "that the new settlers were farmers who had lost their land in their own part of the country. Since they had nothing to lose, these people readily betook themselves to the new region, attracted by the

---

26. The interpretation of the edict follows V. A. Tcherikover, *CPJ* 1:67f.; 2:53f.

27. Here two things must be presupposed: (1) that "Akone" is a transcription of the Hebrew "Hakone" and can be translated as "zealot." (so J. Juster, *Les Juifs dans l'Empire Romain*, II [Paris. 1914], 229); (2) that the inscription dates from the first century C.E. The only thing certain is that the Monteverde catacombs in Rome were already in use in the first century. See M. Hengel, *Die Zeloten* (Leiden, 1961), 71 (Eng. trans. *The Zealots*, trans. D. Smith [Edinburgh: T. & T. Clark, 1989]).

28. J. B. Tyson believes that Jesus' journeys outside Galilee were in part flights from Antipas ("Jesus and Herod Antipas," *JBL* 79 [1960]: 239–46).

29. There were also concessions when Jews settled in Asia Minor (*Ant.* 17.147ff.).

great concessions which Herod granted to every new settler."[30] There is actual evidence for this in the case of Tiberias. According to Josephus, its population was made up of three groups: forcibly resettled subjects of Herod Antipas, officials who were compelled to live in the new capital, and ἄποροι, "poor people, who had been brought there from all over the place, some of them people who were not even definitely born freemen" (*Ant.* 18.37).[31] Six months later these ἄποροι instigated a revolt (*Life* 66).

1.3 *Kinship between these groups and the Jesus movement.* Emigration and new settlement were important for the history of the Jesus movement too. The "Hellenists" left Palestine because of persecution (Acts 8:1; 9:19). So did Peter, who was hardly safe in Palestine after he had been imprisoned by Agrippa I (Acts 12:1ff.). Economic reasons connected with the catastrophic famine under Claudius (ca. 46/47 C.E.) may have driven a group of early Christian prophets beyond Palestine's frontiers to Antioch (Acts 11:27ff.). The same may perhaps be true of Paul's rivals, some of whom after all came from Palestine (see 2 Cor. 11:22). Paul polemically accuses them of materialistic motives (e.g., 1 Thess. 2:5; Phil. 3:19)—and polemic occasionally hits the target.[32] At all events, the mission that reached out beyond the borders of Palestine must be seen in the context of Jewish emigration in general. Resettlements in Palestine, on the other hand, played a lesser part. A few Galilean families probably moved to Jerusalem (Acts 1:14; Mark 15:40f.). But the first congregation probably fled from Jerusalem before the outbreak of the Jewish War (Eusebius *Eccl. Hist.* 3.5.2f.).[33] Where the Jesus movement is concerned,

---

30. A. Schalit, *König Herodes* (Berlin, 1969), 328. On Herod's settlement policy, see pp. 324ff. It is possible that in the confusion at the beginning of Herod's rule (Parthian invasian and civil war) many people became "displaced persons."

31. Josephus's account of Tiberias may be somewhat biased. His experiences with the town had been unfortunate. He writes, for example, that Tiberias had been built on unclean ground—on top of a cemetery. Impurity of this kind was locally and temporally limited (see *Ant.* 18.37). Perhaps these are later prejudices, played up later, against the Tiberias "mob" (σύγκλυδες; see *Ant.* 18.37). Tiberias was founded between 17 and 22 C.E. (thus Avi-Yonah, *Foundation,* 163), probably 19/20 C.E. (thus Y. Meshorer, *Jewish Coins of the Second Temple Period* [Tel-Aviv, 1969], 74f.).

32. Paul's letters were written between 50 and 56 C.E. (see P. Vielhauer, *Geschichte der urchristlichen Literatur* [Berlin, 1975], 70ff., 88f., 175 passim). The famine under Claudius was in the late forties. It is therefore possible that the appearance of rivals in Paul's mission field was partly due to that.

33. S. G. F. Brandon disputes—in my view wrongly—that there was an exodus to Pella (*The Fall of Jerusalem and the Christian Church* [London: SPCK, 1951], 167–73). A flight of some kind surely took place. See G. Sowers, "The Circumstances and Recollection of the Pella Flight," *ThZ* 26 (1970): 305–20; and J. Gunther, "The Fate of the Jerusalem Church: The Flight to Pella," *ThZ* 29 (1973): 81–94.

the settlement of Tiberias in 19/20 C.E. is especially illuminating. It shows that about the time of Jesus' public ministry in Galilee, there were people without any possessions, perhaps without any "home country."

2. Evasive Behavior: The Qumran Community

The people belonging to the Qumran community also saw themselves as emigrants. They had "left" Judah (CD 4:3), were living "in a strange land" (CD 6:5) and were waiting for their return (1QM 1:3). The secular pattern of behavior that we call emigration was taken up by this group and imbued with religious significance. They were not the only ones. There were hermits too, like the desert ascetic John the Baptist (Matt. 3:1ff.; 11:7ff.; *Ant.* 18.116ff.) and the hermit Bannos (*Life* 11f.).[34] Like the Qumran community, these men also wanted to prepare the way in the wilderness for God (Isa. 40:3; Mark 1:3; 1QS 8:13f.).

2.1 *Dissemination.*   Josephus (*Ant.* 18.20) and Philo (*Quod omnis probus liber sit* [*Prob.*] 75) agree in giving the number of the Essenes as four thousand. Even if we add together the Essenes who lived in Qumran and those who were living elsewhere, the number is surely too high. In Qumran about 1,200 burial places have been found.[35] If we assume that the settlement lasted for about two hundred years, and that there was a change of generation every twenty-five years on average, Qumran would have been inhabited by about 150 people. We do not know exactly. The duration of the settlement is illuminating. Since no children were born there, the membership was recruited from people who joined from outside — frequently the children of Essene families (1QSa 1:6ff.), frequently also from non-Essenes (Pliny *Natural History* 5.15 §73). The continuance of the settlement is therefore in itself an indication of the extent of social uprooting in Palestine.

2.2 *Reasons and conditions.*   We learn very little about the motives that impelled people to join the community, but we can perceive or deduce situations of general pressure, political confusion, and economic need.

2.2.1 *Situations of general pressure.*   Only the account in Pliny the Elder goes directly into the reasons that led people to join the community:

---

34. They belonged to the baptist movement (see J. Thomas, *Le mouvement baptiste en Palestine et Syrie* [Gembloux, 1935]), which was certainly very much larger, since groups belonged to it of whom we know no more than the name: Hemerobaptists and Masbotheans (Eusebius *Eccl. His.* 4.22.7).

35. H. Bardtke, *Die Handschriftenfunde am Toten Meer,* II: *Die Sekte von Qumran* (Berlin, 1958), 37: The dead were thirty to forty years old on average. According to Josephus, however, some of the Essenes lived to be over a hundred (*J.W.* 2.151).

On the west bank the Essenes withdraw so far that they cannot be injured. They are a solitary kind of people, different from anyone else in the world. They are without women, have renounced all sexuality, live without property and in the company of palm trees. Day after day the number of those who join them steadily increases, people seeking them out in sufficient numbers: people tired of life, waves of whom are brought here by the fate of their accustomed way of life. In this way this tribe of people into which no one is born — it is unbelievable — has survived for thousands of years. So weariness of life on the part of others becomes for these people a source of fertility." (*Nat. His.* 5.15)

The account is written from the perspective of an outside visitor. He overestimates the age of the settlement, knows nothing about married Essenes, and seeks an explanation for their deviant behavior which ignores their own religious understanding of what they were.[36] It is for that very reason that this testimony is so important for us: outsiders had the impression that Qumran was a gathering of dropouts. What stress situations they had fled from we are not told.

2.2.2 *Political pressure was probably one of the reasons.* This is suggested by a chronological correlation. The settlement was destroyed by an earthquake in 31 B.C.E. and was built up again only during the rule of Archelaus (4 B.C.E.–6 C.E.) — that is, immediately after the "brigands' war" (*J.W.* 2.65), which threw the whole of Palestine into chaos. It would seem plausible to suppose that many people who were uprooted at that time sought refuge in the community, so that the idea of a desert settlement received a new impetus. The same may well apply to all the disturbances of the first century C.E. According to Josephus, newcomers to the community had to swear "to refrain from robbery" (*J.W.* 2.142). The oath would have been superfluous if the Qumran community had not also included former freedom fighters (whom Josephus viewed as "robbers" or brigands).[37]

---

36. Pliny can hardly have been an eyewitness. His visit to Palestine is not certain (see M. Stern, *CRINT* I, 1, 32f.). Since it is only he and Dio Chrysostom who localize the Essenes on the Dead Sea (see Synesius of Cyrene, *Dion Chrysostom* 3.1f.), we may perhaps assume that the account of the journey is based on a written source: localizations belong to the travelogue as genre, just as does the outside perspective and "the yearning of the weary city-dweller for nature and palm-trees" (W. Bauer, "Essener," in *Aufsätze und Kleine Schriften* [Tübingen, 1967], 1–58, here p. 6). In addition we may assume that Pliny's sources about Palestine derive from the first century C.E. Pliny calls the little town that Archelaus founded "Archelais" (*Nat. His.* 13.44).

37. The oath seems like an interpolation between two enjoinments to secrecy (*J.W.* 2.142). Did Josephus interpolate something here in order to emphasize the harmless nature of the Essenes?

2.2.3 *Economic pressure.*   When people entered the Qumran community they were not only giving way to pressure; they were drawn by something too. Many of them were attracted by the Essene production communism: a living for everyone was made in common, and the individual was freed from anxiety about it (*J.W.* 2.122, 127; *Ant.* 18.20; Philo *Prob.* 85f.). Was a community of this kind not especially bound to attract people who saw their livelihood in danger? Josephus testifies that people without possessions were admitted, as well as propertied people (*Ant.* 18.20). Admittedly, the rules for admission (1QS 5:1–6:23) all presuppose that property will be transferred to the community. People with nothing at all are not envisaged here. But one does not have to be entirely without means in order to feel attracted by the poverty ideal practiced in Qumran. This ideal is vouched for by the community's description of itself as "the poor" (1QpHab 12:3, 6, 10; 1QM 11:9, 13; 4QpPs 37 2:8f., 3:9f.; 1QSb 5:21 and frequently),[38] by a radical renunciation of possessions (1QS 6:19f.), and by clothing and life-style (*J.W.* 2.126; 1QS 9:21ff.),[39] as well as by the unadorned graves otherwise found among the poor.[40] It is also shown in the contempt for wealth (*J.W.* 2.122; 1QMyst 1:10f.; 1QS 6:2; CD 8:5).

Of course a poverty ideal of this kind can be developed and practiced by members of the upper classes too. A radical role exchange can give life a new content.[41] But the hate of wealth and the resentment-

---

38. This self-description is of course only one term among others; see L. E. Keck, "The Poor among the Saints in Jewish Christianity and Qumran," *ZNW* 57 (1966): 54–78.

39. The statement in *J.W.* 2.126 that the Essenes gave the impression of being children brought up in fear is confirmed by 1QS 9:21ff.: one should leave outsiders their work and their possessions, meet them humbly as slaves, but inwardly cherish "eternal hate . . . in the spirit of secrecy." This is the behavior of oppressed people who do not have the power to express openly their hate for their oppressors.

40. The dead were buried in simple tombs without inscription or tombstone, clothes or accessories. "Sand tombs of this kind were destined for the poor at all periods, in the Qumran period too" (Bardtke, *Handschriftenfunde*, 2:45).

41. Fundamentally speaking, what H. Kreissig writes is correct: "To describe a certain group of people as poor . . . always makes sense only if at least most of this group is living in poverty in the sociological sense" (*Zusammenhänge*, 51). But we must also reckon with the possibility of a role exchange. Rich men like Petrus Waldus and Francis of Assisi held leading positions in the *paupertas* movement at the height of the Middle Ages too. See K. Bosl, "Potens und Pauper," in *Frühformen der Gesellschaft im mittelalterlichen Europa* (Munich, 1964), 106–34. See p. 123: "The commitment to *paupertas* and *humilitas* (*abiectio*) only makes real sense for people who in reality are neither *pauperes* nor *humiles*. The poverty movement of the high Middle Ages was sustained by the powerful and rich upper classes, who now felt inwardly compelled to present themselves as religious and ethical models and prototypes for the lower orders, now that the almost magical, indeed religious, effect of their power and sovereignty had faded in the wake of Christianization. . . ." Could this not also have been true of the Teacher of Righteousness and his group?

filled fantasies about great massacres at the end of days suggest that here many people interpreted their socioeconomic status religiously, transfiguring it, but also making it fruitful for creative impulses. We must also suppose that the community had members in easy circumstances: the Teacher of Righteousness was probably an aristocrat who had been deprived of his rights.[42] In the Jewish War we find an Essene, John, at the head of the military hierarchy, side by side with two sons of a high priest and the aristocrat Josephus (*J.W.* 2.567). The sympathies of Philo and Josephus for the Essenes are unmistakable, and both of them were members of the upper class.[43]

As a collective, the community was wealthy. For understandable reasons it must have been interested in the property and working capacity of its members. People who were unable to work were not admitted. Religious reasons are given for this in 1QSa 2:3ff., but these have a hard economic core: workers were needed — artisans such as bricklayers, stonemasons, leatherworkers, potters, smiths, bakers, and apothecaries.[44] Farm workers were needed too, for the community cultivated a two-mile-long tract of land in their oasis. Philo mentions farming even before handicrafts (*Prob.* 76). Finally we must also assume that there were people belonging to the higher professions: architects, stewards, scribes, and scholars. The literary production of the community presupposes education, and this is not generally found in the lowest classes of society.

There is therefore, in my view, no reason to doubt Josephus when he says that both rich people and people without any property were to be found in Qumran (*Ant.* 18.20). The strict hierarchy in the community itself also reflects all too clearly the hierarchy in society as a whole, even if the emphases were different; for here "the top people" were priests.

2.3 Kinship between the Qumran groups and the Jesus movement. In the Jesus movement too we find the description "the poor" (Gal. 2:10; Rom.

---

42. See H. Stegemann, "Die Entstehung der Qumrangemeinde," (thesis, Bonn, 1965; typescript 1971).

43. Kreissig in my view reduces the Essenes too one-sidedly to the common denominator of "lower class" and "class conflict" (*Zusammenhänge*, 105f.). Philo ascribes to them a great capacity for coming to terms even with tyrannical rulers (*Prob.* 89ff.). The powers that be (within the community?) are for them from God (Josephus *J.W.* 2.140). An Essene acts as court propagandist for Herod's rule (*Ant.* 15.373ff.).

44. This can be deduced from the archaeological findings; thus Bardtke, *Handschriftenfunde*, 2:78. On Qumran's economic situation, see W. R. Farmer, "The Economic Basis of the Qumran Community," *ThZ* 11 (1955): 295–308; 12 (1956): 56–58. Supplementary material on irrigation can be found in L. M. Pakozdy, "Der wirtschaftliche Hintergrund der Gemeinschaft von Qumran" in *Qumran-Probleme*, ed. H. Bardtke (Berlin, 1963), 167–91.

15:26).[45] Here too we meet a pronounced poverty ethic which finds expression in clothing (Matt. 10:9f.), lack of possessions (Mark 10:17ff.), and contempt for riches (Luke 6:20ff.). It is true that we do not find here any form of production communism, but we do find a "consumption" communism, though it is based on free gifts and not on principle — or this, at least, is the vision (Acts 4:32ff.).[46] Of course the differences are great. In Qumran we have an overdisciplined community; in the Jesus movement loosely organized local groups whose most important authorities are wandering charismatics. The links between the two phenomena, however, permit the supposition that the motives which led people to join the Qumran community could also have been reasons for joining the Jesus movement. The social background of the two was perhaps comparable.

3. Aggressive Behavior: The Brigands

In Josephus it is hard to distinguish between freedom fighters and criminals; for him, both groups are "robbers" — bandits or brigands. In case of doubt, we have in my view to assume a political background. We shall therefore be looking at most of Josephus's statements about these people under the next heading ("The Resistance Movement"). But this leaves us with only a very thin basis for assertions about criminal robbery. We must also remember that some of the "brigands" were merely somewhat untamed tribes. In their case, robbery was not a manifestation of social uprooting. It belonged to their way of life in general.

3.1 *Dissemination.* There were robbers and brigands all over the Roman Empire.[47] Strabo (16.2.18, 20) and Josephus (*Ant.* 15.346ff.) provide evidence that they existed in Iturea and the Trachonitis. Agrippa I or II boasts in an inscription that he had fought to put down robbers (*OGIS* 424). In the New Testament, the parable of the Good Samaritan presupposes the prevalence of robbers or brigands (Luke 10:30ff.). The Essenes reckoned with them, and when they went on a journey took weapons as a protection simply on this account (*J.W.* 2.125). Members of their community had to abjure robbery (*J.W.* 2.142). How widespread

---

45. L. E. Keck, "The Poor among the Saints in the New Testament," *ZNW* 56 (1965): 110–29: these were really "poor" people.

46. See M. Hengel, *Eigentum und Reichtum in der frühen Kirche* (Stuttgart, 1973), 39ff. (Eng. trans. *Property and Riches in the Early Church*, trans. J. Bowden [London: SCM Press; Philadelphia: Fortress Press, 1974]). He assumes — in my view rightly — that there was a certain historical background to the Lukan summing up.

47. See the excursus "Zum Räuberunwesen in der antiken Welt," in M. Hengel, *Zeloten*, German ed., 26–35.

brigandage was it is no longer possible to discover. It is certainly prejudice when the Jews are accused of being a nation of brigands (Strabo 16.2.37; Justin 40.2, 4; cf. Josephus *Ag. Ap.* 1.62).

3.2 *Reasons and conditions.* It is only seldom that we hear anything about the reasons for brigandage in Palestine. In the regions acquired in 23 B.C.E., Herod had to force thievish tribes to adopt a settled way of life and to farm the land (*Ant.* 15.348; 16.271). After about ten years they reverted to their former way of living, for a settled life "did not please them, nor did the land bring them the fruits of their labors" (*Ant.* 16.271). Here remembrance of the earlier life-style — that is, cultural tradition — as well as economic necessity was the reason for brigandage. Often, undoubtedly, the first of these motives would have been lacking; but a failed harvest could result in the growth of brigandage (*Ant.* 18.274). The same may be said of political tensions. After the disturbances under Cumanus (48–52 C.E.), some of the people involved "turned to robbery, so that plundering and, among the more resolute, attempts at rebellion soon became everyday occurrences all over the country" (*J.W.* 2.238). Since a differentiation is made here between robbery and attempts at rebellion, we may probably take it that this passage too refers to brigands in the usual sense.

3.3 *Kinship with the Jesus movement.* There is no kinship between the Jesus movement and the brigands except for the phenomenon of social uprooting. Perhaps Jesus is referring to brigands when he mentions "the foxes' holes" (Matt. 8:20). Caves were places of refuge for brigands (*OGIS* 424; *Ant.* 15.346), but for freedom fighters too (e.g., *J.W.* 4.512f.). If this is a covert reference to these people, then Jesus was describing the homelessness of the Son of man as more complete than the homelessness of the brigands.

4. Aggressive Behavior: The Resistance Movement

4.1 *Dissemination.* We have evidence that there were freedom fighters who resisted the Herodian and Roman regime for a hundred years. The following survey lists the most important happenings.[48] What is of particular interest to us is the continuance of the resistance movement over so long a period, and its size.

---

48. For further details, see Hengel, who has carefully described and analyzed the history of the resistance movement (*Zeloten,* German ed., 318ff.).

47–46 B.C.E.:   Herod kills the brigand captain Hesekiah, who had gathered "a large band" around himself (*J.W.* 1.204; *Ant.* 14.159).

39–38 B.C.E.:   Galilean brigands almost inflict a defeat on Herod (*J.W.* 1.304ff.). The country's caves are thereupon "cleaned up" (*J.W.* 1.310ff.; *Ant.* 14.420ff.). In spite of that, there are two other revolts against Herod in Galilee (*J.W.* 1.314ff, 326; *Ant.* 14.431ff., 450).

4–5 B.C.E.:   After Herod's death the "brigands' war" plunges the country into chaos. Five groups are involved: the group around Judas the Galilean was "by no means small" (*J.W.* 2.56); Varus had to divert part of his army to combat them (*J.W.* 2.68; *Ant.* 17.288f.). Three thousand Herodian soldiers, reinforced by Roman troops, were employed against Simon and his supporters (*Ant.* 17.266, 275). With the "great multitude" that rallied to him (*Ant.* 17.279), Athronges was even able to surround a Roman cohort. In addition, two thousand discharged Herodian soldiers participated in the risings (*Ant.* 17.270), together with another group (*Ant.* 17.277).

6–7 C.E.:   Judas the Galilean agitates against the census (*Ant.* 18.4ff.; Acts 5:37).

ca. 27 C.E.:   Two "robbers" or brigands are crucified together with Jesus (Mark 15:27). When he is taken prisoner, Jesus protests at being treated "like a robber" (Mark 14:48). Shortly beforehand there had been a rising in which Barabbas was involved (Mark 15:6f.).

40 C.E.:   During the disturbances preceding Caligula's death—disturbances triggered off by his attempt to install a statue of himself in the Temple—the Jewish aristocracy is afraid that "because no seed had been sown, banditry would follow, since it would be impossible to pay the taxes" (*Ant.* 18.274).

44–45 C.E.:   Cuspius Fadus kills the brigand captain Ptolemaeus, who had harassed Idumeans and Arabs especially, in southern Palestine. He is (allegedly) able to purge the whole of Judea of "brigands" (*Ant.* 20.5).

46–48 C.E.:   Tiberius Alexander has Simon and Jacob executed, these being two of Judas the Galilean's sons.

48–52 C.E.:   Under Cumanus, "brigands" attack an imperial slave on the public highway (*J.W.* 2.228f.). During anti-Samaritan disturbances, an enraged mob makes common cause with the brigand chief Eleazar ben Dinaeus, "who had been at large in the mountains for many years" (*Ant.* 20.121). Many people join the brigands, so that "from this time on, the whole of Judea was full of bands of thieves" (*Ant.* 20.124). Tacitus also mentions robber bands in connection with these disturbances (*Annals* 12.54).

52–60 C.E.:   Felix has "innumerable" brigands and their sympathizers crucified (*J.W.* 2.253). In addition, through cunning and breach of faith, he captures the brigand chief Eleazar ben Dinaeus, who had gathered a whole corps (σύνταγμα) of brigands around himself (*Ant.* 20.161). But Felix is still unsuccessful. During his rule, the "Sicarii" are active even in Jerusalem itself (*Ant.* 20.165). The attempt on Paul's life (Acts 23:12ff.) is also evidence that groups of terrorists were at work in Jerusalem.

There is no need for us to pursue here the growth of political resistance up to the Jewish revolt. It is obvious enough.[49] What is of greater interest to us is the relative continuity of that resistance. This is shown first of all by the fact that the family of Judas the Galilean showed signs of forming a dynasty. Judas himself may have been the son of the brigand leader Hesekiah, and his sons and grandsons come to the fore in the resistance movements of 46–48 and 66–73 — not only Simon and Jacob, but also the royal claimant Menahem, who was murdered (*J.W.* 2.448), and Eleazar, Masada's defender (*J.W.* 7.253). A second piece of evidence is the long period of activity of Eleazar ben Dinaeus; it lasted for ten years, perhaps twenty. Third, we may point to the argument used by the Jewish aristocracy in 40 c.e.: to say that tax arrears lead to "robbery" presupposes experience over a period of many years. Finally, Josephus himself stresses the continuity of the resistance, stretching from Judas the Galilean to the Jewish revolt (*Ant.* 18.6ff.; *J.W.* 7.253ff.).

One problem remains. Josephus has nothing to tell us about freedom fighters between 10 and 35 c.e., the period of most interest to us. This could be due to a dearth of sources, but it could also be that the country was relatively quiet in these years. Tacitus reports merely: *sub Tiberio quies,* "Things were quiet under Tiberius" (*Historiae* 5.9). Perhaps it is not merely chance that the irenic Jesus movement should have grown up at that particular period.

4.2 *Reasons and conditions.* The resistance movement was influenced by a wide variety of social conditions. For one thing, there was a socio-cultural resistance tradition reaching back to Maccabean times — a fact that should not be underestimated. But apart from that, the main reasons were rivalry between native power elites, the fear of prosecution, and economic necessity. Here the economic motive seems to have been the strongest.

4.2.1 *Rivalry between native power elites.* The Galilean brigands whom Herod fought to put down were probably closely connected with Has-monean groups which had vainly resisted the rise of the Herodians. Hesekiah had influential sympathizers in the Jerusalem upper class (*Ant.* 14.168ff.). His son Judas may even have come forward with dynastic claims during the "brigands' war."[50] He led a pack "of despairing men"

---

49. In the Jewish War the resistance groups were of course unusually large. There were 2,400 Zealots (*J.W.* 5.250) and 960 Sicarii in Masada (*J.W.* 7.400). John of Gischala had 6,000 men under him and Simon ben Giora 10,000 (*J.W.* 5.248ff.).

50. W. R. Farmer assumes that these messianic claimants were Hasmonean in origin ("Judas Simon and Athronges," *NTS* 4 [1958]: 147–55). Since Josephus explicitly stresses that Athronges had no famous forefathers (*Ant.* 17.278), it is possible that the others did in fact appeal to their ancestry. Since Simon, the Herodian slave, hardly comes into

(*Ant.* 17.271). However he may have justified his claims, his followers were probably outcasts. Other leaders of the rebellion were low down in the social scale: Simon was a slave (*Ant.* 17.273), Athronges was a shepherd (*Ant.* 17.278).

4.2.2 *Fear of prosecution.*   After anti-Samaritan attacks, many Jews were forced to escape the prosecution which threatened them by joining the resistance movement (*J.W.* 2.238). During the Jewish War we come across people in Tarichea who had turned to war because of punishable acts they had committed in peacetime (*J.W.* 3.542). Some of them were taken as slaves; others were massacred in an ambush: "Everyone declared that it would be dangerous to let these people go free because, since they had no country of their own to which they belonged, they would certainly not remain quiet" (*J.W.* 3.533). Homelessness was the fate of many people in Palestine.

4.2.3 *Economic necessity.*   Resistance to the Romans had an economic aspect from the very outset. It took the form of opposition to taxation. The argument ran as follows: anyone who paid taxes to the Romans was recognizing lords other than God. The First Commandment in radicalized form was the central message of Judas the Galilean (*Ant.* 18.23; *J.W.* 2.118, 7.410). Refusal to pay taxes was the most important consequence.

A message of this kind could originate and find an echo only where taxes were felt to be a crushing burden. There is evidence that this was in fact the case. Herod was already forced to grant a remission of taxation on two occasions, in order to prevent social unrest (*Ant.* 15.365, 16.64). After his death, an appeal was made to his successor to repeal certain taxes (*Ant.* 17.205), but in vain; it was not until Vitellius that the disputed turnover tax on fruit sold in the Jerusalem market was remitted (*Ant.* 18.90). Complaints to Augustus about unduly high poll taxes were equally unavailing (*Ant.* 17.308). Augustus did remit a quarter of the taxes in Samaria, but not in the main Jewish province, because of the revolts that had taken place there (*Ant.* 17.319). That is to say, a quarter of the tax burden must be viewed as punitive; or, to put it another way: taxation could have been reduced by a quarter. Even after Archelaus had been removed, and after a new tax assessment by Quirinius, taxes remained high. At the time of Jesus, Syrians and Jews together petitioned the emperor Tiberius to remit taxes (Tacitus *Annals* 2.42). It is therefore probable that theological arguments against paying

---

question here, we are left with Judas the Galilean, whose father, Hesekiah, is explicitly named by Josephus. This Hesekiah may have been of distinguished ancestry.

taxes found an echo (*Ant.* 18.6) because the economic situation was crushing for many people; and for this the tax burden was partly responsible. That is why difficulties in raising crops could lead to "brigandage" (*Ant.* 18.274). Farmers and leaseholders who were encumbered with debt often had no alternative except a flight to the resistance groups in the mountains, as a way of escaping the impoverishment that threatened them.

The rich, of course, saw things differently. For them, the freedom fighters were bandits "who had squandered all that they had" (*J.W.* 4.241). This is correct, in the sense that these really were impoverished groups. The idea that a person can become poor without its being his own fault is a notion that has never commended itself to established circles. The freedom fighters for their part knew very well where they had to look for sympathizers. At the beginning of the Jewish War they destroyed the debts register in Jerusalem, "so that they could get the mass of debtors on their side, and could incite the poor to rebel against the rich without fear of punishment" (*J.W.* 2.427).

Josephus believes that these social-revolutionary elements were the real motives of the freedom fighters. He belittles the desire for national independence as an ideological camouflage for greed: "Large bands of robbers made continual attacks, allegedly in order to set up a united country again, but in reality in the hope of private profit" (*Ant.* 18.7; cf. *J.W.* 7.256, 264).[51] In other passages too he reports terrorist actions against the rich (*J.W.* 2.265; 4.334ff.). There can therefore be no doubt that the resistance movement drew its impetus from the socioeconomic distribution struggle between the lower and the upper classes, a distribution struggle that probably took on particular acerbity in times of famine.[52]

We can, at least, discover one illuminating chronological correlation here: Josephus assigns the crucial growth of resistance to the Cumanus period (48–52 C.E.; cf. *Ant.* 20.124). Now, under Cumanus's predecessor a great famine had disrupted the country and had cost many lives (*Ant.* 20.51, 101; Acts 11:27ff.). The anti-Samaritan attacks under Cumanus

---

51. M. Hengel, *Zeloten*, German ed., 46: These were "for the most part people belonging to the socially underprivileged classes, who were fighting among other things for the divinely willed new order in the distribution of property.... The reproach of greed which Josephus levels against the brigands should probably be understood in this light" (trans. directly from the German text). See also ibid., p. 341f.

52. S. Zeitlin, *The Rise and Fall of the Judaean State*, II (Philadelphia: Jewish Publication Society of America, 1967), 269: "It is a phenomenon of economic development that, in such crises, the rich swallow the poor. Many lost their farms and a whole new class of semi-farmers or tenant farmers came into being. Land tenancy on the royal domain had been common. Now private landlords multiplied."

can therefore probably be interpreted as a symptom of an exacerbated economic situation. Despairing people who have little to lose are more inclined to follow extremist slogans than people living in security. At that time, flight from prosecution led many people to join the resistance movement; but this was probably the occasion for the movement's growth, not its true cause.[53]

4.3 *Kinship with the Jesus movement.*   In spite of all the differences, we can detect kindred features in the Jesus and the resistance movements. To be in debt is a situation that is thought about in the Jesus movement too. We come across anxiety about social decline, fear of the debtors' prison (Matt. 5:25; 18:30) and of enslavement as a consequence of debt (Matt. 18:25). The remissions of debt granted by the Unjust Steward in the parable are judged favorably, and even the doubtful means used does not diminish their value (Luke 16:1ff.). The parable of the Wicked Husbandmen reflects the rebellious mood among tenants (?) on great estates (Mark 12:7).[54]

Even the response to the crisis is sometimes comparable. Flight into the mountains was a way of escaping "tribulation" for freedom fighters and Christian groups alike (Mark 13:14ff.), even if Mark 13 is a call to wait for the coming of the Son of man, not a call to resistance. A readiness to leave one's familiar surroundings must have been widespread at that time, even outside these groups. Probably the source of Mark 13 originated in the period of the disturbances preceding Caligula's death.[55] At that time many Jews, with their families, left their homes and all that they had in order to join the protest demonstrations in Ptolemais and Tiberias. Before Petronius, the Syrian legate, these people affirm: "We leave our towns and villages, our houses and possessions, and are prepared to give up goods, money, everything we cherish and all our cattle. We believe that we do not give up, but receive" (Philo *Ad Gaium* 232; cf. 225).

---

53. In 40 c.e. too political resistance may have been increased by threatening economic misery. According to Josephus it had not rained all year (*Ant.* 18.285). But this could be a legendary motif. A sudden rain counts as God's answer when Petronius finally gives way (E. M. Smallwood's view in *Philonis Alexandrini Legatio*, 32). What is less legendary is the fact that the danger is by no means past.

54. For the sociological background of the parable, see M. Hengel, "Das Gleichnis von den Weingärtnern Mc. 12, 1-12 im Lichte der Zenonpapyri und der rabbinischen Gleichnisse," *ZNW* 59 (1968): 1–39.

55. G. Hölscher's view in "Der Ursprung der Apokalypse Mrk. 13," *ThBl* 12 (1933): 194–202. Assentingly, e.g., R. Pesch, *Naherwartungen* (Düsseldorf, 1968), 215–18; L. Gaston, *No Stone on Another*, Suppl NovTest 23 (Leiden, 1970), 23ff.

A statement of this kind is a direct reminder of Mark 10:28–30. And indeed the ethical rigor of the Synoptic tradition has analogies in the ethic of the freedom fighters. Preparedness for martyrdom belongs both to discipleship (Mark 8:34f.) and to resistance. The Sicarii bravely endured torture and torments (*J.W.* 7.417ff.; *Ant.* 18.23f.), simply in order to avoid having to call the emperor "Lord."[56] They were rigorous toward their own people too: the murder of friends and relatives was sanctioned in the service of the cause (*Ant.* 18.23). This is reminiscent of the hate of family which is elevated into a condition for discipleship in the Jesus movement (Luke 14:26). The disrespectful requirement that the dead should be left to bury their dead (Matt. 8:22) finds its analogy in a practice of the freedom fighters, which was to slay deserters and leave them without burial. People who wished to bury their relatives were themselves put to death and remained without burial (*J.W.* 4.381ff.). The condemnation of wealth is common to both movements too, even if the conclusions drawn are very different. For instance, the Jesus movement sharply condemned the murder of the wealthy Zechariah ben Barachiah (Matt. 23:35), whereas the Zealots extolled it as a heroic deed (*J.W.* 4.335ff.).

In spite of diametrically opposite features, the two movements have characteristics that are formally comparable.[57] This can be explained by the fact that the radicalism of the two ethics was the radicalism of socially uprooted people.

5. Subsiditive Behavior: Begging and Vagrancy

Not all beggars are socially uprooted. Some live in familiar surroundings. We can speak of social uprooting only in the case of homelessness and/or a breach with familiar modes of behavior.

5.1 *Dissemination.* The New Testament testifies that beggars existed (Mark 10:46ff.; Luke 14:16ff.; John 9:1ff.; Acts 3:2). Institutional regulatives show that they were a matter-of-course part of society.[58] The Talmud

---

56. M. Hengel thinks that the image of the carrying of the cross could come from the Zealot milieu ("Nachfolge," 64).

57. That is why in Acts 5:35ff. the activity of Judas the Galilean is put parallel to that of Jesus. Celsus (Origen *Contra Celsum* 2.12) still compares Jesus with a στρατηγός and λήσταρχος. See Hengel, "Nachfolge," 43.

58. See S. Krauss, *Talmudische Archäologie,* vol. 3 (Leipzig, 1912; reprint, Hildesheim, 1966), 63–74; J. Jeremias, *Jerusalem zur Zeit Jesu,* 3rd ed. (Göttingen, 1969), 132–34 (Eng. trans. *Jerusalem at the Time of Jesus,* trans. F. H. and C. H. Cave, rev. ed. [London: SCM Press, 1973]). Kreissig disputes—in my opinion rightly—the view that well-organized charitable care for the poor had made begging attractive (*Zusammenhänge,* 51ff.).

tractate Pe'ah VIII 7a lays down precepts about the care for the poor who wandered from place to place: "The poor person who is wandering from place to place should be given not less than a loaf of bread. . . . If he remains overnight, he should be given whatever is necessary for the night." The *Damascus Document* also envisages the support of "the homeless" (CD 14.14f.). Some beggars perhaps pretended that they were unable to work. Pe'ah VIII 9d threatens that sham suffering will become real before they die.[59]

5.2 *Reasons and conditions.*   It is plausible that economic impoverishment should have led to mendicancy. In the parable, the steward who is threatened with dismissal also considers begging as a (theoretical) possibility (Luke 16:3). Generally speaking, unemployment would have been due to illness and handicap. In the *Gospel of the Nazarenes* (frag. 10), the man with the paralyzed hand pleads: "I was a mason and earned (my) living with (my) hands. I beg you, Jesus, to restore me to health so that I do not shamefully have to beg for food." The disabled also included people who were "possessed."[60] The deranged prophet of doom in Jerusalem is fed by charity (*J.W.* 6.307). Others who were mentally sick no doubt existed in a similar way.

5.3 *Kinship with the Jesus movement.*   The early Christian wandering charismatics also lived from charity (Matt. 10:7ff.). They were highly familiar with the piece of beggar's lore that said "Ask, and it will be given you" (Luke 11:9). The rule for dealing with the wandering poor given in Pe'ah VIII 7a is reminiscent of corresponding rules in the *Didache* for itinerant charismatics (13.6): even an "apostle" receives only one loaf to take with him on his journey; in general he remains for only one night. Of course the Jesus movement was not a mendicant movement. But it took up secular patterns of mendicant behavior, varied them and

---

59. W. Grundmann considers that these were "work-shy and a-social people" (*Umwelt des Urchristentums* I [Berlin, 1965], 187). It does not occur to him that a pretended inability to work may be based on the fact that a person has not been able to find work. Judgments of this kind are illuminating—and also depressing.

60. It is worth thinking about J. Klausner's opinion in *Jesus von Nazareth* (Berlin, 1930), 363 (Eng. trans. *Jesus of Nazareth,* trans. H. Danby from original Hebrew ed. [London: Allen & Unwin, 1925]). He sees a connection between deviant behavior and the general social situation: "We have already seen how Palestine, and especially Galilee, had become full of sick and suffering people, neurasthenics and psychopaths, as a result of the continuing wars and unrest, and the frightful oppressions of Herod and the Romans. The enormous chaos and the economic misery which followed in its wake also increased the numbers of the poor, people who had come down in the social scale, and the unemployed, to such a degree that in Palestine, and especially Galilee . . . neurotics, especially hysterical women, and people with all kinds of psychological defects (paralytics, epileptics, idiots, and the semi-insane . . .) increased to an appalling extent" (trans. from German ed.).

reinterpreted them: the radical renunciation of provision for the future was an expression of trust in God's care (Matt. 6:25ff.).

6. Subsiditive Behavior: Prophetic Movements

6.1 Dissemination. We have evidence that prophetic movements were afoot between about 35 and 75 c.e.[61] They seem to have been particularly numerous under Felix (52–60 c.e.). Josephus sums up these prophets succinctly under the heading of deceivers and cheats, "who under the pretext of divine inspiration worked to bring about revolution and revolt, and tried to work the people up into religious enthusiasm, enticing them into the desert with the pretence that there God would proclaim their liberation through miraculous signs" (*J.W.* 2.258ff.). Earlier we meet only two prophets: about 37 c.e. a Samaritan who claimed to have discovered the missing Temple vessels on Mount Gerizim (*Ant.* 18.85), and about 44 c.e. Theudas, who persuaded "a very great number" (*Ant.* 20.97), or four hundred followers (Acts 5:36), to follow him to the Jordan, where the river would miraculously divide. Under Felix there was an Egyptian who promised that the miracle at Jericho would be repeated at the walls of Jerusalem (*Ant.* 20.169). According to *J.W.* 2.261ff. he had thirty thousand followers, according to Acts 21:38f., four thousand. Under Festus, a prophet promised that in the desert all evil would come to an end (*Ant.* 20.188). And at the close of the Jewish War, in Cyrenaica, Jonathan the weaver enticed "by no means a few" into the desert (*J.W.* 7.437ff.). The Romans put down all these movements by force of arms.

6.2 Reasons and conditions. We can do no more than deduce the motives that led people to join movements of this kind. What is certain is that their adherents were recruited from the lower classes. Theudas's followers took all they possessed with them to the Jordan, so it cannot have been much (*Ant.* 20.97). The Egyptian collected δημοτικὸς πλῆθος around him—that is, simple people (*Ant.* 20.169). Jonathan was a weaver. His followers were "people without any property," while his enemies were members of the Jewish upper class (*J.W.* 7.438). The promise that all necessity would be ended points to groups who knew what necessity was (*Ant.* 20.188). The social background would have been the same as that of the resistance movement, especially since there are numerous links between the two groupings: the followers of the Egyptian are called Sicarii ("Assassins") in Acts 21:38f. Jonathan himself was a Sicarius (*J.W.* 7.438).

---

61. See Hengel, *Zeloten*, German ed., 234–51; R. Meyer, *Der Prophet aus Galiläa* (Leipzig, 1940).

6.3   *Kinship with the Jesus movement.*   All the prophetic movements share typical features: A prophet announces a miracle performed by God which is typologically linked with Israel's salvation history. He exhorts people to follow him to the place where the miracle is expected to take place (ἕπεσθαι *Ant.* 20.97, 188; ἀκολουθεῖν *Ant.* 20.188). There the Romans intervene. We find all this in the Jesus movement too. Jesus proclaims a wondrous new Temple which will excel the old one. He calls people to discipleship, goes to the place where he expects the miracle will take place, and is crucified by the Romans. Even in the New Testament his ministry is already compared with the activity of Theudas and Judas the Galilean (Acts 5:36f.). This was probably not simply polemic, for the Jesus movement itself had to warn its members against these prophetic movements. People were cautioned against seeking the Messiah in the desert (Matt. 24:26) and against "following" false prophets (Luke 17:23). If the Jesus movement felt forced to warn people against prophetic movements, does this not suggest that its adherents felt attracted by them?

Of course the differences are great. The national prophets of salvation were hoping for liberation from all foreign rule. The movements set on foot by John the Baptist and Jesus were very much more conversion movements. They demanded repentance in the face of the impending judgment. This critical feature is missing in the message of the nationalist prophets of salvation, as far as we can see.[62]

III. SOCIAL UPROOTING AND SOCIAL CRISIS

We shall now try to arrive at a summary interpretation of social uprooting as anomic behavior.[63] We can talk about anomy, first where

---

62. On the other hand we find it in Judas the Galilean; cf. κακίζων (*J.W.* 2.118) and ὀνειδίσας (*J.W.* 2.433). M. Hengel thinks of prophetic "reproaches" such as we find in the preaching of John the Baptist (*Zeloten*, German ed., 94).

63. E. Durkheim introduced the term "anomy" (or "anomie") into sociology. "It expresses a state in which individuals are no longer able to behave in accordance with the norms of their group. This occurs, for example, in economic crises which shift people into totally different groups, thereby taking from them the assured behavior they have hitherto enjoyed, until they have learned the rules of behavior that correspond to the new groups to which they now belong" (W. Rüegg. *Soziologie,* Funk-Kolleg 6 [Frankfurt, 1969], 40). P. Berger puts this concept at the center of his theory about religion: religion means coming to terms with anomy and overcoming it (*The Sacred Canopy: Elements of a Sociological Theory of Religion* [Garden City, N.Y.: Doubleday; London: Faber & Faber, 1969]). He relates the term to all situations that profoundly disturb values and sense of meaning. It is important to see that the religious renewal movements cited above are not in themselves anomic phenomena. They adopt anomic behavior as a way of overcoming anomy.

members of a society are no longer able to lead their lives according to the norms of the social environment to which they belong; second, where this phenomenon is widespread to a more than average extent; and third, where the groups affected have undergone changes in their status that have led to a disruption of their traditional way of living. Do we find these three conditions in Palestine?

1. Almost all the phenomena in which social uprooting manifests itself are associated with deviant behavior, although this can probably least be said of emigrants and new settlers. For example, when Peter went to Antioch, he was uncertain whether he should eat with Gentile Christians or not (Gal. 2:12ff.). Paul, the diaspora Jew, had little patience with his vacillation; but what Paul calls hypocrisy was probably to some extent difficulty in finding bearings in a strange environment.[64]

2. Whether social uprooting was widespread to a more than average degree in Jewish Palestinian society is a question we can hardly answer, since we do not know what the average was. Here two observations may be of help. First, we can point to the opinion of contemporaries. Josephus considers that the amount of robbery (brigandage) and resistance was extremely unusual (see, e.g., *Ant.* 20.124). The dimensions of the Jewish Diaspora attracted attention (e.g., Strabo in Josephus *Ant.* 14.115; *Sibylline Oracles* 3:271; 1 Macc. 15:15ff.; Philo *Ad Gaium* 281ff.). Pliny was astonished at the vitality of the Qumran community (*Nat. His.* 5.15 §73). Second, we should note the wide variation in the quality of what we have summed up as "social uprooting." There was emigration, robbery, and begging in every society. What is unusual is that in the internal Jewish revival movements this pattern of behavior was imbued with religious significance, that emigration was stylized and transformed into the settlement of a religious community, brigandage into religious and social resistance, and beggars into itinerant charismatics.[65] When deviant behavior becomes the basis for religious renewal, this is probably a characteristic symptom of a society's condition. There was only one revival movement within the framework of normal life, and that was Pharisaism.

3. Anomy is evoked through changes in social status. Here two things are important. First, the process can be upward or downward; inherited

---

64. See P. Berger, *Sacred Canopy,* 50: "Thus travel in areas where there were no Jewish communities was not only ritually impossible but inherently anomic (that is, threatening an anomic disintegration of the only conceivable 'correct' way of living) for the traditional Jew."

65. It must be pointed out, however, that there was a creative interpretation of deviant behavior elsewhere in the ancient world too—for example, among the Cynic wandering philosophers. Here too there was discipleship; see Hengel, "Nachfolge" (cf. n. 1), 27–34.

norms can be called in question by both processes. Second, anomy is not evoked simply by the existence of social pressure; history shows that the unendurable is often endured for an astonishingly long time. People become active if they cherish a hope for better things, or if things threaten to become worse. Anyone who is aware of the standards of a better life reacts more sensitively to a drop in the social scale than someone who has been born in miserable circumstances.

It follows from this that it would be simplistic to limit anomic behavior to a certain class. Every class can be drawn into the whirlpool of social change. The existence of members of the upper classes in the various socially uprooted groups is therefore not an argument against a connection between internal Jewish revival movements and a widespread crisis of Jewish Palestinian society. For example, there were undoubtedly upper-class emigrants. There were aristocrats in Qumran. Hesekiah, Judas the Galilean, and John of Gischala were resistance leaders who may well have belonged to the upper class.[66] In the Jesus movement we meet a *syntrophos* (foster brother or intimate friend) of Herod Antipas (Acts 13:1f.). It is probable that most of these upper-class people had come down in the social scale. The emigrants were political refugees; the Qumran Zadokites were a priestly group who had been deprived of power and evicted by the Hasmoneans. Hesekiah's family was on the decline. His son Judas appears as the leader of a company "of despairing men" (*Ant.* 17.271). John of Gischala may have come from a good family, but at the beginning of his career, at all events, he was a poor man (*J.W.* 2.585). Menahem may perhaps have been involved in the fall of his "friend" Antipas in 39 C.E.

Apart from that, it has no doubt by now become clear that most socially uprooted people came from the middle classes. It was the people who had declined into poverty, rather than the people born in poverty, who set out to pass their lives beyond the boundaries of normal life, or even to seek for ways of renewing society. This is most obvious in the case of the freedom fighters. They were recruited from former farmers (*Ant.* 18.274) who had got into debt (cf. *J.W.* 1.426f.) and had become poor (*J.W.* 4.241). We may assume that the same was true of the Essenes and members of the Jesus movement. We find artisans,

---

66. Acording to Josephus (*J.W.* 4.208), John enjoyed the trust of the Jerusalem aristocracy; also according to Josephus (*Life*, 192), he was a friend of the aristocrat Simon. It is probable that he belonged to the aristocracy himself, though this is not quite certain. Since according to *J.W.* 2.585, he was a poor man at the beginning of his career, we might conclude with G. Baumbach "that he belonged to the ancient country nobility who had been impoverished by the Hellenistic reform of the economy" ("Zeloten und Sikarier," *ThLZ* 90 [1965]: 727–40, here col. 731).

farmers, and fishermen among them. There are some indications that the economic situation of this class had worsened in the first century, that these people were threatened with a drop in the social scale, and were therefore exposed to social anomy.[67]

1. *Political reasons.* From the time when the Romans began to administer Judea directly, tax collection was controlled by them (see the tax administrator Captio in Philo *Ad Gaium* 199), and the taxation policy became more inflexible. Herod had twice granted a remission of taxes, in order to prevent social unrest (*Ant.* 15.365; 16.64). He may perhaps have advanced the necessary payments to the Romans himself. But now requests for any tax remission had to be made in far-off Rome, where no one was familiar with the difficult conditions in Palestine.[68] We do not know whether the plea for tax remissions under Tiberius was successful (Tacitus *Annals* 2.42). It is improbable. Nor do we hear anything about any easing of taxation during the great famine under Claudius.[69] Conditions in the new Jewish settlement areas of Batanea were probably symptomatic. During Herod's lifetime the new settlers were freed from taxation altogether. Under his successor Philip, inconsiderable levies were made (*Ant.* 17.23ff.). Agrippa I and II "oppressed them with taxes," but were even outdone by the Romans (εἰς τὸ πάμπαν) (*Ant.* 17.28).

Here we have direct evidence that the taxation burden increased in the first century. For only the tax levied under Philip can be explained by the cessation of the unavoidable initial concessions to new settlers.

2. *Economic reasons.* There are some indications that property became progressively concentrated in the first century. Herod had acquired an immense quantity of land through confiscation (*Ant.* 17.307).[70] After Archelaus had been

---

67. For the economic situation in Palestine, see F. M. Heichelheim, "Roman Syria," in *An Economic Survey of Ancient Rome,* ed. T. Frank, vol. 4 (Baltimore: John Hopkins University Press, 1938), 121–257; F. C. Grant, *The Economic Background of the Gospels* (London: Humphrey Milford, 1926); Klausner, *Jesus von Nazareth,* German ed., 231–57; H. Kreissig, "Die landwirtschaftliche Situation in Palästina vor dem jüdischen Krieg," *Acta Antiqua* 17 (1969): 223–54; also his *Zusammenhänge,* esp. 17–87; D. Sperber, "Costs of Living in Roman Palestine," *JESHO* 8 (1965): 248–71; 9 (1966): 182–211. In what follows it is not my intention to offer an analysis of the economic situation. My purpose is only to point to signs that the situation of the lower and lower-middle classes had deteriorated in the first century.

68. The Syrian governor Vitellius did grant an alleviation of taxation in Jerusalem, however (*Ant.* 18.90). One wonders whether he had been authorized by Rome to do so?

69. According to Bardtke (*Handschriftenfunde,* 2:72), sixty coins were found in Qumran dating from Agrippa I (37–44 C.E.), only six procurator coins from the time of Claudius (i.e., from 44 to 54 C.E.), but thirty-one procurator coins and one silver coin from the Nero period (54–68 C.E.). This could indicate that during the famine under Claudius the Qumran community had hardly any income but, on the contrary, had to spend their money for the most part — hence the disproportionately few coins dating from this period. But the fortuitous character of the material transmitted permits only very cautious conclusions.

70. Schalit describes him as "perhaps the only large landowner in Judea and his whole country" (*Herodes,* 260). Unfortunately we do not know this so precisely.

deposed in 6 c.e., this property was sold (*Ant.* 17.355; 18.2). We know nothing about the purchasers, but of course they can only have been people with considerable capital. Through these transactions the people who in any case possessed property became richer still.

Now, one thing that marks large estates off from small ones is the fact that they are able to produce far more than enough for their own needs. It was these estates that were able to export. To some degree we have good evidence for this. The balsam export had always been in the hands of the rulers.[71] The Herodian princes supplied the neighboring Phoenician towns with grain (Acts 12:20ff.; Josephus *Life* 119). Oil was exported to Syria (*J.W.* 2.591). We also have evidence that a good profit could be made from the export business. John of Gischala took advantage of a favorable situation and was able to sell oil to Syria at a profit of 700 percent. Salome, Herod's sister, owned the fruitful area round Jamnia and Phasaelis, where Herod had caused about seventeen square miles of land to be irrigated. From this relatively small area he drew an income of sixty talents (*Ant.* 17.321), whereas Herod Antipas, for example, had drawn an income of "only" two hundred talents from the whole of Galilee and Perea (*Ant.* 17.318ff.).

The country's "top people" undoubtedly took the most fruitful areas for themselves, and that meant the export business too. And in the first century export enjoyed an enormous boom. Evidence for this is the swift growth of the port of Caesarea, which was not founded until 10 b.c.e.[72] "The peace of Augustus" was undoubtedly favorable for trade. And it favored above all the people who already possessed property in any case. So when, in the parable of the Talents, the well-funded moneylender (who is evidently modeled on Archelaus) commands good connections abroad too, this is not mere chance. We need add nothing to the pessimistic saying at the end of the parable: "To every one who has will more be given; but from him who has not, even what he has will be taken away" (Luke 19:26).

3. *Ecological reasons.* The concentration of property, and the impoverishment of other people that went with it, was intensified by ecological crises.[73] It is true that most of the famines for which Josephus provides evidence belong to the first century b.c.e.: a drought (65 b.c.e.), a hurricane (64 b.c.e.), an earthquake (31 b.c.e.), epidemics (29 b.c.e.), and a famine (25 b.c.e.). But Matthew (13:8) calls earthquakes and famines signs of the times. And we know that there was a great famine under Claudius (46–47 c.e.). Indeed, during his period of rule there were supply difficulties in the Roman Empire generally.[74] At times such as these, the small farmers declined even more deeply into debt and dependence.

---

71. See Diodorus 2.48.9; Strabo 17.1, 15. According to Theophrastus *Hist. plant.* 9.6.1, the Persian kings evidently already took possession of the balsam plantations. Anthony gave them to Cleopatra. Herod leased them from her (*J.W.* 1.361f.; *Ant.* 15.96).

72. Zeitlin, *Rise and Fall,* 268: "The opening of the Port of Caesarea in 10 b.c.e. made a great change in Judaea's economic life."

73. See the compilation in Jeremias, *Jerusalem,* German ed., 157–61.

74. See E. Haenchen, *Die Apostelgeschichte,* KEK 3 (Göttingen, 1961), 55 n. 4.

Changed political conditions had here too if anything negative consequences. In the severe famine of 25 B.C.E. Herod had been able to prevent the worst by selling property of his own (*Ant.* 15.299–316). We are told nothing about any comparable governmental help in the hard times under Claudius. We hear only about private initiatives (Acts 11:28; *Ant.* 20.51ff.).

Perhaps there was also a disproportion between the potential agricultural productivity of the country and the size of its population. But we do not have sufficient evidence to back up this supposition.[75]

We have therefore good reason to believe that in first century Palestine a few wealthy people had become wealthier still, whereas people lower down the social scale — small-holders, tenant farmers, fishermen, and artisans — found themselves in difficulty. This means that the conditions were ripe for anomic behavior in both groups. Among the "climbers" there may perhaps have been a trend toward assimilation with Hellenistic Roman civilization; there is evidence that this was the case among the Herodians. But we do not know. In the threatened lower-class groups, people reacted to the situation with a latent readiness for social uprooting — even among the *petit bourgeoisie* who had had settled homes (cf. Mark 13:14ff.; Philo *Ad Gaium* 225, 232). Many of them left their homes and their land. Marginal groups particularly probably reacted most sensitively to the social situation as a whole, and especially a group that is notoriously marginal — the young. Josephus stresses that they were receptive to the slogans of the freedom fighters (e.g., *Ant.* 18.10; *J.W.* 4.128). Some of them joined the Essenes. The Qumran burial places testify that the number of young people was relatively high. Other young people would no doubt have followed the Jesus movement, even if this is no more than supposition. Luke 3:23 says that Jesus was thirty years old.

---

75. Grant (*Economic Background,* 81–87) and Zeitlin (*Rise and Fall,* 269) suppose that there was overpopulation. This is a very attractive idea. But in the first place we do not know the absolute population figure; see the highly deviating estimates which A. Byatt has compiled in "Josephus and Population Number in First Century Palestine," *PEQ* 105 (1973): 51–60. Second, overpopulation must always be measured against the economic potentialities of the country. According to B. Colomb and Y. Kedar, 97 percent of the country was cultivated, for example, so that in Galilee a population of one and a half to two million would have been conceivable ("Ancient Agriculture in the Galilee Mountains," *IEJ* 21 [1971]: 136–40). Third, the best indication of overpopulation is really the dissemination of the phenomenon of "social uprooting." That is to say, we should have to deduce the overpopulation from phenomena which the overpopulation in its turn is supposed to explain. It is true that this is not wholly impossible, but methodologically it is not ideal. So we are left with no more than a supposition. There is much in favor of it. An analogy is the widespread social uprooting at the height of the Middle Ages: "In spite of the strong pressure toward keeping medieval people from moving from place to place . . . the simple demographic expansion drove a growing number of individuals and groups out of their familiar surroundings and the conditions in which they had lived" (J. Legoff, *Das Hochmittelalter,* Fischer Weltgeschichte 11 [Frankfurt, 1965], 55).

About twenty years after his call, Peter was still taking long journeys as far as Rome. James the Lord's brother was executed in 62 C.E. One of the disciples who was well known in the Johannine group must have lived for a very long time (John 21:22f.). The Zebedees left a father who was still able to work. But none of this provides firm evidence for the youth of the early Christian itinerant charismatics and their sympathizers.[76]

Let us sum up the results of our thinking. Early Christian discipleship was not molded solely by religious considerations; there were social factors too. When early Christian wandering charismatics left their homes, families, and all that they had, some of them were probably escaping from social and economic pressure. Others may have taken note of social pressure in groups known to them, even if they were not directly affected. But in leaving their familiar surroundings, they all adopted patterns of behavior that already existed as manifestations of social uprooting. We know that the extent of this behavior in society as a whole was striking. In individual cases it may have been conditioned by biographical circumstances arising from the situation. But its proportions can be explained only by a general crisis of society, in which political and economic factors played a special part, as well as ecological and cultural ones. It is often only a few groups who are directly affected by crises of this kind; but these exert an influence on the whole of society and essentially color the general climate of feeling. People become inclined to interpret the world around them as shaken by crisis even if they are not (or not yet) personally affected. Their behavior is determined not merely by the objective circumstances but by their subjective interpretation.[77]

What did objectively exist was an exacerbated distribution struggle between the different classes. This threatened the people lower down the social scale with a further decline and made other people rich. In this process of change, traditional modes of behavior, norms, values, and interpretations of what life is about were all called in question. The whole of society was threatened by anomy. Religiously, this anomy was interpreted as the beginning of the end-time crisis, as the disintegration of law (ἀνομία, Matt. 24:12), family, love, and order—indeed as a

---

76. A counterexample would be Menahem/Manaen (Acts 13:1). Herod Antipas ruled for forty-three years (4 B.C.E.–39 C.E.). In the forties his *syntrophos* must have been about sixty years old.

77. See the so-called Thomas theorem. This says that "people do not make their behavior depend only on the objective facts of a situation, but also, and sometimes for the most part, on the significance which this situation has for them" (K. R. Merton, "Die Eigendynamik gesellschaftlicher Voraussagen," in *Logik der Sozialwissenschaften,* ed. E. Topitsch, 2nd ed. (Cologne, 1967), 144–161; quotation from p. 145).

shaking of the whole cosmos. The eschatological mood of catastrophe is in my view an interpretation of social anomy. To this interpretation not only objective circumstances but the sociocultural tradition of Judaism contributed — apocalyptic, for example. On the one hand, this is a reflection of the crisis; on the other hand, it released the power to overcome crisis. Belief in an impending revolution of everything favors experiment with new, socially deviant forms of living.

Various movements for religious revival tried to overcome the anomic situation by offering people new bearings in life. One of these was the Jesus movement.[78] Like the other movements, it recruited its members especially from marginal groups — groups, that is, on the edge of a class threatened by a decline in the social scale, or people who had to find a new orientation in changed circumstances, as well as outsiders of various kinds, some of them no doubt young people. In all these groups there was a chance for the deviant, often eccentric forms of living which were practiced in the internal Jewish revival movements, and among which generally widespread deviant forms of behavior — emigration, brigandage, and begging — were taken up and creatively modified.

Only the Pharisees succeeded in reconciling religious renewal and normal everyday life. That is their great achievement. In the first century C.E. their influence still prevailed. All the other revival movements came to grief — the Jesus movement among them. That succeeded only outside Palestine, after it had become transformed — under new conditions — into Hellenistic Christianity. Here Paul, the former Pharisee, played an essential part. This success too had as its precondition adaptation to normal, everyday life.[79]

---

78. In my view it is one of the most important functions of religion to preserve people from anomy, or to seek for new values, interpretations of meaning, and forms of living in a given anomic situation. If a religion is neither able to lend form to this longing for new forms of living out of itself, nor to integrate it in itself, then it is probably dead.

79. In closing I should like to indicate, at least briefly, how an understanding of religious autonomy can be interpreted, in view of the practical contingency of religion: (1) As "relative autonomy": The social factors do not determine an existence of discipleship as such, but they do determine it as a variant of social uprooting. They do not decide, for example, whether someone becomes a saint or a criminal. (2) As "functional autonomy": A pattern of behavior can become widespread because of economic motives but can then be taken up by people who are not impelled by them, although their behavior would be inconceivable without these economically conditioned "models" and "analogies." (3) As "oppositional autonomy": Divergences between an autonomous self-understanding and actual contingency can not always be interpreted as a "false awareness." A sense of autonomy, even if it is not autonomous, can in its deviation from reality bring to expression a movement against it and, for example, become a protest against the cohesion of conditions that are exposed to the ravages of "moth and rust" (Matt. 6:19).

3

Jesus' Temple Prophecy

◆

Prophecy in the Tension between Town and Country[1]

HE SANHEDRIN accused Jesus of having said: "I will destroy this Temple that is made with hands, and in three days I will build another, not made with hands" (Mark 14:58). The saying first of all reflects an ambivalent attitude toward the Temple: it is not supposed to disappear entirely, but it will be replaced by a new one. Moreover the prophecy has unfavorable consequences for its author. We shall be looking below at the historical context to which it points. We shall first try to discover the social dynamic that finds expression in this interlocking of opposition and identification, and we shall then go on to look at the results of the prophecy. In a factor analysis, we shall examine the influence of social circumstances on the tradition, while in a functional analysis we shall see the effects of tradition on society. In the factor analysis we shall be maintaining the hypothesis that the Temple prophecy mirrors tensions between town and country—tensions, that is, between Jerusalem and the Jewish people living in the hinterland.[2] The thesis of our functional analysis is that the Temple prophecy was

---

1. I put forward the theses in this essay on 28 May 1975 in Kiel, and on 30 May 1975 in Heidelberg. I am indebted to my colleagues for many stimulating suggestions.

2. The town–country formula oversimplifies Palestine's socioecology. We have to distinguish between Hellenistic city states, land settled by Jews, unsettled deserts and mountains, and the Jewish capital. The socioecological "town" concept must be distinguished from the *polis* notion, which is an idea derived from constitutional law. Jerusalem was not a *polis;* see V. A. Tcherikover, "Was Jerusalem a 'Polis'?" *IEJ* 14 (1964): 61–78. On the urbanization of Palestine, see A. H. M. Jones, "The Urbanization of Palestine," *JRS* 21 (1931): 78–85; also his book *The Cities of the Eastern Roman Provinces* (Oxford: Clarendon Press, 1937), 227–95.

bound to be understood as an attack on the religious and material status quo — and must have been understood in this sense not only by the aristocracy but by the common people too.

Neither of these two hypotheses necessarily presupposes that the Temple prophecy is a genuine Jesus saying. The social context would be the same, regardless of whether the words are the words of Jesus or the formulation of one of the early Christian prophets; for it was only after 70 C.E. that Palestine's social structure underwent any fundamental changes. At the same time, I shall be indicating a number of arguments in favor of the genuineness of the saying. Here the fact that it cannot be derived from Judaism or early Christianity counts as a primary criterion for authenticity. A secondary criterion is its conformity with Jesus' ministry as a whole.

1. It is impossible to trace the Temple prophecy back to Jewish tradition. The combined prediction in a single saying of the Temple's destruction and its renewal is unique, as far as tradition is concerned.[3] And yet *historically* the combination is not without a prototype; for in 20–19 B.C.E., Herod had Zerubbabel's Temple pulled down and a new one built (Josephus *Antiquities,* 15.380ff.). From that time on, prophetic imagination had a model on which to base its visions of the future. This fact may be considered to fix the saying's *terminus a quo,* or earliest possible date.

2. The temple prophecy cannot be derived from early Christianity either. The *terminus ad quem* (its latest possible date) is the destruction of the Temple in 70 C.E., for the saying is not a prophecy after the event:

---

3. Prophecies against the Temple are never directly linked with the promise of a new one. *1 Enoch* 90:38f. refers to Jerusalem, not to the Temple (cf. 91:13; 25:5; 89:73). Here I can only point to L. Gaston's thorough investigation, *No Stone on Another,* Suppl NovTest 23 (1970), 65–243. Gaston thinks that only the second part of the prophecy is authentic. The first part has certainly been at least reformulated. We often meet the Temple saying on the lips of opponents (exceptions are John 2:19; *Gospel of Thomas* 71). It was probably given a form that could bring Jesus into disrepute. The question is whether the first person singular active form goes back to a slanderous reformulation of this kind; for Jesus could be indicted only if he could be taxed with actively wanting to bring about the Temple's destruction (for example, through arson, etc.), not if he proclaimed its destruction in the context of an eschatological turning point. Mark 13:2 replaces the first person active with the third person passive, John 2:19 with the second person plural. These variations are certainly partly due to the context, but they could also indicate that the tradition itself originally varied. See O. Betz, "Die Frage nach dem messianischen Bewusstsein Jesu," *NovTest* 6 (1963): 20–48, esp. 37 n. 2; F. Hahn, *Das Verständnis der Mission im Neuen Testament,* WMANT 13, 2nd ed. (Neukirchen-Vluyn, 1965), 29 n. 3 (Eng. trans. *Mission in the New Testament,* trans. F. Clarke, Studies in Biblical Theology 47 [London: SCM Press; Naperville, Ill.: Allenson, 1965]). E. Linnemann argues for the nonauthenticity of the Temple saying, on the grounds that it is not in line with anything in Judaism and thus could not have been understood by Jesus' listeners (*Studien zur Passionsgeschichte,* FRLANT 102 [Göttingen, 1970], 125–27).

its positive element — the building of a new Temple — was never fulfilled, while the negative element was fulfilled in a different way — it was the Romans who destroyed the Temple, not Jesus.[4] It is improbable that an early Christian prophet formulated the saying *before* 70 C.E. The saying came to be given a different interpretation. Stephen spiritualizes its second part: what he announces is not that the Temple will be rebuilt but that the Mosaic laws will be changed (Acts 6:14). The Gospel of John spiritualizes both parts: the destruction of the Temple and its rebuilding are interpreted as pointing to Jesus' death and resurrection. Matthew's Gospel transfers the whole prophecy into the potential mood: Jesus can destroy and rebuild (Matt. 26:61). The prophecy was probably subjected to this reinterpretation because it had not been fulfilled.

There are other reasons too for rejecting early Christian authorship. The Christian groups were reproached with being hostile toward the Temple; it is almost always on the lips of their opponents that we come across the prophecy (Mark 14:58; Acts 6:14; *Gospel of Peter* 7.26). To have attributed to Jesus what was actually the saying of one of their prophets would have been voluntarily to provide their opponents with ammunition.

3. The Temple prophecy fits very well into the framework of Jesus' ministry. Saying and narrative tradition point in the same direction: the cleansing of the Temple and the Temple prophecy both express aggression toward the Temple and at the same time identification with it — the Temple prophecy in the form of a prophectic saying, the cleansing of the Temple as its associated symbolic prophetic act.[5] The saying is entirely in line with Jesus' expectation of the imminent end, for the destruction and renewal of the Temple were conceivable only in the framework of cosmic change. Finally, the prophecy fits in well with historical events. It explains why Jesus and his followers went to Jerusalem, for other comparable first-century prophets also moved with their supporters to the place where they expected the miracle they had announced to take place.[6] It also explains why the disciples made

---

4. In Mark 13:2 the negative half of the Temple prophecy became a secondary "prophecy after the event"; it was isolated because only this part had been fulfilled. Even so, the original prophecy is recognizable: the Temple was initially destroyed by fire (Josephus, *Jewish War* 6.228ff.), then razed to the ground (*J.W.* 7.1ff.). A pure prophecy after the event would have mentioned both happenings. For another view, see N. Walter, "Tempelzerstörung und synoptische Apokalypse," *ZNW* 57 (1966): 38–49.

5. Thus among others F. Hahn, *Verständnis der Mission*, German ed., 29f.; H. Schürmann, "Die Symbolhandlungen Jesu als eschatologische Erfüllungszeichen," *BiLe* 11 (1970): 29–41, 73–78; J. Roloff, *Das Kerygma und der irdische Jesus* (Göttingen, 1970), 95. In John 2:13-22 the Temple prophecy and the cleansing of the Temple are linked.

6. See Theudas (Josephus *Ant.* 20.97), an Egyptian prophet (*Ant.* 20.169f.; *J.W.* 2.261ff.), a Samaritan prophet (*Ant.* 18.85ff.), Jonathan (*J.W.*, 7.437ff.). See here R. Meyer, *Der Prophet*

Jerusalem their center after Easter, for it was here that they awaited decisive eschatological events.

The following discussion is independent of the problem of the saying's authenticity, however, for the same social factors can determine both history and the history of a tradition — both historical reality and fantasy. Sociological analysis rests on what is typical, recurrent, and structural — that is to say, on what is valid for a number of people and situations, irrespective of whether this is Jesus, early Christian prophets, or congregations. It is just this which sets the limit for this kind of analysis. It is an inadequate tool for grasping what is unique about the Temple prophecy. It can grasp only some of its aspects.

I

One of the most interesting aspects of the Temple prophecy is its opposition to the Temple. I hope to show that this opposition had its main roots among the rural population. At first sight this would seem to be confuted by the fact that during the unrest in 39–40 B.C.E. (when Caligula tried to have his statue set up in the Temple), the country people displayed a devotion to the Temple which even led them to die on its behalf. At that time it was the farmers especially who joined the protest demonstrations, leaving their fields for the purpose. Agriculture was neglected to such an extent that the harvest was endangered, and consequently the payment of taxes too (Josephus *Ant.* 18.274, 287). But it was precisely this intense identification with the Temple that provided the best foundation for a resolute opposition to it: the more sacred an institution, the more stringent the criticism of its actually existing form will often be. Measured against the absolute, any everyday reality inevitably exposes itself as compromise. So it is no contradiction if we find energetic opposition to the Temple side by side with a devoted attachment to it.[7]

If we make a clear-cut, theoretical distinction, we can talk about (a) *prophetic* opposition to the Temple and (b) *programmatic* opposition. A prophet says what *is going to* happen to the Temple; a program says what

aus Galiläa (Leipzig, 1940), 82ff.; G. Theissen, *Urchristliche Wundergeschichten* (Gütersloh, 1974), 242f.

7. See O. Cullmann, "L'Opposition contre le temple de Jérusalem, motif commun de la théologie johannique et du monde ambiant," *NTS* 5 (1959): 157–73. His pupil L. Gaston offers a comprehensive survey of all critical trends against the Temple (*No Stone*, 119ff., 150ff. passim).

ought to happen to it. Prophetic opposition is linked with a particular person; a program is pursued by a group and is independent of the individual members of that group (who may well change, for example, when one generation succeeds another). It is obvious that the two forms of opposition influence each other. We are only separating them for the purpose of analysis.

(a) We can compare the different examples of *prophetic* opposition to the Temple under two aspects. We have to ask first about the people who proclaimed the threats against the Temple. Second, we have to inquire about the situation in which the proclamation was made—that is, the occasions on which the prophecies were uttered.

Jesus was not the only person in Jewish history to proclaim threats against the Temple. We have (or know of) similar utterances by Micah, Uriah, and Jeremiah (Micah 3:9ff.; Jer. 26:20ff.; 26.1ff.). Turning to New Testament times, we may add Jesus, son of Ananus, whose prophecy of doom is quoted by Josephus among portents heralding the destruction of the Temple (*J.W.* 6.300ff.):

> Four years before war broke out, a man called Jesus, son of Ananus, an ignorant countryman . . . came to the feast on which, according to custom, all Jews built booths in the neighborhood of the Temple, to the glory of God. All at once this man began to cry out:
> "A voice from the beginning
> a voice from the end,
> a voice from the four winds,
> a voice over Jerusalem and the Temple,
> a voice over bridegroooms and brides,
> a voice over the whole people!"
> He cried this day and night, running through all the streets of the city. . . .

The mad prophet continued his lament right down to the outbreak of the Jewish War, and was killed during the siege of Jerusalem.

There are five analogies between this and Jesus' ministry: (1) the threat to the Temple; (2) the feast as setting for the proclamation; (3) the prophet's imprisonment by the Jewish aristocracy; (4) his surrender to the Romans. But it is the fifth point which interests us here: all the five prophets who prophesied against the Temple came from the country— Micah from Moresheth (Micah 1:1), Uriah from Kiriath-jearim (Jer. 26:20), Jeremiah from Anathoth (Jer. 1:1), Jesus from Galilee; and the son of Ananus is described as an ignorant countryman.

The picture becomes more complicated when we look at other Temple prophecies, first of all Stephen's. Stephen may have come from the Diaspora, since when he was in Jerusalem it was to the diaspora Jews there that he turned, and since one of his supporters came from Antioch

(Acts 6:5). A more significant point for us is that after his death it was in the country that his adherents initially continued their preaching (Acts 8:1ff.). Were they safer there?

We do not know who the author of the Temple prophecy in Matt. 23:37ff. was.[8] The first part of the prophecy is a rebuke to Jerusalem for stoning its prophets. The second part threatens that God will leave the Temple — perhaps as a preliminary stage to its destruction, for both Josephus and Tacitus report that before the catastrophe a voice in the Temple announced the departure of the divine presence (Tacitus *Historiae* 5.13; Josephus, *J.W.* 6.299; *2 Bar.* 8:1f.). Both writers see this as an omen of the Temple's destruction. Probably the prophecy dates from the years before the Jewish War. At all events, it is uttered from a non-Jerusalem perspective, for the messengers are "sent" to Jerusalem as if they came from somewhere else, and the people of Jerusalem are addressed in the second person plural. The Temple is "your" house.

Finally, we must mention a Samaritan prophet whose proclamation began about 35 c.e.[9] He promised his followers that they would find the missing Temple vessels on Mount Gerizim. This is of course a covert attack on the Temple in Jerusalem. This movement too had its center in the country. People gathered together in the Samaritan village of Tirathana for a procession to Mount Gerizim. According to Josephus, Pilate had the crowd mowed down so mercilessly that proceedings were successfully brought against him (*Ant.* 18.85–89).[10] His intervention shows that he was exceedingly allergic to the slogan "Temple."

All in all, we see that prophetic opposition to the Temple was supported for the most part by people who came from the country, not from Jerusalem itself.

It is not merely his country origin that links Jesus with his namesake, the prophet of doom. Both of them chose a feast day in Jerusalem for their proclamation: Jesus the Passover, the son of Ananus the feast of

8. See O. H. Steck's thorough analysis *Israel und das gewaltsame Geschick der Propheten*, WMANT 23 (Neukirchen, 1967), 48–50, 227–39; he dates the saying between 66 and 70 c.e. It could also of course be older. We are not even certain whether Jesus himself is not after all its author.

9. See M. F. Collins, "The Hidden Vessels in Samaritan Traditions," *JSJ* 3 (1972): 97–116. The Samaritans believed that the Taheb, the Messiah, would reveal the hidden Temple vessels; see John MacDonald, *The Theology of the Samaritans* (London: SCM Press; Philadelphia: Westminster Press, 1964), 365.

10. Michael Grant disputes that the final massacre of the Samaritans was the essential reason for Pilate's recall (*The Jews in the Roman World* [London: Weidenfeld & Nicolson; New York: Scribner, 1973], 112). It is hard to believe that a prefect would have forfeited his office for proceeding drastically against an armed movement. When Vitellius appeared in Palestine after Pilate's recall, the first thing he did was to soothe feelings in Judea and Jerusalem. Here too there had no doubt been problems.

Tabernacles. And we have evidence that it was at the great feasts especially that there were tensions between the urban and the rural population. Four incidents may be mentioned here.[11]

The first of them took place after the death of Herod (4 B.C.E.). At that time disturbances broke out all over the country—in Galilee, Perea, and Judea (Josephus *Ant.* 17.269–84). When the country people poured into Jerusalem for the feast, the unrest spread there too. After the revolt had been put down, people in Jerusalem defended themselves by saying:

> People had gathered in Jerusalem in such numbers because of the feast, and the war had not been begun on their advice; it was only the roistering of outsiders which was responsible. They themselves were beset by the Romans to such an extent that it did not occur to them to beset the Romans. (Josephus *Ant.* 17.293)

Of course this was partly an excuse. But there was a grain of truth in it. The rural population was more rebellious than that of the city.[12] So from that time on, the Roman military presence was reinforced on feast days, "so as to nip in the bud any rebellious movement by the assembled crowd" (Josephus *J.W.* 2.224). These military units were not able to quash the rebellious mood sufficiently, however. On the contrary, the soldiers themselves became the source of new clashes, as we can see from a second incident, which took place fifty years later, under Cumanus (48–52 C.E.):

> For as the people poured into Jerusalem for the feast of Unleavened Bread, a Roman cohort was drawn up above the colonnade of the temple. . . . All at once, one of the soldiers lifted up his cloak, turned his buttocks to the Jews with an indecent gesture, and made the noise appropriate to this position. (*J.W.* 2.224)[13]

---

11. We find a further incident mentioned in Josephus, *Ant.* 17.213f. and 20.118ff. See J. Blinzler, "Die Niedermetzelung von Galiläern durch Pilatus," *NovTest* 11 (1958), 24–49.

12. On the unrest after Herod's death, see M. Hengel, *Die Zeloten* (Leiden, 1961), 331–36 (Eng. trans. *The Zealots,* trans. D. Smith [Edinburgh: T. & T. Clark, 1989]). Hengel rightly stresses the tensions between town and country which became manifest here (see German ed.. p. 335). He also sheds light on the earlier history of these tensions. The predominance of the town over the country developed during the general economic boom in the Hellenistic period; see M. Hengel, *Judentum und Hellenismus,* WUNT 10 (Tübingen, 1969), 101f. (Eng. trans. *Judaism and Hellenism,* trans. J. Bowden [London: SCM Press; Philadelphia: Fortress Press, 1974]). L. Finkelstein went even further, interpreting the whole history of the Jewish religion in the light of the conflict between town and country (*The Pharisees: The Sociological Background of their Faith* [1938; 3rd ed., Philadelphia: Jewish Publication Society of America, 1963]).

13. The soldier's fart may perhaps have been one instance of a widespread anti-Jewish, and general, gesture of contempt. We meet it in Horace's satire 1.9.70: vin tu curtis Iudacis oppedere, "Why will you offend the circumcized Jews?" There the context is the infringement of the Sabbath through business. I am indebted to Prof. P. Vielhauer for drawing my attention to this Horace reference.

A disturbance followed the provocation. Stones were thrown, panic broke out, and many people were killed. There were other disturbances in the country during Cumanus's rule. Incidents under his successor, Felix, may serve as a third example. Felix had successfully combatted the resistance movement in the country — but with the result that it now flared up in the city.[14] Its first victim was Jonathan, the high priest (*J.W.* 2.256); his murder may perhaps have been instigated by the Roman procurator (*Ant.* 20.163). Since one incident leads to another, murders proliferated:

> Since the murder was simply allowed to happen, the brigands came into the city on the feast days quite openly, mingling with the crowds, and stabbing sometimes their own enemies, sometimes other people whom they had been hired to attack. And this did not merely take place in the city; it sometimes happened even in the Temple; for they were so audacious that they murdered even there, without any sense that they were committing an impiety. (*Ant.* 20.165)

What is significant here is that the freedom fighters had no reverence for sacred places and seasons. They used feast days and the Temple for their terrorist activities — probably with a clear conscience, being convinced that they were performing the holy will of God. This dissociation from the Temple also becomes clear in our final example. Under Albinus (62-64/65), freedom fighters forced their way into the city on a feast day, took Eleazar's secretary hostage (Eleazar being the Temple governor), and used him to extort the release of ten imprisoned comrades (*Ant.* 20.208f.). The leniency of the authorities encouraged further ventures of the same kind:

> The brigands now tried in every way to bring any of Ananus's relatives or friends into their power, each time keeping them prisoner until some of the Sicarii were set free. So they grew in numbers once more, and ravaged the whole country with new audacity. (*Ant.* 20.210)

It is quite evident here that the resistance movement which was operating in the country saw the Temple aristocracy as their enemies.[15] For us, the essential fact is this: the country people who poured into the city at the feast days were bound to seem a security risk to the authorities who were responsible for law and order, partly because the rural population was rebellious anyway, partly because the large crowd

---

14. See Hengel, *Zeloten*, German ed., 49, 375f.

15. Nothing supports the suggestion that the people who were coerced conspired with the coercers, as G. Baumbach believes; see his *Jesus von Nazareth im Lichte der jüdischen Gruppenbildung* (Berlin, 1971), 54. On the policy of the high priests, see still E. M. Smallwood, "High Priests and Politics in Roman Palestine," *JThS* 13 (1962): 14–34.

provided cover for agitators. So the latent tensions between town and country continually manifested themselves on feast days.

This also has a bearing on the passion story,[16] though here we are leaving aside the question of how far it was the history of the passion itself that these tensions influenced, and how far it was the history of the tradition. The high priests and the scribes were united in resolving that Jesus should not be arrested on the feast, so that there should be no disturbance among the people (Mark 14:2). Here "the people" can only mean the country people who were pouring into the city for the feast, for the people of Jerusalem were there all the time anyway. Evidently the authorities were afraid that the country people were in sympathy with Jesus. It is consistent with this when the report of his entry into Jerusalem tells us that it was the people who were pilgriming to the feast who cried "Hosanna" (Mark 11:9)—not the people of Jerusalem. And it was not anyone from Jerusalem who took his body; it was Joseph from Arimathea (Mark 15:43). For the authorities, the Jesus movement was only one particular example of the disturbances that infiltrated into Jerusalem from outside, from the country. That is why there was special concern to know where Peter came from, and why he was asked whether he belonged to "the Nazarene, Jesus" (Mark 14:67). The very fact that he was a Galilean (Mark 14:70) made him the object of suspicion. No doubt the authorities had experience in the matter. According to Luke 13:1-3 Pilate had taken measures against Galilean pilgrims in Jerusalem![17]

Our first hypothesis, then, has been based on two series of analogies. In the first place, most of the people who had uttered threats against the Temple came from the country. Second, with his saying against the Temple, Jesus came before the public eye on an occasion when tensions between city and county often showed themselves.

(b) The postulate that Jesus' opposition to the Temple was partly rooted in these tensions between town and country can be further supported if we look at the *programmatic* opposition to the Temple. If we leave the Samaritans out of the discussion, there were two Jewish groups who programmatically opposed the Temple: the Essenes and the Zealots (Zealots here being taken to mean the whole freedom movement). The differences between these groups and the Jesus movement are profound;

---

16. Hengel is correct in his judgment that the antagonism between town and country was also "of essential importance for an understanding of the passion" (*Zeloten*, German ed., 371 n. 1). It was this remark that suggested the present essay.

17. Blinzler gives good reasons for supposing that the incident took place at a Passover ("Niedermetzelung," 24–89). Methodologically, his further reflections make the mistake of drawing too swiftly on the composition of the Gospels for the purpose of historical reconstruction. See also H. W. Hoehner, *Herod Antipas* (Cambridge: Cambridge University Press, 1972), 175f.

but the three do have one characteristic in common: they strove for a renewal of Judaism and were critical of its existing form. Hence their opposition to the Temple.

The Essenes rejected the sacrificial cult in Jerusalem (*Ant.* 18.19).[18] It is true that they sent sacrifical offerings to the Temple, but they were excluded from the sanctuary itself. Josephus's account is confirmed by the Qumran writings. The Essenes rejected the Temple as unclean (CD 4:18; 1QpHab 12:7f., and frequently elsewhere). No Essene was supposed to enter it (CD 6:11-14). It was set over against the community, which saw itself as a human sanctuary, in which the burnt offerings were acts according to the law (4QFlor 1:6f.). It was the community's task to atone for the land (1QS 8:6-10 and frequently). The assertion that they were Israel's real Temple and the interpretation (in 4QFlor 1:1-12) that Nathan's prophecy referred to the Qumran community undoubtedly had a polemical significance: the Qumran community was meant to replace the rejected Temple. What is important for us here is the fact that the home of this opposition to the Temple was located outside Jerusalem — in a desert oasis, and among the Essenes who were scattered throughout the country. It is true that Josephus writes that the Essenes could be met with in every "town" (*J.W.* 2.124), but he often calls Palestine's villages towns. Philo gives a more reliable account of the Essenes from the angle of the city of Alexandria:

> These people live mainly in villages, avoiding the towns because of their characteristic unrestraint, probably knowing that by having dealings with these towns they would be subjecting themselves to a contact with incurable consequences for the soul, like a sickness resulting from poisoned air. Some of them work in the fields, the others in various peaceful trades; and in this way they benefit both themselves and their neighbors. (Philo *Quod omnis probus liber sit* 76)

Philo reports similar objections to urban life among the Therapeutae (*De vita contemplativa* 19ff.). But we must remember that what these writers say may have been colored by the city-dweller's yearning for "the simple life."

There was a socioreligious program behind the terrorist actions of the Zealots.[19] At the beginning of the Jewish War, their "zeal" for the

---

18. On the significance of the Temple for Qumran, see B. Gärtner, *The Temple and the Community in Qumran and the New Testament* (Cambridge: Cambridge University Press, 1965); G. Klinzing, *Die Umdeutung des Kultus in der Qumrangemeinde und im Neuen Testament* (Göttingen, 1971).

19. Hengel has worked out this socioreligious program particularly clearly; see *Zeloten,* esp. 93–150 (German ed.).

law led to Temple reform. Josephus reports that "brigands" who had come to the city from the country (*J.W.* 4.128) seized for themselves the right to choose the high priest, set aside ancient family privileges (*J.W.* 4.147), and finally went on to elect a new high priest:

> Now it so happened that the lot fell on a man whose person was proof enough of the wickedness of their undertakings—a person called Phanias, son of Samuel, who came from the village of Aphtha. Quite apart from the fact that he was not descended from high priests, he was so ignorant that he did not even know what the high priesthood actually was. But they dragged him in from the country against his will. (*J.W.* 4.155f.)

The Zealots did not content themselves with provoking the ancient urban aristocracy in this way: most of these people were actually put to death. And in other ways too the freedom fighters who came in from the country exercised an appalling reign of terror over the urban population, who were more inclined than the country people to come to terms with the Romans, and therefore counted as unreliable. Four rural groups tyrannized the city: Galileans under the leadership of John of Gischala (*J.W.* 4.121ff., 559), Judeans under Simon ben Giora (*J.W.* 2.652; 4.503), the Temple Zealots under Eleazar (*J.W.* 4.135ff.),[20] and the Idumeans (*J.W.* 4.224ff.). Of course these different groups probably included people from Jerusalem too, but for the most part their adherents came from the country. We can understand this reign of terror only if we assume that it was the expression of a long pent-up hate of the city, and especially its aristocracy. Incidentally, as in the case of the Essenes, some of the Zealots also seem to have objected in principle to urban life. Hippolytus reports that Zealots and Sicarii (whom he curiously views as an Essene group) did not touch coins because of the images impressed on them. Moreover, they did not go "into any town, so that none of them was obliged to pass through a gateway on which there were any statues" (Hippolytus *Adversus haereses* 9.26). Here too we find a fundamental dissociation from the town—or, to be more precise, from the Hellenistic town.

Jesus' opposition to the Temple, in contrast, involves no dissociation from the town in principle.[21] Nor is it programmatic: we cannot detect

---

20. M. Smith rightly stresses the rural origin of the Temple Zealots ("Zealots and Sicarii, their Origins and Relations," *HThR* 64 [1971], 1–19), but he is wrong when he interprets them as exponents of a "peasant piety." The Temple Zealots were priests. Thus rightly M. Hengel, "Zeloten und Sikarier," in *Josephus-Studien: Festschrift für O. Michel,* ed. O. Betz et al. (Göttingen, 1974), 175–96, esp. 195; G. Baumbach, "Zeloten und Sikarier," *ThLZ* 90 (1965): 727–40. It must be remembered here that most of the priests had their homes outside Jerusalem. The rural origin of the movement and its priestly character were in no way contradictory.

21. There are a few sayings that indicate a dissociation from urban culture: Matt. 11:7-9,

any program for reforming the Temple in Jerusalem, or discover plans for organizing a new community with a claim to be itself the new Temple.

Both prophetic and programmatic Temple opposition shared one characteristic, however: their roots were in the country. We have evidence for this. We also have evidence that there was an antagonism between town and country which showed itself especially in political attitudes. Beyond this, any conclusions are interpretation. But a well-founded interpretation, in my view, is the inference that in the first century C.E. an emerging opposition to the Temple was nourished by the tensions between town and country and that it is to this field of tension that Jesus' Temple prophecy also belongs. For to suppose that prophecy develops especially where there is social tension is surely plausible enough. Equally plausible, however, is the postulate that prophecy is not explained by and "derived from" this tension; social tension between peoples and nations, classes or other groups, has always existed, but prophets have not always appeared on the scene. It is rather the case that social situations have to be interpreted in the light of particular traditions if they are to determine action.[22] And it is only then that they come to be passed down to us. So here too, opposition to the Temple in Roman Palestine becomes comprehensible only if we remember Israel's radical theocratic tradition: the sense that God himself reigned in Israel as her king. The Jewish Temple state also belonged to this tradition. It saw itself as a "theocracy" (Josephus *Against Apion* 2.165), but in actual fact it was an "aristocracy" (*Ant.* 20.229); for here it was through the mediation of the Temple aristocracy that God ruled. We use the words "radically theocratic" for all movements in which the rule of God is affirmed and brought into play against its theocratic mediators.

What we therefore have to ask in our case is this: How could the Temple appear to be so compromised in the first century C.E. that it roused the opposition of a whole number of different, radically theocratic groups? Three possible reasons may be suggested.

---

where "soft raiment" and "kings' houses" are disparaged; also Mark 13:1, where the disciples are amazed at the Temple buildings. This is a little reminiscent of people from the provinces who seldom come to the capital. D. Claessens vividly describes the astonishment of a villager who comes to a medieval town (*Kapitalismus als Kultur* [Düsseldorf and Cologne, 1973], 84). He has "much to admire: stone houses, and many of them (more than 'three next to one another' was bound to impress as being 'many' at that time), paved roads, glass windows in the houses (bull's eye panes), sizeable churches, a great many people. . . ."

22. See R. K. Merton, "Die Eigendynamik gesellschaftlicher Voraussagen," in *Logik der Sozialwissenschaften,* ed. E. Topitsch, 2nd ed. (Cologne, 1967), 144–61, esp. 145. Here he expounds the Thomas theorem, which maintains that "people do not make their behavior depend simply on the objective circumstances of a situation but also, and sometimes mainly, on the significance which this situation has for them."

1. Opposition to the Temple could be opposition to its builder. For strict believers, Herod, the Idumean, was no Jew in the true sense. He was not dynastically legitimate. His pro-Roman assimilation policy was bound to make him the object of suspicion.[23] He was certainly not the ideal builder for the Jewish sanctuary. Now, we hear from Josephus that initially the plan to build the Temple roused unrest (*Ant.* 15.388)—though allegedly only because people feared that after the old Temple had been torn down Herod would lack the means to build a new one. Did this fear perhaps conceal a much more fundamental rejection of the Herodian plan to build a Temple?

2. Opposition to the Temple could also be opposition to the style of the building. Its Hellenistic form symbolized Herod's cautious assimilation policy. This was palpable in the golden eagle over the gateway (*Ant.* 17.151), because the eagle was the symbol of the Roman imperium, the emblem of the legions and the emperor.[24] It also contravened the prohibition of images. Shortly before Herod's death there was even a plot to remove it, a plot that ended with the execution of the conspirators (*Ant.* 17.149–67). But after Herod's death, the conspirators' sympathizers gathered in the Temple, demanding revenge for the execution from Archelaus, Herod's designated successor. In this case they were supported by the country people (*J.W.* 2.9ff.; *Ant.* 17.213ff.). Archelaus had to intervene with all his forces in order to prevent the rebels who poured in from the country from joining forces with the rebels who were gathered in the Temple.

3. Finally, opposition to the Temple could also be opposition to the Temple aristocracy. The disapprobation of the Essenes was directed not least against the non-Zadokite Hasmonean high priests. So in order to exclude the Hasmoneans, Herod first fell back on a legitimate high priestly family (*Ant.* 15.22, 40). But he soon arbitrarily installed whomever he liked. It was only the Temple Zealots who once again appointed a Zadokite to the high priestly office.[25]

There were therefore a number of substantial reasons for opposition to the Herodian Temple, reasons which could play a part in both Jerusalem and in the country, but which were probably of more lasting influence in the country. In the city there were good reasons for tolerating the Herodian Temple—indeed, for identifying with it.

---

23. On the problems associated with the Herodian monarchy, see A. Schalit, *König Herodes* (Berlin, 1969), esp. 146ff., 403ff., 483ff.

24. On the golden eagle, see Schalit, *Herodes,* 734.

25. See J. Jeremias, *Jerusalem zur Zeit Jesu,* 3rd ed. (Göttingen, 1969), 215–18 (Eng. trans. *Jerusalem in the Time of Jesus,* trans. F. H. and C. H. Cave, [London: SCM Press; Philadelphia: Fortress Press, 1969; rev. ed. London: SCM Press, 1973]).

II

The Temple prophecy cut across the interests of the whole Jerusalem community far too radically for it not to have roused opposition.

The Temple brought the priestly aristocracy a sizable income: regular taxes (above all, tithes and firstfruits), shares in the sacrifices, irregular donations, for example in connection with oaths and penances.[26] How these things were shared out was a matter of dispute. Shortly before the Jewish War, there were violent quarrels about their distribution. The high priests were supposed to have appropriated the priests' share of the tithes by force, so that some of the poorer priests starved (*Ant.* 20.181, 206f.).[27] It is most likely that it was among the "minor clerics" (both urban and rural) that latent opposition to the Temple was strongest. The Zealots who barricaded themselves in the reformed sanctuary were probably drawn from these groups.

But it was not only the priests who had a financial interest in the Temple. Cattle dealers, money changers, tanners and shoemakers all more or less lived from the sacrificial cult. The many pilgrims were dependent on the services of the Jerusalem population; spending was required and encouraged, for apart from the tithe that had to be paid to the priests, the law theoretically demanded a second tithe, which every Israelite was supposed to eat in Jerusalem (Deut. 12:11ff.). For the people of Jerusalem this was not an extra burden — in fact it was a source of profit for their businesses. In addition, they tried to achieve a tax dispensation on the grounds that Jerusalem was a holy city. This emerges from an alleged edict of the Syrian king Demetrius, which among other things assured the city of Jerusalem freedom from taxation, because of its holiness (1 Macc. 10:25-45).

Of course these were fantasies prompted by wishful thinking. Now and again, however, these desires may actually have been crowned with success. Vitellius repealed a turnover tax on fruit sold in the Jerusalem market (*Ant.* 18.90; 17.205). Agrippa I dispensed with a property tax levied on Jerusalem houses (*Ant.* 19.299). But the country people were

---

26. On the earnings, see E. Schürer, *Geschichte des jüdischen Volkes im Zeitalter Jesu Christi,* 4th ed. (Leipzig, 1901–1909), 2:301–12 (Eng. trans. *The History of the Jewish People in the Age of Jesus Christ,* revised and ed. G. Vermes et al. [Edinburgh: T. & T. Clark, 1973]); F. C. Grant, *The Economic Background of the Gospels* (London: Humphrey Milford, 1926), 94–96; Jeremias, *Jerusalem,* German ed., 120–24.

27. A. Büchler traces this distribution struggle back to "an unusual increase in the tithing"; see *Der galiläische 'Am-Ha'ares des zweiten Jahrhunderts* (Vienna, 1906; reprint, 1968), 17 n. 1. It is more probable that the "takings" had diminished and that the distribution was therefore more bitterly disputed.

imposed upon all the more. When there were tax arrears before the Jewish War, Jerusalem successfully resisted a levy on the Temple treasury (*J.W.* 2.293–96). Instead, representatives of the city's aristocracy went out to the villages in order to raise the money needed to meet the amount due (*J.W.* 2.405). If these two actions are related to the same tax debt, the difference in the sums involved would be illuminating: Gessius Florus, the Roman procurator, demanded seventeen talents; the aristocracy collected forty. Did the difference count as "commission"? If this was tax owed in different years, the increased sum would indicate that there was a growing unwillingness to pay taxes.

However that may be, the people of Jerusalem enjoyed advantages because theirs was a holy city – that is, because of the Temple. So to question the religious status of the city was bound to jeopardize the economic situation of its people too.

It is therefore understandable that people should have been hypersensitive to any attempt to infringe the city's "holiness." It so happens that it is for the Pilate era that we actually have evidence of this. He tried to bring emblems of Roman sovereignty into Jerusalem secretly, but failed twice because of popular opposition (Philo *Ad Gaium* 276ff.; Josephus *Ant.* 18.55–59),[28] even when all he wanted to do was to put up signs bearing the emperor's name inside a Roman administrative building. After Pilate had been recalled, demands went further still. The Syrian legate Vitellius was even told to dispense with emblems of Roman sovereignty throughout Judea (i.e., not only Jerusalem). Vitellius thereupon paid the price of a big detour, in order to have peace in the hinterland of his Nabatean campaign (*Ant.* 18.121).

This zeal for the holiness of Jerusalem undoubtedly had a religious basis. It was religious motives that brought to Jerusalem men and women, money, material goods, and trade.[29] But if the economic importance of Jerusalem was initially based on religion, then there were practical economic reasons for strengthening those religious motives, since it

---

28. On the two incidents, see C. H. Kraeling, "The Episode of the Roman Standards at Jerusalem," *HThR* 35 (1942): 263–89; P. L. Maier, "The Episode of the Golden Roman Shields at Jerusalem," *HThR* 62 (1969): 109–22; Maier rightly assumes that there were two different events. S. G. F. Brandon sees them as indicating a trend toward a broader interpretation of the prohibition of images (*Jesus and the Zealots* [Manchester: Manchester University Press, 1967], 68ff.); S. H. Perowne detects a growing decline in Pilate's authority (*The Later Herods* [London: Hodder & Stoughton, 1958], 51ff.).

29. See the conclusions of Jeremias (*Jerusalem,* German ed., 1–98, esp. 41, 65, 82, 97). My comments on the social and economic situation in Jerusalem are based especially on this admirable book. It incidentally shows that sociological questions were always a component of historical-critical research.

was to them that Jerusalem owed its special status. In my view, no one can properly forbid us to ask whether the religious zeal of people in Jerusalem should be judged any differently in principle from the agitation of the Ephesians when they were afraid that their souvenir industry would suffer as a result of Christian preaching (Acts 19:23ff.). Interactions that are readily conceded where heathen cults are concerned cannot be excluded a priori in the case of the Jewish and Christian religion. This applies to Jesus' Temple prophecy too.

III

Here we can pin these interactions down more precisely. When Jesus announced that the Temple was going to be destroyed and then rebuilt, everyone concerned with its building was bound to feel personally affected.

Building had been going on ever since 20/19 B.C.E. The outer courts and inner Temple had been finished by 9/8 B.C.E. But even after that time, building steadily continued. The Gospel of John refers to this. There "the Jews" react to the Temple prophecy by saying: "It has taken forty-six years to build this Temple, and will you raise it up in three days?" (John 2:20). The truth of the matter is that building went on for over eighty years, before the Temple was finished under Albinus (62–64 C.E.). Why this prolonged construction period? And what was the reason for the disproportion between the ten years needed to put up the most important buildings and the further seventy years of extension work?[30]

The problem becomes more complex still when we look at what Josephus has to say about the number of workmen engaged on the building. Herod took on eleven thousand. After eighty years the eleven thousand had become eighteen thousand (*Ant.* 15.390; 20.219). If we assume that Josephus is exaggerating to the same extent in both passages — and there is no doubt that he does exaggerate — we can calculate that the number of workmen grew by 63.5 percent in eighty years, even though a great part of the work was already finished after ten. We can then also draw up the following (though highly fictitious) sum: if we assume that Jerusalem, including its suburbs, had a population of about 220,000 (A. Byatt's view, and he trusts considerably to the accuracy of Josephus's information about size, thus offering a matching estimate[31]),

---

30. There were setbacks during the building: see Josephus *Ant.* 17.260ff.; *J.W.* 2.49f.; S. H. Perowne, *The Life and Times of Herod the Great* (London: Hodder & Stoughton, 1956).

31. A. Byatt, "Josephus and Population Number in First Century Palestine," *PEQ* 105 (1973): 51–60. The population is generally considered to have been much smaller. In

then by the time the Temple was finished, 8.2 percent of all Jerusalem masons would have worked on it. About 20 percent of the city's population would have been directly dependent on the building, if we calculate that every workman had a family of two or three people. And this would account for only some of the people whom the Temple supported.

How, then, did this come about? How could the Temple expand its "capacities" to this degree? The development had both an economic and a social angle. Financially, the Temple could regulate its affairs regardless of economic aspects. The building was financed by the Temple treasury, which was considerable (Josephus *J.W.* 5.187, 189; Tacitus *Historiae* 5.8); its income came from the whole Diaspora and was relatively independent of local crises, and it would certainly have increased during the long peaceful era following Augustus. At all events, the Temple accumulated considerable capital. When Sabinus looted the Temple treasury, he carried off four hundred talents (*Ant.* 17.264). It was undoubtedly economically wise for Herod to make this capital productive once more. In addition, the building of the Temple had social aspects. In this way Herod provided work for a great many people, especially many of the poorer priests; for the eleven thousand workers on the Temple included one thousand priests who were entrusted with the building of the inner Temple. These men were evidently poor, for Herod saw to it that they were provided with priestly clothing as well as with the tools necessary for building and carpentry (*Ant.* 15.390). These social aspects of the building of the Temple emerge even more clearly on the work's completion:

> About this time the Temple was finished. When the people now saw that the builders (more than 18,000 in number) had no work, they expected that they would be in difficulty about wages, since they had hitherto earned their living by working on the Temple. Moreover there was an unwillingness to horde any more money for fear of the Romans, so the intention was to draw on the Temple treasury to satisfy the masons; for if one of them had worked for no more than a single hour in the day, his wage was paid out to him immediately. So people petitioned the king to restore the eastern portico. (*Ant.* 20.219f.)

Agrippa II rejected this proposal, though he did allow roads to be paved. But later on, new Temple buildings were evidently begun after all (*J.W.* 5.36ff.). We can deduce from this that the Temple workmen were

---

"Die Einwohnerzahl Jerusalems zur Zeit Jesu," *ZDPV* 66 (1943): 24–31. J. Jeremias puts it at twenty-five to thirty thousand; in his *Jerusalem* (German ed., 96) his estimate is fifty-five to ninety-five thousand. L. Finkelstein thinks in terms of seventy-five thousand (*Pharisees*, 609).

an influential group. They could make their further employment a political issue, and could induce King Agrippa II to revise an edict. And they were probably well paid. We read in *b. Yoma* 38a about Temple workmen (producers of shewbread and incense) who went on strike and returned to work only after their wages had been raised by 100 percent. The wages were "fantastic."[32] But what is important for us is not merely the amount but the fact that the Temple workmen were aware of their own interests, and were prepared for conflict.

If we take these interests into account, we can also understand the vigorous reaction to attempts by the Roman prefects or procurators to use part of the Temple treasury for their own purposes. For example, Pilate had the sensible plan of building a long aqueduct to Jerusalem. The project was to be financed by the Temple treasury, which was quite legitimate. But the plan roused popular anger. There were tumults, incidents, and a number of deaths (*Ant.* 18.60–62). In my view, it is plausible to suppose that it was the Temple workmen especially who had good reason to oppose the new project, although we have of course no way of proving this. These workmen could profit from the Temple treasury undisturbed only if it was used for exclusively "sacred" purposes.[33]

A second incident took place under Gessius Florus (about 66 C.E.). When the province was in arrears with its tribute, the procurator wanted to take the missing money from the Temple treasury "on the pretext that the emperor needed money." The people thereupon poured angrily into the Temple and insulted the procurator. Some of them went around begging alms "for poor unhappy Florus" (*J.W.* 2.293f.). In this incident too the interests of all the people who were paid directly out of the Temple treasury were at stake—especially the people working on the building, whose employment and brisk payment (according to *Ant.* 20.219f.) was explicitly justified by fear of Roman "encroachments" of this kind.

---

32. Thus Jeremias, "Einwohnerzahl," 28. A table with all the wage scales for which we have evidence in the period may be found in D. Sperber, "Costs of Living in Roman Palestine," *JESHO* 8 (1965): 248–71. Taking *b. Yoma* as basis, he reckons on 1.2, 2.4, or 4.8 denarii. That would be above average, if we remember, for example, that Matt. 20:1-16 gives a day's wage as one denarius.

33. It cannot have been the Temple aristocracy who opposed the undertaking. They must have agreed that the aqueduct should be financed from the Temple treasury. If Pilate had taken the money by force, he would have had to enter the Temple precincts, which were taboo—and we should certainly hear of this. Morever, according to *Šeqalim* 4.2, the Temple was obliged to ensure that the city was provided with water; see Jeremias, *Jerusalem*, German ed., 16f., n. 11. The protesting groups must therefore be sought among the common people, not among the aristocracy. It was perhaps the latter who informed Pilate about the impending demonstration. At all events Pilate was well prepared. See P. L. Maier, *Pontius Pilate* (Garden City, N.Y.: Doubleday, 1968), 357.

So if someone stood up in Jerusalem, prophesying against the Temple and announcing its destruction, this was bound to seem a challenge to the people who had built the Temple with their own hands and whose social well-being was dependent on it. Did this not fundamentally call in question the legitimacy of their work? The prophecy of a miraculously raised new Temple was not in line with their interests either—at least not the erecting of a Temple "not made with hands." It cannot have been difficult to present the Temple prophecy as an attempt to sabotage the Temple building. And this made it possible to appeal to the existential fears of a great many people in Jerusalem.

In this context we must point to the striking fact that Jesus was arraigned on two counts, both at his cross-examination by the sanhedrin and in the crucifixion scene. In both passages, the Temple prophecy is the first accusation leveled against him; his messianic claim is mentioned only afterwards (Mark 14:57-64; 15:29-32). Moreover, the two charges are ascribed to different groups: the reproach of the messianic claim is made by the high priest (14:61), or by the high priests and the scribes (15:31); the accusation of the adverse Temple prophecy, on the other hand, is made by anonymous spokesmen, τινες in Mark 14:57, παραπορευόμενοι in 15:29f. Since in 15:31 the Temple aristocracy is distinguished from "the passersby" by the word ὁμοίως, we may assume that the authors of the second accusation were simpler people, who were not members of the aristocracy.

Sociological factors would suggest that this differentiation is quite within the bounds of possibility. The people at the head of the state were mainly concerned about the political aspect of the Jesus movement, which was tied up with the messianic idea. Every messianic movement could call in question the autonomy of the institutions that were dominated by the aristocracy (see John 11:49). For that reason, when Jesus is brought before Pilate, it is only the messianic claim that plays any part. There we hear nothing at all about the Temple prophecy (Mark 15:1-5). The ordinary people, on the other hand, could hardly have been enlisted against Jesus on the grounds of his messianic claims or expectations. There, economically based fear for the Temple and the Temple building was the moving force. Later on, Stephen too was lynched by "the people," who were roused by his critical remarks about the Temple (Acts 7:54ff.).[34] If it is in any way true that the aristocracy successfully stirred up the mob against Jesus (Mark 15:11), it would have possessed an excellent tool in the Temple prophecy.

---

34. On Stephen, see M. Hengel, "Zwischen Jesus und Paulus," *ZThK* 72 (1975): 151–206, esp. 188ff.

* * *

None of this is intended to be a claim that the passages in question are historical. All that we can be certain of is that they are historically possible. It is equally certain that there is no reason for the widespread conviction that these are, largely speaking, quite unreliable historical texts. But we must again remember that the structural factors to which I have drawn attention can have influenced both history and the history of the tradition.[35]

At all events, the Jesus movement stirred up against itself all the groups associated with the Temple, and these groups were not confined to the leaders or "the best circles." This means that we must perhaps correct an idea which many people have come to cherish, the notion that Jesus came into conflict only with the aristocracy of the Temple state and with the Romans — that what we see here is a member of the lower classes who clashed with the class above him. It may be said in general that social conflicts cannot be reduced to antagonisms between the lower and the upper classes. This fundamental antithesis is continually overlaid by other tensions: interethnic aggressions, generation conflicts, the rivalry between power elites or — as in our case — by ecological antagonisms between town and country. For on the urban side we do not find merely the leaders; we find ordinary people too. Conversely, Jesus' sympathizers were not confined to the simple country people; they also included the "councillor" Joseph of Arimathea.

I hope that the factor and functional analysis I have put forward has been able to show that the Temple prophecy belongs to an area of tension generated by profound conflicts, and that while the prophecy is on the one hand rooted in these, it on the other hand influences the field of tension itself.

Finally, let me stress that according to its own intention the Temple prophecy transcends the social context I have outlined. For what it expresses is the longing for a Temple that is *not* bound up with the network of human interests but comes directly from God. It is the radically theocratic longing for God's immediate presence and rule that is articulated in political metaphor through the proclamation of the

---

35. If I view some unduly self-assured historical skepticism with a degree of reservation, this is not a regression — a retreat from the recognitions of form criticism. The skepticism of form criticism is determined by sociological reflections: it assumes the existence of a *Sitz im Leben* — a real-life situation — which has molded tradition. But it is on the basis of sociological considerations that I incline here and there to a somewhat greater confidence in the historicity of the traditions. So my argumentation belongs within the framework of form criticism.

βασιλεία, and in cultic metaphor through the Temple prophecy. So in this tradition we are brought face to face with the fundamentally double character of all religious tradition:[36] it is conditioned by its social context (and generally to a much greater degree than religion's own self-understanding would like to believe); yet at the same time it is the utterance of a "call to liberty" — liberty from all determining outside influences. And this call can be heard all the more insistently, the more that critical analysis reveals tradition's practical, material dependence.

---

36. The concept of "double character" is borrowed from T. W. Adorno, *Ästhetische Theorie* (Frankfurt, 1970), 334–87. *All* mental phenomena are both autonomous and contingent, not just aesthetic ones. The analysis of the contingency of mental processes is not designed to undermine the sense of autonomy; its aim is to let autonomy become recognizable as oppositional autonomy. I am unfortunately unable to discuss here these and other hermeneutical consequences of sociological inquiry for New Testament interpretation. The example of a sociological analysis put forward here can probably show better than any theoretical discussions that sociological questionings merely deepen historical-critical research. They are not a radically new approach. Up to now, I have not come across any argument against the legitimacy of sociological inquiry in exegesis which is not fundamentally aimed at historical-critical research in general. Antisociological emotions (which can be found among both orthodox Marxists and orthodox Christians) are simply further evidence for the fact that historical-critical awareness is unlikely or unusual, and by no means something we can take for granted.

4

Nonviolence and Love of Our Enemies (Matthew 5:38–48; Luke 6:27–38)

———————◆———————

The Social Background

"DO NOT resist evil!" and "Love your enemies!": these requirements to renounce violence and to love people who are hostile to us radically call in question our normal behavior. So it is quite understandable that these demands should themselves continually be called in question. Today, this questioning is prompted particularly by criticism of the ideology behind them. The reproach made is that these demands encourage Christians to avoid conflict and that this has harmful consequences, both psychologically and socially. Psychologically, these requirements stand in the way of a realistically necessary ability to achieve one's objectives, and prevent the integration of aggressive impulses; while socially, the people who benefit for all practical purposes are the dominating groups; for love of enemies mitigates the social tensions that could jeopardize the position of these groups.[1]

---

1. As an example of psychological criticism, see F. Nietzsche, *Zur Genealogie der Moral* I, 13 (Leipzig, 1924), 273: "When, with the vindictive cunning of impotence, the oppressed, the downtrodden and the abused tell themselves: 'Let us be different from the wicked, let us be good! And everyone is good who abuses no one, hurts no one, attacks no one, does not retaliate, who leaves vengeance to God' . . . then this, if we listen to it coolly and without prejudice, in real truth means nothing but: 'We weaklings simply are weak; it is well if we do nothing which we are not strong enough to do'; but thanks to that counterfeit and self-deception of impotence, this bitter fact . . . has clothed itself in the grandiloquence of forbearing virtue which serenely bides its time . . ." (this passage translated directly from the German; Eng. trans. *The Genealogy of Morals*, trans. H. B. Samuel, in Nietzsche, *Works*, vol. 14 [Edinburgh and London: J. N. Foulis, 1910]; also *On the Genealogy of Morals*, trans. W. Kaufmann and R. J. Hollingdale [New York: Random House, 1969]).

The following inquiry cannot solve these far-reaching problems, nor is that its purpose. What I should like to do, however, is to throw some light on the historical background. We shall look at the reasons originally given for loving one's enemies and for nonviolence, as well as at the underlying historical situations in the early Christian groups. This is not an attempt to shift responsibility for our own ethical conduct on to the past. We ourselves have to take responsibility for what we do. But in order to assume this responsibility, we have to be as clear as possible about the historical background of our ethical tradition.

Our investigation falls into two parts. In the first part, we shall consider the motives prompting love of enemies and nonviolence. In the second part we shall look at the social situations to which they belong. The first part therefore concentrates on the psychological side of the problem, the second on its sociological aspect. But the two elements cannot be separated completely. Indeed we may presume from the outset that a difference in motivation structures can be connected with a difference in the structures of social life.

I. THE MOTIVES FOR LOVING ONE'S ENEMIES
AND FOR NONVIOLENCE

In the early Christian texts dealing with love of enemies, the motives suggested can be divided into four groups: (1) imitation, the purpose being to imitate God; (2) differentiation, which stresses superiority compared with other groups; (3) reciprocity, a motive based in principle on belief in the reversibility of human behavior; (4) eschatological reward. There are traces of other motives too, but they are not so marked. We may suspect that in actual fact all four motives probably underlie all the texts, but they are stressed in different ways. In Matthew, the imitation and differentiation motives are dominant; in Luke, reciprocity and reward.

As an example of sociological criticism, see H. Adam, *Südafrika: Soziologie einer Rassengesellschaft,* Suhrkamp edition 343 (Frankfurt, 1969), 94, where the ethic of nonviolence, which is deeply rooted among black leaders who have had a Christian education, is made partly responsible for the stability of this race dictatorship. See also Mao Tse-Tung, *Reden auf der Beratung über Fragen der Literatur und Kunst in Yenan* (Peking, 1961), 49, where love of enemies is declared to be an impossibility in class society: "But at present this love does not exist. We cannot love our enemies, cannot love the detestable phenomena in society" (quoted in H. P. Hasenfratz, *Die Rede von der Auferstehung Jesu Christi,* FThL 10 [Bonn, 1975], 241). See also *Mao-Tse-tung on Literature and Art,* 3rd ed. (Peking, 1967).

A. *The Imitation Motive*

In Matthew, the *imitatio dei,* the imitation of God, is the central reason for loving one's enemies. Love of enemies is sovereign behavior, behavior that makes human beings godlike. It elevates them far above their situation—as high as the sun, which shines on good and evil alike:

> Love your enemies and pray for those who persecute you, so that you may be sons of your Father who is in heaven; for he makes his sun rise on the evil and on the good, and sends rain on the just and on the unjust. (Matt. 5:44-45)

If we compare other early Christian versions of this command to love our enemies, we shall notice two things. First, it is only here that we meet the phrase "sons of God" used in a clearly ethical sense. A person becomes God's son through ethical conduct. This is a Wisdom concept of divine sonship (Ecclus. 4:10; Wisd. of Sol. 2:18; 5:5). Ultimately speaking, it is a generalization of the kingly claim to be God's son (Ps. 2:7; 2 Sam. 7:14), except that here it is wisdom and right conduct that create the sonship, not power. But for all that, the son-of-God concept still has a royal echo. Wisdom is royal wisdom, the wisdom of King Solomon, to whom most of the Wisdom writings are attributed—wisdom that confers kingly rank (Prov. 4:8f.; Wisd. of Sol. 6:21).[2] The Stoic sage was also a king.[3] So we might say that to love one's enemies is an expression of a kingly demeanor; it is the sign of God's sons. In Luke it is different. There the son-of-God concept is eschatologically defined, not ethically: ". . . and your reward will be great, and you will be sons of the Most High; for he is kind to the ungrateful and the selfish" (Luke 6:35).

The sentences that follow in Luke are also thinking of eschatological judgment (6:36ff.). So whereas in Matthew the divine sonship is the *goal* of human conduct, in Luke it is the reward.[4] In the later texts which talk about an *imitatio dei,* the son-of-God idea is missing completely (see *Didache* 1.5, Justin *Apology* 1.15.13; *Dialogue* 96.3), although Justin does pick up the parable of the sun.

A second observation confirms the special position adopted by the Gospel of Matthew. There the *imitatio dei* is interpreted in a general and

---

2. Kings rule through wisdom (Prov. 8:15); wisdom crowns (Prov. 4:8f.); wisdom teaches the king clemency (*Letter of Aristeas* 207). See B. Mack, *Logos und Sophia: Untersuchungen zur Weisheitstheologie im hellenistischen Judentum,* StUNT 10 (Göttingen, 1973), 87f. On the Wisdom background of the Sermon on the Mount in general, see U. Luck, *Die Vollkommenheitsforderung der Bergpredigt,* ThEx 150 (Munich, 1968).

3. E.g., Epictetus *Discourses* 3.22, 72.

4. C. Dietzfelbinger, *Die Antithesen der Bergpredigt,* ThEx 186 (Munich, 1975), 46.

fundamental sense. It is not simply a matter of imitating this or that divine behavior, if we want to follow Jesus. The Christian ought to be perfect as God himself is perfect—and this perfection is not limited to particular acts. The other early Christian definitions of the *imitatio dei* are different: they mention practical forms of conduct. We need only put the different formulations side by side:

> You must be perfect, as your heavenly Father is perfect. (Matt. 5:48)

> Be merciful, even as your Father is merciful. (Luke 6:36)

> Give to everyone who asks you and do not ask it back. For the Father will give to everyone from his own gifts. (*Did.* 1.5)

> Be kind and merciful as your Father also is kind and merciful. (Justin *Apol.* 1.15.13; cf. *Dial.* 93.3)

The generalization in Matthew has a special point. He puts the demand for perfection at the close of the series of antitheses, so that in this way it applies to each one of the forms of behavior required in the six antitheses. Taken as a whole, the antitheses illustrate the fulfillment of the law (Matt. 5:17), the better righteousness (5:20), the required perfection (5:48); and here there is a clear upward progression from the surmounting of inward aggression (5:21ff.) to—as climax—the practice of loving one's enemy (5:43ff.).[5]

In Matthew, therefore, love of enemies means a sovereign mastery of the situation by way of the *imitatio dei*. In the ancient world there are many analogies in which benevolence and love are judged to be an expression of inward excellence.[6] Seneca quotes the view: "Si deos, inquit, imitaris, da et ingratis beneficia, nam et sceleratis sol oritur et piratis patent maria" ("If, he says, you would imitate the gods, give benefits even to the ungrateful, for the sun shines even on the wicked, and the seas

---

5. In Matthew, love of enemies is put at the end of a consciously contrived composition, whereas in the Sermon on the Plain it introduces the practical commandments (Luke 6:27ff.). The same may be said of the *Didache* (1.3ff.). Love of enemies is always given a prominent place in the composition. The sequence in Q is disputed. The order in Matthew is presupposed as original by R. Bultmann, *Geschichte der synoptischen Tradition*, 7th ed. (Göttingen, 1967), 100; Eng. trans. *The History of the Synoptic Tradition*, trans. John Marsh (Oxford: Basil Blackwell; New York: Harper & Row, 1963); and S. Schulz, *Q: Die Spruchquelle der Evangelisten* (Zurich, 1972), 120f. The Lukan order is considered to be the original by H. Schürmann, *Das Lukasevangelium*, HThK III/1 (Freiburg, 1969), 341–66; and D. Lührmann, "Liebet eure Feinde (Lk 6,27-36/Mt 5,39-48)," *ZThK* 69 (1972): 412–38.

6. See H. Kosmala, "Nachfolge und Nachahmung Gottes I. Im griechischen Denken," *ASTI* 2 (1963): 38–85, esp. 64, 56f. Not available to me were H. Haas, *Idee und Ideal der Feindesliebe in der ausserchristlichen Welt* (Leipzig, 1917); and M. Waldmann, *Die Feindesliebe in der antiken Welt und im Christentum* (Vienna, 1902).

are accessible to pirates too") (*De beneficiis* 4.26.1). Seneca admittedly goes on to qualify this: God is unable to confer certain gifts on those who are worthy of them without automatically giving them to the unworthy too (*De ben.* 4.28.1). But fundamentally speaking, the idea is there: love in *imitatio dei* is an act of superfluity. The emperor Marcus Aurelius admonishes himself in the same sense: "Love the human race—follow God" (7.31), and in this love he includes in principle even unpleasant, hostile people (2.1). Pliny the Elder even sums the matter up by saying: "It is God, when one mortal being helps another" (Deus est mortali iuvare mortalem) (*Natural History* 2.5 §18). The *Letter of Aristeas* exhorts the ruler to imitate God (210), especially in his clemency (207), his compassion (208), and his justice (209). In a sense, Christianity applies this ideal of kingly virtue to every human being:

> But whoever takes upon himself the burden of his neighbor, whoever is willing to do good to someone who is poorer in that wherein he himself is better off, anyone who gives to the needy that which he himself has received and possesses from God, thus becoming a god for the recipient—he is an imitator of God. (*Epistle to Diognetus* 10.6)

All these analogies speak against the thesis that the requirements to renounce violence and love one's enemies are a resentful reaction against the virtues of the strong and that they express "the vindictive cunning of impotence," which disparages aristocratic virtues because they are completely out of reach. Love of enemies is not what Nietzsche thought: it is an act of sovereignty, not the reaction of people who are ground down; it is the generalization of a sovereign attitude which even someone who is outwardly inferior can adopt. Nietzsche, the acute critic of Christian ethics, indicates this himself, when he outlines a utopia in which love of enemies is an act of the strong, an act without resentment: ". . . here alone the real '*love* of his enemies' is possible—if indeed it is possible at all on earth. How much reverence a noble person feels for his enemies! And such reverence is already a bridge to love."[7]

B. *The Differentiation Motive*

The relationship to other people as well as the relationship to God can provide reasons for loving one's enemies and renouncing violence. To set oneself apart from other groups is plainly an important spur toward realizing these demands. In Matthew, the Gentiles and the tax collectors are mentioned in this connection: "For if you love those who love you, what reward have you? Do not even the tax collectors do the

---

7. Nietzsche, *Genealogie der Moral*, German ed., I, 10, 266.

same? And if you salute only your brethren, what more are you doing than others? Do not even the Gentiles do the same?" (Matt. 5:46f.).

Matthew is talking from a Jewish point of view. Here "brethren" means fellow Jews.[8] Gentiles are all the rest. But other versions name different outsiders. Justin mentions prostitutes (they love the people who love them) and tax collectors, who insist on the payment of money they have lent out (*Apol.* 1.15.9, 10). Luke mentions "sinners" three times. This is the most general category that can be formulated, and it cannot really be identified with any specific social group.[9] In Luke and Justin, the people mentioned are groups from which Gentile Christians could dissociate themselves too. So the differentiation motive can be found everywhere. But it is especially marked in Matthew, because he puts the renunciation of violence and love of enemies in the antithetical form of Old Testament commandments. By doing so, he stresses dissociation from the "old" righteousness — from the Pharisees and scribes (5:20), whose interpretation of the law he is criticizing here.[10] The "new thing" is sharply differentiated from the old, but the old takes concrete form sociologically in specific groups.

Difference compared with other groups is based either on conduct per se or on its result. The conduct required is set apart from the behavior of other people as something "special." (Matt. 5:47: περισσόν here is clearly picking up περισσεύσῃ in 5:20), or as something "new" (Justin *Apol.* 1.15.9f.). In contrast, the *consequences* of this divergent behavior are described in the words μισθός (Matt. 5:46; Luke 6:35) and χάρις (Luke 6:32, 33, 34; *2 Clement* 13.4; Ignatius *To Polycarp* 2.1; *Did.* 1.3). Here μισθός is plainly directed toward the eschatological reward, whereas χάρις can also be interpreted as the approval of other human beings (see below).

---

8. Dissociation from the tax collectors, who after all were also Jews, is not a counter-argument. For one thing the "brethren" in 5:47 are contrasted with the Gentiles, whereas the tax collectors are contrasted *not* with the brethren but "with those who love you." Moreover, tax collectors and Gentiles could easily be associated with one another. For brethren in the sense of fellow countrymen see the arguments in H. von Soden, *ThWNT* 1:145 (cf. *TDNT* 1); J. Jeremias, *Die Gleichnisse Jesu*, 7th ed. (Göttingen, 1965), 108 n. 2 (Eng. trans. *The Parables of Jesus*, trans. S. H. Hooke, 3rd rev. ed. [London: SCM Press, 1972]). More cautiously, J. Friedrich, *Gott im Bruder* (Stuttgart, 1977), 233.

9. K. H. Rengstorf (*ThWNT* 1:332 [see *TDNT* 1]) would like to identify "sinners" with "Gentiles" (i.e., as in Gal. 2:15). But the parallels in Luke speak in favor of a more general meaning; see Luke 5:8; 7:37, 39; 13:2; 15:1f., 7; 18:13; 19:7, where "sinners" always refers to people belonging to Judaism. Luke perhaps deliberately chooses the more general word (Schulz's view in *Q*, 129f.).

10. See esp. C. Burchard, "Versuch, das Thema der Bergpredigt zu finden," in *Jesus Christus in Historie und Theologie: Festschrift für H. Conzelmann* (Tübingen, 1975), 409–32, esp. 422ff.

It is just this seeking for human approval that is the reverse side of the differentiation motive. We find the anticipated reaction of other people as a reason for Christian behavior very early on.[11] Matthew already says: "Let your light so shine before men, that they may see your good works and give glory to your Father who is in heaven" (5:16). In *2 Clem.* 13.4, the link between love of enemies and social approbation is stated even more directly:[12]

> When they hear about you that God says: "You have no thanks (χάρις) when you love those who love you, but you have thanks when you love your enemies and those that hate you"—when they hear that, they will be astonished at your extraordinary goodness; but if they see that not only do you fail to love those who hate you, but that you do not even love the people who love you, then the name (of Christians) will be mocked.

Justin immediately follows the commandment to renounce violence by demanding: "Let your good works shine before men" (*Apol.* 1.16.2). It is not just chance that in the early church we find love of enemies mentioned in the apologetic writings particularly—indeed, that here this tenet finds a new *Sitz im Leben,* or real-life situation. For the effect on outsiders was a decisive motive from early on: anyone who wants to be different from other people also wants to impress them.[13] But this, admittedly, is to get caught up in a contradiction; for when Matthew contrasts love of enemies so sharply with the behavior of Pharisees, scribes, tax collectors, and Gentiles, he seems to negate that breakdown of inner and external groups which is the very purpose of the command to love our enemies. Perhaps further analysis of the sociological background of love of enemies in Matthew can make this inconsistency comprehensible.

C. *The Reciprocity Motive*

Critics of love of enemies and nonviolence occasionally take objection to this kind of behavior on the grounds that it is one-sided: this is love not offered in expectation of returned love. According to Luke,

---

11. W. C. van Unnik, "Die Rücksicht auf die Reaktion der Nicht-Christen als Motiv in der altchristlichen Paränese," in *Judentum, Urchristentum, Kirche: Festschrift für J. Jeremias* (Berlin, 1957), 221–34.

12. According to H. Köster, *2 Clem.* 13.4 is dependent on Luke (*Synoptische Überlieferung bei den Apostolischen Vätern,* TU 65 [Berlin, 1957], 75–77); but this is not certain (see pp. 110f.).

13. On apologetics as the *Sitz im Leben* for the later mention of the commandment to love one's enemies, see W. Bauer, "Das Gebot der Feindesliebe und die alten Christen," in *Aufsätze und kleine Schriften* (Tübingen, 1967), 235–52.

love of an enemy is like lending money without ever getting it back. Yet it is also Luke who stresses a fundamental reciprocity even in the love of enemies and in nonviolence. For in Luke these commandments come under the general heading of the golden rule (i.e., "Do as you would be done by"). Whereas Matthew cites this rule in a different context (7:12), Luke puts it at the center of a brief compendium of Jesus sayings, where it is preceded by, and followed by, sayings about love of enemies and nonviolence: "And as you wish that men would do to you, do so to them" (Luke 6:31).[14]

It is not only the way the passage is built up that links the golden rule with its context; it is also the language that is used. For in the phrases about loving one's enemies, the catchword "do" (ποιεῖν) is explicitly picked up at the very points which are missing in Matthew. Only Luke continues the commandment "Love your enemies!" with the further exhortation "Do good to those who hate you" (καλῶς ποιεῖτε, Luke 6:27). Only Luke raises the question: "If you do good to those who do good to you (ἀγαθοποιῆτε τοὺς ἀγαθοποιοῦντας), what credit is that to you? [What thanks do you have?] For even sinners do the same" (Luke 6:33). Only Luke reiterates: "But love your enemies, and do good (ἀγαθοποιεῖτε), and lend, expecting nothing in return." In my view, it is clear enough: Luke interprets love of one's enemies and nonviolence as ultimately speaking an expression of the golden rule—that is, as expressing a fundamental reciprocity in human behavior. One person really expects the same conduct of the other. Reciprocity is the hope, though not a condition or a calculation.

Luke emphasizes this reciprocity motive in another way too. He stresses three times that to love an enemy expects "thanks." Scholars dispute whether "thanks" here means God's approbation or the approval of human beings,[15] and, further—if human thanks are meant—whether these are the thanks of the people directly concerned or the general approval of others. What speaks in favor of interpreting "thanks" as divine reward is the substitution of μισθός for χάρις when the command to

---

14. Probably the golden rule was already given this position in Q. This is also S. Schulz's opinion (*Q*, 121), although he otherwise considers that Matthew is the original.

15. Most scholars think of a divine reward. See H. Conzelmann, *ThWNT* 9:382 (see *TDNT* 9); W. Grundmann, *Das Evangelium nach Lukas*, ThHNT 3 (Berlin, 1969), 149. W. C. van Unnik rightly sees that the human *quid pro quo* is at least also present, as implicit background ("Die Motivierung der Feindesliebe in Lukas VI,32-35," *NovTest* 8 [1966], 284–300, esp. 295ff.): if Christians only act in the same way as sinners, they can expect only human thanks! And what kind of thanks is that! But different kinds of human "thanks" could also be meant: if one pays back in full what has been lent, human thanks will not be the same in quality as if the lender renounces repayment entirely. See Luke 7:40ff., where Luke discusses this problem, taking two different debtors as illustration.

love one's enemies is repeated (Luke 6:35). Here reward clearly means eschatological reward.[16] Yet the variation of the word used could itself suggest that there is actually a transition here from an immanent to a transcendent reward. The following arguments would suggest that "thanks" should be interpreted as recognition by human beings:

(1) χάρις is the technical term used in Hellenistic literature for an act performed in return for other good deeds: cf. χάρις ἀποδιδόναι (Xenophon *Memorabilia* 2.2.1, 2) or ὁ δράσας τὴν χάριν (Thucydides 2.40.4).[17]

(2) In early Christian parallels to the commandment to love one's enemies, χάρις is always understood in immanent rather than transcendent terms. See Ignatius *To Polycarp* 2.1: "When you love good pupils, what thanks do you have?" In *Did.* 1.3, the following two sentences are parallel and mutually interpretative: "What thanks do you deserve when you love those who love you?" and "But love those who hate you — then you will have no enemy." Are thanks here not expected especially from the people whom one loves in spite of their hostility?

(3) Luke is familiar with the interpretation of χάρις as human thanks: "Does the lord thank the servant because he did what was commanded?" (Luke 17:9). This parallel is in line with what is being said here: what we are in duty bound to do anyway entails no thanks.[18]

Luke is at least thinking of human thanks *as well*. The ποία indicates this too: "What kind of thanks do you deserve?" This is hardly the way anyone would talk about God's grace! Now, we might object that the very point Luke wants to make is that we should renounce any kind of return. The three rhetorical questions would seem to suggest this. But the third question (which Luke may perhaps have added) makes the meaning of these questions clear. The point is to renounce any expectation of the *same* return (Luke 6:34). Anyone who performs good deeds must not act in expectation of receiving corresponding good deeds. Anyone who lends money must not reckon with repayment of the same amount. This does not exclude the possibility that he may earn thanks. Luke is concerned with the quality of the other person's reaction — the kind of thanks love of an enemy may expect. He adheres to reciprocity in principle.

---

16. "Reward in heaven" was mentioned shortly before (Luke 6:23).

17. See van Unnik, "Motivierung," 292ff.

18. It is true that in 1 Pet. 2:20 the term χάρις is related to divine recognition; but there "God's approval" has to be added, for the very reason that "thanks" just by itself would have been understood as human thanks. See van Unnik, *Motivierung*, 296.

In this he is not unique in early Christian writings. In the *Didache* too the golden rule, love of enemies, and the renunciation of violence are combined (1.2–5).[19] Love of enemies aims at reciprocity or — to put it more cautiously — aims at making the enemy stop being an enemy.[20] "What thanks do you deserve when you love those who love you. Do not the Gentiles do this too? But love those who hate you! In that way you will have no enemies!" (*Did.* 1.3).

Renouncing the demand for repayment of a loan is probably based on the same reciprocity motive, carried a little further: "You cannot do it either!" (*Did.* 1.4), meaning "you too are powerless to pay back what is required of you." (But there are other possible interpretations here.)[21]

In Matthew, on the other hand, reciprocity and nonviolence are related to each other in a completely different way: "You have heard that it was said, 'An eye for an eye and a tooth for a tooth'. But I say to you, Do not resist one who is evil" (Matt. 5:38f.).

The new behavior demanded is sharply contrasted with the *ius talionis* of old, which required practical reciprocity in retaliation. We find this contrast only in Matthew. It unintentionally stresses the renunciation of reciprocity. Nor is a new, ideal kind of reciprocity in view. On the contrary, the new conduct has God as lodestone and model, the aim being to imitate his "asymetrical" and unilateral behavior toward human beings. Anyone who unilaterally renounces resistance, anyone who loves his enemies and prays for his persecutors, is imitating God, who lets his sun shine on the good and the evil, irrespective of their reactions. It is just this that sets a person far above other human beings. Luke, on the other hand, stresses that this new behavior has as its purpose a new (ideal) kind of reciprocity. This behavior distinguishes a person not from any particular, socially definable groups but from "sinners" in general. But everyone can be, and can become, a sinner. So while in Matthew the practical reciprocity of earlier times is broken through,

---

19. This comment stands, quite apart from literary or textual criticism of the passage. *Did.* 1.3–2.1 is probably an interpolation, either by the author himself or by a later hand. But in either case the golden rule would have been the reason for the interpolation. The interpolation theory therefore underlines the connection between golden rule and love of enemies. On the literary or textual problem, see P. Vielhauer, *Geschichte der urchristlichen Literatur* (Berlin, 1975), 730, 733, and the literature cited there.

20. For this there are many parallels in Judaism. These are cited in A. Nissen, *Gott und der Nächste im antiken Judentum*, WUNT 15 (Tübingen, 1974), 312ff. See esp. *Testament of Benjamin* (ed. R. H. Charles), 21f.; 5, 1 "The good man hath not a dark eye; for he showeth mercy to all men, even though they be sinners. And though they devise with evil intent concerning him, by doing good he overcometh evil. . . . If, therefore, ye also have a good mind, then will both wicked men be at peace with you. . . ."

21. See H. Köster, *Synoptische Überlieferung*, 229; R. Knopf, *Die Lehre der zwölf Apostel*, HNT suppl. vol. 1 (Tübingen, 1920), 9.

in Luke we are confronted instead with the goal of a new, ideal reciprocity.

D. *The Motive of Eschatological Reward*

The reciprocal behavior postulated is an anticipation. To be unable to count on this reciprocity from the outset is an instrinsic element in loving an enemy. The reciprocity may well remain an anticipation, without any echo on the part of the other person. Here the idea about the heavenly reward now comes into play — the idea, that is, of an *eschatological* reciprocity which takes account of the longing for a return, even if this longing is never fulfilled in this world. Immanent reciprocity and eschatological reciprocity do not necessarily rule each other out. In Ecclus. 12:2 they complement each other: "Do good to a godly man, and you will be repaid — if not by him, certainly by the Most High." Similarly, Luke passes from immanent to eschatological reciprocity without any pronounced breach. He stresses the eschatological aspect far more than Matthew, however. Matthew certainly also uses the term "reward" (5:46), but in this Gospel, love of enemies has an intrinisic value of its own, since it is an imitation of God. Luke, on the other hand, gives the *imitatio dei* idea a different focus: "Be merciful, even as your Father is merciful. Judge not, and you will not be judged; condemn not, and you will not be condemned; forgive, and you will be forgiven; give and it will be given to you" (Luke 6:36ff.).[22]

Here "be merciful" is obviously parallel to "judge not." Luke is not thinking merely of imitation of God's *present* acts. He is thinking too of God's acts in the future, in judgment. We might paraphrase and say: Be merciful, even as your Father is merciful in the eschatological judgment.

The eschatological judgment proceeds according to a *ius talionis.* So we might say that in Luke love of enemies aims at a *ius talionis* in the future, whereas in Matthew it is confronted with the *ius talionis* of old. In Luke, therefore, the reciprocity motive influences both present and future. He is not alone in this, in the early days of Christianity. In *1 Clement* too (13.2), mercy, forgiveness, and kindness are actuated by a hope for reciprocity.[23] Here as well, eschatological judgment is the guiding idea. But when we find echoes of the golden rule in the middle

---

22. Schürmann distinguishes these sayings too sharply from the preceding words about love of enemies (*Lukasevangelium*, 342–66); for the idea of the *imitatio dei,* which is already present in Luke 6:35, is taken up again here in v. 36, so that it is impossible to talk about a cleft between v. 35 and v. 39.

23. On *1 Clem.* 13.2, see Köster, *Synoptische Überlieferung,* 12–16.

of this collection of the Lord's sayings, this indicates how little future and present can be separated:

> For so he [Jesus] said:
> Be merciful so that you may find mercy.
> Forgive so that you may be forgiven.
> As you do, so will it be done to you.
> As you give, so will you be given.
> As you judge, so will you be judged.
> If you show kindness, kindness will be shown to you.
> With the same measure with which you measure, will it be measured unto you.

Matthew quotes the corresponding words "Judge not, that you be not judged" at a different point (7:1ff.), detached from problems about loving one's enemies. When he is speaking about loving enemies, he does not talk about the eschatological judge. He talks about the Creator and his sovereignty over good and evil, the Creator whom it is good to imitate, quite apart from the consequences. Justin is different. He picks up Matthew's "sun" image but does not content himself with the imitation motive, adding a reminder of the consequences at the judgment;

> for we see the Ruler of all too as one who is kind and merciful, letting his sun rise on the ungrateful and the just, and letting it rain on the good and the bad, all of whom he will one day judge, as he has taught. (*Dial.* 96.3)

This reminder of the eschatological judgment is highly illuminating; for Justin does not merely touch on the eschatological reward. He also points to the impending judgment on the ungrateful and wicked, a motive often suggested in connection with exhortations to be ready to forgive enemies, but which is actually missing in the Synoptic statements about nonviolence and love of enemies. We find this motive in two variations. The idea of God's judgment *either* leads to thoughts about the punishment of the wicked—that is, it involves an outward-turned aggressiveness—aggressiveness toward others; *or* it reminds us of our own guilt—that is, it intensifies the inward-turned aggressiveness inherent in the sense of guilt in general. The first idea makes it possible to put off revenge until the coming of the eschatological era; the second sharpens our sense of being dependent on forgiveness ourselves.[24]

1. The motive of arriving at an eschatological postponement of vengeance can be found in Paul in a comparable context "Vengeance is mine, I will repay, says the Lord" (Rom. 12:19). Here aggressiveness is undoubtedly being "delegated" to God. He takes over the wish for

---

24. On the following passages from Jewish sources, see A. Nissen, *Gott und der Nächste,* 308ff.

revenge and by so doing relieves men and women of the burden of aggressiveness. The idea is widespread. In the *Testament of Gad* 6.3ff. (ed. R. H. Charles), we can read:

> If a man sins against thee, cast forth the poison of hate and speak peaceably to him, and in thy soul hold no guile; and if he confess and repent forgive him. . . . And if he be shameless and persist in his wrong-doing, even so forgive him from the heart, and leave to God the avenging.

The same theme is stated even more clearly in *2 Enoch* 50:3f. (ed. R. H. Charles):

> Endure for the sake of the Lord every wound, every injury, every evil word and attack. If ill-requitals befall you, return them not either to neighbour or enemy, because the Lord will return them for you and be your avenger on the day of great judgment, that there be no avenging here among men."

2. The other variant of the judgment motive is as follows: a person who, faced with the divine judgment, is conscious of his own guilt, cannot urge the guilt of other people and insist on that, not even if it is the guilt of his enemy. For he himself is in danger of divine punishment:

> He that takes vengeance will suffer vengeance from the Lord, and he will firmly establish his sins. Forgive your neighbor the wrong he has done, and then your sins will be pardoned when you pray. Does a man harbor anger against another, and yet seek for healing from the Lord? Does he have no mercy toward a man like himself, and yet pray for his own sins? If he himself, being flesh, maintains wrath, who will make expiation for his sins? (Ecclus. 28:1-5)

Both reasons for forgiving enemies can be found in the Gospels. We need think only of the fantasies of vengeance in Matt. 10:11-15, where—in direct contradiction to the command to love our enemies—hostile places are threatened with eschatological punishment, an end that will be worse than the end of Sodom and Gomorrah. But just because of this—just because themes of this kind can be found in the Jesus tradition—their omission in connection with love of enemies is striking, especially in the Lukan version, where we almost feel bound to postulate them, because of the context; for the preceding Beatitudes, which call the poor, the hungry, and the mourners blessed, are set over against "woe" proclamations against the rich, the satisfied, and those who laugh. It would correspond to this if the final Beatitude— "Blessed are the persecuted" — were followed by a "woe!" to the persecutors. Instead we find a "woe!" to the people who are not persecuted: "Woe to you, when all men speak well of you, for so their fathers did to the false prophets" (Luke 6:26). The eschatological judgment to which the "woe!" refers does not in this case suggest thoughts about the punishment of our enemies. It makes us critical about our own behavior. Not to have evoked rejection means that we must have behaved wrongly! This is the equivalent of saying that the second motive ("self-criticism as a prevention against aggression and aggressiveness") is much more in line with what we find in the Gospels than the first. For a central verse in the Sermon on the Mount reads: "And forgive us our debts, as we also forgive our debtors" (Matt. 6:12). Yet we do not find this reason explicitly given in the context of love of enemies. And that is important. There a positive motive is dominant: the *imitatio dei*, excellence compared with others, hope for "thanks" and the expectation of an eschatological reward. We cannot sense any negative motivation here — neither fear of judgment nor the danger of evil consequences in the future. This too confirms our impression that these commandments are sustained by a great, positive self-confidence — and are therefore anything but a resentment-inspired attack by the weak on "the victors."

Finally, let me point to two motives which play a prominent part in the closest classical parallels to the comandment to love our enemies, and which find only a partial correspondence in early Christianity. We come across these parallels in the Stoic demands to do good to one's opponent[25] and especially in what Epictetus says about the Cynic: "He must allow himself to be kicked like a dog, and while he is being kicked he must go on loving them like a father of them all, like a brother" (*Discourses* 3.22.54).

Two motives are important here: first, the Stoic's independence of outward suffering; and, second, the tie binding together all human beings. The independence motive is the theme of the whole passage about the true Cynic. In an exemplary way, he lives out Epictetus's basic conviction that we should concentrate on the things that we can control and should disengage ourselves from the things over which we have no influence. It depends on ourselves whether we feel humiliated by the scorn of another person or not (*Encheiridion* 20); and if someone ill-treats us, we should view this as a chance to practice inner detachment

---

25. As well as the passages cited, see Seneca *De ira* 2.32.1; 3.34.2; *De otio* 1.4. On the comparison between Stoic and early Christian "love of enemies," see R. Bultmann, *Jesus* (1926; 3rd ed. Gütersloh, 1977), 77–84 (Eng. trans. *Jesus and the Word*, trans. of 2nd ed. by L. P. Smith and E. Huntress Lantero [New York: Scribner, 1934; London: Fontana Books, 1958]). But Bultmann's interpretation of love of enemies as the climax of self-mastery (German ed., p. 79) is not adequate, for it is precisely this theme that is missing from the early Christian texts. For criticsm of Bultmann's interpretation, see the arguments adduced (in my view rightly) in L. Schottroff, "Gewaltverzicht und Feindesliebe in der urchristlichen Jesustradition Mt 5,38-48; Lk 6,27-36," in *Jesus in Historie und Theologie: Festschrift für H. Conzelmann* (Tübingen, 1975), 197–221.

(*Dis.* 3.20.9ff.). This motive of arriving at a sovereign inward control can be found only twice in early Christian writings. Renunciation of self-defense presupposes control of inward aggressive impulses:

> Abstain from carnal (and bodily) desires. If anyone strikes you on the right cheek, offer them the other and you will be perfect. (*Did.* 1.4)

> To him who strikes you on the cheek, offer the other too, and to him who takes your shirt, do not refuse your cloak. But whoever is angry deserves the fire. If someone compels you to go one mile, accompany him for two. (Justin *Apol.* 1.16.1)

Here the buildup of the passage makes it clear that this is a reflection on the psychological presuppositions for loving an enemy and for renouncing self-defense: desire and anger have to be controlled. We encounter this theme very seldom, and even then it is no more than hinted at.

There is a certain tension between the second Stoic motive and the first. The requirement to be independent of everyone else is counterbalanced by the sense of a profound bond between all human beings, even if they are hostile. The tormented Cynic ought to behave toward his tormentors like a father and brother. Marcus Aurelius emphasizes this particularly:

> Say to yourself in the early morning: I shall meet today inquisitive, ungrateful, violent, treacherous, envious, uncharitable men. All these things have come upon them through ignorance of real good and ill. But I, because I have seen that the nature of good is the right, and of ill the wrong, and that the nature of the man himself who does wrong is akin to my own (not of my own blood and seed, but partaking with me in mind, that is in a portion of divinity), I can neither be harmed by any of them, for no man will involve me in wrong, nor can I be angry with my kinsman or hate him; for we have come into the world to work together, like feet, like hands, like eyelids, like the rows of upper and lower teeth. To work against one another therefore is to oppose Nature, and to be vexed with another or to turn away from him is to tend to antagonism. (2.1; see also 9.27; Marcus Aurelius, *Meditations*, ed. and trans. A. S. L. Farquarson (Oxford: Clarendon Press, 1944)

Nowhere in the early Christian writings do we find an appeal to a natural kinship between all human beings as reason for loving our enemies. Our likeness is only before God, who lets his sun shine on good and evil alike.

We can now sum up the first part of our investigation.

Matthew clearly emphasizes the "imitation" motive. This includes a "social" superiority, for anyone who through *imitatio dei* becomes "a son of God" is above the people who are *not* sons of God. In this way, the imitation motive and the differentiation motive are connected, quite apart from the fact that dissociation from Gentiles and tax collectors, Pharisees and scribes can actually be interpreted as "negative" *imitatio.* For to imitate God means *not* imitating other human groups. The two motives display a certain asymmetry. Both see the value of the behavior required as inherent in the behavior itself.

Luke is different. Here the outcome of what a person does plays the decisive part; and he clearly stresses reciprocity motives: thanks and eschatological reward, human and divine approval, are hoped for and expected, in exchange for the conduct demanded. Anyone who loves and forgives is in principle dependent on an echo of love and forgiveness, even if, in the event, this response is never given. In Luke, then, we notice an insistence on symmetry. And that, now, brings us face to face with the question: Are these different motivation structures reflections of different structures in social life?

II. LOVE OF ENEMIES AND NONVIOLENCE:
THE SOCIAL CONTEXT

It is impossible to determine what love of enemies and nonviolence mean apart from the social situation in which these demands are made and practiced. Now, it is clear from the outset that historically speaking the Matthean and Lukan traditions belong to different religious milieus and have as background two different types of righteousness.[26] In the one we find an idea of righteousness based on an asymmetrical relationship between superior and inferior—a *iustitia salutifera,* which claims the help of the strong for the weak, and which springs from ancient oriental tradition. In the other we see a Western type of righteousness, which insists on the establishment of symmetry and mutuality between equals: the *iustitia distributiva.* The two types arise from different kinds of social experience. The one derives from life under an oriental monarchy, the other from life in a Hellenistic republic.[27]

But this does not tell us much. In the Synoptic Gospels, both types of righteousness are transcended. Love of enemies—in itself asymmetrical—is now expected of people who have very little power. They are expected to adopt the sovereign attitude of a king and to forgive out of a consciousness of inward superiority. It is the virtue of kings and

---

26. See the comparison in Hasenfratz, *Auferstehung,* 212–26.
27. See H. Bolkestein, *Wohltätigkeit und Armenpflege im vorchristlichen Altertum* (Utrecht, 1939; reprint, Groningen, 1967), 418ff.

the powerful to help the weak. This axiom is now turned upside down: it is the persecuted person, of all people, who takes over the royal role as "son of God."

But the Hellenistic mutuality ethic is modified too; for love of enemies means accepting the possibility that reciprocity between human beings may fail to materialize. The unilateral love of enemies is not restricted by the golden rule, as one might perhaps think. It is actually radicalized; for the golden rule makes it clear that this is not a particularist ethic. It is behavior that, basically speaking, is expected of everyone.

This means that to point to the two different types of righteousness and their different social backgrounds does not take us very far, for the two types are linked with each other and modified. We must ask more specifically about the *Sitz im Leben* of love of enemies and nonviolence — their background in real life. It is obvious, on the face of it, that it makes an ethically relevant difference whether the victor is the one who is supposed to "love" his defeated enemy and to renounce vengeance, or whether it is the person who has been vanquished who wins through to this attitude. In an important essay, Luise Schottroff has traced this idea through and has classified the parallels from the ancient world in a convincing typology — a typology whose distinguishing criterion is the real-life situation. According to this classification, the renunciation of vengeance, moderation toward enemies, or even a kindly and well-disposed attitude to them, can be found in three different contexts:[28]

1. The "defeated" person ought to be a person without rancor (ἄχολος). He must accept the situation as it is — and of course this is a counsel of wisdom, for it is often "not very useful to avenge injustice" (Seneca *De ira* 2.33.2). It is true that in the ancient world to submit to a situation could also be censured as the expression of a slavish mentality, but this is no contradiction: it was quite openly accepted that there were different rules of conduct for the dependent and the free (ibid. 2.34.1).

2. The "victor" renounces revenge. Seneca writes here:

> Though it is honorable in the case of good deeds to requite goodness with goodness, one should not requite wrong by wrong. In the first case, to let oneself be excelled is a reason for contempt — in the second, to excel. There is an inhumane word "revenge" (even though this is admittedly considered to be justice). And vengeance is not very different from wrong-doing except in the sequence of events. (*De ira* 2.32.1)

3. The philosopher suffers wrong rather than commit it. The great model is Socrates (Plato *Crito* 49Aff.). The philosopher is above the social

---

28. Schottroff, "Gewaltverzicht," 207–13. I should like to emphasize how much I am indebted to this essay for important and stimulating suggestions.

hierarchy, allowing himself to be classified neither evidently below nor above. Many anecdotes illustrate his sovereign indifference to abuse:

> But Socrates, after Aristocrates had kicked him, neither retaliated nor reproved him in any way except to say to the passersby: "This man has been infected with mule disease." But when someone threatened "I will kill you!" Plato turned around and threatened him in return: "I will appease you." (Themistios *Peri aretes* 46)[29]

We now have to ask where we should place the early Christian groups whom we can glimpse behind the precepts about renouncing violence and loving enemies. Here we have to distinguish between the Matthean and the Lukan congregations, and also the groups behind the logion tradition (including Q). After that we must ask where the historical Jesus stands.

A. *The Matthean Congregations*

Matthew put nonviolence and love of enemies side by side, as two separate, antithetically formulated demands. But even in Matthew the two commandments are closely connected. This emerges from the buildup of the series of antitheses.[30] We twice meet the extended introductory formula "You have heard that it was said to the men of old . . ." (5:21 and 5:33), and this formula divides the series into two groups of equal size, a division that is underlined also by the introductory πάλιν ("again") in v. 33. In both groups the last two antitheses are closely linked in form as well as content. Both are introduced only by an abbreviated opening formula. Both deal with connected subjects — adultery and divorce on the one hand, the renunciation of violence and love of enemies on the other. So although the renunciation of violence and the love of enemies are stated separately, this must not lead us to conclude that they are not closely related in substance.

The analysis of the structure is illuminating in another way too. The first group of antitheses is casuistically formulated: πᾶς plus participle ("every one who") is followed in each case by an assertion of guilt. The

---

29. Themistios lived ca. 317–388 c.e. His speech *On Virtue* (cited here) was translated into German by J. Gildemeister and F. Bücheler under the title "Über die Tugend" in *Rheinisches Museum für Philologie* NF 27 (Bonn, 1872): 438–62. The quotation is taken from p. 461. There appears to be no published English translation. Themistios is recounting older anecdotes. Plutarch also recounts the last story but tells it about Eukleides (*De cohib. ira* 14). Themistios himself tells it again about Socrates in another passage (7.95a).

30. See R. Guelich, "The Antithesis of Matthew V,21-48: traditional and/or redactional?" *NTS* 22 (1975): 444–57; also G. Strecker, "Die Antithesen der Bergpredigt (Mt 5,21-48 par)," *ZNW* 69 (1978): 36–72.

positive requirement is never stated — only the conduct condemned. The second group of antitheses, on the other hand, is apodictic. The behavior required is described positively with the help of infinitives or imperatives. Whereas the first group of antitheses now turns to "all" (πᾶς), the second is directed to a particular group. The second person plural, which is never used in the first group outside the formula of address "But I say to you," etc., now occurs frequently. All the commandments are either formulated as infinitives dependent on λέγω ὑμῖν ("I say to you") and are thus in the second person plural, or they are directly formulated in the second person plural (5:44, 46, 47, 48; 5:37). We may conclude from this that the negative assertions of guilt apply to everyone. But the positive commandments are emphatically directed to a particular group.

We must now try to throw some light on the situation of this group, drawing on the help of features that are peculiar to Matthew. The situation of the Matthean congregations must emerge from the statements in Matthew that go beyond Luke or from other elements that are special to him.

1. Matthew goes beyond Luke in the demand: If any one forces you to go one mile, go with him two miles (5:41); ἀγγαρεύειν is a technical term of Persian origin which was used for services to the state rendered under duress. The only parallel we have (Mark 15:21) is thinking of the soldiers who, meeting Simon as he comes back from the fields, force him to carry Jesus' cross. Epictetus also talks about soldiers in connection with the word (*Dis.* 4.1.79):

> You should treat your whole body like a heavily laden donkey as long as this is possible and permitted. But if there is "aggareia," and a soldier takes hold of it, let it happen. Do not resist and do not grumble. Otherwise you will be beaten, and will lose your donkey notwithstanding.

The many rabbinic parallels[31] also have as their background services enforced by the state. The foreign word μίλιον (translated mile) is a special pointer to the Romans, for this is the only time the word occurs in the New Testament, the usual term being στάδιον.[32] All this suggests

---

31. See P. Fiebig, "ἀγγαρεύω," *ZNW* 18 (1917–18): 64–72; also his "Jesu Worte über die Feindesliebe," *ThStKr* 91 (1918): 30–64, esp. 51ff.

32. See W. Bauer, *Griechisch-Deutsches Wörterbuch zu den Schriften des Neuen Testaments,* s.v. μίλιον (cf. *A Greek-English Lexicon of the New Testament and Other Early Christian Literature,* 2nd ed. rev. and augmented by F. W. Gingrich and F. W. Danker from the 5th German ed. 1958 (Chicago and London: University of Chicago Press, 1979). The measure στάδιον, on the other hand, can be found in Matt. 14:24; Luke 24:13; John 6:19; 11:18; Acts 14:20; 21:16. So it is striking that a foreign, Latin word should turn up at this particular point.

that in the situation of the Matthean congregations, compulsory services enforced by the Romans (i.e., by Roman soldiers) were a real and pressing problem.[33]

2. In Matthew, all four examples of a nonviolent reaction to injustice are introduced in the same way: "Do not resist one who is evil!" (5:39). But the examples that follow in fact require more than nonresistance. In each case they demand that the opponent be voluntarily offered more than he asked for. They call for a paradoxical complaisance — meeting the other person more than halfway. The Matthew text implies this "more," for after the command not to resist, the examples that follow are all introduced by the word "but" (ἀλλά). The negative demand not to offer any resistance is supplemented and exceeded by a positive one.[34] So Matthew too is not thinking merely of passive submission. All the same, it is characteristic that he should mention nonresistance first of all.[35] Here it will surely be permissible to ask whether this does not reflect the situation of a subjugated people? It is the same situation for which Josephus wrote his *Jewish War* (ca. 75–79 C.E.), his purpose being to warn the Jews and all the other Eastern peoples against resisting the Roman Empire. He puts his ideas on this subject into the mouth of Agrippa II, in a great speech before the outbreak of war:

> For one must try to win over the powers that be, and not enrage them. But if you magnify minor misdemeanors through violent abuse, then you certainly expose those you abuse as far as you yourselves are concerned; but all that you accomplish is that they will now ruin you openly through the injuries which they have up to now only secretly and unobtrusively done you. Nothing puts an end to blows as quickly as patient endurance, and the submission of the victim makes the tormentor mend his ways. Even if we assume that the Roman officials are really unbearably harsh, this does not mean that

---

33. Here I am picking up P. Hoffmann's important suggestions in P. Hoffmann and V. Eid, *Jesus von Nazareth und eine christliche Moral*, Quaestiones Disputatae 66 (Freiburg, 1975), 147–67. He rightly asks (p. 158): "Are these changes a response to the desperate situation after the Jewish revolt had been crushed?"

34. Rightly Hoffmann, *Jesus*, 159: "The sayings are a call not merely to acceptance but also to a paradoxical activity. It is precisely this which makes their interpretation so difficult."

35. The renunciation of resistance must not be restricted to the legal sector (as C. Burchard rightly stresses in "Versuch," 424 n. 62). Only one of the practical examples can be interpreted as a renunciation of legal rights. It must be said in general that the specific examples cannot be summed up under the heading of "renunciation of resistance," for what is being talked about here in each given case goes beyond this renunciation. Consequently we do not feel that the final example — the requirement to give — is completely out of place, even though it has nothing to do with nonresistance against either wickedness or the wicked.

all the Romans are injuring you — even the emperor himself. Yet it is against them that you mean to wage war. (*J.W.* 2.350–52)

It is quite conceivable that when Matthew speaks against offering resistance, the background of his demand is the very situation which Josephus is addressing, except that Matthew is thinking not merely of submission but of a paradoxical reaction. The general mood underlying the passage could well be the same.

3. Another feature peculiar to Matthew is the antithetical formulation, which contrasts the new ethic with a strict *ius talionis* and hate of one's enemies. Here again we may ask whether war and the postwar era did not offer illustrations enough for notions of revenge and for hate of the enemy. We may ask too whether this war did not spread and intensify the preconceived notion that the Jews hated other nations. Tacitus at least gives eloquent expression to this prejudice:[36]

Moses, quo sibi in posterum gentem firmaret, novos ritus contrariosque ceteris mortalibus indidit. . . . Apud ipsos fides obstinata, misericordia in promptu, sed adversus omnes alios hostile odium. (In order to secure the people for the future, Moses introduced new rites which were contrary to those otherwise customary in the world. . . . Among themselves, unshakable loyalty and readiness for compassion ruled, whereas toward all others there was hostility and hate.) (*Hist.* 5.4, 5)

If we compare this with what is said in Matthew, we find that the general tenor is the same: the commandment of love applied among the Jews themselves, but the enemy could be hated — all this on the basis of the Mosaic law. If the Matthean congregations are dissociating themselves here from the scribes and Pharisees, they are no doubt dissociating themselves at the same time from the prejudice to which a defeated people was subjected.

4. Finally, we must point to the parallels between Matt. 5:44f. and 5:9: "Love your enemies and pray for those who persecute you, so that you may be sons of your Father who is in heaven" (5:44f.). This promise can be found again in 5:9 under the heading "peace": "Blessed are the peacemakers, for they shall be called sons of God." Both passages are based on the Wisdom son-of-God concept, which has an ethical definition. In the one passage the sonship is seen as presentative force (5:44f.), in the other as eschatological gift (5:9). Once again, we have to ask whether we are not bound to understand intervention for peace in practical terms: peacemaking and love of enemies go together, and both are

---

36. Burchard assumes that Matt. 5:44 was "formulated under the influence of a *topos* which was not precisely pro-Jewish, such as Tacitus, *Hist.* V 5" ("Versuch," 425 n. 65).

associated with the son-of-God title. Should not peace hold good for enemies too? Could love of enemies mean among other things standing up for peace in the years after the Jewish war?[37]

In my view, these four observations permit us to assume that experiences of the Jewish War and the postwar era are reflected in the way traditions about loving our enemies are formulated in Matthew.[38] This situation could well explain all the particular features found in Matthew—which does not mean that these features have always been contributed by an editor. On the contrary, Matthew is reproducing the traditions of Jewish-Christian congregations. And these congregations drew on the tradition about loving enemies as a way of coming to terms with the situation of a subjugated and humiliated people. The asymmetry in the motives for loving enemies and for nonviolence which we find in Matthew would then have a certain correspondence in real social conditions. These too were asymmetric, since they were the conditions existing between victors and vanquished. What is important is that in a countermove to this somber and depressing state of affairs, the Matthew tradition shows the awareness that renouncing violence and loving one's enemies means rising above the situation and being superior to one's antagonists, "the Gentiles." This makes it understandable that these "Gentiles" should have been looked down on. Even ethically, it makes a difference whether we look down on the people whom we in any case excel, or whether the underdog preserves his dignity by knowing himself to be inwardly superior to the victor. Remembrance of the God who is above good and evil forbids us to assume that this attitude is prompted by resentment.

There are other indications in the Gospel of Matthew which support our postulate that Matthew's version belongs to a special social situation. The traditions it contains reject the Jewish rising with unmistakable clarity. Matt. 23:35 sharply condemns the Zealots' murder of the rich

---

37. Fiebig rightly points out that Matt. 5:43-48 is thinking about national enemies ("Jesu Worte über die Feindesliebe," 37f.): "'Tax-collectors' and 'Gentiles,' who are used here as antitype, were after all the national enemies of the Jews!" (p. 38). If, now, with J. Dupont (*Les Béatitudes,* II [Paris, 1973], 633–64), we relate to one another the sayings about love of enemies and the sayings about peacemakers (Matt. 5:43ff. and 5:9), but—in the case of the first—think of national enemies too, the inference is that peacemaking also is not confined to the private sphere. It is more than love of our neighbor and compassion (though for another view, see Dupont, pp. 644–54). Does the son-of-God title—that is, the generalization of ancient messianic tradition—not suggest this? It is the king's function to create peace. We find εἰρεινοποιός used above all as an attribute of the mighty (W. Foerster, *ThWNT* 2:417f. (see *TDNT* 2)). Here this function is expected of everyone. See H. Windisch, "Friedensbringer—Gottessöhne," *ZNW* 34 (1925): 240–60.

38. As far as I know this thesis was put forward for the first time by Hoffmann in *Jesus,* 147–67, esp. 158ff.

Jerusalem citizen Zechariah, son of Barachiah.[39] The rebels are denigrated as "murderers" (Matt. 27:7). And conversely, the picture of the Messiah in Matthew is completely nonpolitical, not to say "anti-Zealot."[40] The Messiah "will not wrangle or cry aloud, nor will any one hear his voice in the streets" (Matt. 12:19f. = Isa. 42:1ff.). He comes riding on a donkey, without violence (Matt. 21:5; Zech. 9:9). He is a son of David — but what marks him out are his miraculous healings, not his political ambitions (Matt. 12:23; 9:27; 15:22).[41] Whichever way we look at it, the Matthean traditions are in many respects molded by the Jewish situation after the catastrophe of 70 C.E.

B. *The Lukan Congregations*

We have seen that in Luke the emphasis lies on an ideal reciprocity which is then also intended to provide a standard for practical behavior, even if the other person does not abide by this standard.[42] God, at all events, will even things out. If we now ask about the social situation behind this variant of the tradition about loving our enemies, we have to start from what is especially characteristic of Luke: the Hellenistic

---

39. See the investigations in O. H. Steck, *Israel und das gewaltsame Geschick der Propheten,* WMANT 23 (Neukirchen, 1967), 33–40. It is only the Matthean version that is no doubt thinking of the murder of Zechariah son of Barachiah. Luke more probably has in mind Zechariah son of Jehoiada (2 Chron. 24:20-22).

40. Hoffmann, *Jesus,* 163: "Matthew was evidently writing under the impression of the catastrophic failure of the messianic revolt against Rome. His Gospel therefore paints Jesus throughout as the Messiah who was humble and meek, nonviolent and peaceable, self-abasing and good — in deliberate contrast to the Zealot messianic ideal...." Here one can most readily discover the nonpolitical messianic ideal, which also had its traditions, as K. Berger shows; see his "Die königlichen Messiastraditionen des Neuen Testaments," *NTS* 20 (1973): 1–44, and "Zum Problem der Messianität Jesu," *ZThK* 71 (1974): 1–30.

41. See C. Burger, *Jesus als Davidssohn,* FRLANT 98 (Göttingen, 1970), 72ff.

42. A. Dihle rightly points to a tension between a reciprocity ethic and love of enemies (*Die Goldene Regel: Eine Einführung in die Geschichte der antiken und frühchristlichen Vulgärethik,* Studien zur Altertumswissenschaft 7 [Göttingen, 1962], 113ff.). He would therefore like to interpret the golden rule in Luke 6:31 in an indicative sense. But then the contrast to the imperative context would have to be stressed by way of the appropriate particles. The tension disappears, however, if we remember that it is not the actual behavior of the others that is intended to be the standard of one's own practical conduct; it is the ideal behavior expected of them. But it would then follow from this that one really expects from the others too love of enemies, nonretaliation, and the renunciation of repayment. This was not excluded from the outset, however. The ancient world gradually surmounted the idea of retaliation — in principle too. A. Dihle has worked this out in his important study (pp. 41ff., 61ff.). The ethical norm existed, even if practical behavior — there as everywhere — lagged behind.

conceptuality, and the problem about lending money, to which Luke gives a prominent place.

It is a striking fact that Luke expresses Jesus' ethical demands with the help of traditions and concepts drawn from Hellenistic popular ethics.[43] The golden rule was formulated by the Sophists toward the end of the fifth century B.C.E. It made its way into Judaism in the second century B.C.E. (*Letter of Aristeas* 207; Tob. 4:15), and it is presented in Matthew as the summing up of "the law and the prophets" (7:12). Luke cites this rule as a general axiom, not as a specifically Jewish tradition. Of course it is difficult to decide whether he even knew that it was a generally held precept. But it is Luke, if anyone, whom we should most readily expect to be aware of this, since he deliberately adopts Hellenistic ideas in other places too (cf. the Areopagus speech, Acts 17:22ff.). But above all, it is at the very points where he is affirming the demand to love our enemies that he draws on terms taken from Hellenistic ethics: καλῶς ποιεῖν and ἀγαθοποιεῖν (6:27, 33, 35) and χάρις (6:32, 33, 34). The essential point is that, consciously or unconsciously, the Lukan congregations appeal to generally accepted standards of conduct. The Christian ethic can stand comparison with the standards of the world.

There is another special feature in Luke too: his stress on lending money.[44] First, unlike Matthew, he stresses: "Give to *everyone* who asks of you" (Luke 6:30), and—going beyond Matthew—he insists that one should not ask anything back.[45] Moreover, he takes up the theme in three passages that have no parallel in Matthew, for example, in his third rhetorical question: "And if you lend to those from whom you hope to receive, what thanks do you have? Even sinners lend to sinners, to receive as much again" (Luke 6:34). On the analogy of the first two rhetorical questions, we should expect: Do not lend only to those who lend to you. But the general sense of what we read is: Do not lend only to the people from whom you hope to get back what you have lent! So here the idea is not lending in expectation of a similar service (i.e., reciprocity).[46] What

---

43. See van Unnik, "Motivierung," passim.

44. On the following passage, see W. Stegemann's important comments in W. Stegemann and L. Schottroff, *Jesus von Nazareth — Hoffnung der Armen* (Stuttgart, 1978), 144–48 (Eng. trans. *Jesus and the Hope of the Poor* [Maryknoll, N.Y.: Orbis Books, 1986]).

45. Both divergences can also be found in *Did.* 1.5, however. If the conclusion to be drawn is a matter of dispute, can we postulate dependence on Luke (Köster, *Synoptische Überlieferung,* 230ff.)? Or is it permissible to conclude that these are independent variants in the tradition (H. T. Wrege, *Die Überlieferungsgeschichte der Bergpredigt,* WUNT 9 [Tübingen, 1968], 82–94)?

46. The theme of lending against return can be found elsewhere too; see Ecclus. 29:1ff., where the lender is promised: "on every occasion you will find what you need" (29:3); Athenagoras, suppl. 12, 3: "For if you love those who love you, and lend to those who

comes through here is instead the simple fact that the people who can lend are seldom the people who themselves borrow.

Luke repeats the admonition to love enemies in 6:35. Although he takes up 6:27f. again, everything is not repeated. We hear nothing about blessing or praying for our enemies. Instead the subject is once again the lending of money.

But as if that were not enough, he stresses this problem yet a third time, going beyond what Matthew says.[47] Matthew writes in 7:1f.: "Judge not, that you be not judged. For with the judgment you pronounce you will be judged, and the measure you give will be the measure you get." There is no mention here of financial problems. It is different in Luke. After the demand not to judge, he goes on: "Forgive [your debtors], and you will be forgiven; give, and it will be given to you; good measure, pressed down, shaken together, running over, will be put into your lap. For the measure you give will be the measure you get back" (6:37f.).

With four attributes, Luke emphasizes the measure that the giver will receive. This measure is not the judicial one, but the measure for restoring what has been given (cf. the relationship between δόδοτε, δοθήσεται, and δίδωσιν).

There can therefore be no doubt that in the Lukan congregations love of enemies and money problems belong closely together. Ecclus. 29:6 had already said earlier that the debtor becomes an enemy (ἐχθρός) and pays back in curses and abuse. Ecclus. 4:3 talks about the anger of people who are refused a gift. Unlike Matthew, therefore, Luke is not thinking of "the nation's enemy." But what we meet here as "private" hostility is ultimately the outcome of socioeconomic differences. As we know, Luke was somewhat sensitive to tensions caused by differences of this kind. That comes out in his accounts of the quarrel between Hellenists and Hebrews (Acts 6:1-6) and the disturbances in Ephesus (Acts 19:23ff.). In both cases, tensions in the Christian congregations themselves were involved, as well as tensions between Christians and non-Christians.[48]

---

lend to you, what thanks will you have?" If Luke does not bring this formulation (which suggests itself from the context), it will surely be because he is not thinking of mutual lending. For a different view, see I. Howard Marshall, *The Gospel of Luke: A commentary on the Greek text*, New International Greek Testament Commentary (Exeter: Paternoster Press, 1978), 257–67, esp. 263.

47. The change in this passage goes back to Luke. Thus rightly W. Stegemann, *Jesus*, German ed., 148. H. Schürmann takes a different view (*Lukasevangelium*, 363). He believes that Matthew was stressing a single, coherent idea, putting the theme of judgment at the center and leaving everything else out.

48. W. Stegemann (*Jesus*, German ed., 148) limits this to relationships within the congregation: "Luke therefore relates the demand to love one's enemies to the charitable

Now, Luke is not the only person to link the problem of giving money firmly with the commandments about loving our enemies. We find a similar link in the *Didache*.[49] But here the stress is different. If somebody snatches something away, one should not ask for it back. After all, one has no power to enforce the demand anyway (1.4). This does not precisely suggest that the people concerned were prosperous and influential. In the case of the requirement to give to everyone who asks, without asking for anything back, the main stress is on an emphatic "woe" to the people who take without real need — that is, the impostors or sham beggars. Since there is no way of asking alms back from these people, they are threatened all the more emphatically with the eschatological judgment, when everything will have to be given back, down to the last penny (1.5). Overflowing openhandedness is therefore required; yet the final demand actually turns this upside down (1.5) "Let your alms sweat in your hand until you know to whom you are giving" (1.6). Luke is different. He is appealing to congregations in which people lend money. His problem is not alms given to beggars but credit granted to someone poorer than oneself (the heading "lend" is missing in the *Didache*). Luke is presupposing people who lend and are able to lend, and who should forgo asking for a return.[50]

Here then we see an appeal to motives belonging to Hellenistic reciprocity ethics and an appeal to money-giving and money-lending Christians; and these themes can well be combined. The Lukan congregations represent a Christianity which has made its way into the upper classes too, and which can therefore face the world around with the claim

---

behavior of Christians among themselves." But Luke explicitly stresses that one should give to everyone (6:30). This includes non-Christians too. He also thinks of an attack by robbers (6:29). This is hardly conceivable among Christians. Luke formulates the commandment in entirely general terms. But this does not exclude the possibility that quite concrete social relationships are in the background. To this degree I believe that W. Stegemann's sociological interpretation is correct: Luke is appealing to prosperous Christians to provide for a social adjustment in their congregations. This problem may well have concerned Luke. But as far as his explicit intention is concerned, he is formulating quite general commandments.

49. See J. P. Audet, *La Didachè: Instructions des Apôtres* (Paris, 1958), 268ff.

50. Whether it is permissible to offer a sociological explanation for the change of addressees in the Sermon on the Plain (6:20ff. is addressed to the disciples, 6:27ff. to all listeners) may remain a matter of dispute (see W. Stegemann's interpretation, *Jesus*, German ed., 91ff., 102, 144). There is in fact a much simpler explanation. The Beatitudes are addressed to the disciples (Luke 6:20-23), but the "woe" admonitions to the rich and satisfied (6:24-26). Afterwards Luke turns to the disciples once more. The rich and satisfied are after all hardly the proper addressees for talk about loving enemies. But in this case there would be no need to assume a change of addressee between 6:20ff. and 6:27ff. On the contrary, after a change of addressee in vv. 24ff., Luke turns once more to the original addressees.

of a fundamental equality. This self-confidence is the mark of all Luke's writings. We need only point to one feature: the prologue shows that this is a work claiming literary merit which is prepared to compete with other writings. It therefore takes over general literary conventions. It is dedicated at the same time to a certain "most excellent Theophilus," who was probably a member of the upper classes.[51] So in Luke the social situation is quite different from the one reflected in Matthew. In Luke we find nothing more about the problems of a subjugated people. Here a greater social symmetry in the relationship between Christians and their environment corresponds to the symmetrical element in the motives suggested for loving one's enemies.

C. *The Transmitters of the Sayings Tradition*

Luke and Matthew are reproducing a common tradition, probably a written source, even though it is impossible to see all the divergences between Luke and Matthew as editorial changes. It is more plausible to assume that variants in the tradition also played a part.[52] For that very reason, we may view the logia, or sayings, tradition shared by Matthew and Luke as a coherent tradition stratum which had its original home in Palestine before the Jewish War. For one thing, the Semitic background is still evident in the language (so that a localization in Palestine is probable). For another, the destruction of the Temple is not yet presupposed (so that a date before 70 C.E. is possible).[53] If we wish to discover where this tradition really belongs socially—its *Sitz im*

---

51. Luke points out with a certain pride that the church had upper-class members as well—in addition to Theophilus, we may think of Joanna, the wife of Chuza, who was one of the stewards of Herod Antipas (Luke 8:3), Menahem (Manaen), his friend (Acts 13:1), the centurian Cornelius (Acts 10:1ff.), Dionysius, an assistant judge in Athens (Acts 17:34), and so on. See M. Hengel, *Eigentum und Reichtum in der frühen Kirche* (Stuttgart, 1973), 69 (Eng. trans. *Property and Riches in the Early Church,* trans. J. Bowden [London: SCM Press; Philadelphia: Fortress Press, 1974]).

52. It is impossible to enter here into the dispute about Q. The strongest argument in its favor is still the sequence of sayings in Matthew and Luke. But it is a puzzle to me how anyone proposes to explain the deviations between Matthew and Luke without the influence of independent variants in the tradition (just as Tim Schramm [*Der Markus-Stoff bei Lukas* (Cambridge: Cambridge University Press, 1971)] has made the influence of tradition variants on the Lukan redactional work seem probable). I find it even more puzzling how anyone can profess to distinguish between tradition and redaction in Q, which can only be extremely hypothetically reconstructed.

53. The Temple saying (Luke 13:34f./Matt. 23:37f.) presupposes that the Temple is not yet destroyed. Here the threat is only that it will be forsaken. But it is impossible to say more than that about the date of Q. It is a puzzle to me how some people purport to know that it can be dated about 50 C.E.

Leben—three deductive methods are open to us, one analytical, one constructive, and one comparative.

1. The analytical method of deduction draws from the texts indications about a probable *Sitz im Leben* which is earlier than the Matthean and Lukan congregations in which the texts were used. At the present moment we cannot advance beyond presumptions and probabilities here. But Luke 6:29 does point to a quite particular context: "To him who strikes you on the cheek, offer the other also; and from him who takes away your coat do not withhold even your shirt." Here, as we know, Luke is thinking of a holdup: the thieves seize the victim's coat first, and then reach out for his shirt. (Matthew is thinking of a court trial, and he reverses the order.) But an attack of this kind generally took place on the open highway. That is to say, Luke was thinking about the situation of wayfarers and travelers. In doing so he was probably reproducing the saying in its traditional sense, for his own real concern was a different problem—the problem of lending money.

In Matthew, we might ask whether the admonition "If any one forces you to go one mile, go with him two miles" is not especially understandable on the lips of itinerant Christians. For here there is no mention of the animals that people needed for their work. These animals played an important part when services were enforced by the authorities,[54] but itinerant missionaries would hardly have been expected to own any. All the same, the admonition has a point even for Christians who were settled in one place.

We should also note the parable of the sun. It inevitably reminds us of another nature parable in the Jesus tradition—the lilies of the field (Matt. 6:25-34). In both cases, nature is made the model for human behavior, and in both cases what was originally a pessimistic image is remolded. The fact that the sun shines in just the same way on good and bad would rather be a cause for resignation over the ethical irrationality of a world in which good and bad often receive the same treatment.[55] Similarly, animals' freedom from anxiety would seem to be a reason for pessimistic reflections about human beings, who have to earn their bread laboriously.[56] In the Jesus tradition, both of these originally

---

54. See Epictetus *Dis.* 4.1.79. See Fiebig, "Jesu Worte über die Feindesliebe," 52: "'ἀγγαρεία is the equivalent of death': that was a common assertion among the Jews, where it was related to requisitioned animals, which the Romans naturally did not spare."

55. See Hoffmann, *Jesus,* 154. The preacher Solomon especially ponders over all the senseless things that take place under the sun (Eccles. 1:13; 2:11, 18, 22, etc.).

56. See the rabbinic parallels to Matt. 6:25ff. in H. L. Strack and P. Billerbeck, *Kommentar zum Neuen Testament aus Talmud und Midrasch,* I (Munich, 1922), 435f.: "Rabbi Simeon ben Eleazar (ca. 190) said: Have you ever in your life seen a wild animal or a bird who

pessimistic images are turned into something positive. Men and women who follow Jesus can be as carefree as the birds and the lilies, who neither sow nor reap nor gather into barns, do not work and do not spin (Matt. 6:26, 28). There is no talk here about people working—and very certainly nothing about people looking for work.[57] On the contrary, one of the privileges of discipleship seems to be not to have to work, because disciples are sustained by God; for the search for the kingdom of God is more important than work. So the people who are the subject of this passage are early Christian wandering charismatics. Since the parable of the sun is a reshaping of what is really a pessimistic tradition—a reshaping comparable to what we find in the images of the lilies and birds—this would seem to suggest that the command to love our enemies (which is linked with the parable of the sun) belongs to the same historical context as Matt. 5:25ff. and had its real-life situation among the itinerant charismatics, who had no home and did not work.

2. The analytical method of deduction offers us no more than a presumption. This presumption can be transformed into a justifiable theory by way of a constructive deduction. For in the tradition that preceded Matthew and Luke, the commandment to love our enemies was closely linked with the final beatitude: "Blessed are you when men revile you and persecute you and utter all kinds of evil against you falsely on my account. Rejoice and be glad, for your reward is great in heaven, for so men persecuted the prophets who were before you" (Matt. 5:11f.).

Matthew says that the people who are persecuted are blessed. In Luke it is the people who are hated. In each case, the commandment about loving enemies is formulated correspondingly: Matthew talks about the people "who persecute you" (διώκειν, Matt. 5:12, 44), Luke about the people "who hate you" (μισεῖν, Luke 6:22, 27). The *Gospel of Thomas* unites the two variants "Blessed are you when they hate you and persecute you" (logion 69). This agreement in the key headings[58]—in Matthew

---

pursued a trade? And yet they are fed without any tormenting anxiety; and are they not created solely in order to serve me? And I was created for the service of my Creator. Must I not then be fed without tormenting anxiety? It is only because I have marred what I do that I have interfered with my sustenance" (*Kid[dushin]* 4, 14). A parallel tradition (*pKid.* 4, 66b, 38) puts it even more clearly: "And who made me earn my bread in sorrow? Answer: my sins. Because I have marred what I do, I have interfered with my sustenance."

57. L. Schottroff takes a different view (*Jesus,* German ed., 56f.). She interprets Matt. 6:26ff. with the help of the parable of the laborers in the vineyard in Matt. 20:1ff. But one can hardly find anything about looking for work in Matt. 6:25ff.

58. See Lührmann, "Liebet eure Feinde," 415. Even someone who rejects a written logia source (Q) can interpret this link between key words as sign of a link in tradition; for it is these very key-word links that have been used as an argument against the existence

throughout a long section — shows that there was a direct link here in oral or written tradition: loving enemies was something for people who were persecuted and hated. But who were these people? Who are the persecuted Christian prophets about whom Matthew in particular talks so plainly?[59] Christians in general can hardly be meant here, because the reference to the prophets would then be almost pointless.[60] If we now gather together everything that is said in Matthew about Christian prophets and everything said there under the heading "persecute," one thing becomes evident: in every case the people in question are wandering charismatics without any settled home:

> He who receives a prophet because he is a prophet shall receive a prophet's reward. (Matt. 10:41)

Here there is no doubt that the passage is talking about itinerant prophets, who are to be given shelter and food. Prophets of this kind have, of course, left house and home:

> A prophet is not without honor except in his own country and in his own house. (Matt. 13:57)

> Behold, I send you prophets and wise men and scribes [Luke 11:49: prophets and apostles], some of whom you will kill and crucify, and some you will scourge in your synagogues and persecute from town to town (διώξετε). (Matt. 23:34)

Luke also uses the key word "persecute" here, although he does not interpret it to mean being driven from town to town. In Matthew, the passage is once again talking about itinerant prophets who are forced to move from place to place because of persecution. The same situation underlies Matt. 10:23, although in this passage the term "prophet" is not used:

---

of a logia source; see J. Jeremias, "Zur Hypothese einer schriflichen Logienquelle Q," in *Abba: Studien zur neutestamentlichen Theologie und Zeitgeschichte* (Göttingen, 1966), 90–92 (selections from this vol. trans. J. Bowden, C. Burchard and J. Reumann as *The Prayers of Jesus* [Naperville, Ill.: Allenson; London: SCM Press, 1967]).

59. For a comparison of the two versions, see Steck, *Israel*, 20–26, 257–60; Dupont, *Béatitudes*, 1:227–50.

60. Steck argues rightly in my view when he writes: "But why this reminder of the corresponding prophetic fate at all? If this is simply the fate of the righteous — the community or congregation — it is incomprehensible; for as far as the righteous are concerned . . . verses 22-23b are a completely sufficient statement to which nothing can be added, theologically. But if we go back to the tradition of ideas which underlies the Deuteronomistic utterances about the prophets, the answer is simple: the final beatitude is parenesis not simply for suffering Christians as such, but because they are acting as preachers in Israel and experience abusive and slanderous rejection by Jews in what they do for their own people" (*Israel*, 259).

When they persecute you in one town, flee to the next; for truly, I say to you, you will not have gone through all the towns of Israel, before the Son of man comes. (Matt. 10:23)

If we add the beatitude in Matt. 5:10, we have then listed all the passages that talk about Christian prophets or about persecution. The assumption everywhere (except in Matt. 5:10-12) is that Christian prophets will be leading itinerant lives. We may therefore postulate that this is the assumption behind Matt. 5:10-12 too, whereas the Lukan parallel, 6:22f., may perhaps be more closely related to Christians living a settled existence. Now, we might object that this social situation, this *Sitz im Leben*, is particularly clear in Matthew—that is to say, in the form Matthew gives to the final beatitude (Matt. 5:11f.) and in the special Matthean tradition (Matt. 10:41; 10:23). But there are sufficient pointers to wandering charismatics in Luke too. Indeed, supporters of the theory that wandering charismatics were the most important transmitters of the tradition have been actually reproached with basing their theory mainly on passages in Luke.[61] But this reproach is without foundation. The rules for early Christian wandering charismatics are passed down to us in the missionary charge, which can be found in both Q and Mark (6:7ff.), is at least to some degree presupposed in 1 Corinthians 9, and appears to some extent in the *Gospel of Thomas* too—with a clear reference to itinerant Christians: "And if you go into any country and wander about there and people receive you, eat what is put before you. Heal the sick among them" (logion 14).

Wandering charismatics were a widespread phenomenon, in different variations.[62] The phenomenon is not restricted to Q, nor is it an ideal

---

61. Thus W. Stegemann, *Jesus*, German ed., 106. Also his important essay on itinerant radicalism in early Christianity, "Wanderradikalismus im Urchristentum: Historische und theologische Auseinandersetzung mit einer interessanten These," in *Der Gott der kleinen Leute, Sozialgeschichtliche Auslegungen*, II: *Neues Testament*, ed. W. Schottroff and W. Stegemann (Munich and Gelnhausen, 1979), 94–120 (Eng. trans. *God of the Lowly*, trans. M. J. O'Connell [Maryknoll, N.Y.: Orbis Books, 1984]). In this criticism of the theory about itinerant radicalism, the phenomenon itself is not disputed, but it is restricted to the Q stratum and is explained in much more strongly economic terms.

62. Everything suggests that the early Christian wandering charismatics came from the Syro-Palestinian area. This movement was the social background of Q, which must probably be located in Palestine. Clear indications in Q are Matt. 10:5ff.; 8:18-22; 6:25ff.; 10:37ff. (with Lukan parallels in each case). The Gospel of Matthew talks about wandering charismatics in special traditions (Matt. 10:40-41; 10:23), and therefore probably also assumes that this is a living phenomenon. This is E. Schweizer's view in *Matthäus und seine Gemeinde*, SBS 71 (Stuttgart, 1974), 142ff. In the *Didache* we again come across the movement, where it is quite clearly presented as a contemporary phenomenon (*Did.* 10.7; 11.4ff.). Now Q, Matthew, and the *Didache* are not linked solely through a network of traditions. They probably all belong to the Palestinian or Syrian area. Here, accordingly,

Lukan picture, which has to be given a literary interpretation. All that
we are still able to discover about the original social location of love
of enemies—its location, that is, before it was given a fixed written form
in Matthew and Luke—points to an itinerant charismatic movement:
persecuted early Christian prophets, who often had to escape their
enemies by moving from place to place. It was these prophets who talked
about loving enemies!

3. A comparative deduction enforces our findings. The closest analogy
to the command to love enemies and to renounce violence can be found
in what Epictetus says about the Cynic's life (*Dis.* 3.22). He is talking to
a young man who expresses an interest in this way of life, and he warns
him about the difficulties involved, describing (in idealized terms) the
extreme demands made by a life of this kind:[63]

> Think the matter over more carefully, know yourself, ask the Deity and do
> not make the attempt without God. For if he advises you to take up this life,
> be sure that he either wishes for you to be great, or for you to receive many

---

a certain continuity can be shown, down to the pseudo-Clementine letters (see G.
Kretschmar, "Ein Beitrag zur Frage nach dem Ursprung frühchristlicher Askese," *ZThK*
61 [1964], 27–67).

Mark and Luke must perhaps be judged somewhat differently—that is, the two Gospels
which possibly show a greater distance from the Syro-Palestinian area. Luke dissociates
himself in 22:35ff. for the period after Jesus from certain radically ascetic commandments of the itinerant charismatics and condemns their proclamation of the kingdom
of God as imminent in this era (Luke 10:9), describing it as the heresy of prophets who
come forward in Jesus' name and whom the faithful should not follow (Luke 21:8). That
is to say, the special Lukan traditions or redactional changes betray a critical detachment from the still existing phenomenon, or variant of that phenomenon. But otherwise Luke continues its traditions of social criticism by painting an idealized picture
of the past. Clear pointers to the itinerant charismatic movement can also be found
in the Gospel of Mark: 1:16ff.; 2:14; 3:13ff; 6:7-13; 9:41; 10:28-30. The traditions of the
wandering radicals were therefore widespread; and this being so, it is hardly possible
to assess these traditions as belonging exclusively to redaction history, even though the
individual evangelists may have added their own particular stresses. To limit the
phenomenon to Q does not accord with the wide dissemination of the sayings. Criticism
of the itinerant radicalism theory made by L. Schottroff and W. Stegemann (*Jesus,* German
ed., 54ff., 106 and frequently elsewhere) hardly takes sufficient account of the development of the historical Jesus by way of Q to Matthew and the *Didache,* and fails to recognize
that Luke does not merely develop an idealized picture of the early Christian wandering charismatics but also criticizes them.

63. See also the idealized description in Themistios *Peri aretes* ["On Virtue"], chap.
22. "But they go about confidently and cheerfully, enjoying the good things for which
their own hands have done nothing. For there the sound of one coin striking another
is never heard, and no glint of gold is seen in their baggage, and only these wanderers
are not tormented by the fear of robbers, nor do changing circumstances and violence
descend to them from castles. And if they do so descend, then they return shamed, because
they have attacked men whom nothing defeats." This is considered to be the way taken
by Antisthenes, Diogenes, and Crates (chap. 21).

blows. For that too is a very fine trait which is woven into the Cynic's life: he has to allow himself to be kicked like a dog, and while he is being kicked he must go on loving those who kick him, like a father of them all, like a brother. (*Dis.* 3.22. 53–54)

Epictetus requires the Cynic to lay aside all anger (3.22.13) and to be rocklike in the face of insults: "No one reviles him, no one strikes him, no one ill-treats him. He has put his body at everyone's disposal, so that anyone may use it as he wishes" (3.22.100). The analogies with ideas found in the Jesus movement are obvious, and so is the comparable social background. Epictetus is undoubtedly talking about a real itinerant existence (3.22.45ff.). He warns his discussion partner against exploiting his hosts: "But you seem to want to visit someone's house for a while, simply in order to eat your fill" (3.22.66). Here a piece of prosaic reality shows through Epictetus's idealizing descriptions (cf. the warning against early Christian wandering charismatics in *Did.* 11.3ff.). He also makes it clear that the itinerant Cynic philosopher must do without a family (3.22.67). But he has a new family instead, since all human beings are now his family (cf. Mark 3:34f.; 10:30[64]):

---

64. W. Stegemann has put forward an alternative interpretation of Mark 10:28-30 in *Gott der kleinen Leute* (Eng. trans. *God of the Lowly*). He thinks of a change of religion in the place where one is settled, not of the change from a settled way of life to an itinerant existence. He points here to Philo *De specialibus legibus* 1.52, with the admonition to receive the proselytes particularly kindly: "Since they . . . have left country and friends and relatives for the sake of virtue and piety, they should not be denied new towns and housemates and friends." Tacitus considers ideas of this kind to be an offense against obligations toward the gods, country, and family (*Hist.* 5.5). Now, Philo is also familiar with a real, practical abandonment of house and home: in describing the disturbances under Caius, he tells how protesting men and women left their villages (*Ad Gaium* 225), declaring: "We are leaving our towns, abandoning our houses and land, our possessions, money and everything we cherish. And everything else we have will we voluntarily contribute. We believe that we do not give but receive" (*Ad Gaium* 232). They also declare that they are prepared to sacrifice their wives, brothers, sisters, sons, and daughters (*Ad Gaium* 234). All this is meant quite literally. But in Mark 10:28f. the literal interpretation is also the obvious one. For in the Markan context it is undoubtedly an itinerant group that is under discussion. The same is true of the pre-Markan tradition, since it is hardly possible to detach Peter's question: "Lo, we have left everything and followed you" (v. 28) from the pericope (see the remote parallel John 6:66ff.). The leaving is meant literally and, according to everything we know, corresponds to the historical reality.

The second part of the saying must then be interpreted in a transferred sense, inasmuch as the brothers, sisters, mothers, and fathers who are restored a hundredfold obviously cannot be literally and physically members of the family. This is simply "the family of God." The supposition that the Christian congregations are meant here, or groups sympathizing with the Jesus movement, is just as plausible as the assumption that the people who moved from place to place and from congregation to congregation would more readily enjoy the benefit of "a hundredfold" restoration of what has been abandoned than the people who remained in a single place. If we add to this that the itinerant Cynic

Good man, [the Cynic] has made all human beings his children. The men are his sons and the women his daughters. He approaches everyone he meets in this way, and this is the way he cares for everyone. Or do you think that it is for petty reasons that he scolds the people he meets? He does so as a father, as a brother and as a servant of Zeus, the Father of us all. (3.22.81–82)[65]

The way these itinerant Cynic philosophers live cannot be separated from their message. They are sent by God to teach other people about good and evil (3.22, 23). They do this not least by showing through their own example what true liberty and independence are (3.22.45ff.). And in this very way they participate in the sovereignty of God (3.22.95: ὡς μετέχων τῆς ἀρχῆς τοῦ Διός). Something similar can be said about the early Christian wandering charismatics. The very way they live is a sign of liberty. Here message and life-style are inseparable.[66]

If — by way of the three deductive methods we have followed — we assign the commandment to love enemies and renounce violence to the early Christian wandering charismatics, we find that one puzzle has been solved: the curious fact that in the patristic church we meet these commandments preeminently in the apologetic writings[67] (if we except the *Didache*, which is still completely under the influence of wandering charismatics). Indeed it is in these apologetic writings that we have to look for the literary *Sitz im Leben* of these commandments. As W. Bauer has shown,[67] writings meant for use in the congregations treat these

---

philosopher also viewed his listeners as his family, as substitute for the family he had forsaken (Epictetus *Dis.* 3.22.81f.), then there is nothing against relating Mark 10:28f. to wandering charismatics too (similarly R. Pesch, *Das Markusevangelium*, HThK II/2 [Freiburg, 1977], 2:145), even though readers of the Gospel in the congregations probably thought that they themselves were meant.

65. The passage of course also throws light on important differences between early Christian itinerant charismatics and Cynic itinerant philosophers: the criticism of anyone who compromises, indeed the contempt in which he was held, was apparently typical of these wandering philosophers; see Epictetus *Dis.* 3.22.10, where the prosaic reality is clearly evident. It is also significant that the itinerant philosopher ascribes to himself the superior role of father. In the Jesus tradition, in contrast, we read: "Call no man your father on earth" (Matt. 23:9).

66. Itinerant charismatics and local congregations enjoyed a complementary relationship. Luise Schottroff ascribes to me the view that "the non-itinerant majority of the population" was unable to make anything of the ethic of the itinerant charismatics (*Jesus*, German ed., 67). But I have never put forward this view where Palestinian conditions are concerned — not even in the passages in my essays to which L. Schottroff refers. There seems to be a misunderstanding at this point.

67. Justin *Apol.* 1.15.9–13; 1.16.1–2; *Dial.* 35, 85, 96; Aristides 15.5, cf. 17.3; Athenagoras *Legatio pro Christianis* 11.1; 12.3; Theophilus *Ad Autolycus* 3.14; Diognetus 5.11; 5.15; 6.6; Tertullian *Apologeticus* 13.37. See W. Bauer, "Das Gebot der Feindesliebe," esp. 242. There he suspects that "its usefulness for the defense of the new religion may already have won for love of enemies its relatively important place in the Lukan writings." But in the Gospels the development into an apologetic *topos* is heralded only hesitantly.

commandments with considerably more reserve. Indeed certain utterances show that they really went against the grain. Outwardly, people no doubt plumed themselves on the commandment about loving enemies, since this counteracted the reproach of misanthropy. But when the commandment was applied to internal conditions in the congregations themselves, judgments could be highly critical, as we see from *2 Clem.* 13.4. That is to say, the commandment was alive and active in the early period, among the wandering charismatics, but in the local congregations it then acquired a new *Sitz im Leben,* which was much more literary. It now had an apologetic function and was used to counter anti-Christian prejudices. This change of function may already begin in the Gospels, when the Gospel of Matthew tries to dissociate itself from Old Testament retaliation thinking and hate of enemies (and hence also from Judaism — denigrated by the popular view). Or when Luke words the commandment in such a way that it is formally in line with Hellenistic reciprocity ethics.

But the original real-life situation, or *Sitz im Leben,* is of great importance for the way love of enemies and nonviolence is evaluated. The Christian who was settled in one place became increasingly dependent if he gave in to his enemy, for he had to expect that their paths would cross again and again. In this situation, giving way often means inviting cheating and slights to continue. Nonresistance increases the likelihood that attacks will be repeated. And yet the person in this situation too is faced with the great demand that he love his enemy. This requirement could be much more convincingly met by the wandering charismatic. He was really free. He could leave the place where he had been defeated and humiliated. He need never expect to meet his opponent again. By moving on, he was able to preserve his independence and liberty. The price for that liberty was rigorous asceticism — a life barely at subsistence level. But the gain was great. The wandering charismatic also acted vicariously for his friends in the local congregations, practicing on their behalf that love of enemies which links human beings with the love of God.

D. *The Historical Genesis*

To have found a real-life situation for a tradition does not tell us anything about the origins of that tradition. It tells us only about the function it exercised. We have to distinguish between these two things. The probability that a tradition does not derive from Jesus grows, the greater the difference between what can be shown to be the real-life situation and Jesus' proclamation. If this difference cannot be established—if indeed the discovered real-life situation can be explained only if we can ultimately trace it back to Jesus himself—then nothing forbids us to ascribe authenticity to a tradition. And that is the case here. The life of early Christian wandering charismatics in no way contradicts Jesus' ministry, but was based on his call to discipleship and was prototypically embodied in his own wandering life. And there is no reason for questioning Jesus' call to discipleship.[68] This call was probably linked from the outset with participation in Jesus' own mission by the people who were called. It is only this which justifies the abrupt break with the family that is demanded, contrary to the most elementary ethical principles (Matt. 8:22)—that is to say, only if the person called was entrusted with a task that was more important than anything else in the world.[69] So through his call to discipleship Jesus founded the early Christian itinerant charismatic life. If love of enemies and nonviolence breathe the spirit of this wandering charismatic life, then this is ultimately the spirit of Jesus.[70]

But we can push the question further. Love of enemies and nonviolence (the latter especially) fit excellently into the contemporary situation in which Jesus lived. Where nonviolence is concerned, we can find two datable analogies, the first from 26/27 c.e., the other from 39 c.e. And Jesus' public ministry falls between these two dates. The two analogies show that the ideal of nonviolence was at least in the air—and at that time especially. For soon the tensions between Romans and Jews, the resistance movement and the aristocracy, became accentuated, and increasingly fostered a readiness for war and violence. But let us look at the analogies.

When in 26 c.e. Pilate took up his new post as prefect, or governor, of Judea, he soon found himself confronted with a problem that was typical of his new environment, a problem that he had evidently grossly underestimated. For he secretly attempted to introduce images of the emperor into Jerusalem.[71] These images counted as images of false gods,

---

68. M. Hengel shows that the idea of discipleship cannot be derived either from Judaism (the rabbinic teacher–pupil relationship especially is quite differently structured) or from early Christianity: it is impossible to "follow" the Exalted One in the literal sense ("Nachfolge und Charisma," BZNW 34 [Berlin, 1968]).

69. Ibid., 82ff.

70. Where the question about historical authenticity is concerned, D. Lührmann's comments are worth consideration ("Liebet eure Feinde," 427–36).

71. See the accounts in Josephus *Ant.* 18.55–59; *J.W.* 2.169–74, with the comments by E. Schürer, *Geschichte des jüdischen Volkes im Zeitalter Jesu Christi*, I (5th ed.; Leipzig, 1920), 489 (Eng. trans. *The History of the Jewish People in the Age of Jesus Christ*, rev. and ed. by

quite apart from the fact that images were in any case forbidden. The population of Jerusalem was up in arms: this was surely a deliberate provocation, intended to show from the outset who was the stronger! At that time Pilate was in his palace in Caesarea. Josephus now tells that the Jews poured into Caesarea, surrounded Pilate's palace, and knelt outside for five days and nights without intermission, without moving. After five days Pilate had them brought into an arena, where he sat himself down on a judgment seat. Everyone now expected him to decide the disputed question. Instead of that, he had the demonstrating Jews surrounded by soldiers, three ranks deep, and tried to put them under pressure. But they still refused to tolerate images of the emperor. Pilate went further. He threatened to put them to death, and ordered his soldiers to draw their swords:

> But the Jews threw themselves down on the ground (as they had previously agreed to do), stretched out their necks to the swords, and cried that they would die rather than disobey the laws given them by their fathers. Profoundly astonished by the fervor of their piety, Pilate ordered that the standards should at once be removed from Jerusalem. (Josephus *J.W.* 2.174)

The Jews' nonviolent resistance was successful. Even the powerful Romans showed that they were vulnerable. That must have made a tremendous impression on contemporaries, and it was at that very time (or shortly afterwards) that Jesus began his public ministry and taught: "Voluntarily offer your enemy your cheek when he strikes you!" How would people at that time have interpreted this saying? It must surely have been taken to mean that this formulated the principle of behavior also underlying the demonstration against Pilate: in a paradoxical antithesis to customary ways of reacting, a vulnerable point is offered, in the hope that one's opponent will come to his senses.[72] But what

---

G. Vermes et al. [Edinburgh: T. & T. Clark, 1973–87]); M. Stern in S. Safrai and M. Stern, *The Jewish People in the First Century*, I (Assen, 1974), 351.

72. The hope that the other person may come to his senses is not directly expressed in the Jesus tradition, but it is no doubt implied by the composition: in Luke through the appended golden rule. But the way the words are put together in the logia tradition already shows that there was no thought here of a simple giving in. The requirement to give (Matt. 5:42) has often been set aside as a saying that does not fit the context, because it talks about giving to another person, not about the renunciation of resistance. But if the Jesus movement always understood the sayings about nonviolence to mean that the other person was thereby to be changed, the logical breach between Matt. 5:40-41 and 42 diminishes: for to give something to another person means that his existence is altered in some way or other. The buildup of the sayings would therefore have a certain point, if nonviolence also aims at changing something in the other person. (John 8:1ff. incidentally offers an illustration, where Jesus tells the onlookers to stone the defenseless adulteress, and where, for that very reason, they all come to their senses.)

happened there, in the framework of a political-religious conflict, is formulated by Jesus in quite general terms, so that the rules of conduct he gives can certainly include conflicts of this kind, but apply beyond them. It is certainly far from my intention to maintain that Jesus was influenced by the events in Caesarea I have described. That is no doubt within the bounds of possibility, but it cannot be proved. What can surely be maintained, however, is that Jesus' contemporaries were not bound to reject as ridiculous from the outset the notion that the enemy could be "disarmed" by demonstrative nonresistance. This behavior strategy was successful. But successful behavior is apt to be imitated. It often determines our mental climate in highly indirect ways. It influences the opinion of men and women about what is pointless and what is not. It has later repercussions.

Later events under Gaius Caligula show the truth of this. Caligula had the lunatic plan of setting up his statue in the Temple in Jerusalem. Again this meant that the Romans would be contravening a religious commandment. Once again the Jews put their once-tried conflict strategy into effect. The Syrian governor Petronius was entrusted with setting up the statue. But he hesitated. Again the people streamed to the governor. And again the governor threatened to use force. Petronius asked the Jews:

> "Do you want to wage war against the emperor, without remembering his arms and your helplessness?" But they answered: "We do not wish to wage war at all, but we would rather die than act against the Law," and at these words they threw themselves on the ground, offered their necks to the sword, and declared that they were prepared to die at that very moment. So they went on for forty days, without planting the ground, although it was seed-time; and they adhered to their words and to the resolution to die rather than to see the statue erected. (Josephus *Ant.* 18.271f.; cf. *J.W.* 2.195–98)

Petronius was so impressed by the readiness of the Jews to sacrifice themselves that he finally formally requested that the command be withdrawn. Luckily Caligula was killed before the conflict could come to a head. All this happened in 39/40 C.E., about thirteen years after the events at the time of Pilate. We may assume that in these years the notion of nonviolent reistance was alive, and at this time particularly. It is surely not by chance that Tacitus writes about Palestine "sub Tiberio quies" ("Under Tiberius all was quiet," *Hist.* 5.9).[73] Although we know that

---

73. See rightly P. W. Barnett, "'Under Tiberius all was quiet,'" *NTS* 21 (1974–75): 564–71: "... by comparison with what happened later it was a quiet period, broken only by those incidents we have noted" (p. 571). But these incidents are unduly played down. Barnett identifies three disturbances under Pilate (p. 568): his "misappropriation" of the Temple

everything was *not* completely quiet, tensions must have been less at that time than beforehand or afterwards. We need only think of the rise of the resistance movement after the introduction of direct Roman administration in 6 C.E., and the growing tensions under Cumanus, after the death of Agrippa I (44 C.E.). If there was a favorable time at all to preach nonviolence in the Palestine of that time, stamped as it was by social and political tensions, then it was the time of Jesus.

If this historical setting for Jesus' words about nonviolence is correct, we shall have to modify our picture of Jesus in one respect. His preaching of nonviolence is often all too one-sidedly seen as being in contrast to his time.[74] This is certainly not wrong. Jesus' proclamation was an alternative to the Zealot resistance movement and to Essene fantasies about the great war of the future (1QM). But Jesus and his movement were not an isolated part of Judaism. There were other forces that worked for a nonviolent solution of conflicts. And we do not have to look for these forces merely among an aristocracy suspected of collaboration (during the events under Caligula one does not have the impression that the aristocracy was in full control of the demonstrating mob).[75] On the contrary, the forces who inclined toward compromise can no more be accused of collaboration with the Romans than Jesus, whom the Romans executed as a political criminal and whose peace-promoting views on nonviolence would hardly have made much impression on Pilate, even supposing that he was aware of them at all. Pilate had discovered personally that great power can emanate from nonviolence and that this power can be no less dangerous politically than violent resistance.

It is in Jesus above all that we find precisely the three patterns of behavior whose combination can endanger any power: (1) the courage for public criticism (and a corresponding echo); (2) preparedness for provocative acts through which the existing rules are discredited; and

---

treasure (Josephus *J.W.* 2.175–77; *Ant.* 18.60–62), the massacre of the Galileans (Luke 13:1f.), and the revolt in which Barabbas was involved (Mark 15:6-7). This is hardly possible. But in spite of these tensions there was hope that problems could be solved without the use of violence; otherwise the Jewish War would have already broken out in 39/40 C.E.

74. E.g., in M. Hengel, *Victory over Violence*, trans. D. E. Green (London: SPCK, 1975), 71–85, where Hengel quite rightly rejects the view that Jesus was a kind of crypto-Zealot.

75. There is some evidence to support the theory that the Jesus movement belonged to "the doves" (P. Hoffmann's view in *Studien zur Theologie der Logienquelle*, NTA NF 8 (Münster, 1972), 74–78, 332. But one must not, of course, restrict this "peace party" to the aristocracy or reckon with an organized, socially homogeneous "party" at all. All that is meant is that the Jesus movement was one of the forces that worked for peace rather than war—and was defeated. The condemnation of the Zealot murder of Zechariah (Matt. 23:35) definitely takes sides against the rebels and their militant core in Jerusalem. L. Schottroff (*Jesus*, German ed., 80f.) is critical of Hoffmann's thesis.

(3) demonstrative defenselessness. Jesus did not develop these behavioral elements into a systematic strategy for solving conflicts, any more than did his contemporaries, when they forced Pilate to withdraw a particular measure. But he did inspire a mode of conduct which neither gives way to the strong nor resorts to violence. And this makes clear the only way open to us, if we are convinced both about the urgency of social changes and about the necessity of preserving peace, inwardly and outwardly.

* * *

We can now sum up. Jesus formulated the commandment that we should love our enemies and renounce violence at a time when his demands could fall on fruitful ground, since nonviolent conflict strategies had proved effective against the Romans. But Jesus' demand goes far beyond every specific situation. It is general. It takes no account of effectiveness or noneffectiveness. It does not merely demand the renunciation of violence. It demands that the enemy be loved, without any reservation. Just because it was formulated generally and apodictically, it could continually be brought up to date. Jesus' disciples—roving, itinerant charismatics—were able to relate his commandment to their situation; the persecuted prophets were thus able to free themselves from hate for their persecutors. The congregations behind the Gospel of Matthew bring the commandment up to date in the period following the crushing of the Jewish revolt, in order—as people outwardly defeated—to meet the victors as inwardly sovereign. The Lukan congregations associate love of enemies with conflicts between the people who lend money and their debtors. In the second century, the commandment became the apologetic argument which was intended to assure a mistrustful public that the Christians were free of a sectarian misanthropy. The protean forms of the practical social contexts to which the commandment to love our enemies and to renounce violence belongs show that this commandment cannot be restricted to a particular sector. Economic, political, and religious enemies are all meant. Private and social tensions, persecutions of minorities, and the suppression of the majority of a nation all have to be seen in this light. In all situations the commandment to love enemies holds good. It is general.

But it is general in another sense too. It formulates in a uniquely clear and emphatic way what we continually find in germ in the ideas of the nations: the attempt to overcome retaliation and hate. Babylonian wisdom already admonishes: "Do not act wickedly toward your adversary. If someone does you wrong, repay him with good."[76] Egyptian

---

76. H. Gressmann, *Altorientalische Texte zum Alten Testament,* 2nd ed. (Berlin and Leipzig, 1926), 292, nos. 21 and 22.

wisdom sayings point in the same direction: "Practice no retaliation, so that God does not requite the injustice you have done" or: "A good man repays no wrong lest he too should be repaid."[77] A Chinese sage says "Repay rancor with virtue."[78] The Jewish proverbial wisdom of the Old Testament demands that the idea of retaliation be overcome: "If your enemy is hungry, give him bread to eat; if he is thirsty, give him water to drink" (Prov. 25:21).[79]

But the need to surmount the idea of retaliation is overmasteringly maintained in two places, and it is formulated as a principle: in Greek philosophy and in Jesus — on the threshold separating Judaism and Christianity.[80] Although even in Plato the positive demand that the adversary be loved is still missing, we find this in Epictetus (*Dis.* 3.22.54). In all cases a merely gradual surmounting of the notion of retaliation is replaced by an abolition of the idea in principle. Vengeance is not merely mitigated (either because it is impossible to calculate the results, or because an act appears in a new light if we take the reasons for it into account, or because one is oneself dependent on the renunciation of retribution). Retaliation is now apodictically excluded. It is better to suffer wrong than to commit it (cf. Plato *Crito* 49Aff.; *Gorgias* 474Bff.; *Politeia* 332Eff.). And this applies as unconditionally as the command to love our enemies and to renounce violence.

This parallelism is very important theologically. We should not object that the whole background is different in the two spheres. The differences between the Platonic, the Stoic, and the early Christian interpretation of reality are undoubtedly great, but they are no greater than the differences between the interpretative horizon of a modern Christian and that of early Christian convictions. Anyone who considers it basically legitimate to interpret early Christian concepts afresh in a modern context — and indeed that this is required of us — cannot from the outset reject as illegitimate a possible translation of early Christian ideas into Stoic conceptuality. Indeed, he will perhaps be able to adopt the Stoic

---

77. W. von Bissing, *Altägyptische Lebensweisheit* (Zurich, 1955), 116 = Pap. Insinger (*Das demotische Weisheitsbuch des Phibis*), chap. 23.

78. Lao Tsu, *Tao te ching,* chap. 63. Other translations have "Repay enmity with good deeds."

79. See Prov. 24:17; 24:29; Ecclus. 28:1-7; Pseudo-Phocyl:.ies 140–42.

80. The distinction made in the following passage between the gradual surmounting of the idea of retaliation and its surmounting in principle is taken from Dihle, *Die Goldene Regel,* 41ff.: "This fundamental conquest of the idea of retaliation was twice achieved in the geographical and historical area with which we are concerned, and in different ways: in Platonic philosophy, through the definition of the ontological character of good and evil, and in the New Testament, with the doctrine that the empirical human being is living under the special conditions of an eschatological existence" (p. 60).

idea of a profound relationship between all human beings as an enrichment of his own ethical and religious awareness.

But if it is an indisputable phenomenon that a religion of revelation and a religiously engaged philosophy arrive at similar conclusions, this should make us think. Does it not raise the question whether the two are not fundamentally dependent on one another? The contradiction between philosophical thinking and common modes of behavior, on the one hand, and the contradiction offered by revelation, on the other? It would seem that we are very well capable of the vision of surmounting vengeance by love of our enemies. But the more we are possessed by this vision, and the more we recognize it to be a binding obligation, the more we become entangled in difficulties from which there seems no way out. In measuring ourselves against this new standard, we should either have to despise ourselves or deny the standard — if it were not for the experience of grace.

PART II

---◆---

STUDIES ON PAULINE THEOLOGY AND THE SOCIAL REALITY OF THE FIRST CENTURY

5

Soteriological Symbolism in the Pauline Writings

◆

A Structuralist Contribution

S OTERIOLOGY is talk about redemption. It announces a turn
from disaster to salvation.[1] Paul proclaims this turning point in
images that he draws from day-to-day life, transferring them to
a process which is designed to refashion that life from the roots up.
From human life he takes images of liberation, justification and reconciliation, transformation, life, death, and union; and he carries these
images over to the event of salvation. We can therefore call his soteriology
symbolic. It is symbolic in a quite fundamental sense, for it resists any
kind of translation into nonmetaphorical language. Salvation is not
described except in transferred images, nor do these images fade into
concepts out of which all metaphorical content has been evacuated by
reflection and usage. We can therefore also call Paul's soteriology symbolic if we understand "symbol" to mean the outcome of a metaphorical
process in which whatever is metaphorical does not evaporate into
nothingness but remains present in intensified form.[2]

---

1. No distinction will be made here between salvation that is already realized and
future salvation. Eschatology is future soteriology, and the same soteriological images
can apply to what is present and to what is future.

2. What I am saying here is based on Paul Ricoeur's definition of the symbol; see his
De l'interprétation: Essai sur Freud (Paris, 1965), 25: "Il y a symbole lorsque le langage produit
des signes de degré composé où le sens, non content de désigner quelque chose, désigne
un autre sens qui ne saurait être atteint que dans et par sa visée" ("Symbols are present
when the language produces signs of complex degree in which the meaning, not content with signifying something, signifies another sense which cannot be arrived at except
in, and by means of, its aim"). (Eng. trans. *Freud and Philosophy: An Essay on Interpretation*,
trans. E. Savage [New Haven and London: Yale University Press, 1970].) Of course we

159

Here I should like to analyze this symbolism with the help of structuralist methods. By "structuralism"[3] I mean a method of approach based on four distinctions and relations: the relation between the signifier and what is signified (in the language of linguistics, the significans and the significatum); the relation between element and structure; the relation between syntagma and paradigm; and the relation between synchrony and diachrony.

The distinction between the signifying term and the thing signified is important for the choice of relevant Pauline texts. The texts that are significant for the subject we are considering are texts with a metaphorical structure of meaning, and that means texts where there is a complex relationship between significans (or signifying term) and significatum (what is signified). This complex relationship can be more closely defined in two respects. Religious symbolism is based on the fact that, on the one hand, what is a significatum in "normal" human speech can again, in its turn, become a significans: for example, the human judge meant in the parable (the first significatum) becomes transparent, and thus the significans or signifier for the divine judge (as a second significatum). On the other hand, the second significatum acts retroactively on the first, for the familiar figures of everyday life are often exaggerated to the point of improbability, so that they may be a transparent medium for a revelation of "the holy." The earthly model may perhaps be "One will hardly die for a righteous man — though perhaps for a good man one will dare even to die" (Rom. 5:7). Here the earthly model is already improbable in itself. But the improbability is intensified further if it is to become transparent for the saving event: Christ died even for his enemies. We continually discover these symbolic intensifications of earthly reality in religious symbolism, heightenings

---

have to realize that today the concept of symbol is often interpreted quite differently and can mean conventional signs which have a merely superficial relation to the thing to which they refer. In that case, what is here called symbolism would have to be described as metaphor. I have decided to use the term symbol for two reasons: (1) The present essay was suggested by Paul Ricoeur's *La symbolique du mal* (being the second part of *Finitude et culpabilité*, which is vol. 2 of *Philosophie de la volonté* [Paris, 1950–60]; Eng. trans. *The Symbolism of Evil*, trans. E. Buchanan [New York: Harper & Row, 1967]). I have also taken up Ricoeur's terminology. (2) The concept of symbol has a long tradition, especially in Germany. See *Allegorie und Symbol: Texte zu Theorie des dichterischen Bildes im 18. und frühen 19. Jahrhundert,* ed. B. A. Sörensen; Ars poetica, Texte 16 (Frankfurt, 1972). On the theory of metaphor, see H. Weinrich, "Semantik der kühnen Metapher," *Deutsche Vierteljahrschrift für Literaturwissenschaft und Geistesgeschichte* 37 (Vienna, 1963): 325–44; T. Gardner, "Zum Problem der Metapher," *Deutsche Vierteljahrschrift . . .* 44 (1970): 727–37.

3. From the considerable literature on structuralism in literary studies, I will here mention only H. Gallas's brief and informative article "Strukturalismus in der Literaturwissenschaft," in *Grundzüge der Literatur- und Sprachwissenschaft,* vol. 1, ed. H. L. Arnold and V. Sinemus, Deutscher Taschenbuch Verlag 4226 (Munich, 1973), 374–88. His definition is as follows: "The basic operation of the structural method is to replace the horizontal, syntagmatic chain (which in itself has no meaning) by a vertical, paradigmatic system" (p. 381).

in which the images taken from human life are to some degree "alienated" from themselves. In this sense there is something ambivalent about religious symbolism. On the one hand, it projects human life into the sphere of the holy. On the other hand, it gives human life a strange, alienated shape in the light of the holy.

The second step, methodologically, is to relate element and structure. We can extract from the Pauline texts recurring metaphorical units in which the whole turn from disaster to salvation is considered under a particular aspect. A distinct soteriological symbolism of this kind is composed of three elements: a description of the disastrous condition, a description of the turn to salvation, and a description of salvation itself. These elements have to be related to one another through a particular aspect. This relationship is clear enough in the descriptions of disaster and salvation, since these correspond to one another in the form of a negative and a positive. The relations to the images describing the redemptive turning point itself—that is, the Christ-event—are less explicit. The symbol of justification, for example, is closely linked with the image of the accursed death, while the transformation symbolism is linked with the Adam/Christ typology. We have first of all to describe these various symbolic meaning-units in themselves.

Our next task is to analyze their complex relationships to one another. For this we have to make two further methodological distinctions. We must first distinguish between relationships that are syntagmatic and relationships that are paradigmatic. In the sequence of the language, all the relations are syntagmatic. Here Paul often slips directly from one symbolism to another—for example, from the justification symbolism in Gal. 2:19 ("I through the law died to the law") by way of the symbolism of death and life ("I died that I might live to God. I have been crucified with Christ") to the symbolism of union and reconciliation ("It is no longer I who live, but Christ who lives in me; and the life I now live in the flesh I live by faith in the Son of God, who loved me and gave himself for me," Gal. 2:20). Apart from these links in the sequence of the text, there are other, less obvious connections cutting right across the texts that have come down to us, for liberation, justification, and reconciliation are substantially related. These symbols present redemption on the analogy of processes that take place between human beings, whereas the symbolism of transformation, death and life, and union draws on images that have to do with life as "organism." There is a protean wealth of relations of this kind, so that it can be said that whenever Paul talks about salvation, the whole gamut of soteriological symbols is implicit, whether this is syntagmatically brought out or not. We may compare a grammatical paradigm, which is always implicit in all its differentiated forms whenever any one of these forms is employed. So anyone who is watching for them, and reads between the lines, can find justification symbols everywhere; and anyone who is on the lookout for something different will everywhere find the symbolism of death and life. This means that the dispute whether Pauline soteriology should be interpreted juridically and ethically or physically and mystically can hardly be unequivocally settled—not even by distinguishing between tradition and its modifications.

This brings us to the final methodological distinction, which is the differentiation between synchrony and diachrony. The object of our investigation is the structure of the symbolic meaning-units in Pauline soteriology. That is to say, what we are considering is a relational web of simultaneously existing elements, where we have to characterize every element by way of its position in the network. What interests us here, therefore, is not so much the earlier history of the individual elements — for example, the important question whether the union symbolism is drawn from gnostic, mystery, or other traditions. In a structuralist investigation we can leave these questions on one side, for methodological reasons. After all, in taking over these elements Paul made them his own spiritual possession, whatever the sources from which they may have reached him. There is no evidence that he found the traditions he took over unimportant. And it is certainly a questionable proceeding to deduce the intention of what he said solely from the modifications to which he subjected traditions. To do this is to arrive at a picture of Paul in which the critic of Enthusiasm pushes out the Enthusiast, the preacher of the eschatological proviso represses the proclaimer of the eschaton, the ethicist dismisses the sacramentalist, and the refashioner of mythical ideas suppresses the artificer of a fascinating mythical world of significance. Arguments of this kind have led to an almost general consensus that the dispute between a juridical-ethical and a physical-mystical interpretation of Pauline soteriology can be settled by assigning what is physical and mystical mainly to tradition, and what is juridical and ethical to Paul himself. Here a structuralist approach could offer an alternative to the solution suggested by tradition history. For it is conceivable that the intention of Pauline soteriology can be found not in any single symbolism or any individual themes but in a network of all the symbols — that is, in the structure of a comprehensive field of soteriological meaning-units.

What we wish to investigate, therefore, is the field of soteriological symbols, which is differently elicited and realized in the individual texts. This field can be illuminated by way of four methodological distinctions: the distinctions between significans and significatum, between element and structure, between syntagma and paradigm, and between diachrony and synchrony. The field of soteriological images pegged out by these methodological procedures can accordingly also be defined as a network of synchronic and paradigmatic relationships linking all the metaphorical meaning-units in Pauline soteriology. We must first work out the meaning-units each for itself. We then have to investigate the relationships between them. Methodologically, the two stages belong together, for it is only the disclosure of a network of relationships between the units that permits us to distinguish clearly from one another the different elements in the imagery. Element and structure determine each other mutually.[4]

---

4. It is therefore necessary for methodological reasons to consider Paul's soteriology

1. SOCIOMORPHIC INTERACTION SYMBOLISM

The symbolism of New Testament soteriology is drawn largely from various patterns of social conditions. For example, God may appear as a king and the angelic host as the royal household. And if what this king himself does is incomprehensible, hopes are all the more pinned to his son. The son, it is hoped, will overcome all evil, subdue hostile rebels, and establish justice. In Paul, we find a sociomorphic[5] (or socioform) interaction symbolism of this kind in three different configurations; for redemption is presented as liberation, as pardon, and as reconciliation.

A. *Liberation Symbolism*

In this symbolism, images of social power are paramount. Salvation is liberation, iniquity means oppression. Satan, death, sin, and law are the enslaving powers. Satan counts as "the god of this aeon" (2 Cor. 4:4), and death as "the last enemy," who tyrannizes over human beings with his sting (1 Cor. 15:26, 56). Sin is a personal power (Rom. 5:21) who rewards its slaves with death (Rom. 6:23), tricks and destroys them (Rom. 7:7-12). In the same way the law is presented as a numinous force, one of those "elemental powers" in the world which the Galatians serve as idols (Gal. 4:3). Redemption from this subjugation to alien powers is won by a stronger power still. It comes about through a "change of government." This phrase is open to misunderstanding.[6] It suggests that here salvific power merely takes the place of a power that is hostile, the

---

as a whole. It is not possible to base the argument merely on examples. This means that for reasons of space I have dispensed almost entirely with a discussion of other viewpoints.

5. The term "sociomorphic" was coined by E. Topitsch in *Vom Ursprung und Ende der Metaphysik* (Vienna, 1958): 1–32. Topitsch distinguishes between biomorphic, sociomorphic, and technomorphic models. In order to take in inanimate nature as well, I have preferred to talk here about physiomorphic symbols instead of biomorphic ones.

6. The interpretation of Paul which E. Käsemann inaugurated and summed up in his commentary on Romans moves the symbolism of a change of government into the center of Pauline theology, interpreting the justification symbolism in the same light (see P. Stuhlmacher, *Gottes Gerechtigkeit bei Paulus* [Göttingen, 1965]). In my view we are indebted to the trend of this interpretation for two major insights: (1) its discovery of a neglected theme of Paul's theology, which necessarily determines his theology as a whole to some degree (although I am unable to identify the whole of Pauline theology with this theme); (2) the rejection of the existential interpretation, which fails to do justice to Paul's cosmic and mythical assertions. See E. Käsemann, *An die Römer*, HNT 8a (Tübingen, 1973) (Eng. trans. *Commentary on Romans*, trans. G. W. Bromiley [Grand Rapids: Eerdmans; London: SCM Press, 1980; 2nd corrected impression 1982]).

dependency structure remaining the same. The inner logic of a thinking in terms of power categories (shown, for example, in the frequent
use of the word ὑπό, "under") would certainly seem to point in this direction. So it is all the more significant that Paul should have cut through
this logic. When he is talking about slavery as a metaphor illustrating
the disastrous human condition, he uses contrasting images of liberty
and independence to describe salvation. The hope of redemption is that

> the creation itself will be set free from its *bondage* to decay and obtain the
> glorious *liberty* of the children of God. (Rom. 8:21)
>
> For you did not receive the spirit of *slavery* . . . , but you have received the
> spirit of *sonship*. (Rom. 8:15)
>
> So with us; when we were children, we were *slaves* to the elemental spirits
> of the universe. But when the time had fully come, God sent forth his Son . . . ,
> to redeem those who were under the law, so that we might receive adoption
> as *sons*. (Gal. 4:3-5)

What is significant is the way the two images—slavery and sonship—
overlap, or even clash. Whereas the purchase of a slave is basically
reversible—since the slave can be sold again—the son's coming of age
is once and for all. The son is irrevocably destined for liberty, but he
can still become a slave: "So, brethren, we are not children of the slave
but of the free woman. For freedom Christ has set us free; stand fast
therefore, and do not submit again to a yoke of slavery" (Gal. 4:31–5:1).
Now, Paul can of course also talk about "slaves of Christ" (e.g., Rom. 1:1),
because even the redeeming power involves obligation on the part of
the redeemed. But he generally uses this image to express a paradox
between final, ultimate liberation, and empirical social status: "For he
who was called in the Lord as a slave is a freedman of the Lord. Likewise
he who was free when called is a slave of Christ. You were bought with
a price; do not become slaves of men" (1 Cor. 7:22-23).

The point of what he says here is not that redemption makes people
Christ's slaves but that freemen become bondsmen and bondsmen free.
He is not talking about a change of masters in a continuing structure
of domination. He is talking about a restructuring of the relations of
domination through the saving event (see also Gal. 3:28). In order to
bring out the unique character of this "change of government" Paul on
one occasion even cuts through the logic of what he is saying. In Rom.
5:17 he begins: "If, because of one man's trespass, death *reigned* through
that one man"—and we should expect the conclusion to be "How much
more will life reign." But instead he goes on: "how much more will those
who receive the abundance of grace and the free gift of righteousness
reign in life through the one man Jesus Christ." It is only in a single

passage that Paul talks about changing from an old dependency to a new one. In Rom. 6:15-25 he expounds the thesis that redemption turns the slaves of sin into slaves of righteousness. The passage provides the main support for interpretations that put a change of government at the center of Pauline theology. But in fact it actually speaks against this interpretation. For Paul writes explicitly: "But having been set free from sin, you have become slaves of righteousness. I am speaking in human terms, because of the weakness of your flesh (*RSV:* "your natural limitations"; Rom. 6:18f.). This proviso clearly refers to continual talk about a change of government in a structure of domination that still remains what it was. For Paul, this kind of talk belongs to "the weakness of the flesh."

How, then, does he think of the changeover from slavery to freedom? Here Paul uses two christological images — the image of exaltation and the image of purchasing a slave's freedom. This corresponds to the two possible ways of achieving liberation. Either the enslaving forces are vanquished, or the people who have been enslaved are snatched out of their power. The concept of exaltation is unmistakably based on the political image of the mighty ruler who subdues his enemies. The "purchase" image, on the other hand, is drawn from the commercial world of the slave market, where a financially potent purchaser could buy someone's freedom ("redeem" him). Power categories are present in both images. But the characteristic thing is the way Paul remolds them; for both exaltation and purchase are linked with humiliation. But humiliation means that the redeemer himself was subjected to the enslaving powers — that he himself took the form of a slave on himself (Phil. 2:7), was slain by "the rulers of the world" (1 Cor. 2:8), and was subjected to the law (Gal. 4:4f.). It is only through this humiliation that the exaltation can take place. It is *because* the redeemer has abased himself that God has exalted him above all other powers (Phil. 2:9). The exaltation Christology is part of the liberation symbolism, and the point of it is that the person subjected becomes the ruler, the failure becomes the universal lord, and the slave becomes the liberator. What Paul is saying is that the new lord who replaces the subjected powers was himself the victim of these very powers. Is there not an implicit longing here — the longing that, for once, not only should the rulers be changed but that rule itself should lose its subjugating character?

The image of purchasing the slave's freedom is also linked with the humiliation. The purchaser, the redeemer, was "born under the law, to redeem those who were under the law, so that we might receive adoption as sons" (Gal. 4:4f.). Paul does not write that Christ was victorious *over* the law, so that he might buy the freedom of those whom the law had enslaved. He writes that Christ was put "under" the law in order that he could make the purchase. In other passages too the prefix ἐξ in ἐξαγοράζειν (Gal. 3:13; 4:5; cf. 1:4) stresses the snatching *out of* a relationship of dependence. And where only "buy" is used, there is an emphatic addition: "Do not become slaves of men" (1 Cor. 7:23). In the same way, Rom. 7:14 says that the human being is sold *under* sin, not sold *to* sin. So because the "dependence" categories are dominant in the image of the bought and freed slave, the image can easily be integrated into the liberation symbolism. And for the same reason, the question of what the purchase cost can also fade into the background. The vanquishing of the hostile powers makes this question superfluous.

In one respect, however, the purchase metaphor does bring out a particular nuance. To eliminate subjugating powers certainly implies liberation of the people who have been subjected, but to buy a slave's freedom does not imply that the slave's former masters have been eliminated. They go on existing. So the notion of a purchased freedom can directly lead to the admonition not to become slaves (1 Cor. 7:23). The sale of a slave is reversible. The conquest of power is final. So the parallelism between the idea of exaltation and the idea of buying the enslaved in order to free them corresponds to the parallelism in the metaphor of son and slave.

Whatever sector the images in the liberation symbolism come from, they all have as their theme the problem of domination and might, dependence and independence. They are images of social power. Their logic is an "underdog" logic, the logic of "ὑπό."

B. *Justification Symbolism*

The justification symbolism has a different theme: the problem of guilt. Here the disastrous human condition has been caused by trespasses against the law. Salvation means pardon in the face of the well-deserved death penalty. Indictment and pardon take place in a judicial proceeding before God (Rom. 14:10) or Christ (2 Cor. 5:10). Judgment is pronounced in accordance with "the law," without respect of persons (Rom. 2:11). But problems arise at this point. Was "the law" not confined to a particular group of people, the Jews (see Rom 2:17ff.; 9:4)? Could judgment really be pronounced on the basis of the law, without respect of persons?

Two different notions of justice do in fact come up against one another in the justification symbolism. Justice can be understood as a neutral concept, independent of the power and status of the people involved in the legal process. It is obvious that this concept has a specially good chance of being implemented when power is controlled and restricted—

as it was in the Greek city-states, with their republican constitutions.[7] But in the ancient east, conditions were more authoritarian. There justice always meant an act of grace on the part of the mighty. Right was might, justice was mercy (cf. Matt. 6:1). So the notion of a "gracious" justice which creates salvation does not *transcend* the judicial sphere. It merely premises a different experience of justice and injustice.

Paul uses the neutral concept of law in order to prove the universal guilt of all human beings. With the help of this concept he can show that the law is valid quite apart from election (quite apart, that is, from "personal relationships"); see Rom. 2:11. But if he wants to proclaim pardon in the face of the judgment that threatens every man and woman, then other nuances come to the fore in his understanding of justice. Then justice can mean showing mercy, and the righteousness of God is revealed "outside the law" (Rom. 3:21). Here the law is not binding on the judge. For this judge, "faithfulness to the community" (i.e., "personal relationships"), with the resulting obligation to provide help, has a higher status still. What is new about the Pauline proclamation is now that he proclaims justice interpreted as grace as also having universal validity. The justice and righteousness of God which brings about salvation applies to the Gentiles too, if they believe in Christ— not to the Jews alone. For the substantial basis of Paul's proclamation is to be found here, in the Christ-event: the death of the redeemer has surmounted law and guilt. Christ is the end of the law (Rom. 10:4).

If we want to understand this inner link between justification and the death of the redeemer, we must look at Paul's analysis of the law. He describes it as negative in three different ways.

1.   The law brings with it "knowledge of sin" (Rom. 3:20). It makes people aware that they have transgressed the law, even if this awareness differs in the case of Gentiles and Jews. The Gentiles do not know the divine norm that has been revealed, but their inner conflict of conscience betrays that they are nonetheless bound to a law that condemns them (Rom. 2:12). The Jews deny that they have transgressed the law, but by condemning the world of the Gentiles they show that they have a keen eye for the law's contraventions. In condemning other people they are, objectively speaking, condemning themselves too (Rom. 2:1). Both Jews and Gentiles go along with the law's condemnation. So the law is negative first of all because it leads people to pronounce the death penalty on themselves, even

---

7. On the differences between Greece and Rome on the one hand and the ancient east on the other, see H. Bolkestein, *Wohltätigkeit und Armenpflege im vorchristlichen Altertum* (Utrecht, 1939; reprint, Groningen, 1967).

if unconsciously. "Knowledge" of sin is therefore more than a subjective awareness. It is a recognition of sin.

2. The law is also negative because it leads people in the wrong direction — toward their "own righteousness." It promises life under certain conditions, which are formulated as imperatives. And in this way it allows people to forget that it has a merely regulative function for the community existing between Yahweh and human beings. This community or fellowship (the covenant with Abraham, for instance) precedes the law (Moses); see Romans 4; Galatians 3. It cannot be a result of the law's fulfillment; fulfillment of the law can only be a result of this fellowship. Here the misdemeanor is not the transgression against the law. On the contrary, the fault lies in the very will to regulate the relations between God and men and women, for this desire can undoubtedly be seen as a step toward human self-sufficiency — that is, inward human independence of a God who personally claims and pardons. It is here that the law is contravened, at a deeper level than human intention, and contrary to that intention. For the more human beings try to fulfill the divine norm in order to arrive at community with God in the lives they live, the less they notice how — contrary to their intention — they are missing the very point of the norm, which *is* community with God in human life: "Israel who pursued the righteousness which is based on the law did not succeeed in arriving at the law" (Rom. 9:31). It is only when Paul is talking about Israel that he develops the idea that the law is negative because it wrongly leads people to seek "their own righteousness" (Rom. 9:30–10:4) and therefore deceives them (2 Cor. 3:13).

3. Third, the law is negative because it exercises a deadly power as soon as human beings encounter it in the form of an imperative commandment. This idea is developed in Romans 7. Here Paul defines the law as negative first of all because the prohibition rouses the prohibited desire (7:7-8). But this is not enough for him. He repeats: the coming of the law does not mean only that desire and sin revive. Law means the death of the self (7:9-11): "But when the commandment came, sin revived and I died; I found that the very commandment which promised life for me led to death." Here the law does not kill human beings only because of the offenses against the law they have already committed. It kills through its very coming, simply because it confronts human beings as an imperative norm. But it is given deadly power through the sin which has lent it its own aggressive force. "For sin, finding an opportunity through the commandment, deceived me and killed me through the commandment"

(Rom. 7:11). Of course the law is in itself holy, just, and good (Rom. 7:12). But in confrontation with human beings, the descendants of Adam, it is used by sin, so that sin can unload its aggressiveness on to the self, under the guise of the law's holiness. Here the norm is recognized as introjected aggressiveness, the law (and with it all morality) is revealed in all its ambiguity, and the curse of the law (Gal. 3:13) is made conceptually clear. (It may be noted, at least in passing, that the three forces νόμος, ἐγώ, and ἁμαρτία — law, self, and sin — which clash here in a dramatic process correspond roughly to the three "authorities" of psychoanalytical anthropology, ego, superego and id.)

The law is therefore negatively defined in three respects. First, it is "knowledge of sin," the recognition of a norm that quite properly condemns the human being. Second, it seduces men and women to seek their "own righteousness." Third, it is the deadly power of the imperative. In the symbolism of justification, the human condition is disastrous because men and women are living under this condemnatory, cheating, and deadly power — under the curse of the law. The expiatory death "for us" is the vicarious assumption of the curse of the law; that is to say, it is not merely the punishment that follows our offenses against the law which is assumed. It is the deadly aggressiveness of the law's imperative as well, the aggressiveness that issues from the confrontation between law and sinner.[8] This deadly aggressiveness expended its force on Christ. The law can now no longer condemn anyone who is "in Christ," and it can no longer lead anyone astray. It has been unmasked. Its imperative has lost its deadly force. It is in this sense that Christ is the end of the law (Rom. 10:4).

Most of what is said about this accursed death of Christ (and most of these statements are incidentally without the ὑπερ, "on behalf of," formula) has a recurrent structure: the redeemer takes the iniquity and doom of human beings upon himself so that they may achieve salvation. The soteriological intention of the assumption of this iniquity and doom is described in each case through a final (or purpose) clause, or a substantival final construction:

---

8. According to E. Käsemann, Gal. 3:13 and 2 Cor. 5:21 "do not speak of punishment but of the deep ignominy of the incarnation"; see "The Saving Significance of the Death of Jesus in Paul," in *Perspectives on Paul,* trans. Margaret Kohl (London: SCM Press; Philadelphia: Fortress Press, 1971), 32–59, quotation from p. 43. The concept of suffering as a punishment is certainly inadequate, because punishment would endorse the law, not end it. But in my view we clearly find the idea of Christ's condemnation, which in Rom. 8:3 is, as I see it, clearly distinguished from the incarnation.

Christ redeemed us from *the curse* of the law having become a curse for us . . . so that in Christ Jesus *the blessing* of Abraham might come upon the Gentiles. (Gal. 3:13-14)

For our sake he made him to be sin who knew no *sin,* so that in him we might become the *righteousness* of God. (2 Cor. 5:21)

[God sent his Son] in the likeness of sinful *flesh* and for sin, he condemned sin in the flesh, in order that the just requirement of the law might be fulfilled in us, who walk not according to the flesh but according to the *Spirit.* (Rom. 8:3f.)

There is always a precise correspondence between disaster and salvation. The redeemer overcomes curse, flesh (σάρξ), and sin. More indeed: he himself becomes curse, flesh, and sin, so that the redeemed may receive blessing, Spirit (πνεῦμα), and righteousness. In my view, the disputed passage Rom. 3:24f. must be interpreted along the same lines: in his expiatory death Christ was subjected to the wrath of God stored up in the past, so that God might bring about his saving righteousness.[9] "Him God put forward as an expiation . . . to prove at the present time that he himself is righteous and that he justifies him who has faith in Jesus" (Rom. 3:25f.).

Whether we interpret the accursed and atoning death of Christ as a vicarious death or an expiatory one is not important. The animal victim differs from the human representative only because the victim does not voluntarily assume its fate; it remains passive. It does not participate in the sacrificial event, as its determining subject. But in the passages just quoted, Christ is undoubtedly viewed passively. None of these passages says that he died in order to redeem us. The determining subject of the happening is generally God. Christ is merely the object of God's action. We can therefore quite well talk about a sacrificial death, the more so since in the framework of the justification symbolism the subsequent fate of the victim plays no part. The death of the victim is redemptive in itself. The resurrection does not belong to the logic of the sacrificial idea. The assertions quoted above stress only the salvific consequences for those who are redeemed. We hear nothing about the further fate of the redeemer. That distinguishes these passages from most of the ὑπέρ ("on behalf of, for the sake of") ones. The ὑπέρ utterances stress that the redeemer deliberately accepted his death. But these utterances belong to a different symbolism.

---

9. See O. Kuss, *Der Römerbrief,* 2nd ed. (Regensburg, 1963), 155–61; Käsemann, *An die Römer,* German ed., 84–94.

C. *The Reconciliation Symbolism*

In this symbolism, the theme is the antithesis between hostility and peace, hate and love, separation and community. The most important texts are Rom. 5:1-11; 8:31-39; and 2 Cor. 5:14-21, the key words being reconciliation, peace, and love (καταλλαγή, εἰρήνη, and ἀγάπη).

The symbolism of liberation and justification is thinking in vertical categories: the human being is "under" sin; Christ is "above" other powers; the judge and the sinner are on absolutely different levels. But in the reconciliation symbolism we find images of relationship, on a horizontal level. The new note is heard most clearly in 2 Cor. 5:20f. Here the apostle admonishes his readers in God's stead; he *begs* on Christ's behalf—be reconciled! Where a word becomes a plea, the thought categories of dominance and subjection, superordination and subordination are left behind. So Paul can illustrate the event of reconciliation through the example of dying for another person: "Hardly anyone will die for a righteous man . . ." (Rom. 5:7). Yet Christ died for the weak (5:6), for sinners (5:8), indeed for enemies (5:10). But in spite of this three-stage progression, or intensification, which carries the earthly model to improbability point, the relationship between redeemer and redeemed is, for all that, the relationship between reconciled enemies, not the relation of victor and vanquished. This aspect is characteristic of the reconciliation symbolism, and it comes out again when we encounter here the cosmic powers that otherwise belong to the symbolism of liberation. These powers are now seen as negative, not because they oppress human beings but because they could separate the redeemer from those he has redeemed. But separation has nothing to do with the usual vertical network of relationships, with its superordinations and subordinations; height and depth now become irrelevant:

> Who shall *separate* us from the love of Christ? . . . Neither death, nor life, nor angels, nor principalities, nor things present, nor things to come, nor powers, nor height, nor depth, nor anything else in all creation, will be able to *separate* us from the love of God in Christ Jesus our Lord. (Rom. 8:35, 38f.)

To have peace with God therefore means preeminently that access to him is not barred by any division: "Since we are justified by faith, we have peace with God through our Lord Jesus Christ. Through him we have obtained access to this grace in which we stand . . ." (Rom. 5:1f.). In the Deutero-Pauline epistles this reconciliation symbolism is developed even further. In the hymn in Colossians, for example, reconciliation is described as a cosmic event. The conflict between all the powers is finished and peace has been established. For here—in contrast to the hymn in Philippians—the aim of redemption is "peace," not subjugation (Col. 1:20).

In the reconciliation symbolism, the death of Christ is presented not so much as an accursed, vicarious death, but rather as the surrender of love. It is God's love that this death reveals, not his wrath. Here the event of redemption manifests itself as a *mysterium fascinosum,* not a *mysterium tremendum.* What is initially striking is that the "dying" formula ἀποθανεῖν ὑπὲρ ἡμῶν (and similar phraseology)[10] is always linked with the key word "love":

> The life I now live in the flesh I live by faith in the Son of God, who *loved* me and gave himself for me. (Gal. 2:20)

> But God shows his *love* for us in that while we were yet sinners Christ died for us. (Rom. 5:8)

> For the *love* of Christ controls us, because we are convinced that one has died for all. (2 Cor. 5:14)

> He who did not spare his own Son but gave him up for us all, will he not also give us all things with him? ... Who shall separate us from the *love* of Christ? (Rom. 8:32, 35)

The contextual link between "love" and the "dying" formula is less direct where love is being talked about in a parenetic context. There what is meant is not the love of God or Christ, which manifests itself in a death for us, but the love of Christians, which takes its bearings from this death:

> If your brother is being injured by what you eat, you are no longer walking in *love.* Do not let what you eat cause the ruin of one for whom Christ died. (Rom. 14:15)

> "Knowledge" puffs up, but *love* builds up. ... And so by your knowledge this weak man is destroyed, the brother for whom Christ died. (1 Cor. 8:1, 11)

In the context of the "dying" formula in 1 Thess. 5:10, we find (5:8) the exhortation to take the shield of faith and love. Here the "dying" fomula is linked with the idea of love only very loosely, but the connection is not entirely missing.

When Paul talks about "dying for us," what he is thinking of is generally a surrender in love in which Christ himself is the subject of the surrender. He can certainly also tell us that God did not spare his Son; but this can be called both an expression of God's love in Christ (Rom. 8:39) and an expression of Christ's own love (Rom. 8:35). Surrender

---

10. On the "dying" formula, see K. Wengst, *Christologische Formeln und Lieder des Urchristentums* (Gütersloh, 1972), 78ff.

means that God's Son "loved me and gave himself for me" (Gal. 2:20). If this personal participation on the redeemer's part were lacking—if his own subjectivity were not involved—we could not find the dying "for us" in a parenetic context, that is, as an appeal for deliberate action. The dying "for us" which follows the self-surrender of love can therefore be clearly distinguished from the accursed death.

The difference is brought out once again in a second characteristic of the surrender in love: it is only the dying that is important in the accursed and sacrificial death. Where reconciliation is concerned, it is a different matter. Reconciliation, love, and peace could not be brought about by a dead person. So inasmuch as reconciliation is not only *brought about* by the redeemer but *is* at the same time reconcilation between him and the redeemed, a final separation would be a flagrant contradiction. For it is precisely separation that is to be overcome. So according to an inner logic, an intrinsic part of the symbolism of reconciliation is new life beyond death. And in the framework of the reconciliation symbolism we do in fact often find the "dying" formula linked with the idea of resurrection. The statement that Christ "was put to death for our trespasses and *raised* for our justification" (Rom. 4:25) introduces a passage in which images of peace, love, and reconciliation are predominant. The way in which the idea of a life beyond death is taken up again in Rom. 5:10 confirms that the link here is not a fortuitous one: "If while we were enemies we were reconciled to God by the death of his Son, how much more, now that we are reconciled, shall we be saved by his *life*." The reconciliation throws open a perspective beyond death. The "dying for us" in Rom. 8:31ff. is extended in a similar way. First of all we hear only about a surrender for us (8:32). This is followed by a question: Should God not then give us everything with this surrender? Christ has died, more:—Paul corrects himself—he has also been *raised* and intercedes for those he has redeemed. Nothing can separate us from his love, not even death.

This text shows particularly well how the symbolism of reconciliation is bound to transcend the idea of dying. For if separation is the doom that has to be overcome, then death has to be overcome as well, since death means eternal separation. In 2 Cor. 5:15 too the "dying" formula is characteristically expanded. Christ died for all, "so that all those who live might live no longer for themselves but for him who died for them and *was raised*." The ὑπὲρ αὐτῶν ("for them") does not refer merely to ἀποθανόντι ("died"). It refers to ἐγερθέντι ("was raised") too. Otherwise we should expect the article to be repeated (i.e., καὶ τῷ ἐγερθέντι, "and the one who was raised").

Finally, we have a comparable expansion in 1 Thess. 5:10. There a soteriological purpose clause is added to the "dying" formula: Christ died "so that whether we wake or sleep we might *live* with him." So in the reconciliation symbolism, death is the self-surrender of love which creates enduring community between the redeemer and the redeemed. Here we almost always meet the key word "love" in the context of the "dying" formula. And this formula is often expanded by a perspective that reaches beyond death.

2. PHYSIOMORPHIC TRANSFORMATION SYMBOLISM

The symbolism we have analyzed up to now is based on images of social interaction. The relations between slave owner and slave, father and son, judge and accused, friend and enemy—that is the pictorial background. Redemption is portrayed as a change in personal relationships. The change can come about because the redeemer is paramount, potent, and sovereign—that is, because there is an *asymmetry* between the redeemer and those he redeems.

These sociomorphic (or socioform) interaction symbols are augmented by a series of symbols depicting physiomorphic (or physioform) transformation. Here the images are drawn mainly from the organic sector. In this symbolism, redemption establishes a *symmetry* between the redeemer and the redeemed, and the two are assimilated and become one. Here redemption is not merely a transformation of relationships; it is a transformation of essential qualities and characteristics too. It is typical that the metamorphosis of essence is generally brought about through the force of "mythical analogy."[11] What happens to the redeemer happens to the redeemed as well, because there is a kinship between them, a kinship brought into being through sacramental acts and a comparable fate. For modern thinking, similarity and power, correspondence and efficacy, analogy and assimilation are concepts expressing very different relations between two things. But in mythical thinking, what is related and analogous also has the power to mold and transform. This power is released when the correspondence between redeemer and redeemed is visibly or palpably established—especially by way of sacramental acts. Here human beings take upon themselves the redeemer's death, assume his form and literally re-present his sufferings in body

---

11. On the phenomenon of "mythical analogy," see E. Cassirer, "Die Begriffsform im mythischen Denken," in *Wesen und Wirkung des Symbolbegriffs* (Oxford: B. Cassirer, 1956; 4th ed., Darmstadt, 1969), 50f.

and blood. The physiomorphic transformation symbols are therefore often linked with sacramental ideas, although they can also be found separately.

A. *Change-of-Form Symbolism*

It is in 2 Cor. 3:18–4:6, 1 Cor. 15:35-57, and Rom. 5:17-21 especially that we encounter the symbolism of a change of form (form here meaning the person's Gestalt, or total configuration). The most important key words are εἰκών ("image" or "likeness"), μορφή ("form") and δόξα ("glory"). The notion of mythical analogy is found most clearly in 2 Cor. 3:18: "And we all, with unveiled face, reflecting the δόξα of the Lord, will be changed into his εἰκών from δόξα to δόξα; for this comes from the Lord of the Spirit" (or: "who is the Spirit"). The analogy is first described in visual terms: the relationship between redeemer and redeemed is like the relation between a picture and its reflection. This perfect analogy is confined to those who stand before the Lord with unveiled face—that is to say, those who have been illumined by "the light of the gospel" (2 Cor. 4:4). The correspondence between mirror and mirror image now has a direct, energy-laden dynamic, for the human being is transformed into the εἰκών of the redeemer, into community with his very being or essence. The analogy effects assimilation. Some of the physiomorphic images in 2 Cor. 3:18 are drawn from the world of natural law, or the technical world of "the maker" (e.g., the mirror). Others are organic. The face (πρόσωπον) is one of the main characteristics of the human form. The εἰκών concept is an organic one too.

This emerges especially clearly in 1 Cor. 15:38-49, where v. 49 emphatically brings out the real point of the change-of-form symbolism: "Just as we have borne the εἰκών of the man of dust, we shall also bear the εἰκών of the man of heaven." This change of form or Gestalt is then illustrated in 15:39-41 by a wealth of comparisons taken from the world of nature:

> For not all flesh is alike, but there is one kind for men, another for animals, another for birds, and another for fish. There are celestial bodies and there are terrestrial bodies; but the glory of the celestial is one, and the glory of the terrestrial is another. There is one glory of the sun, and another glory of the moon, and another glory of the stars; for star differs from star in glory.

What Paul wants to say here is that just as different organisms obviously differ in form (and he evidently sees the heavenly bodies as animated or "ensouled" too), there is also a difference between the form and essence of human beings as the descendents of Adam, and their form and essence as the redeemed. Without redemption, human beings are confined to the form they have inherited from Adam. It is this which their species continually reproduces. The background here is undoubtedly the biomorphic symbolism of a generative renewal of form. It serves to describe the way in which men and women are confined to their nature as descendants of Adam. This nature is excluded from redemption: flesh and blood cannot inherit the kingdom (1 Cor. 15:50). That is why Paul longs for a radical transformation (1 Cor. 15:52f.), a redeeming "mutation" of human nature in which human beings can change the structure they have inherited.

This notion about restriction to the human nature inherited from Adam is given a deeper dimension in Rom. 5:12-21. Here it is no longer the εἰκών (or image) that is stressed as characteristic of the human condition. The characteristic thing is now infringement of the divine commandments. At this point the physiomorphic change-of-form symbolism is deepened by a sociomorphic metaphor which has to do with commandment and transgression.

Here too the premise is the mythical analogy between Adam and his descendants. Death acquired its sovereignty because Adam sinned. All other human beings have sinned like him, so all must die. This postulate is now qualified: some human beings did not sin ἐπὶ τῷ ὁμοιώματι τῆς παραβάσεως Ἀδάμ ("after the similitude of Adam," 5:14 AV). By saying this, Paul is endorsing the general "similarity" between Adam and other human beings—a similarity, moreover, which has a real potency, because here the analogy both assimilates and determines (cf. Rom. 6:5).

Of course we must not think of this determination "mechanistically," since it rests on a mythological analogy, and since it includes a personalist element too: what is determined by the mythical prototype is imputed to the individual self. Any kind of mechanistic (or biological) determinism is foreign to mythical thinking, so there is nothing for Paul to correct here. In fact, his modification of the mythical analogy between Adam and the descendants of Adam moves rather in the opposite direction. For he qualifies his "personalistic-sounding" assertion that death was passed on to all human beings because all sinned (5:12), and it is really his own qualification that sounds deterministic: between Adam and Moses men and women sinned without the law, so their transgression of the law could not be held against them (5:13). Death nevertheless reigned in that era, but it did so without any legal legitimation. At this point the mythical analogy between Adam and his descendants is set aside, not because human beings between Adam and Moses were individually responsible for their mortality but because they were subjected to a fate that had no judicial basis. Here reflection about guilt comes up against a fate that has nothing to do with human responsibility.

There is no disputing the fact that in Paul human beings are responsible for a mortality that is at the same time outside their sphere of responsibility, for according to the mythical analogy, the sin that causes death is inescapable; and yet it is still laid at the door of the individual self. According to Paul, the human being must assume responsibility for the nature he has inherited from Adam. This does not have to be the pathological self-accusation of religious masochism. If death and the other limitations of human existence are not simply accepted as inevitable, as a fact of nature, this is an expression of the longing that even the irrevocable finality of the human condition may *not* after all be irrevocable—a longing which for Paul has already become the realization that for him the redemptive turning point has already happened. The transformation of human beings has already begun, but it has not yet been completed.

In Rom. 8:29 too the physiomorphic character of the Gestalt symbolism is deepened by sociomorphic imagery. Paul says about the redeemed: "For those whom he foreknew he also predestined to be conformed to the image of his Son, in order that he might be the first-born among many brethren." Here the natural background is obvious. The form is the same because the ancestry is the same. The redeemer and the redeemed are brothers; the redeemer is the firstborn. But the reason for the similarity of form is expressed by a sociomorphic image. It is due to a sovereign divine resolve. As an image, this would hardly seem to hold water, for it suggests that through will power a father could determine the form his sons will take. And yet the image fits, for all that. For the sociomorphic metaphors are not aiming to stress the personal and ethical character of a similarity of form. The point is that a man or woman's destiny to become a redeemed Gestalt precedes all human will and responsibility. The sociomorphic metaphors underline the finality aspect which is brought out by the physiomorphic change-of-form symbolism.

In this symbolism, therefore, salvation is thought of as the stamp of the redeemer's nature which is impressed on human beings. Redemption is not due to any particular act on the redeemer's part. It comes about because his nature appears, becomes efficacious, and drives out the human nature which is antagonistic to it. The form of Christ replaces the form of Adam, and his glory replaces the glory of Moses. So the Adam/Christ typology and the Moses/Christ typology are part of the change-of-form symbolism. What is of essential importance here is not the antitype but the fact that Christ is the true εἰκών or likeness of God, and has the power to change men and women into an εἰκών of himself.

B. *The Symbolism of Death and Life*

Paul often depicts redemption as new life following a death that has been anticipated. Life and death are organic processes that can be pictorially grasped. They are biomorphic and physiomorphic symbols. This becomes clear in Rom. 6:5, where Paul talks about the σύμφυτοι γίγνεσθαι. The redeemed have "grown together" with the Gestalt of Christ in his death, and in the same way they will become joined to his risen Gestalt too. In 1 Cor. 15:35-37 images from the plant world are used in a similar way to illustrate death and resurrection: "You foolish man! What you sow does not come to life unless it dies. And what you sow is not the body which is to be, but a bare kernel, perhaps of wheat or some other grain."

Of course the symbolism of death and life is closely linked with the change-of-form (or Gestalt) symbolism. But the two can still be clearly distinguished from one another. New life after death does not necessarily involve a change of Gestalt. Above all, a change of Gestalt does not necessarily imply a previously assumed death. On the contrary: "Lo! I tell you a mystery. We shall not all sleep, but we shall all be changed" (1 Cor. 15:51). This is surely the essential difference. Dying with Christ is not part of the inner logic of the change-of-form symbolism. The εἰκών of Christ is the εἰκών of the exalted Lord. But in the symbolism of death and life it is the Gestalt and destiny of the humiliated One that have formative power. It is only "the fellowship of his sufferings" which confers the right to share in his life:

> If we have died with Christ, we believe that we shall also live with him. (Rom. 6:8)
>
> ... that I may know ... the fellowship of his sufferings, becoming like him in his death, that if possible I may attain the resurrection from the dead. (Phil. 3:10f.)
>
> ... if children, then heirs, heirs of God and fellow heirs with Christ, provided we suffer with him in order that we may also be glorified with him. (Rom. 8:17)
>
> For we are weak in him, but in dealing with you we shall live with him by the power of God. (2 Cor. 13:4)
>
> ... always carrying in the body the death of Jesus, so that the life of Jesus may also be manifested in our bodies. (2 Cor. 4:10f.)

Redeemer and redeemed belong together, but this is something that can be interpreted with different categories. So in 2 Cor. 4:10f. we see the idea of an epiphany of the redeemer in the redeemed person, and in 2 Cor. 13:4 the concept of mystical identity. But in each case the prefix σύν ("with") is used, and in my view this distinguishes clearly enough the community of redeemer and redeemed in a common destiny from true and complete identity. This community in destiny can be understood only by way of the category of mythical analogy: baptism and suffering move the Christian into correspondence with Christ, and this correspondence allows the "assimilating" power of Christ's fate to act. Here the mythical analogy does not come into play between the glorified form of the redeemer and the redeemed, as it does in the change-of-form symbolism. Its field is the fellowship of suffering and death shared with the humiliated Lord. So in this symbolism a simple confrontation between the form of human beings as the descendants of Adam, and their form as those who have been redeemed, is not sufficient. Instead we are told how human nature "in Adam" — the body of sin (Rom. 6:6) — is destroyed with Christ in his death, so that his life can also become efficacious. Of course there is nothing automatic about the efficacy of this new life. Rom. 6:4 talks about it in imperative terms: "so let us walk in a new life."

The subject of the change-of-form symbolism, then, is the surmounting of the irrevocable finality of human existence, its inescapable imprisonment in the human condition, which means imprisonment in sin and death. But the subject of the symbolism of death and life has to do with the conquest of human finitude. What comes through here is the yearning that life might begin again from the start — not merely individual human life but creation in general. This is the longing for the "new creation" (Gal. 6:14; 2 Cor. 5:17). And according to Paul, this longing is satisfied in the Christ-event. In that event the old creation has finally passed away and the new creation has already begun. The symbolism of death and life is matched by the Christology of cross and resurrection. Because the redeemer has assumed and vanquished the finitude of human existence, the men and women he has redeemed may also hope for victory over human finitude.

C. *Union Symbolism*

Union symbolism talks about overcoming the separation of human beings and their isolation in their own selves. In life we see union in the shape of two fundamental, vital processes: sexuality and eating. In Paul both these processes become metaphors for the event of salvation. And in 1 Cor. 6:13 he puts the two side by side as parallels, even if his purpose is a polemical one: "'Food is meant for the stomach and the stomach for food'. . . But the body is not meant for immorality, but for the Lord, and the Lord for the body." Here Paul is probably criticizing a slogan that was going the rounds in Corinth. But his very rejection of the slogan betrays the parallelism of the two processes. This parallelism is even more marked when food itself serves to represent a person, as it does in the Lord's Supper.

But let us look first at the erotic metaphors that Paul develops immediately after the verse just quoted:

> Do you not know that your bodies are members of Christ? Shall I therefore take the members of Christ and make them members of a prostitute? Never! Or do you not know that he who joins himself to a prostitute becomes one body with her? For, as it is written, "The two shall become one flesh." But he who is united to the Lord becomes one spirit with him. (1 Cor. 6:15-17)

Here Paul uses the word κολλᾶσθαι both for sexual intercourse with a prostitute and for union with the redeemer. The common ground between the two elements in the comparison is the union in a single person of two people who have hitherto been separate. The objective fact behind this is the perception (which almost sounds psychoanalytical) that the relationship to the Lord is a transmuted eroticism, a sublimation of the longing—alive in all sexuality—to cross beyond the limits of one's own person in the direction of another "Thou." Unity with the Lord is in fact given a more elevated description: the believer is with him one πνεῦμα (or spirit), whereas with the prostitute he is one σῶμα (or body). But no undue weight should be attached to this distinction, for the word σῶμα can also be used to express unity with the Lord.

The structural link between the erotic and the believing relationship emerges from 1 Cor. 7:34 too. If it were not for this link, the two relationships could not become rivals: "The unmarried woman . . . is anxious about the affairs of the Lord, how to be holy in body and spirit; but the married woman is anxious about worldly affairs, how to please her husband."

In using the sexual metaphor to describe a union beyond the limits of individual personhood, Paul is not thinking individualistically. What he means is a union of a whole community. When he asks "Do you not know that your bodies are members of Christ?" the plural in "your bodies" suggests several people. And the term "member" in itself implies a relationship to other members too. So union with the redeemer is always from the outset union with other people who have also been redeemed. Consequently the sexual metaphor can be used for the relationship between the redeemer and the whole community of his people: "I betrothed you to Christ to present you as a pure bride to her one husband" (2 Cor. 11:2). And in another passage sexual relationships appear as only one possible form of social relationship among others;

and yet they do all the same provide the model for the others: "There is neither Jew nor Greek, there is neither slave nor free, there is neither male nor female, for you are all one in Christ Jesus" (Gal. 3:28). The word "one" (in "you are all one") does not mean "you are all united." It means you are all *one person*. All together form a single person, as if the personal frontier has been broken down — as if the other man or woman is as close as one's own self. The pictorial background for this unity between persons is certainly not the relationship between Jews and Gentiles, slaves and freemen. The real point is that the crossing of the personal frontier experienced in sexual union is now transferred to other social relationships too. For the erotic metaphor is more suited than any other to express this longing for the barriers of the personal ego to be overcome and self-isolation surmounted.

But the union symbolism draws on other images as well. Eating and drinking also illustrate physical union between the body and other things — other "bodies," in the case of meat. This is also true when what we are talking about is the spiritual food of the Lord's Supper, which is united with the person of Christ (see 1 Cor. 10:4). So eating can become a symbol for the overcoming of the barriers that separate one person from another: "The cup of blessing which we bless, is it not a participation [or communion] in the blood of Christ? The bread which we break, is it not a participation in the body of Christ?" (1 Cor. 10:16). Here as well, the two communities are indissolubly linked with one another: the community between the redeemer and the redeemed, and the community among the redeemed themselves. We can call this mysticism, but it is a mysticism of social relationships in which many people are involved.

This "mysticism" of the one body of Christ finds its finest development in 1 Cor. 12:12-27. The redeemed are joined together like the members or limbs of a body: "If one member suffers, all suffer together; if one member is honored, all rejoice together. Now you are the body of Christ and individually members of it" (1 Cor. 12:26-27).

This union symbolism, whether the metaphors on which it draws are sexual or whether they have to do with eating, undoubtedly includes an ecstatic element, if by ecstasy we mean a stepping out beyond the frontiers of one's own person. But it is not ecstasy in the general sense of the word. It is the ecstasy which goes out to other people. In this respect Paul may perhaps have been correcting the "Enthusiasts" in Corinth, but he was not attacking their enthusiasm as such. For Paul himself is an enthusiast, in every sense. But among all the different forms of enthusiasm, it is the enthusiasm of love which he values most. He is an ecstatic, but he prizes the ecstasy of love more than any other ecstasy.

This ecstatic element comes out most clearly when Paul expresses his awareness of the barrier between people: "For what person knows a man's thoughts except the spirit (πνεῦμα) of the man which is in him?" (1 Cor. 2:11). What is within a person is inaccessible from without. Everyone is closed in within his own self. No one can ultimately put himself in the place of anyone else. It is only in the redeemed person that this frontier is surmounted. The person who has been redeemed has the spirit—the πνεῦμα—of Christ.

The same awareness of the frontier of the individual person is expressed in the "dwelling" metaphor. Here the human being is depicted as a structure, a kind of building which can shelter different things: sin (Rom. 7:17, 20), the Spirit (Rom. 8:9; 1 Cor. 3:16), even Christ himself (Rom. 8:10). These take the place of the human being as determining subject, so to speak. So Paul explicitly corrects himself: "It is not I that do it, but sin which dwells within me" (Rom. 7:20). What corresponds to this in the person who has been redeemed is: "It is not I who live, but Christ who lives in me" (Gal. 2:20). The self is driven out. That is the ecstatic element. But of course it cannot last. Even the phrase "Christ lives in *me*" (Gal. 2:20) retracts the complete dispossession of the self by another power. But Paul wants to hold fast to the phrase, so he goes on, correcting himself: "But the life I now live in the flesh. . . ." In Rom. 7:18 the self is limited in rather the same way by a pointer to the flesh (σάρξ): "For I know that nothing good dwells within me, that is, in my flesh." In both passages the σάρξ concept serves to show that there is a limit to a complete substitution of the self either by sin or by Christ. But in both passages it also becomes clear that what redemption strives for is the ultimate transcending of the σάρξ as well. For the σάρξ is itself the dwelling in which the human being lives. Σάρξ means that human beings are isolated in their own selves:

> You are not in the flesh, you are in the Spirit, if the Spirit of God really dwells in you. Any one who does not have the Spirit of Christ does not belong to him. But if Christ is in you, although your bodies are dead because of sin, your spirits are alive because of righteousness. (Rom. 8:9-11)

Unity with the spiritual Christ presupposes that the σάρξ has been transcended. This is possible because the redeemer is comparable to a "corporate personality" who integrates in himself the men and women who have been redeemed. In him they are all one person (Gal. 3:28). The Christology that belongs to the union symbolism is the idea of the σῶμα Χριστοῦ, the body of Christ. In the Deutero-Pauline letters this Christology is developed further still, and its cosmic components emerge more clearly. Here Christ is a macroanthropos who embraces all things and beings. We can sense that Paul is moving toward something similar, but the idea is not yet explicit. Paul brings out a particular aspect, however, when he points out that an enthusiastic and ecstatic transcending of the limits of the person is not in itself as yet redemption. It only becomes redemption when it is the enthusiasm of love, which ecstatically transcends the limits of personhood by reaching out to the other person who is "in Christ" too (cf. 1 Cor. 13).

3. THE STRUCTURE OF THE FIELD
OF SOTERIOLOGICAL SYMBOLISM

Each of the individual symbolic units already has a unique inner logic of its own. This is the focus through which the often different pictorial elements are ordered and related to one another. This logic can be illustrated by the characteristic preposition used in each case. The liberation symbolism is based on a logic of ὑπό ("under"), and the justification and reconciliation symbolism on a logic of ὑπέρ ("on behalf of," "for the benefit of"). The typical preposition in the transformation symbolism is ὡς ("as"), while in the symbolism of death and life it is σύν ("with"). The phrase that recurs in the union symbolism is ἐν Χριστῷ, "in Christ." In each case the relation between redeemer and redeemed is defined in particular, more or less pictorial categories.

All the symbols are related to one another in a multiplicity of different ways, however. The whole field of soteriological symbolism has an inner "logic" of its own, which emerges from the different classifications and antitheses. In analyzing the different symbolisms, we have already distinguished between a sociomorphic interaction symbolism and a physiomorphic transformation symbolism. The sociomorphic symbolism puts what happens between people at the center. The physiomorphic symbolism describes the assimilation of different beings. In the one we can talk about a soteriology of redeeming action; in the other about a soteriology of redeeming participation.

There is another important distinction too. The conditions of power, justice, and personal existence drawn upon in the sociomorphic images can change, according to human experience. If we are talking about the pictorial half of the image, we can say that human beings can even initiate the "redemption," the pardon, and the reconciliation themselves. Consequently these symbols are also extremely pictorial. However much the reality may be symbolically heightened, these images are still clearly drawn from human activity. The physiomorphic images, on the other hand, are based on what is outside the "personal" human sector. They have to do with human life in its natural, organic, and vital aspects. The transformation images found here have no pictorial analogy in day-to-day life. The human being's Gestalt is largely constant; his life runs its course with inexorable irreversibility; his egocentric isolation is permanent. Here structures of the human condition are touched on which lie deeper than human action, and precede it. These structures can hardly be altered by anything that human beings can do—or only to a minimal degree, for they are to be found in the finality of the Gestalt that human beings have inherited, the finitude of their time, and the isolation of the human self. In order to be able to express transformations in this fundamental sector—even if the expression is no more than an *expressed yearning* for that transformation—language must reach beyond the limitations of the field of action open to men and women. The non-human "other" (above all, organic nature) becomes the metaphor for the human being's transcending of himself. These symbols are certainly less pictorial than the sociomorphic interaction symbols, but what they aim at is something more fundamental.

A second difference between sociomorphic and physiomorphic symbolism emerges more clearly once we perceive that the substance of a symbolic unit in the first group always has a specially close relationship to a symbolic unit in the second. Liberation and transformation symbolism obviously belong together. Both stress the position of sovereignty held by the redeemer and the redeemed. The human being's new Gestalt is "glory" and "power" (1 Cor. 15:43). This is the εἰκών of the firstborn Son (Rom. 8:29), the sign of his freedom, just as the εἰκών of Adam was the sign of his dominant position in the world. But the redeemed εἰκών of the new human being is participation in the εἰκών of the exalted Lord, who vanquishes the powers and buys the liberty of the enslaved (redeems them). Both symbols stress one aspect of "the holy," an aspect which can be described as domination, sovereignty, and majesty. The sociomorphic symbolism ascribes this aspect preeminently to the redeemer but the physiomorphic symbolism shows that redeemed human beings too are destined for a position of sovereignty—by virtue of their redeeeming participation in the redeemer's nature.

The relation between sociomorphic justification symbolism and the physiomorphic symbolism of death and life is similar. The justification of the godless has to do with death and life, condemnation and pardon. The symbolism of death and life talks about taking on the death of Christ. This brings out another side of "the holy," that absurd, somber, and terrifying side which has been called the *mysterium tremendum*. An innocent person is exposed to the wrath of God. The way to salvation is only by way of death and suffering.

Finally, we should notice the connection between the symbolism of reconciliation and union symbolism. Both have to do with the overcoming of separation. In both, the bright and winning side of the event of redemption is the subject — the *mysterium fascinosum*. The reconciliation symbolism describes this as a quality of the redeemer, but the union symbolism ascribes it to the redeemed as well. This means that we can divide the field of soteriological symbolism into six, as shown in the accompanying chart:

Sociomorphic Interaction Symbolism	**Physiomorphic Transformation Symbolism**
Liberation Symbolism Salvation as liberation from enslaving power through exaltation and redemption	*Change-of-Form Symbolism* Salvation as the surmounting of the fixed and final character of human nature through the Gestalt of the redeemer
Justification Symbolism Salvation as the remission of guilt through the accursed death of the redeemer	*Death-and-Life Symbolism* Salvation as the surmounting of finitude through participation in the death and resurrection of the redeemer
Reconciliation Symbolism Salvation as reconciliation with enemies through the loving surrender of the redeemer	*Union Symbolism* Salvation as the surmounting of the isolation of the self through unity in "the body of Christ"

We can now define somewhat more closely the relationship between sociomorphic interaction symbolism and physiomorphic tranformation symbolism. The act of redemption conceived of in sociomorphic terms occupies a position of priority, objectively speaking. The redeemer initiates action which dominates and fascinates, and accepts absurdity. These acts are addressed to human beings, and their response to them is the theme of physiomorphic symbolism. According to this symbolism, human beings too are destined for a position of sovereignty, participate in the absurdity of the divine suffering, and share in the love which in its "enthusiasm" crosses barriers. But in order to do this, men and women would have to transcend the limitations of the human condition which they have inherited, and would have to participate in the nature of the redeemer and be "assimilated" by him.

It has often been assumed, under the banner of the demythologization program, that Paul intended what he said to be understood existentially. In my view, this assumption may be regarded as confuted, if it means to assert that Paul deliberately employed his cosmological and mythological symbols as a way of setting certain existential processes going, and that in so doing he attached no importance to their mythical content. Paul still fully accepted the world of myth. He believed in the action of supernatural forces transcending the human sphere. Whether what he says has an existential function — perhaps without his intending it — is another question. Is what he says not perhaps unconsciously determined by a "logic" drawn from human life? Is it not profoundly influenced by the fundamental problems of human existence? It has been the aim of the structuralist analysis I have put forward here to throw a little light on this hidden logic. Paul was no more aware of this logic than we are aware of the structure of our language when we are talking. But without his intending it, that logic determined what he said.

Finally, it must be stressed that our results are by no means unambiguous. On the one hand the symbolism of Pauline soteriology brings out a fundamental existential problem. But on the other hand it takes its impress from the structure of the holy, as a reality above human beings which both attracts and oppresses them. This raises a question that we cannot discuss here — the question about the truth of religious tradition. For one person, this tradition witnesses to the acts of God. For another, it testifies to unconscious existential social and historical processes. No third position would seem possible. Or is one after all conceivable? Could it not be that in the encounter with the holy men and women feel impelled to draw on symbolism, as a way of transcending an existence deeply impressed with the stigma of domination, guilt and aggression, finality, finitude, and isolation? Could it be that, even though the soteriological symbolism developed by Paul is certainly a world of meaning constructed by human beings, it nonetheless evolved as an answer to the riddling and alien reality of the holy? For this is a reality that should not be disputed, even if its sociomorphic and physiomorphic interpretations take the form of human — all too human — images.

6

Christology and Social Experience

———————————◆———————————

Aspects of Pauline Christology in the Light of the Sociology of Knowledge

S OCIOLOGICAL INVESTIGATIONS of early Christianity are often suspected of attributing religious faith to nonreligious factors, although this is not their intention. The suspicion is voiced with particular acrimony, however, in the case of studies based on the sociology of knowledge.[1] These studies start from the assumption that religious convictions become plausible only in the context of particular social structures, or that different social structures influence the choice and acceptance of religious convictions. They investigate the social "plausibility structure" or "plausibility basis" of religious convictions;[2] that is, they consider all the social conditions and factors which allow a conviction to seem obviously tenable. Here the social conditions that influence religion contribute to the picture, as well as the effect that

---

1. On the basic problems connected with investigations of the New Testament based on the sociology of knowledge, see K. Berger, "Wissenssoziologie und Exegese des Neuen Testaments," *Kairos* 19 (1977): 124–33; also his *Exegese des Neuen Testaments,* Uni-Taschenbücher 658 (Heidelberg, 1977), chap. 8, "Soziologische Fragen," 218–41. On p. 218 he quotes L. L. Schücking's apt dictum on reductionism: "The mud does not produce the eel, as Aristotle thought, but the view that where there is no mud there is no eel either, comes closer to the truth."

2. The term "plausibility structure" is taken from P. L. Berger, *A Rumor of Angels: Modern Society and the Rediscovery of the Supernatural* (Garden City, N.Y.: Doubleday, 1969; Harmondsworth: Penguin, 1971), 42ff. If I here prefer to use the term "plausibility basis," that is in order to make it clear that the plausibility of religious ideas does not depend on their inner structure alone but is conditioned by nonreligious factors. It is precisely this that Berger means by the term "plausibility structure." There should be no need to stress that the term "plausibility structure" does not imply any reductionism: a house's foundation is not its cause. And "plausibility" is not identical with truth.

religious convictions have on social reality. For no society is entirely static. Every society changes, and in every society there are processes that promote these changes. If, now, religious ideas have their plausibility basis in social changes, no one can precisely assess how far these religious ideas are an *expression* of the changes, and how far their motive power — how far they are conditioned by the changes, and how far they themselves exert an influence. All we can ever do is to detect the interaction and mutual influence of religion and society. And this interaction generally makes a mockery of every attempt to pin down any particular aspect as the "first cause" of social and religious happenings.

A changing society can be viewed from a number of micro or macro sociological angles.

1. Role analyses ask about the positions and patterns of behavior of the people holding certain religious convictions and about the mutual influence of roles and beliefs. An example of a theory on this level of observation might be the assumption that the Son-of-man Christology had its real-life situation (its *Sitz im Leben*) among homeless itinerant charismatics who — like the Son of man himself — stood sovereign above the normal standards of society but were also condemned and rejected by that society.[3]

2. Analyses of groups and institutions investigate larger social units. They consider these as a network of different roles and positions and try to define their relationship to other groups and institutions. Here too there is often a correspondence between social movements, congregations and churches, and the religious convictions held there. An example of an investigation of this kind is J. H. Elliott's sociological interpretation of 1 Peter, his postulate being that the structure and function of the "household" in the ancient world provides the plausibility basis for the epistle's theology.[4]

3. The analysis of society takes in the social system as a whole — its stratification, its potential for conflict, the chances it offers for mobility, and its legitimation problems. We may assume that religious movements which spread through the whole of a society have aspects of that whole society as their plausibility basis. Early Christianity was one of the movements that had a significance for society as a whole.

---

3. I have outlined this thesis in *Soziologie der Jesusbewegung*, ThEx 194 (Munich, 1977), 26ff. (Eng. trans. *The First Followers of Jesus*, trans. J. Bowden [London: SCM Press, 1978]; in U.S. under the title *Sociology of Early Palestinian Christianity* [Philadelphia: Fortress Press, 1978]).

4. J. H. Elliott, *A Home for the Homeless: A Sociological Exegesis of 1 Peter: Its Situation and Strategy* (Philadelphia: Fortress Press, 1981).

This brings us to the most interesting question for a sociology of early Christianity: To what degree did aspects of society as a whole provide the plausibility basis for the early Christian faith? What I should like to do here is to try to show from Paul's Christology that there was indeed a correlation between processes of change in society as a whole and early Christian faith. Since this is not a question of correlations between static social structures and religious ideas, but has to do with the connection between social changes and acts of faith, the problem of sociological "reductionism" will, I believe, hardly arise in acute form. For when social changes find expression in human awareness, this in its turn affects the changes themselves — even if it is only that the social process is strengthened and encouraged.

The object of our investigation is Pauline Christology or, to be more precise, two christological images. On the one hand Paul presents Christ as the master who has voluntarily assumed the position of a slave. But on the other he pictures Christ as a "mystical body" in which all Christians participate. We shall call these two Christologies "position" and "participation" Christologies.[5]

Position Christology interprets the Christ-event on the analogy of a radical change in social position. It works with sociomorphic (or socioform) images: Christ is a slave and a master, a condemned prisoner and a judge; he is viewed as enemy and reconciler. He successively assumes complementary roles which can be fitted into a hierarchical order. The master is "more" than the slave; the judge is above the condemned prisoner; the reconciler is (generally) someone who is superior to the rest. In real life it is impossible for anyone to assume both roles toward the same human counterpart. But the christological images present this as something that really happens. The slave becomes the master; the condemned prisoner becomes the universal judge; the object of human hostility becomes the reconciler.

Participation Christology, in contrast, works with physiomorphic (or physioform) metaphors. Here we shall confine ourselves to the image of the body. In the ancient world, this metaphor was widely used as a way of describing social units, especially the state. But in the mind of the Christian congregations, the image is more than a metaphor. For the congregation is not just "a" body. It is the body of Christ, who is present in marvelous fashion in the community of his people as risen Lord. Sacramental rites incorporate members into this body: "We were

---

5. I have entered in more detail into the distinction between two groups of christological images (which I have here called position and participation Christology) in "Soteriological Symbolism in the Pauline Writings," chapter 5 above.

all baptized into one body—Jews or Greeks, slaves or free" (1 Cor. 12:13). The Lord's Supper binds the members together because they eat the same bread: "We who are many are all one body, for we all partake of the one bread" (1 Cor. 10:17). This christological image too goes beyond anything in real life. Of course integration processes can be found everywhere, but no one can be permanently bound as closely to another person as a limb is bound into a larger organism.

Although the images used in the position and participation Christologies transcend social reality, they were nevertheless plausible in particular social contexts. So what was their plausibility basis in the society of the ancient world?

1. POSITION CHRISTOLOGY
AND ITS PLAUSIBILITY BASIS

When the Son of God is humiliated to the status of slave, so as then to rise to be Lord over all the powers, this inevitably reminds us of social mobility processes—upward or downward movements that were found not only in the symbolic world of early Christian faith but also, in less extreme form, in society. This suggests that real upward and downward processes may have provided the plausibility basis for belief in the exalted and humiliated Lord, even if the term "correspondence" is an inadequate way of describing the relation between social reality and religious symbolism.

What do we know about social mobility in the Roman Empire at the time of the principate (i.e., the era under Augustus and his successors)?[6] First of all, we must beware of projecting modern experiences of social mobility into the ancient world. The chances of rising were limited. All the same, they were greater at that time than in other periods. Social mobility is an urban phenomenon, and with the flowering of the mediterranean *polis* civilization in Hellenism and the Roman Empire, the chances of rising no doubt increased.

A rise of this kind extended over several generations. The slave could

---

6. See G. Alföldy, *Römische Sozialgeschichte*, 2nd ed. (Wiesbaden, 1979), 83–138, esp. 133ff. (Eng. trans. *The Social History of Rome*, trans. D. Braund and F. Pollock [London: Croom Helm; Totowa, N.J.: Barnes & Noble Books, 1985]); H. W. Pleket, "Sociale Stratifie en Sociale Mobiliteit in de Romeinse Keizertijd," *Tijdschrift voor Geschiedenis* 84 (Groningen, 1971), 215–51; H. Castritius, "Die Gesellschaftsordnung der römischen Kaiserzeit und das Problem der sozialen Mobilität," *Mitteilungen der TU Braunschweig* 8 (1973): 38–45; K. Hopkins, "Elite Mobility in the Roman Empire," in *Studies in Ancient Society*, ed. M. I. Finley (London and Boston: Routledge & Kegan Paul, 1974): 103–20.

be freed. As *libertus* — a freedman — he still had a blemish. But his son could already move up into the urban aristocracy of the decurions, or city councillors. The Vitellii were a classic example for the rise of a family. According to Suetonius, they were descended from a freed slave who became a cobbler (*Vita* 2.1ff.). The cobbler's son made a fortune, with the help of which the grandchildren became *equites* ("knights"), or members of the equestrian order. His great-grandchildren were senators. One of them was the Syrian legate who deposed Pontius Pilate, the prefect, or governor, of Judea and Samaria. His son was even emperor for a short time (69 C.E.). Of course there were cometlike careers as well, but those were the exception. Pertinax was the son of a freed slave and became first an *eques*, then a senator, and finally emperor, following Commodus in 193 C.E. and reigning for three months.

So there were limited opportunities for rising. How often these were actually realized is not so important. The essential point is that people's expectations could be shaped by the fact that anyone could move up to the next rung on the ladder during his lifetime. For slaves living in the towns and cities this was almost the rule during the principate. They could expect to be freed after about thirty years, and often sooner.

The important thing is not simply the fact that there were chances for rising in the world. The decisive point is the force behind the rise. Of course personal capability and energy were an important factor. But loyalty to a master was more important still — very much more so than in modern society. A man had his master to thank for his advancement. He either moved up the ladder together with that master, or the master promoted his advancement, or he acquired a new master who had a higher rank than the old one. A rise in the world was the reward for personal loyalty to an individual, so we might talk about an "advancement loyalty," even if the force behind social mobility cannot be explained by that alone. Since in my view this advancement loyalty is of vital importance for an understanding of early Christian Christology, I should like to give a few examples.

1. A slave could rise in the social scale even if he remained a slave.[7] His prestige depended on the prestige of his master. If he was sold to a master who was an important man, he improved his status. As an imperial slave — that is, as a member of the *familia Caesaris* — he could even occupy a position higher than that of his former master. Epictetus

---

7. P. R. C. Weaver, "Social Mobility in the Early Roman Empire: The Evidence of the Imperial Freedmen and Slaves," in *Studies in Ancient Society*, ed. M. I. Finley, 121–40. There was again a clear hierarchy among the imperial slaves themselves. Those who played a part in government were of course at the top of the tree.

illustrates this in his story about a slave belonging to his own former
master Epaphroditos:

> Epaphroditos owned a cobbler who was no use, so he sold him. By some
> strange chance this man was bought by a high imperial official, so that he
> became cobbler to the emperor. You should have seen how Epaphroditos
> buttered him up! "How is my excellent Felicio?" and: "I love you!" And then
> if somebody asked us: "What is your master doing?" the answer would be:
> "He is in conference with Felicio!" Yes — but had he not sold him because he
> was no use? Who had suddenly turned him into a sensible man? (Epictetus
> *Discourses* 1.19.19–22)

2. One of the most widespread examples of upward mobility was the
manumission of slaves.[8] Most slaves in the towns and cities could hope
for this. Slaves were generally freed before they were thirty-five years
old, but this did not make them the equivalent of freemen. The *libertus*
was still dependent on his patron, to whom he owed certain services
(*operae*) and whose "clientele," dependents or protégés, he enlarged. To
free his slaves was in the master's own interests, for the prospect of being
freed as a reward for faithfulness was an incentive for slaves to serve
their master accordingly. Masters also profited from the work and
support of the *libertus*. We can therefore say that the system was "simply
a more refined form of exploitation than slavery without manumission."[9]
But the system was effective. It bound slaves to their masters and defused
possible social conflicts, because it did not deprive the disfranchised
slave of all hope. In Nero's time, the senate discussed whether the obligation of the freed slave, the *libertus,* toward his patron should not be given
increased rigor by the threat of sanctions. The one party argued:

> It was not expecting particularly much of the freedmen that they should retain
> their liberty at the price of the same compliance (*obsequium*) through which
> they had attained it. On the other hand, obvious evil-doers would deservedly
> be reduced to the status of slave once more, so that fear would keep within
> due limits those whom kindness had not been able to reform. (Tacitus *Annals*
> 13.26.3)

The opposite side warned against reducing freed slaves to slavery
again, arguing that these people were important for society as a whole:

> The freedmen constituted a very large group. As a rule, the general body
> of citizens, the decurions, the assistants to the highest officers of state, and

---

8. See G. Alföldy, "Die Freilassung von Sklaven und die Struktur der Sklaverei in der
römischen Kaiserzeit," in *Rivista Storica dell'Antichità*, vol. 2; ed. M. Sordi et al. (Bologna,
1972), 97–128; also printed in *Sozial- und Wirtschaftsgeschichte der römischen Kaiserzeit*, ed.
H. Schneider, WdF 552 (Darmstadt, 1981), 336–71.

9. Thus Alföldy, *Römische Sozialgeschichte,* German ed. 125.

the priests, as well as the cohorts in Rome, were all freedmen; while most of the equestrian order and very many senators were also descended from men of this rank. If freedmen were eliminated, the lack of those born free would become evident. (*Annals* 13.27.1)

This view won the day. But the debate shows that the manumission system was built up on loyalty and was an important factor in the mobility that extended over several generations. Here again, a freed slave had great advantages if his master enjoyed an exalted status. As the *libertus* of a Roman citizen, he generally received citizenship himself, while as the *libertus* of a *peregrinus* (a freeman not enjoying Roman citizenship) he remained a *peregrinus*.

3. Even a free citizen could improve his status through loyalty to someone who was more powerful than himself. He could be the "client" or protégé of a respected patron. This involved mutual obligation. Pliny the Younger, for example, begs full citizenship (under the *ius Quiritum*) for his three clients:

> Sir: Valerius Paulinus has left a will making me the patron of his Latin freed men [i.e., freed men of inferior status], passing over his son Paulinus. I beg you to confer full citizenship on three of them first of all, since I am afraid that it might be immodest to ask your favor for all of them at once. For the more generously you treat me, the more moderately I must appeal to that generosity. The names of the men for whom I am asking your favor are C. Valerius Astraeus, C. Valerius Dionysius and C. Valerius Aper. (Pliny the Younger *Epistulae* 10.104)

4. Finally, the army must be mentioned as an important factor in social mobility.[10] Anyone from the provinces who served in the army for twenty-five years could acquire Roman citizenship on his release. A man could rise from the ranks and become a centurion; and then, in the carefully thought-out hierarchy of the centuriate, he could rise to the rank of *primipilus,* or senior centurion of a legion, thus acquiring the rank of *eques,* or "knight." Of course these opportunities were limited. In the middle of the second century there were about two thousand centurions. But even a private soldier could move up the social ladder by way of his military service. As a veteran he enjoyed modest privileges (the *immunitas*), and received money or land as a reward for his services. It can therefore be said that "the Roman citizen had the greatest, and

---

10. See B. Dobson, "The Centurionate and Social Mobility during the Principate," in *Recherches sur les structures sociales dans l'antiquité classique* (Paris, 1970), 99–116; also his "The Significance of the Centurion and 'Primipilaris' in the Roman Army and Administration," *ANRW* II, 1 (Berlin, 1974), 392–434.

indeed for most people the only, chance of improving his status if he allowed himself to be recruited for a legion or the militia."[11]

Loyalty to master, patron, and emperor (as the supreme commander of the army) was undoubtedly an important mobility factor in Roman-Hellenistic society. Ordinary people could see from their own situation, and by looking at other people, that the individual had a chance to rise only if he had a good master or acquired a better one. A rise in the social scale was the reward for loyalty. This loyalty was based on mutual obligation. Anyone who was rich and powerful was in duty bound to stand up for the people who were dependent on him, and to work for the community as a whole. An astonishing "donation" mentality made it possible for urban administrations to cope with communal tasks in spite of a modest public revenue.

Real social structures are often reflected in religion, in symbolically intensified form. What in reality is present only in germ, and subject to many limitations, can develop with much less hindrance in the symbolically interpreted "world" of religion. The advancement loyalty actually experienced in society inevitably created fundamental structures of religious feeling and thinking. Anyone who became a Christian acquired a new master who was above all other masters. Beforehand, that person had been the slave of sin. Now he was a slave of the mightiest of lords (Rom. 5:16). Before, he was subjected to the powers of the world. Now he was a "son" who had come of age (Gal. 4:1-6). Earlier, he had been a servant of human beings. Now he was "Christ's freedman," who had been bought for a high price (1 Cor. 7:21ff.). As Christ's soldier he fought for his master (2 Cor. 10:4-6). The metaphors of religious faith are taken from real upward mobility and point to an objective connection between society and religion; for the advancement loyalty experienced in social life was the plausibility basis for faith in the exalted Lord. But here religious symbolism reached out far beyond the limits of reality. Let me illustrate this in four ways.

First, faith in the exalted Lord was an offer of advancement loyalty for everyone, whatever his or her existing social status. In Christ there was "neither Jew nor Greek, neither slave nor free, neither male nor female" (see Gal. 3:28). The bond with Christ gave the very lowest of all a chance, for the Christ-event represented an "advancement" process which burst the bounds of all experience: the one who was executed becomes the universal Lord; the one condemned, the divine judge; the scapegoat, a high priest.

---

11. F. Vittinghoff, "Soziale Struktur und politisches System der hohen römischen Kaiserzeit," *HZ* 230 (1980): 30–55; quotation from p. 38.

A second difference between society and religion has to do with the place of personal "performance." In the ancient world, competence and achievement did not play the dominant role that they do in modern times (or in the modern mind). But all the same, without some degree of personal *virtus* there was hardly any chance to rise, even if, in case of doubt, the decisive factor was personal loyalty. This was the situation in which Paul preached his message of justification; and his message was a radical one. It said that works and achievements do not decide anything at all about a person's status before God. All that counts is πίστις – that is, loyalty to the crucified Master who is now above all masters.

A third characteristic of faith is its radicalization of "status dissonance."[12] Status dissonance is a result of mobility processes: the same person can be assigned a higher or lower status according to the context. As an imperial *slave*, Felicio was inferior to his former master, Epaphroditos; as an *imperial* slave and a member of Caesar's household, he was above him. Since the ancient world, much more than modern societies, clung to the "given" and existing boundaries of origin and legal status, and yet at the same time permitted a mobility extending over several generations, almost everyone found himself in a position of "status dissonance" in one way or another. This status dissonance actually experienced in everyday life provides the plausibility basis for the belief that Christ had a diametrically opposite status before God and before the world: in the world, the only-begotten Son of God was "a slave," who suffered the shameful death of crucifixion (Phil. 2:6ff.). He took upon himself the greatest possible status dissonance.

Finally, we should remember one more peculiarity of early Christian faith. In social life, the chances of rising were spread over several generations. Within the span of a single lifetime everyone could hope to advance at least one step. The dependent son could hope to become independent on his father's death. The slave could hope for manumission. The *libertus,* the freed slave, could prosper economically and could become a member of the associations of the "Augustales" (associations devoted to the cult of the emperor). His son could become a decurion. The *peregrinus* (or *Latinus*) could acquire full Roman citizenship.[13] But the

---

12. For the term "status dissonance," see Weaver, "Social Mobility," 122, 125, 129f. W. A. Meeks supposes, probably rightly, that there were many people with "status dissonance" in the early Hellenistic Christian congregations (*The First Urban Christians: The Social World of the Apostle Paul* [New Haven and London: Yale University Press, 1983], esp. 70ff.). He interprets this as a sign of upward mobility (p. 73).

13. On this gradual upward mobility, see Vittinghoff, "Soziale Struktur," 52; also Alföldy, *Römische Sozialgeschichte,* German ed. 134f.

early Christian faith was an offer of advancement loyalty that conferred everything all at once, in a single step. With baptism, the Christian became a "son of God," a freedman and a soldier of Christ, a citizen of the heavenly *polis*.

To sum up: real processes of advancement in Roman-Hellenistic society provide the plausibility basis for Pauline position Christology. Faith in the exalted Lord is an offer of advancement loyalty for everyone. It demands only loyalty — neither works nor achievements. It leads to radical status dissonance, for the position of the Christian before the world can be diametrically opposite to his status before God. Faith gives in a single act what is otherwise the improbable outcome of a process spread over generations.

2. PARTICIPATION CHRISTOLOGY AND ITS PLAUSIBILITY BASIS

We shall confine ourselves here to one of the metaphors used in participation Christology: the image of the body and its members. In the ancient world, this was a widespread image for the political commonwealth.[14] We meet it especially in exhortations to social concord, in situations where the city-states were threatened by conflict (see the fable of Menenius Agrippa in Livy 2.32).[15] In the Hellenistic period, the image could then acquire a wider scope. The Hellenistic empires, extending over many nations and civilizations as they did, provided a genuine foundation for cosmopolitanism. All could be viewed as members of a cosmic commonwealth, irrespective of the state or people to which they belonged. During the Roman-Hellenistic period which is of particular interest to us here, we find the body metaphor used in this sense in the Stoic writings especially. Stoicism was a philosophy widely held among the ruling elite of the empire, and some of the authors whom we find using the image of the body and its members were themselves members of that elite.[16]

This may be said of Cicero, who succeeded in rising from the rank of *eques* to that of senator. For him, everyone belonged to a body that embraced the whole of humanity, not merely the citizens of one's own

---

14. H. Schlier offers a general survey in his article "Corpus Christi," *RAC* 3 (1957): 437–53; also E. Schweizer, "σῶμα," *ThWNT* 7 (1964): 1024–91 (cf. *TDNT* 7).

15. W. Nestle, "Die Fabel des Menenius Agrippa," *Klio* 21 (1927): 350–60.

16. A. Wikenhauser collected and translated into German the most important texts in *Die Kirche als mystischer Leib Christi nach dem Apostel Paulus* (Münster, 1940), 130–43.

country (*De officiis* 3.19–20; *De finibus* 3.19, 64). Seneca enjoyed the same social status as Cicero, he too rising from *eques* to senator. After 54 C.E., he and Burrus were the most important men in the Roman Empire. In his writings he several times insists on the close ties existing between all human beings: "Just as there is sympathy between all the members of the body, because the preservation of the whole is important for each individual part, so human beings should cherish every individual, because we were born to be a community" (*De ira* 2.31.7). All are "members of a great body" (see Seneca *Epistulae* 95.51f.; 92.30). The emperor Marcus Aurelius goes on to deduce from the body metaphor the notion that we are all destined to work together (2.1, 3). For him, the fact that we all belong together as members of one body is the reason for loving all human beings (7.13). Epictetus, the freed slave, occasionally uses the image of the body and its members in a cosmic sense (see *Dis.* 2.5.24ff.; 10.3f.). He is the only one of these writers who did not belong to the imperial upper class. But thanks to his pupil Arrian (an administrator and general who later rose to the rank of senator), we are in possession of his "discourses." His teaching found a lively echo among the ruling elite of the Roman Empire, as did the teaching of the Stoic philosophers generally.

In my view, the cosmopolitical body metaphor used in Stoic philosophy has a clearly discernible plausibility basis in Roman-Hellenistic society. The Roman Empire was not a single, homogeneous society. It was rather a conglomeration of different "societies," upon which a unified political superstructure had been imposed.[17] The era of the principate was remarkable for successfully integrating the provincial aristocracies more and more into the imperial upper class, or for linking them closely to it. The emperor played a decisive part here, binding to himself the key figures in the city aristocracies by conferring privileges on them, or attaching the few satellite princes (like the Herodians) through personal loyalty. The Stoic picture of the cosmopolitical "body" of humanity has its *Sitz im Leben*—its real-life situation—in the upper class of decurions, "knights," and senators. These people experienced in practical terms a cosmopolitical integration process, which—encouraged by the principate—cut across the boundaries of peoples and cultures.[18]

---

17. F. Vittinghoff's view in "Soziale Struktur," 30: "For in the empire there were an indeterminable number of societies, with varying structures, which existed as ethno-cultural units." Moreover: "In the countries outside, Roman society . . . was only a superstructure, as it were" (p. 30).

18. The relative integration of the upper class is stressed by G. Alföldy, who maintains that the stability of Roman society was based on the fact that "the leading classes among former aliens could be integrated into the upper classes of Roman society"; see

This link between the metaphor of the (cosmo)political body and the integration of a ruling elite through the principate is directly referred to in the writings that have come down to us. The emperor is depicted as the head of the body politic and the guarantor of its stability. This is the way Seneca addresses Nero, for example: "Your goodness of soul has gradually become known and talked about throughout the whole body of the empire (*imperii corpus*), much being shaped according to your image. A state of health starts from the head (*a capito*)" (*De clementia* 2.2.1).

In another passage, again addressing Nero, he says: "tu animus rei publicae tuae es, illa corpus tuum" (You are the soul of your commonwealth, and that commonwealth is your body) (*De clem.* 1.5.1). Comparable utterances about the emperor and the empire can be found in Tacitus (*Annals* 1.12.3 and 13.4), Curtius (*Hist.* 10.9.1ff.), and Plutarch (*Galba* 4). The emperor is the essential integrating factor, "since without their head the members [he means the provinces] would shiver into dissension" (Curtius 10.9).

The Roman-Hellenistic ruling elite, in which the (cosmo)political body metaphor had its real-life situation, disapproved of early Christianity. For Tacitus (*Annals* 15.44) and Pliny the Younger, both of them Roman senators and legates, the Christian faith was a superstition. Pliny writes (*Epistulae* 10.96.8): "Nihil aliud inveni quam superstitionem pravam, immodicam" (I have found nothing but miserable superstition, immoderately pursued). The fact that we come across a comparable body metaphor in the early Christian writings too would seem at first sight to contradict the assumption that the metaphor had a plausibility basis in the upper classes. But if we look more closely we find that the assumption is endorsed, for the Pauline image about the body of Christ can in fact be clearly distinguished from the cosmopolitical body metaphor.

1. The Stoic image about the body and its members is cosmopolitical. It takes in all human beings. Their unity is already existent. Early Christianity, in contrast, restricts the image to little Christian groups. And here, it is not a question of bringing out a kinship between human beings that had always existed. Here a new bond is created by way of baptism

---

his "Die römische Gesellschaft — Struktur und Eigenart," *Gymnasium* 83 (1976): 1–25. K. Christ criticizes this view; see his "Grundfragen der römischen Sozialstruktur," in *Studien zur antiken Sozialgeschichte: Festschrift für F. Vittinghoff* (Cologne and Vienna, 1980), 197–228. He assumes (p. 215) that the *decuriones* were still locally oriented and that only senators and *equites* made up the imperial upper class, which was controlled by the emperor. It nevertheless proved possible to bind the *decuriones* of the cities loyally to this imperial upper class. Rome acted as protector of the institutions of the city republics.

and the Lord's Supper. Baptism binds together "Jews and Greeks, slaves and free" (1 Cor. 12:13). The Lord's Supper brings together rich and poor (1 Cor. 11:17ff.).

2. In the examples outside the New Testament, either all the members of the body are presented as equal, or they are subordinated to one dominating member (the stomach or the head; see Livy, 2.32). In Paul too one member has a special position, but here it is not the most powerful of the members; it is the weakest. Regard for the weakest member becomes the criterion for the unity of the body.

These two features correspond to the specific plausibility structure of early Christianity. For whereas the upper classes were involved in an integration process encouraged by the principate, any comparable integration processes were lacking in the lower and middle classes. There the individual social groups had a varying relationship of loyalty to members of the upper class — as slaves, freedmen and "clients." But the various groups with their different concerns and interests had no feeling of belonging together.[19] It was only in the little fringe groups of the early Christian congregations that we can discern the germ of this sense of solidarity. It is therefore understandable that the image of the body and its members should be restricted in early Christianity to small groups and should depict a new unity which did not yet exist, but which was in the process of evolving.

This new social unity was produced not through loyalty to the emperor but through loyalty to a completely different Lord, who had been executed by the forces of the state. Nor was it promoted by the objective and functional needs of rule. Instead it had a common point of reference among the victims of that rule: among the weakest members. In this image, the other, suffering man or woman takes the place otherwise held by the strongest member and guarantees the integration of the whole body (1 Cor. 12:22ff.).

Parallel to the integration of the ruling elite, an integration process took place in the empire among small fringe groups who did not participate in government or administration. As long as the upper classes had enough coherence and were able to bind the disunited groupings in the lower classes to themselves, the integration movement in early Christianity (which offered an alternative to that of the upper classes) remained a phenomenon confined to fringe groups. But the great crisis in the third century changed the structure of society. The upper classes crumbled — senate, decurions, and army confronting one another mistrustfully as alien groups. On the other hand, the lower classes became

---

19. Alföldy's view in *Römische Geschichte,* German ed. 135.

unified.[20] The old distinctions between slaves, freedmen, and freemen disappeared. Is it merely chance that it was now that Christianity was able for the first time to become a leading spiritual power?

To sum up: Paul's position and participation Christology has a social plausibility basis in the mobility and integration processes of Roman-Hellenistic society.[21] The structure and dynamic of society shape the forms taken by religious experience and thought. But at the same time religious faith transcends society. Belief in the exalted Lord offered advancement loyalty to everyone, even the least important. Incorporation in the body of Christ offered integration for all, even for the lower classes, who had a very much smaller share than the upper echelons in the integration processes taking place throughout the empire.

The analysis I have put forward here is based on the sociology of knowledge. It makes no claim to be an exhaustive treatment of Pauline Christology. It does not even cover all its interconnections under the aspect of the sociology of knowledge. All I should like to do is to suggest that the Christology of the early congregations should not merely be seen in correlation with mobility and integration but also shows unmistakable links with social conflicts. The crucifixion itself is the expression of a conflict with the ruling class. And other aspects might be mentioned as well.

In closing, I should like only to draw attention to the hermeneutical importance of investigations of this kind. In Roman society, people could directly experience that to acquire a better master led to more freedom and a wider variety of possible ways of behavior. Advancement loyalty raised status. Men and women today are bound to experience personal dependencies very differently. They see again and again that it is the will to achieve and "to get on" that leads to careers which move up the ladder of success — and that this will "to get on" is often linked with a degree of *disloyalty* to superiors and colleagues. In actual fact, dependence on the people above plays an important part; but people's attitude to this dependence is ambivalent. It is not simply accepted and affirmed. Not infrequently, it leads to great emotional problems.[22] In other words,

---

20. Ibid., 153ff. He stresses that "the lower classes manifested a more and more unified structure" (p. 158).

21. H. Gülzow, independently of myself, has developed the thesis of a connection between social mobility in Roman society and the spread of new (oriental) religions or cults. He put this forward in Heidelberg on January 1, 1983, in a lecture to the Patristische Arbeitsgemeinschaft. In my view this is a highly interesting theory.

22. This is not intended to mean that in the ancient world the relationship to "masters" could not also be extremely ambivalent. Juvenal and Martial give eloquent expression to the feelings of those protégés who were more self-confident and intelligent and who felt that they were humiliatingly treated by their patrons.

a modern man or woman cannot understand why it is supposed to be so liberating to have a new master. Modern people suspect that this offer made in Christian preaching veils a threatening "authoritarian" dependence — and the suspicion is not always unjustified. In our modern context, the proclamation of redemption as a "change of regime" can be the expression of an authoritarian intention which obscures rather than expresses the real motives of the original Christian faith.

This does not mean that position Christology is inaccessible for modern men and women; for what they are yearning for is indeed a society in which people in the highest positions can take the lowest, and the lowest can take the highest, and in which the solidarity of all human beings proves itself in the weakest member of society. Up to now there has never been any such society — except in the symbolic world of religion. But people who believe in the reality of religious symbols will seek for a society of this kind in a different way from those for whom it is no more than an empty dream.

7

Judaism and Christianity in Paul

◆

The Beginning of a Schism and Its Social History

*For Hartwig Thyen on his sixtieth birthday, April 21, 1987 ***

IN PAUL the paths of Jews and Christians clearly diverge for the first time. As a missionary, he founded congregations which no longer required that their members should first be converted to Judaism (through circumcision) as a condition for admission. As a theologian, by making an antithesis of "faith" and "law" (or "faith" and "works"), he drew a dividing line between the new faith and the religion that had given it birth. Yet in Paul we can also see the first attempt to bring the paths of Jews and Christians together again; for he struggled to find a reason and an interpretation for the parallelism of the two religions, borne up by the hope that at the end God would unite the two once more (Romans 9–11).

If we consider Paul's life's work from the viewpoint of social history, we discover the same theme that emerges from this judgment drawn from the history of theology: there again we can see the beginnings of the schism between Judaism and Christianity. We cannot light up the social history of this schism completely. For that, we lack too many of the building blocks for a sociology of the Jewish and Christian congregations in the ancient world. The reflections that follow are merely a provisional attempt.

In the first section, I shall outline three models for determining the relationship between Judaism and Christianity. New Testament

* This essay is intended as a greeting to Hartwig Thyen on his sixtieth birthday. He is one of the few German-speaking New Testament scholars who in their work have taken up questions relating to the Jewish–Christian dialogue. The present essay is a small token of thanks for stimulating ideas in this sector and in others.

Christianity can be interpreted as a parallel to Judaism; as its de-restriction, or opening; and as its transformation.

In a second section we shall look at Paul's interpretation of the relationship between Jews and Christians. All three models discussed in section one can be shown to have a place in Paul, in their theological form.

In a third section we shall formulate a sociological hypothesis for each of these models. Our main thesis here is that the theological interpretations of the relationship between Jews and Christians that we find in Paul were the more plausible because they also had a basis in social reality.

I. THREE MODELS FOR DETERMINING THE RELATIONSHIP BETWEEN JUDAISM AND CHRISTIANITY IN NEW TESTAMENT TIMES

A. *The First Model: Christianity as a Parallel to Judaism*

From the viewpoint of the detached observer, the advance of Judaism and Christianity in the Roman Empire was part of the spread of oriental cults generally.[1] From the turn of the era on, we can observe an "orientalization" of culture and society. In his book *Wohltätigkeit und Armenpflege im vorchristlichen Altertum* ("Charity and the Care of the Poor in the Ancient World before Christ"; 1939),[2] Hendrik Bolkestein also shed sociological light on this process, taking as an example the charitable ethic of oriental civilization. His thesis is that, whereas the West stresses the mutual obligation of people on the same social level, the Orient is preeminently familiar with the obligations of the strong toward the weak; and here reciprocity is not always expected. The western ethic, which is based on equality, presupposes in principle citizens who enjoy equal rights. That is to say, it is linked with the social structures of the republican city-state, the *polis*. The oriental ethic based on compassion, on the other hand, is molded by the authoritarian social structures of the East, where the socially weak are dependent on the benevolence of the more powerful. When — through the mediation of Jews and

---

1. See *Die orientalischen Religionen im Römerreich,* ed. M. J. Vermaseren, Études préliminaires aux religions orientales dans l'empire romain 93 (Leiden, 1981).

2. H. Bolkestein, *Wohltätigkeit und Armenpflege im vorchristlichen Altertum,* trans. from Dutch by F. A. Ledermann (Utrecht, 1939; reprint, Groningen, 1967). For a critical assessment, see W. Bauer, GGA 202 (1944): 358–68; M. Dibelius, *DLZ* 69 (1948): 85–87; I. Weiler, "Zum Schicksal der Witwen und Waisen bei den Völkern der Alten Welt," *Saeculum* 31 (1980): 157–93.

Christians — the oriental "compassion" ethic now spread in the West as well, this was bound up with an orientalization of the structures of society in Greece and Rome. The institutions of the *polis* declined in influence, devalued by the overriding authoritarian structures of the Roman military monarchy. In the third century C.E., in a long drawn-out crisis, this process led to the transformation of society; for at the end of the crisis society became Christian. In other words, the shift toward an authoritarian society at the turn of the era called for new patterns of human solidarity, and these were provided by Judaism and Christianity.

Paul would fit into this pattern in the following way.[3] His preaching of grace gave theological expression to the new values. The compassion of the strong toward the weak which was required is radicalized into God's grace toward the sinner, and is deduced from this grace, as the human behavior corresponding to it. For us, it is important to see here that in a conception of this kind, Jews and Christians are viewed as parallel variants in a world of oriental conviction. The differences between them individually are just as much ignored as are the differences between the two of them and their environment. Yet there can be no doubt that Christianity and Judaism were very different indeed from the world around. Both were monotheistic heresies in a polytheistic world. Both demanded from their members a high degree of consistent conduct, deviating from the social customs otherwise practiced. Both held a special position among the oriental cults which were then thrusting into the Roman Empire. For that very reason they would seem to be parallels.

B. *The Second Model:*
Christianity as a De-restriction or Opening of Judaism[4]

The question remains: What distinguishes the two groups from one another? Why was it that only one of them — Christianity — "conquered" the world? Why not Judaism? Wolfgang Schluchter looks for an explanation (and his analysis is not confined to Judaism in ancient times) in the "fringe" position occupied by Jews in society. He writes:

---

3. This conclusion is not found in Bolkestein, but in my view emerges of itself from his viewpoint.

4. W. Bousset, *Kyrios Christos* (Göttingen, 1913; reprint 1967) coined the phrase about Christianity as "diaspora Judaism that had become universal and de-restricted" (p. 291). But he initially means by this only a certain type of early Christian faith: the rational, ethically directed Christianity of *1 Clement,* which finds its continuation in the apologetic writers. But according to Bousset, what dominates earliest Christianity is the "mystery" cult of the kyrios. In the terminology of this essay, this is not merely a de-restricted Judaism. It is Judaism that has been transformed.

Whatever view one may take of the inward situation of this people in the different historical eras and in the different countries, as far as their outward situation is concerned, the Jews — as a special society, largely ascriptively recruited [i.e., recruited by birth — G.Th.], "closed" to the outer world by ritual barriers, without an autonomous political organization — would seem to have remained in an alien and self-imposed fringe position; not individually indeed, but nonetheless collectively.

Schluchter makes this fringe position responsible for the fact that "diaspora Judaism combines a high capacity for innovation with a scant capacity for diffusion."[5]

It is in fact true that only Christianity developed the power of diffusion which was one day to allow it to penetrate the whole of society. Unlike Judaism, it dispensed with certain divisive norms — circumcision and (some) dietary laws — two complexes, that is, which could intervene divisively in the most elemental relationships between people: marriage and the fellowship of shared meals. In this way it created the preconditions that later enabled it to break away from the fringe position in which — just like Judaism — it had long existed. Seen in this light, Christianity was a Judaism that was accessible to non-Jews as well. The decisive change was the social opening made possible by the abandonment of some dividing norms.

In this context Paul's historical importance could be defined by saying that he conceived a Judaism for non-Jews. He provided a theological foundation for the renunciation of dividing norms and made this renunciation prevail in the policies of the church. The question remains: Does this opening of Judaism to society not at the same time represent a profound inward transformation? And did not Paul more than anyone else push forward this transformation of Judaism into Christianity?

C. *The Third Model:*
Christianity as a Transformation of Judaism

This brings us to a third way of defining the relationship between Judaism and Christianity: Christianity is a Judaism that has been transformed in its inner structure, because it has become open to non-Jews. In his work on the sociology of religion, Gustav Mensching described this transformation as the path from a national, or ethnic, religion to a religion that is universal.[6] When a religion takes this path, it is not

---

5. W. Schluchter, "Altisraelitische religiöse Ethik und okzidentaler Rationalismus," in W. Schluchter (ed.), *Max Webers Studie über das antike Judentum* (Frankfurt, 1981), 11–77, esp. 52.

6. G. Mensching summed up his distinction between national and universal religion

merely its social "catchment area" that expands; its conception of salvation changes too. In national religions, salvation is conferred by membership in a community into which a person is born. The task is to guard that salvation and to live up to it. Universal religions, on the other hand, assume that the individual is more independent of society and nature. Salvation is not conferred by any "given" social affiliation. On the contrary, what is "given" is a state of iniquity. A person can move out of this disastrous condition and arrive at a state of salvation only by way of a fundamental change and transformation. A characteristic of universal religions is therefore the idea of redemption.[7]

We see this transition from national to universal religion taking place in Paul's theology. When he formulates for the Gentiles Jewish belief in God and his Messiah, he cannot assume that his Gentile addressees already stand in a positive relationship to God. They have to be converted; they have to turn away from the many gods to the one and only God. They have to change profoundly before they can arrive at a positive state of salvation. They need redemption — through faith and sacramental mediation.

This idea of a sacramentally mediated transformation of the human being, which also heralds a transformation of the whole cosmos, distinguishes Pauline Christianity from Judaism.[8] It is undoubtedly a variant of the notion of redemption that Mensching considers constitutive for universal religions.

II. PAULINE INTERPRETATIONS OF THE RELATIONSHIP
BETWEEN JEWS AND CHRISTIANS

In our second section, we shall now ask how Paul himself viewed the relationship between Jews and Christians. Here we shall take our bearings from the three models that I have just outlined. We find these models in Paul as well, although his intention in using them is certainly to

---

in *Die Religion: Erscheinungsformen, Strukturtypen und Lebensgesetze* (Stuttgart, 1959), 65–77 (= "Folk and Universal Religion," in *Religion, Culture and Society: A Reader in the Sociology of Religion,* ed. L. Schneider (New York: John Wiley & Sons, 1964), 254–61. See also G. Mensching, *Volksreligion und Weltreligion* (Leipzig, 1938), and *Soziologie der Religion* (Bonn, 1947), 25ff.

7. Mensching's account is more differentiated. Above all he sees the transition from a national to a universal religion as already being prepared by the prophets and in Judaism.

8. This agrees with the structural differences between rabbinic Judaism and Paul that E. P. Sanders has worked out under the heading of "participationist eschatology." See his "Patterns of Religion in Paul and Rabbinic Judaism: A Holistic Method of Comparison," *HThR* 66 (1973), 455–78, and *Paul and Palestinian Judaism: A Comparison of Patterns of Religion* (London: SCM Press; Philadelphia: Fortress Press, 1977).

interpret the relationship between Jews and Christians theologically, not historically.

A. *The Parallelism between Judaism and Christianity: Jews and Christians in the Same Role*

Paul often sets the Christian and Jewish faiths over against one another, as if they were antitheses. But this must not blind us to the fact that antitheses of this kind are only possible at all if a relationship between the two has previously existed. The relationship is the "given." Even in the Epistle to the Galations, Jews and Christians are interpreted as "brothers," even if hostile brothers. Abraham's two wives, Sarah and Hagar, with their children, become "types" of the two religions, although only a forced allegorical interpretation makes it possible to equate Hagar with Judaism.[9] This parallelism is brought out even more strongly in Romans 9-11,[10] where Paul sees Jews and Gentiles (Gentile Christians) standing in a highly curious rivalry to one another: Gentile Christians have already arrived at the goal of a righteousness for which they have never striven, whereas Jews, who deliberately strove toward this goal, have not "attained it" (9:30f.). They have stumbled, have taken offense at the stumbling block (9:32f.). In 9:16 Paul already used the "race" image, which echoes through this passage. He picks it up again in 11:11 as a way of saying something more positive: the Jews have certainly stumbled in their race, but they have not fallen. Paul then changes the image for describing the rivalry of Jews and Gentile Christians, now applying the more general (economic?) notion of "penury" and "riches" to their relationship. The poverty of the Jews is wealth for the Gentiles. For it is only because the Jews took offense at the message that it came to the Gentiles. Their conversion, or so Paul hopes, should then in its turn act as a spur to some Jews to be converted as well (11:11-15).

At the end of chapter 11, the meaning of this shifting "rivalry" situation

---

9. See P. Vielhauer, "Paulus und das Alte Testament," in *Oikodome: Aufsätze zum Neuen Testament* 2, TB 65 (Munich 1979), 196–229, esp. 200; in spite of the catchword "allegorical," what we really have in Gal. 4:21-31 is typology.

10. B. Klappert gives a good survey of basic types of interpretation of these three chapters; see his "Traktat für Israel (Römer 9–11): Die paulinische Verhältnisbestimmung von Israel und Kirche als Kriterium neutestamentlicher Sachaussagen über die Juden," in *Jüdische Existenz und die Erneuerung der christlichen Theologie*, ed. M. Stöhr, Abhandlungen zum christlich-jüdischen Dialog 11 (Munich, 1981), 58–137 (survey on 59ff.). It is in my view obvious if one reads Romans 9–11 as a whole that in these chapters Paul is not intending to accuse Israel, but is trying to seek for God's hidden plan of salvation for Israel. He does, however, also show one danger of every positive "salvation history" interpretation of Israel's destiny: if Jews do not behave in a way that accords with this interpretation, they find themselves in the role of accused. In 10:1ff Paul is forced to stress deliberately his role as Israel's "advocate," in order to offset this impression.

is then interpreted, this time without the race metaphor. Jews and Gentiles alike are supposed to experience themselves as equal before the gracious God. Both go through a phase of disobedience. Here there is no difference between them. But neither does God make any difference when he has mercy on everyone.

In what is probably his final utterance about the relationship between Jews and Christians, Paul sees them on their way to the same goal. They take on the same role, one after the other. Both are branches on the same stem, even if these branches are very different. It is only after a process of struggle that Paul arrives at this view of Jews and Christians, whose paths meet only in God, as parallels meet only at infinity. The conception stands at the end of an extensive development, as I hope to show in what follows.

B. *Christianity as De-restricted or Open Judaism: Gentile Christians in the Role of the Jews*

To see Jews and Christians (Gentile Christians) as parallel to one another was a revolutionary insight for a Jew like Paul, who in Gal. 2:15 distinguishes himself proudly from "Gentile sinners." Paul won through to this insight with his call. Through faith in Christ, Gentiles too can enter into God's history with his people, without their having to become Jews first. The role of the Jews is open to the Gentiles without circumcision. We can make this clear to ourselves when we see that Paul formulates all the prerogatives of Israel listed in Rom. 9:4f. in such a way that they are available not only to Jews but to Gentile Christians too: sonship, glory, covenants, law, worship, the promises, and the patriarchs. The "sonship" is available to all human beings through the Spirit (Rom. 8:14ff.; Gal. 4:6). The "glory" shines forth for all in Christ (2 Cor. 3:18; 4:4). The new covenant is sealed for all in the Lord's Supper. All have a law. It is written in the hearts of the Gentiles (Rom. 2:14ff.). All perform the "worship that accords with reason" (Rom. 12:1ff.). And Abraham is "the father of us all" (Rom. 4:16). Gentile Christians now belong to "the Israel of God" (Gal. 6:16). They are the people who were not God's people once, but who have now become so (Rom. 9:25 = Hos. 2:25). This transference to Gentile Christians of what was said about the Jews is at the very center of the Pauline message.

C. *Christianity as a Transformation of Judaism: Jews in the Role of Gentiles*

When salvation is widened out to take in the Gentiles, this was bound to have a retroactive effect on the understanding of salvation. Gentiles had to be converted from many gods to the true God. Acceptance of the message presupposed a more fundamental transformation in their case than it did in the case of Jews. For Jews, to accept the message meant accepting the endorsement of promises given from time immemorial. What for the Gentiles was "redemption" was for the Jews "fulfillment." Jews had reached the goal of a long pilgrimage. But Gentiles had started to take their bearings from a goal that was entirely new.

In his letters Paul now formulates the idea of redemption not merely for Gentiles but for all human beings without distinction. All men and women — Jews too — are living in a comparable state of iniquity. This universalization of the idea of redemption comes about through an exchange of roles: Jews who do not accept the gospel take over the role of the unredeemed Gentiles. Gentiles who believe the gospel take over the role of the Jews. We find the evidence for this role exchange in a number of passages.

In 1 Thess. 1:9-10 Paul talks about "the wrath of God," which all the Gentiles will experience if they do not become converted to the true God and are not saved by his Son. A little later, in 1 Thess. 2:16, he transfers the threat of judgment to the Jews as well. Because of their opposition to the gospel, they too (as well as unbelieving Gentiles) will be delivered over to the ὀργὴ εἰς τέλος.[11]

In Galatians 4 Paul throws light on the relationship between Jews and Gentiles with the help of the Sarah–Hagar typology. Philo appealed to Abraham's marriage with the two women in order to deduce from it the need for Jews (= Sarah) and Gentiles (= Hagar) to live peacefully together.[12] But for Paul, in contrast, the non-Jewish Hagar has become a "type" of Judaism, and Sarah the "type" of the Christian (both Jewish and Gentile). Nor does he interpret their relationship as a peaceful living together. He stresses the tension between the two.

In Romans 9 he proceeds similarly. Here he introduces the contrasting pairs Sarah and Hagar, Jacob and Esau, Moses and Pharaoh.

---

11. The interpretation of εἰς τέλος is disputed. The phrase can be translated in a substantive sense; in this case τέλος is the "end" of history (= *usque ad finem,* "up to the end"), whereby the phrase can include this "end" or exclude it. In the latter case we should have to translate "until the end, but not after that." If one takes an adverbial translation, one can either stress the quantitative or the temporal aspect: the wrath goes forth completely (not merely partially), or finally (and irrevocably). A clearly different sense emerges only from the "exclusive" interpretation for which J. Munck pleads; see his *Christ and Israel: An Interpretation of Romans 9–11,* trans. from Danish by I. Nixon (Philadelphia: Fortress Press, 1967). H. Hyldahl confutes this view in "Paulus og joderne ifolge 1 Thess 2,14-16," *Svensk exegetisk arsbok* 37/38 (Lund, 1972–73), 238–54.

12. Philo *De congressu eruditionis gratia.* See P. Borgen, "Philo of Alexandria" in *Jewish Writings of the Second Temple Period,* ed. M. E. Stone, CRINT II, 2 (Assen, Netherlands: Van Gorcum; Philadelphia: Fortress Press, 1984), 233–82, esp. 254–56.

Traditionally, Hagar, Esau, and Pharaoh represent the Gentiles. But in Paul they become representatives of unbelieving Israel. This is particularly striking in the case of Pharaoh. He, the arch enemy of Israel, actually becomes the image of unbelieving Israel, because of his hardness of heart.

In Rom. 11:25f. we again find a similar exchange of roles. The presupposition for this is admittedly that we see the idea about "the full number of the Gentiles coming in" as a reminiscence of the pilgrimage of the nations. For according to the traditional idea, it is the salvation of Israel that first makes possible, or triggers off, the flocking in of the nations. But in Romans the process is reversed: the "coming in of the nations" is the precondition that makes it possible for all Israel to be saved.

This transference to the Jews of the role hitherto occupied by the Gentiles is so bold a step that we may be permitted to doubt whether Paul went as far as this from the very outset. Would he not originally have expected most of the Jews to accept the new message? Then the problem that arises here would never have presented itself—the problem whether Jews too had to undergo the fundamental transformation from disaster to salvation which was necessary for Gentiles. We may suspect that Paul's development was this: originally he conceived his idea of redemption solely for Gentiles. It was only in a second step that he generalized it, so that it applied to Jews as well.[13] Two factors may well have led to this step: on the one hand, the hostility of non-Christian Jews to his mission to the Gentiles; and on the other, the rivalry of Christian Judaists in his Gentile mission.

In the fifties of the first century, it could surely no longer have been a matter of doubt that the mission to the Gentiles was not merely more successful than the ministry to the Jews, but that it was up against the actual resistance of Jewish diaspora congregations. The mission disturbed the precarious equilibrium between Jews and their environment,

---

13. J. Gager (*The Origins of Antisemitism* [New York: Oxford University Press, 1983]) is in my view wrong when he disputes the universalized idea of redemption in Pauline theology in the form in which we now find it in the epistles. He maintains that redemption through Christ is only for the Gentiles. For Jews the way of the Torah still applies. But he may be right as far as the beginnings of Pauline theology are concerned (beginnings no longer accessible to us). The following hints suggest this: (1) According to the agreement at the Council of the Apostles in the forties, Paul was commissioned to bring the gospel (only) to the Gentiles. Must Paul himself therefore not once have believed that his renunciation of certain tenets of the law as the condition for membership of the congregation applied only to Gentiles, but not to Jews? At least he once accepted this view. (2) In the earliest Pauline epistle (1 Thessalonians, ca. 52 C.E.), the perception that not only Gentiles (1:9f,) but Jews too (2:14-16) are subject to the wrath of God is expounded as if it is a new recognition. (3) In Galatians we undoubtedly find a generalized doctrine of justification (2:15ff.; 4:21ff.), but here Paul is primarily speaking against Gentile Christians who (subsequently) wish to adopt the law.

partly because it threatened to draw off the sympathetic "outsiders" (the "God-fearing"),[14] who were so important for the Jewish congregations; partly because the tensions in the Jewish congregations caused by Christian preaching led to intervention by the state and the magistrates—as we can see from Claudius's edict, for example. But if the Jewish congregations became the most important and most competent opponents of the mission to the Gentiles, then Paul was bound to find it increasingly plausible to assume that they too (like the Gentiles) were living in a state of iniquity. In 1 Thessalonians, this train of thought is still evident: because Jews try to prevent the mission to the Gentiles, they are delivered over to "the wrath of God" just as much as unbelieving Gentiles (2:16).

The plausibility of the generalized idea of redemption was for Paul further intensified by the rival judaistic mission to the Gentiles; for the postulate of this mission was that salvation can be attained only by affiliation with the people of Israel. Gentiles must become Jews if they want to be full members of the Christian congregations. Christianity for Gentiles as Paul conceived of it was, they claimed, no more than a preliminary step, which had to be "completed"—just as the status of "the God-fearing" was a preliminary step to full Judaism. Paul reacted to this rival mission to the Gentiles by postulating that Jews were just as much in need of redemption as all other human beings. In order to show this, he reduced the importance of the Torah: it could lead to the same bondage as heathen idolatry, even if its real intention was salvation.

The utterances of Paul that we possess probably all belong to the same ten years of his life, and by that time he had already universalized the idea of redemption by exchanging the roles of Jews and Gentiles. This is a constant in what he says. But within this constant there is, I believe, a clear development.[15]

---

14. H. Gülzow has brought out clearly the importance of the "God-fearing" for the early Christian mission to the Gentiles and its relationship to Jewish congregations ("Soziale Gegebenheiten der altkirchlichen Mission," in *Kirchengeschichte als Missionsgeschichte*, vol. 1, *Die alte Kirche*, ed. H. Frohnes and U. W. Knorr [Munich, 1974], 189–266, esp. 194–98: "With the drifting away of their God-fearing adherents, the synagogue was not merely threatened with isolation and the religious devaluation associated with that. Even more painful for the Jews must have been the loss of numerous patrons who provided essential help, not merely materially, but above all through their propaganda in the struggle against anti-Semitism" (p. 196).

15. In my view a development is indisputable, which does not necessarily exclude a hidden continuity within this development. See G. Lüdemann, *Paulus und das Judentum*, ThEx 215 (Munich, 1983), who sees the constant in the theological axiom of a church of Jews and Gentiles: in 1 Thess. 2:14ff. the mission to the Gentiles is threatened; Rom. 11:25ff. reflects about the possible loss of Jewish Christianity. In spite of the contradictoriness of what is said, the intention is the same: to preserve the unity of the church.

In his earliest letter, 1 Thessalonians, only the negative side of the idea of redemption is transferred to the Jews: they too are delivered over to the wrath of God. Paul does not yet say that theirs will also be the righteousness of God which creates salvation (as repeal of his wrath). On the contrary, Paul gives the impression that this "wrath" is final, ὀργὴ εἰς τέλος, "wrath to the end" (2:16).

In the letters of the middle period (Galatians and the correspondence with Corinth), Paul talks in more neutral terms. We repeatedly encounter "impartial statements" which in principle relativize the difference between Jews and Gentiles: in Christ there are neither Jews nor Greeks (Gal. 3:28; 1 Cor. 12:13). Circumcision or noncircumcision is irrelevant (Gal. 5:6; 6:15; 1 Cor. 7:19). Jews and Gentiles have the same chance to be converted. It is true that at present there is still a veil over the hearts of the Jews. But from the Old Testament Paul draws the hope that "when he [i.e., Moses] turns to the Lord the veil will be removed" (2 Cor. 3:16). There is no longer any talk about a final punitive judgment.

Then, in the letter to the Romans, "his last will and testament,"[16] Paul takes a final step. Here, on the one hand, the universalized idea of redemption is consistently carried through. Paul repudiates all objections that Jews will surely enjoy a preference in God's final judgment. Yet on the other hand he considers it vitally important to reconcile the universalized idea of redemption with "the priority" of Jews. Side by side with statements of impartiality, and in their place (as in 10:12), Paul asserts a πρῶτον (a "first") for Jews (1:16; 2:9). This is presented in vivid pictorial form in the parable of the olive tree (11:17ff.). This πρῶτον still stands, in spite of Jewish disbelief. For through that very disbelief they have brought about salvation for the Gentiles. At the end, the Christ who comes in his parousia will redeem Israel and forgive all her sins, even her enmity toward the mission to the Gentiles. Paul can win through to this positive utterance because he is able to interpret the role exchange in a new way. He now sees in it a hidden parallelism: Jews and Gentiles have both fallen into a state of iniquity which makes both dependent on God's grace. Both are *simul iustus et peccator*, as it were — righteous and sinners at the same time. Jews are God's enemies because of their resistance to the mission to the Gentiles; and they are God's beloved, because of the patriarchs (11:28). But the same may be said of all human beings, including the Gentiles. All of them have been from time immemorial "God's enemies" (5:10), yet beloved for Christ's sake. This is the way we might paraphrase what is said in chapters 5–8.

---

16. Thus G. Bornkamm, "Der Römerbrief als Testament des Paulus," in his *Geschichte und Glaube*, Pt. II = *Gesammelte Aufsätze* IV, Beiträge zur evang. Theologie 53 (Munich 1971), 120–39.

If I see the matter rightly, we can therefore partly postulate and partly observe the following development. As missionary to the Gentiles, Paul begins with the message that salvation is now available to Gentiles as well. This message is "de-restricted or open Judaism." Jewish resistance to this "de-restriction of Judaism" leads him to generalize the idea of iniquity. All, both Jews and Gentiles, are living in a state of iniquity. The idea of redemption applied to Judaism transforms the structure of Jewish belief: Jews too must undergo a profound change before they arrive at salvation. But at the end Paul renews the universalized idea of salvation — and, quite explicitly, even for Jews who reject the gospel. Their rejection is seen as one phase of the parallel paths leading Jews and Christians to salvation, paths that will finally converge only at the parousia. Here Christianity is a parallel to Judaism.

III. THE SOCIAL REALITY OF JUDAISM AND THE CHRISTIANITY OF NEW TESTAMENT TIMES

The interpretation of any group is always bound up with social reality. Interpretations have to have a "plausibility basis" in the social world that is under consideration. In this third section, we shall therefore fit Paul's interpretations — Christianity as a parallel, a de-restriction, and a transformation of Judaism — into the social reality of the Jewish and Christian congregations as far as we can discover it. This does not mean that our aim is to *derive* the interpretations from the social background. To see religious convictions in a context of social conditions means something different from reducing conviction to social phenomena.

A. *The Parallelism of Judaism and New Testament Christianity*

Even to a viewpoint based on social history, Jews and early Christians appear to be "brothers." Their relationship is shown in the combination of a diastratic and a diasporal cohesion — a structure, that is to say, that cuts right across social strata or classes and right across geographical regions. These two characteristics are sometimes named as the particular sociological feature of New Testament Christianity. In reality they were inherited from Judaism.

The Diastratic Cohesion
Early Christianity brought men and women belonging to different classes closer together than was otherwise possible in the society of the day (except in Judaism). It formed a diastratic unity, spanning different

social classes; but it was not a representative cross section of society as a whole. It did not penetrate the imperial upper class, nor was it equally distributed in town and country. Among the local upper classes, it appealed mainly to the periphery. As far as numbers are concerned, most of the congregations were in any case drawn from the lower classes. Here what is said by Christians themselves (1 Cor. 1:26ff.) coincides with the statements of outsiders. Since there is a large measure of agreement about the question of a "diastratic structure" (although emphases differ) there is no need to develop this point any further here.[17]

This diastratic cohesion in the early Christian congregations was something new in pagan society. Associations and mystery cults certainly brought people together in the ancient world. For example, we find freemen and slaves side by side. But in spite of their different legal status, these people were often socially on much the same level. Above all, however, it was only the Christian (and Jewish) congregations that tried to influence the whole of everyday life with their norms and convictions. They did not merely hold a few meetings in the course of the year; shared meals were held every week. The congregations were communities covering the whole of life, offering mutual help in cases of sickness and death, looking after children and old people, and providing help on journeys and in business transactions. In this way the first Christian congregations made a new "social offer" in pagan society: diastratic solidarity.[18]

In this respect Christianity was a continuation of Judaism, and its parallel. The Jewish congregations too included people of varying rank in civil life:[19] Roman citizens, citizens of the various cities, resident aliens without civil rights, and foreigners. Most of them were at the same time members of the various Jewish *politeumata* — social communities with a limited autonomy, which were recognized and protected by the Romans.

---

17. The term "new consensus" was coined by A. J. Malherbe in *Social Aspects of Early Christianity* (Baton Rouge and London: Lousiana State University Press, 1977), 31. Representative are, among others, E. A. Judge, *The Social Pattern of the Christian Groups in the First Century* (London: Tyndale Press, 1960), and W. A. Meeks, *The First Urban Christians: The Social World of the Apostle Paul* (New Haven and London: Yale University Press, 1983), as well as my own contributions on the sociology of early Christianity.

18. I have no intention of disputing that other associations and cults satisfied a similar social need, but they did not make the same comprehensive claim on the life and thinking of their members.

19. For Egypt, see A. Kasher, *The Jews in Hellenistic and Roman Egypt*, Texte und Studien zum antiken Judentum (Tübingen, 1985; Hebrew 1978), esp. the chapter "The Status of the Jews in the Roman Civic Stratification" (pp. 75–105). On the Diaspora in general, see S. Applebaum, "The Legal Status of the Jewish Communities in the Diaspora," in *The Jewish People in the First Century*, ed. S. Safrai and M. Stern, CRINT I, 1 (Assen, Netherlands: Van Gorcum; Philadelphia: Fortress Press, 1974), 420–63.

As well as these differences in legal status, there were differences of rank which were economically conditioned. Some conflicts in the Jewish congregations can be attributed to internal differences between poor and rich — for example, the revolt of Jonathan the weaver and his lower-class followers in Cyrenaica, which the Jewish upper class tried to suppress (Josephus *Jewish War* 7.437ff.). But generally speaking the Jewish congregations managed to build up an astonishing solidarity, over and above internal tensions. Inwardly this solidarity was based on the solidarity ethics of the Torah; outwardly it was sustained by the special role of the Jews in society. Even outsiders noticed this. Tacitus confirms that "in Jewish circles there is an unshakable faithful solidarity and helpful compassion, whereas they are marked by hostile hate toward all others" (*Historiae* 5.5.1). It may be mentioned here, if only in passing, that this interpretation of the Jews' self-imposed special role as *adversus omnes alios hostile odium* (Tacitus's "hostile hate toward all others") was an anti-Jewish prejudice that was soon transferred to Christians too (see Tacitus *Annals* 15.44.4).

The diastratic structure of Jewish and Christian congregations was bound to encourage the relativization of status differences. In the earliest Christian congregations, it was one of the fundamental maxims of behavior that the first should be prepared to take over the role of the last. Philo is also expressing a comparable "change of position" when he interprets the Sabbath rest, which the Torah commands should be given to slaves too, as an exchange of roles between master and servant:

> He [i.e., Moses] desires to accustom the masters to put their own hands to work, and not to wait for the ministries and services of slaves, so that, should untoward circumstances one day come about in the changeable course of human life, they should not grow early tired because they are not used to work for themselves . . . ; the slaves, however, should not give up their splendid hope but — since a living spark and glimmer of liberty is given them in the rest they enjoy after six days — they should cherish the expectation that, if they steadily show themselves good and affectionate toward their masters, they may achieve complete liberty. But if from time to time freemen undertake slaves' work, and if servants are granted a share of leisure, human life is ennobled in the direction of the most perfect virtue; for those who find themselves in a more splendid position in life, and those who find themselves in one more lowly, may be reminded of the equality of all, and may dutifully pay their debts to one another. (*De specialibus legibus* 2.67f.)

Could not Philo also have said, like Paul, that in the Lord's sight there are neither slaves nor freemen? One reason why Philo saw his idea of Jewish life embodied in the fringe group of the Essenes was because they consistently rejected all forms of slavery (*Quod omnis probus liber sit* 75–87). So was Paul right when he saw the abolition of differences between slaves and freemen in the congregation as a fulfillment of the promise to Abraham — as a Jewish inheritance (Gal. 3:28)? The trend in both passages is the same, as well as the unmistakable tendency to outstrip real conditions with utopian assertions.[20]

The Diasporal Cohesion

A solidarity that cut across class distinctions was complemented by supraregional communication. Although the cults of the ancient world were widespread, unlike Judaism and Christianity they did not develop any forms of organization above local level.[21]

As early as the forties of the first century, representatives of various Christian congregations met in Jerusalem for a supraregional synod, known to us under the name of "the Council of the Apostles" (Gal. 2:1ff.). There people struggled to lend the new movement cohesion and solidarity. It was agreed that a collection should be made, and mission fields were pegged out. In the period that followed, there were interventions in foreign congregations. Ambassadors from Jerusalem appeared in Antioch (Gal. 2:11ff.), while in the fifties rival missionaries continually turned up in the Pauline congregations. The conflicts they caused presuppose that all sides were striving to arrive at a unity of conviction which would override geographical boundaries. At the same time they show that there was already a lively going and coming; journeys were frequent. In Asia Minor at the end of the second century, Bishop Abercius's epitaph extols this supraregional congregational solidarity:[22] "Everywhere I found brethren in the faith, for I had Paul in my chariot." Perhaps he carried a Pauline manuscript with him, which proved him to be worthy of trust. At all events he found accommodation. "The faith" was his quartermaster. "Everywhere *pistis* drew me on, and set before me as food at every place the fish from the spring, exceedingly great

---

20. "Diastratic solidarity" certainly did not lead to merely utopian assertions. In both Jewish and Christian congregations there was an effective counterbalance. Both, parallel to each other, developed systems of social welfare for the poor and for widows. We only have to compare Acts 6:1ff. with the *Testament of Job* 10–15. We even meet the term *diakonia* in both writings. The Mishnah tractate Pe'ah is familiar with a well-developed system of care for the poor (although we must not presuppose that this was already in existence in New Testament times; see D. Seccombe, "Was there organized charity in Jerusalem before the Christians?" *JThS* 29 (1978): 140–43). In his letter to Arsacius (*Sozom. hist. eccl.* 5.16), Julian the Apostate mentions the charitable activity of Jews and Christians side by side.

21. See R. MacMullen, *Paganism in the Roman Empire* (New Haven and London: Yale University Press, 1981). Chapter 4, "Conversion" (pp. 94–112), shows that the pagan cults were lacking a uniformity that would have been lent by some central control.

22. See H. Strathmann and T. Klauser, "Aberkios," in *RAC* 1 (1950), cols. 12–17, which reproduces the inscription and translates it into German.

and pure, caught by a spotless virgin. . . ." So it is not by chance that—apart from the Gospels—the letter became the most important literary genre in the early congregations; it meant communication between people who were separated from one another.

W. A. Meeks views these supraregional relations as the special mark of early Christianity.[23] But in my own view it is a Jewish inheritance. All the Jewish diaspora congregations were linked with Jerusalem, as center. A common calendar of feast days had to be agreed upon, even if we do not hear much about it in New Testament times. Every year the Temple tax was taken to Jerusalem. Every year many Jews made a pilgrimage to the sanctuary. Conversely, the authorities in Jerusalem tried to intervene on behalf of Jews in the Diaspora. After the destruction of the Temple, the patriarchate gradually developed, as a new central authority for Judaism, parallel to the institutions that developed in Christianity above local level; in these, certain bishops and episcopal synods were assigned a more than regional importance.

But Jews and Christians were also diasporal in the sense that they interpreted their ecumenical distribution as "a dispersion" and "an exile." In the various towns (and villages) of the Roman Empire, Jews formed a special group, which retained an astonishing degree of internal autonomy. They had their own laws, their own lawcourts, their own tax; indeed, they even claimed for themselves the right and the duty, enjoyed by free citizens in a free city, of dying for the laws of their fathers. The Jewish idea of martyrdom preserves this claim of a free polity, even in a situation of political dependence.[24] Christians inherited it from Jews. They too felt that in their earthly country their duty was to a country that was different. Their *politeuma*, or commonwealth, was in heaven (Phil. 3:20). They too were living in exile on earth. They too knew the conflict between the demands of the earthly and the heavenly *polis* (Hermas *Similitudes* 1) and expected of their members a readiness for martyrdom.

In the ancient world Jews and Christians can undoubtedly be seen as "parallel phenomena," and not in the sense that they are merely two variations within a general oriental world of conviction. They also

---

23. W. A. Meeks, "Die Rolle des paulinischen Christentums bei der Entstehung einer rationalen ethischen Religion," in *Max Webers Sicht des antiken Christentums*, ed. W. Schluchter (Frankfurt, 1985), 363–403, esp. 373. The supraregional cohesion of Judaism, even at the time of the Second Temple, has however been carefully shown by S. Safrai; see his "Relations between the Diaspora and the Land of Israel," in *The Jewish People in the First Century*, ed. S. Safrai and M. Stern, 184–215.

24. See here the highly illuminating comments by H. G. Kippenberg, "Die jüdischen Überlieferungen als πάτριοι νόμοι," in *Die Restauration der Götter*, ed. R. Faber and R. Schlesier, (Königshausen, 1986), 45–60.

resemble each other in having a unique position as monotheistic heresies. But in other respects too Jewish and Christian congregations are related to one another in their social structure. Both embody a new offer of diastratic and diasporal solidarity.

Are these new patterns of human solidarity the expression of an "orientalization of society," as Hendrik Bolkestein thought? Are asymmetrical social obligations stressed because the ideal of citizens with equal rights had ceased to provide a plausible basis for social life?

We can also see the matter differently. The ideal of citizens with equal rights had its original real-life situation — its *Sitz im Leben* — in the small privileged class of free citizens. It now freed itself from this situation and was also adopted by groups who had hitherto been excluded from it: foreigners, slaves, and women. It cannot be mere chance that in the letter to the Galatians Paul names the three social categories which were underprivileged in civil life, but enjoyed equality in the congregation: Jews and Greeks (i.e., foreigners to one another); slaves over against freemen; and women over against men (Gal. 3:28). Even if these people have no place in the assembly or *ekklesia* of the political community, they have their place in the *ekklesia* of the Lord. Here they have the freedom of the heavenly Jerusalem (Gal. 4:1ff.). What is happening here is a "downward transfer of upper-class values." An ideal of equality and freedom hitherto accessible only to the privileged is now made available to the underprivileged as well and is transformed in the process — not merely into an internalized spirituality "of the heart" but into the social reality of the congregation. The model for this was provided by Jewish congregations, in which a self-chosen and assigned special role united men and women beyond the limitations of status.

At the same time, there is no doubt that this downward transfer of upper-class values was fostered by the breakdown of the barriers of ancient privilege. Once the local upper classes of free citizens had come to be outshone by an imperial upper class, sections of the local upper class (with their values) could move closer to the classes below. But the link between diastratic solidarity and diasporal cohesion does not fit at all into Bolkestein's picture of a change of values as reaction to an authoritarian change of structure. This supraregional cohesion too can be seen as a downward transfer of upper-class values. For to have contacts extending over the *oikoumenē* — the whole inhabited world — was otherwise a characteristic of the imperial upper class. The elite that had the power was recruited from a few families — the families of senators and men belonging to the equestrian order (the *equites*, or "knights"). These occupied the decisive posts everywhere and thus built up a whole network of acquaintances, friends, and relations. Among the lower classes, supraregional contacts of this kind existed at most among dispersed national groups and where the requirements of commerce created professional links. But nowhere were supraregional ties of this kind as evident as they were among Jews; and nowhere were they so much a matter of course — even in the lower and lower-middle classes — as among Christians. This meant that among Jews and Christians patterns of behavior can be found, right down to the lower classes, which we otherwise tend to find rather in a cosmopolitan upper class. These patterns of behavior undoubtedly matched the supraregional structure of the Roman Empire better than locally restricted traditions of behavior.

In this way Jews and Christians offered forms of solidarity that corresponded to the social change. Christians could deduce these directly from the center of their faith. The *kyrios* they adored was the prototype of a radical change of position: equal to God, yet assuming the role of a slave; and as the one crucified becoming the Lord of the world. As Lord of the world he was the ruler over all powers, and over men and women "of every tongue" — that is, men and women belonging to all the different countries and civilizations that met in the Roman Empire (see Phil. 2:6-12).

B. *New Testament Christianity as a De-restricted, Open Judaism*

In spite of all the parallels, there was one important distinction between Jews and Christians. Jews were an *ethnos*. Their way of life was based on an age-old tradition. Christians, in contrast, were interethnic. They were proud of embracing different nations and peoples. Their way of life was based on a decision for the Christian faith, and that meant deciding against other traditions. Our question is: How can this distinction between Judaism and Christianity be defined in terms of social history?

First of all, in this respect too, Christianity in its earliest form is to be seen as part of Jewish history. It belongs to a series of Jewish attempts at acculturation to the Gentile environment. These attempts were characteristic of the Hellenistic and Roman period.[25] Acculturation is not assimilation. The Hellenistic attempt to bring about a reform in Jerusalem in 175 B.C.E. had features suggesting an attempt at assimilation. For — according to what its opponents said — its aim was to eliminate

---

25. M. Hengel has analyzed the whole of Jewish history in the Hellenistic age under the heading of "acculturation"– even where Jewish forms of religion and life deliberately strive against the advancing Hellenism (*Judaism and Hellenism*, trans. J. Bowden [London: SCM Press; Philadelphia: Fortress Press, 1974, reprint 1991]).

the things that distinguished Judaism from its environment. According to the way the movement itself saw what it was doing, this reform too will have been rather a matter of "acculturation." But we may leave that on one side here. The important point is that acculturation is an adaptation to the environment without a renunciation of one's own identity. So what was special about the early Christian attempt at acculturation? A comparison between Philo and Paul is illuminating at this point.

Philo takes over far more from his pagan environment than Paul. In his writings we find Stoic, Platonic, and Pythagorean ideas. He knows and quotes many ancient writers. He is familiar with the language of the mystery religions. It is true that in Paul we clearly hear an echo of certain ideas drawn from his environment. But the most essential things he has to say can be traced back to Jewish tradition. And yet for all that, Philo, with his basic ideas, is far more firmly anchored in Judaism than Paul, the missionary to the Gentiles. Why?

The essential reason is not the number of ideas each adopts. What is essential is the structure of the acculturation process. Philo selects pagan ideas from his environment, giving them a new interpretation in the framework of his Jewish faith. His most important method here is the allegorical interpretation of the Bible. He certainly describes — much more clearly than Paul — the "mystery" process of the transformation and divinization of the human being. But the one who is transformed into a divine being is Israel herself. The "mystery" is Jewish worship of God. He uses the language of the mysteries to formulate the claim of Jewish faith to an exclusive and universally valid access to the one and only God.[26]

In Paul, the acculturation process has a different structure. Paul does not so much select from the ideas of his Gentile surroundings — ideas that for the most part, no doubt, actually reached him by way of Jewish Hellenistic tradition. He chooses from the Jewish traditions with which he was familiar. From these he takes the elements that can be universalized and dispenses with elements that resist any such universalization, especially circumcision and dietary commandments as a precondition for the conversion of Gentiles to the true God. His choice and reformulation of Jewish traditions is made from a viewpoint that outreaches these traditions; for it is based on the conviction that the coming of

---

26. See Borgen, "Philo of Alexandria," 269–72. Of course Philo's "philosophy" can be interpreted as a transformation of Judaism into a mystery religion. This was the view taken especially by E. R. Goodenough; see *By Light, Light: The Mystic Gospel of Hellenistic Judaism* (New Haven: Yale University Press, 1935). But it must never be forgotten that Philo remained a convinced Jew.

Jesus has brought about a new situation in salvation history: now the biblical promises are fulfilled for all nations and peoples.

Both in Philo and in Paul we can see a "selective acculturation" of Judaism to its environment.[27] Philo selects external ideas, Paul internal traditions. Philo chooses from among pagan traditions, from a Jewish standpoint; Paul chooses from Jewish traditions, from a viewpoint that goes beyond these traditions. As a result, although all the individual elements of Paul's theology can be "derived" from Jewish traditions, the opening toward the Gentiles which we find in him is very much greater than it is in Philo, even though Philo has surrendered himself very much more fully to the elements of pagan education.

This social opening of Judaism for non-Jews can easily be linked with relationships in society as a whole. The Roman Empire was faced with the task of integrating many different peoples into a society that had come into being for the first time. For the empire really existed initially merely as a nonregional "superstructure" on the top of a multiplicity of different individual societies. Religious movements that were well suited to break through the frontiers dividing peoples and cultures were in line with an objective task with which this society was faced. This is true even if the new religious movements in which an answer to this task could be found stood at a considerable distance from the upper class which sustained the state, and which had the greatest interest in integrating many peoples into the sphere of Roman domination. The very parallelism of this supraregional claim—bound in the one case to the emperor, in the other to the *kyrios*—makes it easy to understand why conflicts arose between this new movement and the imperial upper class.

C. *New Testament Christianity as a Transformation of Judaism*

We have seen that the viewpoint from which Paul selected from Jewish traditions pointed beyond these traditions. Let us, in closing, try to discover more closely what this viewpoint was. Here we come upon aspects of New Testament Christianity that can hardly be summed up under the heading of "a de-restriction of Judaism." And at this point we can directly pick up Paul's own statements.

Paul himself tried to reduce the difference between Judaism and Christianity to the antithesis between πίστις and νόμος (which we translate

---

27. I have taken over the term "selective acculturation" from D. L. Balch, "Hellenization/Acculturation in I Peter," in *Perspectives on First Peter,* ed. C. Talbert (Macon, Ga.: Mercer University Press, 1986), 79–101.

as "faith" and "law").[28] He relativized this antithesis in two ways. On the one hand, the νόμος is both Scripture (γραφή) and commandment (ἐντολή), and as Scripture it contains not only commandments but also promises, the purpose of which is faith. As Scripture, νόμος is not an antithesis to πίστις, but witnesses to it. But on the other hand, even as commandment, the νόμος is not merely an antithesis to πίστις. For the whole νόμος is summed up in the commandment of love. The πίστις which is effective through love is thus the fulfillment of the law. In spite of this twofold relativization of the antithesis, we again and again find πίστις contrasted with νόμος in Paul, or "faith" contrasted with "works."

It is therefore no wonder that even today we are still puzzling as to where the antithesis lies. Where are we supposed to look for "the servitude of the law," from which faith in Jesus liberates us? What is so negative about the law? Is it the fact that it is practically speaking never fulfilled? Or the fact that it is in principle unfulfillable? Is it negative because it is misused, as a way of disparaging others, out of self-conceit? Is Paul rebelling against the deadening and aggressive character of commandments when they act *against* human beings? Or is he criticizing a wrong type of religious behavior which is bound up with the law? And here the question arises: Did this wrong behavior always exist in conjunction with the law, or is it a reaction to Jesus' coming? Or does Paul really object to the law only because adherence to it hinders the recognition of a new revelation?[29]

---

28. W. Wrede interprets the antithesis of "faith" and "works" in this sense ("Paulus" [1904] in *Das Paulusbild in der neueren deutschen Forschung*, ed. K. H. Rengstorf, WdF 24 [Darmstadt, 1969], 1–97): "It was however a recognition of the very first rank when Christianity was grasped as being a religion with a principle of its own — that is, as something completely new" (p. 69). He admittedly sees that "the view of Jewish religion is somewhat caricatured in the process" (p. 69). Wrede sees the doctrine of justification as a militant doctrine directed against Judaism. But this fails to take account of the following: (1) In Galatians the doctrine of justification is polemically directed against Christian Judaists, that is, against the attempt to bind Gentiles to the Jewish law. (2) In Romans 9–11, the doctrine of justification is critically directed against Christian anti-Judaists, who view unbelieving Judaism as "rejected." The doctrine of justification has primarily a socially integrative function: it is intended to make it possible for Jews and Gentiles to live together in the Christian congregations.

29. It is only possible to touch briefly on the debate about this point, which is central for a Christian theology. E. P. Sanders assigns Paul's often contradictory statements to three different question complexes (*Paul, the Law, and the Jewish People* [London: SCM Press; Philadelphia: Fortress Press, 1983]): (1) Paul answers the question about how one enters the community of salvation by saying: not through fulfillment of the law, but through faith in Christ. (2) He answers the question about the task still remaining for the God-given law by saying: it serves sin — although in Paul the relationship between law and sin varies. (3) He answers the question about how one can remain in the community of salvation by saying: through fulfillment of the law summed up in the

We can be certain of only one thing: toward Gentiles "the law" can certainly not exercise the function it has in Israel, where, on the basis of God's election, it testifies to his faithfulness and requires the faithfulness of men and women as response. For Gentiles could not live in awareness of an election of their people preceding all human activity. If they were to take over the law, it would become a *Heilsweg,* a "way of salvation," in the sense that the state of salvation would be constituted by fulfillment of the law. The law would no longer be what it was in Judaism: a saving gift—that is, the sign of a salvation given ahead of all human acts, a sign that has to be guarded and cherished.

So what, then, takes the place of membership in the chosen people of the Jews, a membership preceding anything that human beings can do? Its place is taken by the πίστις ("faith") of the human being and its transforming power, which becomes evident in the sacrament. In other words: for Gentile Christians, the indicative of membership of the chosen people by birth is replaced by the indicative of a transformation of human beings in and with Christ. That is the reason why πίστις and νόμος can be formulated as if they are antitheses.

The antithesis between the two can also be explained with the help of some reflections drawn from the sociology of religion. Here Paul is playing off against each other two different forms of religious legitimation. We can correlate these with the three forms of legitimation of authority and rule which Max Weber distinguished, as types:[30]

1. Legitimation on the grounds of tradition: authority is justified by its origin—that is, through inheritance, succession, tradition or custom.

2. Charismatic authority: this, on the other hand, is not derived from anything outside itself; it rests on the presence of an unusual personal power, which has the ability to win recognition without compulsion.

---

commandment of love. There is agreement between what Sanders says here and my own view in the following central point. The substantial reason for criticism of the law is faith in Christ, who makes no distinction between Jews and Gentiles. In the terminology used above, this recognition is defined thus: the personal charismatic relationship to Jesus is available to everyone, independent of their status and origin. The central position of this recognition distinguishes Judaism from Christianity. However, unlike Sanders, I assume that Paul's criticism of the law is prompted by other reasons as well. The law is also criticized because it leads to "zeal for the law" and to "self-glorification." That these objections do not do justice to the Jewish religion should meanwhile be sufficiently well known.

30. These three forms of legitimation of rule are further developed in W. Schluchter, *Die Entwicklung des okzidentalen Rationalismus* (Tübingen, 1979), 122–203.

3. Legal authority: this ultimately proceeds from rules which are not arbitrary, which enjoy validity independent of persons, and which can be made plausible in themselves.

Judaism and Christianity are both based on a traditional authority: Scripture. A "legitimation struggle" flared up between Jews and Christians about its interpretation. Both sides claim to have the only true legitimation. Paul sees a "veil" over the hearts of the Jews which hinders the true understanding of Scripture and the law. Jews have rejected the Christian interpretation of Scripture as arbitrary and ungrounded. But for both Jews and Christians, the νόμος as "Scripture" (γραφή) counts as undisputed authority.

On this common legitimation basis of tradition, two structurally different forms of religious legitimation developed in the Hellenistic-Roman period. On the one hand, Judaism was penetrated through and through by the rabbinic movement (to which Paul also belonged before he became a Christian). This gave Judaism a legal structure of authority based on Scripture which made it possible to know the will of God independently of the cult and which, after the destruction of the Temple, was actually able to replace the cult. With the help of controllable hermeneutical procedures, people sought for nonarbitrary rules for a life before God, rules that made it possible to achieve a priestly holiness even in the everyday life of the world. People wanted both: to live up to practical requirements, pragmatically; and also to win a share in the holiness for which the cult was otherwise the mediator.[31]

The schism between Judaism and early Christianity went so deep just because, on the common basis of the Bible, the first Christian congregations simultaneously developed a religion with a different legitimation structure. In this religion, God's will was discovered not by way of legalistic hermeneutical procedures but through a personal, charismatic bond with Jesus, and with the Spirit who was experienced in this bond. In justifying theological and ethical convictions, the ultimate court of appeal was the presence of God in Jesus. It is this personal, charismatic relationship that Paul calls πίστις — an intensive inner bond with Jesus, to the point of mystical union. It is in the light of this relationship that he reads Scripture, choosing from the Jewish and Old Testament traditions whatever could be universalized. This personal charismatic relationship is the standpoint from which he undertook his "selective acculturation" of Judaism.[32]

---

31. See the picture of rabbinic Judaism in J. Neusner, *Das pharisäische und talmudische Judentum*, Texte und Studien zum antiken Judentum (Tübingen, 1984).

32. There is personal charismatic authority in Judaism too. G. Vermes sets Jesus in a charismatic Galilean milieu (*Jesus the Jew* [London: W. Collins; New York: Macmillan,

Three characteristics of the new religion can be explained, in my view, by this basic charismatic structure: its character as a universal religion; its character as a religion of conversion; and its character as a religion of redemption.

1. Personal charismatic relationships can be entered into without any preconditions; they do not have to be "achieved" in any way in advance. The recognition of a more-than-everyday power in someone is something very simple. It is not necessary first of all to become incorporated in a particular national culture. No education is required. The Spirit seizes everyone irrespective of national and social barriers. On the basis of a simple, personal, charismatic relationship to Jesus, non-Jews too could enter into the Jewish role. Through "faith," Gentiles acquire a share in God's history with his people. The personal charismatic relationship of faith seems to be a way of bringing to its conclusion the trend to universality already inherent in Judaism.

2. No one is born into personal charismatic relationships. They require "conversion," a deliberate commitment to the mediator of revelation. This has, of course, particularly far-reaching consequences when this commitment means taking over totally new tenets of faith — that is, when Gentiles are converted to monotheistic belief. Now, Judaism already showed the signs, or first beginnings, of a religion of conversion. It was highly attractive to people in the surrounding world. Many adopted it. Yet conversion was a supplementary mode of acceptance, parallel to the normal case, which was to be born a Jew. In early Christianity, what was a supplementary mode of acceptance in Judaism now became constitutive. Here too trends in Judaism are taken further.

3. If salvation is mediated through a personal charismatic bond in which a person has not always lived, then before he entered into this relationship, his condition is bound to have been evil. "Faith" effects redemption. A religion that, like early Christianity, puts a personal charismatic relationship at the center, becomes a religion of redemption. The new, salvific relationship does not merely change the person's conduct. It changes his or her complete nature. The person undergoes a transformation (especially as a Gentile Christian). Here again it must be stressed that the idea of redemption is a further development of tendencies already prepared in Judaism. In apocalyptic circles this idea was vividly associated with the expectation of a transformation of the

---

1973; 2nd ed. London: SCM Press, 1983]). It is very illuminating to see how rabbinic Judaism fits personal charismatic authority into its own system of reference. See W. S. Green, "Palestinian Holy Men: Charismatic Leadership and Rabbinic Tradition," *ANRW* II, 19, 2 (Berlin, 1979), 619–47.

whole world. Paul believed that in Christ this expectation had been fulfilled for all who believed.

Let us sum up. Paul is a figure of decisive importance for the parting of the ways of Jews and Christians. His Christianity is personal, charismatically transformed Judaism. Rabbinic Judaism, on the other hand, is a legally, hermeneutically developed Judaism. On the same foundation of tradition, the two religions developed forms of belief with different structures of authority. Paul recognized that when he antithetically set νόμος over against πίστις, as a way of distinguishing the two religions. Yet he saw too that it is impossible to construct an absolute opposition here; indeed he tried to relativize the contrast. For the two forms of religion are doubtless different, but not directly antithetical.

In order to make it clear that the interpretation of first- and second-century Christianity and Judaism I have put forward here is no more than relative, let me stress again: If Judaism is ascribed a legal, hermeneutical authority structure, and Christianity a personal charismatic one, this is merely a way of defining the dominating "organizational principle" of the two religions, which were now becoming independent of each other. It is certainly not intended to mean that there were no charismatics in Judaism and no law in Christianity. But the Jewish charismatics were clearly subject to the Torah and its interpretation. This is shown by the fine story of Rabbi Eliezer ben Hyrkanos, who was able to offer three miracles and even a voice from heaven—a *bat kol*— to support a halakic decision, but who was nevertheless defeated by the majority of his scripturally versed colleagues. In that hour God is said to have laughed in heaven and to have said: "My children have defeated me, my children have defeated me" (*Baba Meṣiʿa* [bBM 59b]). What is viewed as the highest authority here is not the charisma of miracle but the interpretation of the law, free of personal caprice. Conversely, in early Christianity there very soon came to be the beginnings of a legal structure. The *First Epistle of Clement* and the orders of the early church make this evident. But the center of Christianity was always the simple relationship of faith to Jesus Christ.

In closing, we may ask: Can the personal charismatic transformation of Judaism in early Christianity be seen as part of the transformation of the total social structure which took place in the era of the principate? The following link between the two movements would seem to suggest itself. The Roman Empire brought with it a devaluation of many national cultures. What conferred personal status was not the existing affiliation to one's native culture but adherence to the Hellenistic Roman culture, which was something that had to be acquired. To belong to the Hellenistic Roman culture conferred positive status. In the Roman

Empire, for people belonging to most national cultures, a move upward in the social scale meant that they had to detach themselves from their ethnic and cultural origins. This fact no doubt gave plausibility to the notion that the human being's point of departure is a negative one and that salvation has to be sought through redemption from this status. Since upward mobility also meant entry into a new cultural world, and cultural change, the religious expectation that salvation was to be achieved through a change in people seemed plausible. Upward mobility was often achieved through personal loyalty toward members of the upper class. The experience of social reality therefore offered a basis for the belief that a "personal charismatic bond" with a particular master could have positive results — indeed could bring "salvation."[33] If the Christianity of New Testament times can be understood as personal, charismatically transformed Judaism, then in this transformation it corresponds to certain aspects of the total social reality of the time.

With this transformation, it separated itself from Judaism. It is perhaps only today for the first time that Christians can understand, and see as a positive possibility, the fact that Jews lay more stress on faithfulness to their tradition than on adaptation to the "modern society" of the time. For today Christians, out of faithfulness to their tradition, must continually resist seductive attempts at adaptation to "the modern world." Having for centuries looked down with unshaken pride on the Judaism that had been "surmounted," viewing it as "the old covenant," they are today forced to discover that *their* convictions are now disparaged as "old" and "superseded." If we look at the way the paths of Jews and Christians diverged in the first century, seeing these in the light of social history and the sociology of religion, we can surely understand why Christians saw themselves as belonging to the "new" (and of course "better") religion. But if we put aside their own understanding of what they were, the following interpretation suggests itself. At that time the religion of the Bible changed, and two forms of the biblical faith came into being: Judaism and Christianity. This historical interpretation could also contribute to a new theological assessment of the relationship between the Jewish and the Christian faith. But at present that is still, perhaps, an all-too-utopian hope.

---

33. On the link between upward mobility and early Christianity, see Meeks, *The First Urban Christians,* esp. 70ff., and my essay "Christology and Social Experience," pp. 187–201 above.

PART III

---◆---

STUDIES ON EARLY CHRISTIANITY
AND THE SOCIAL REALITY
OF THE FIRST CENTURY

8

Sociological Theories of Religion and the Analysis of Early Christianity

◆

Some Reflections

ANY ATTEMPT to arrive at a sociology of early Christianity is faced with two fundamental problems, both of which require systematic discussion. The first of them is methodological: How can we extract sociologically relevant evidence from the New Testament's sociography and historiography, and from its parenetic, poetic, and mythological utterances? The second problem is theoretical, and it is this problem which we shall be considering here: What religio-sociological theorems should we take as our basis, what heuristic assumptions should we make, what categories should we choose, what questions should we ask, so that in the light of all these things we may gather together and weigh up all the different pieces of evidence, which in themselves are never more than fragmentary?

The need for theoretical reflections of this kind cannot be ignored, if texts are interpreted in a way that runs counter, for the most part, to what they themselves are intending to say. Existential interpretation involves a comparable basic problem: if mythical texts are interpreted (contrary to their own intention) as objectifications of human existence,[1] we are dependent on an anthropology that cannot be derived solely

---

1. R. Bultmann certainly maintains that "myth has to be interpreted, not cosmologically but anthropologically or, better, existentially" ("Neues Testament und Mythologie," in *Offenbarung und Heilsgeschehen* [Munich, 1941], 27–69, quotation from p. 36). But in my view recent discussion has shown that the New Testament statements are undoubtedly meant "cosmologically," and that here an understanding of the world and an understanding of the self are indissolubly linked.

from the texts themselves, since this anthropology is intended to serve as the *framework within which* these texts are to be critically interpreted. Similarly, the sociological evaluation of New Testament texts requires a theory about the sociology of religion. For here it is quite obvious that we are approaching our subject in the light of our own questions, that our scientific, or scholarly, research contains a constructive element, and that in order to be able to analyze the reality we are dependent on model-like constructions.

Theories are never based exclusively on empirical and historical data. They transcend the facts on which they rest (which can always be tested to an only limited degree). They go beyond the facts, for example, in such general statements as: "Religion is a search for human authenticity" (and existential interpretation is in my view based on this simple theory of religion). It will hardly be disputed today that in theoretical generalizations of this kind, values and preconceived ideas are always involved. What is a matter of dispute are the conclusions to be drawn from this acknowledgment.

One possibility, for example, is the hermeneutically tolerant standpoint,[2] which concedes to every "prior understanding" the chance of "comprehending" the subject under discussion. Everything in human history, we are told, exists as a potential for ways of human understanding, not as an object per se or a *Ding an sich* (in Kant's sense). This theory may be somewhat complicated, but its consequence is clear: it would mean that every prior understanding is a source of possible truth.

Today people often advance a step further and arrive at the standpoint of "involved perception": since all perception is determined by interests or concerns, we have to discover in advance, by way of theoretical, scientific reflection, what the "true" interests are, and have to analyze our object in that light. According to this theory, not every prior understanding would be a source of possible truth. This can be said only of the aspects that we have declared to be "emancipatory" or "theologically appropriate."[3]

A third option puts forward the position of "critical examination." Provided that theoretical assumptions do not contradict themselves, it is irrelevant whether they derive from an everyday prior understanding, from a "conservative" or a "progressive" attitude, or from a positive or

---

2. See H. G. Gadamer, *Truth and Method,* trans. W. Glen-Doepel, translation edited by G. Barden and J. Cumming (London: Sheed & Ward; New York: Seabury Press, 1975). The original German edition was already published in 1960.

3. For the theological exegesis, see P. Stuhlmacher, "Thesen zur Methodologie gegenwärtiger Exegese," *ZNW* 63 (1972): 18–26.

negative attitude to the subject of our examination—provided only that the assumptions are so formulated that they can be tested (and if necessary confuted) by confrontation with the sources.[4] The legitimacy of assumptions in the scientific process depends primarily on their verifiability, which is tested in scientific discussion. For the data presented by reality never raise any direct objection to the theories brought to bear on them. Their objection is always communicated by way of the alternative interpretations of other scientists or scholars. As long as different researchers with different preconceived ideas are engaged in the scientific process, mutual correction is always possible.[5] The requirement is therefore that in this process, scientists with approaches, concerns, and prejudgments that are as divergent as possible should participate competitively. It is at all events illegitimate to choose between theoretical assumptions before these are tested against the data offered by reality. So in analyzing the New Testament, it is an absurdity to object from the outset to a certain approach because it is "psychologizing," "historicizing," "sociologizing," or "positivist." All these catchwords are often no more than intellectual taboos which are set up as "no trespassing" signs, whenever scientific questions could endanger preconceived notions. Whether and how a sociological way of looking at early Christianity is possible, and how far it is appropriate, can be decided only on the basis of the sources at our disposal, not by way of reflections about the "nondisposability of faith" or the "nonobjectifiability of the kerygma" and other formulas which—however legitimate they may be in other contexts—could here be misused as a way of stifling scientific curiosity.

The purpose of our present essay cannot be to give a historical survey of the different theories in socio-religious research.[6] We shall confine ourselves to offering a systematic outline, with generalizations and simplifications based on what is typical or "ideal." It must be remembered here that the purpose of our investigation is not to analyze and describe these different theories about the sociology of religion. What we wish to discuss is the contribution they can make to an analysis of early Christianity.

---

4. This is the viewpoint of critical rationalism. See K. Popper, *The Open Society and Its Enemies*, 2 vols. (London: Routledge & Kegan Paul, 1945; Princeton: Princeton University Press, 1950; 5th rev. ed. 1966); H. Albert, *Traktat über kritische Vernunft* (Tübingen, 1968), and *Konstruktion und Kritik* (Hamburg, 1972). It seems to me an advantage that from this standpoint one can very well also practice "hermeneutical tolerance" and "involved perception."

5. See Popper, *Open Society*, vol. 2.

6. J. Matthes gives a brief survey; see his "Religionssoziologie," in *Die Lehre von der Gesellschaft*, ed. G. Eisermann, 2nd ed. (Stuttgart, 1969), 218ff., esp. 230–39.

The function of any theory about the sociology of religion is to bring individual, sociologically relevant data into a coherent systematic structure, or to construe connections that can be tested against individual pieces of evidence. The structure can be formally defined in very different ways: according to its intention; in the light of its cause or genesis; or from the aspect of its function. And three corresponding approaches can be distinguished, all within the viewpoint of the sociology of religion.[7]

1. The approach from the phenomenology of religion.[8] One can start from the self-understanding of religious phenomena — the intention prompting them. Religion is then an "encounter with the holy," with a reality of a unique kind beyond the bounds of human society. This reality doubtless affects society and is institutionalized in various forms; but it nevertheless remains at heart inaccessible to sociological analysis.

2. The reductionist analysis. The connection between the various pieces of evidence offered by the sociology of religion (and especially the connection between religion's own understanding of what it is and its social basis) can also be defined causally or genetically. The intentions behind religious phenomena are then traced back to nonreligious factors. If that involves the claim that in this way we can grasp the whole meaning and social significance of religion, we can talk about a reductionist theory of religion.[9] A classic example is the Marxist theory of religion, in its orthodox form.

3. The functionalist analysis[10] combines elements of the phenomenological and the reductionist approaches. It takes into account both

---

7. A fourth approach might be termed evolutionist. We find this where the sociology of religion is pursued under the aspect of "secularization," and this process is said to be "evolutionary in the universal sense"; that is to say, it is viewed as an irreversible, anthropologically founded process of growing rationalism and world mastery. See G. Dux, "Religion, Geschichte und sozialer Wandel," *IJRS* 7 (1971): 60–94, esp. 65ff.

8. See J. Wach, *Sociology of Religion* (Chicago: University of Chicago Press, 1944; London: Kegan Paul, Trench, Trubner & Co., 1947); G. Mensching, *Soziologie der Religion* (Bonn, 1947). Here one can also talk about the sociology of religion as an interpretative human science: see J. Matthes, *Religion und Gesellschaft* (Hamburg, 1967), 21ff.

9. In a dispute with functionalist sociology of religion, G. Carlsson pleads for rather more "reductionism"; see "Betrachtungen zum Funktionalismus" in *Logik der Sozialwissenschaften*, ed. E. Topitsch, 4th ed. (Cologne, 1967), 236–61. He is undoubtedly justified if this means, for example, the search for correlations between variables belonging to different sectors of reality. This is something different from the denial of a variable's independence, which we find in M. Robbe, *Der Ursprung des Christentums* (Leipzig, 1967), 219f.: "In the Christian religion there are thus reproduced in illusory form the antitheses of the highly developed slaveowning society. The concept of 'Christianity' is therefore problematical in itself. As a unified movement or community, it never existed." See also his essay "Marxismus und Religionsforschung," *IJRS* 2 (1966): 147–84.

10. See O. Schreuder's clear account, "Die strukturell-funktionale Theorie und die Religionssoziologie," *IJRS* 2 (1966): 99–134.

the causal or genetic contingency of religion and the intentionality of religious phenomena. But it analyzes these with a view to the contribution they make to the solution of fundamental social tasks. If we assume that a religion has developed for particular social reasons, this always raises the problem: Why did it go on growing even after the causes of its genesis ceased to apply? Early Christianity, for example, initially came into being as an inner-Jewish revival movement in the rural areas of Palestine. But it spread preeminently, as an independent religion, in the towns and cities of the Mediterranean world—that is, in places where the social conditions that had molded the Palestinian Jesus movement no longer existed. Yet it found an echo there. In the course of time, even the Synoptic traditions spread here too, although these traditions had their home in the Palestinian area. In my view, a functionalist analysis provides better theoretical categories than a reductionist approach for making a transformation like this comprehensible; for if something proves its vitality, we may heuristically assume that it fills some function or other in its particular social context. That is to say, it has an objective purpose, of which the people involved are not always aware, whether this purpose be to stabilize the order of a society, or whether it be to react to its conflicts and tensions by bringing about change.[11] According to this approach, a sociology of early Christianity would have to show how far the early Christian movement which grew up in Palestine could be "functional" in totally different conditions.

The missionary intention of the early Christian movement was undoubtedly to build a bridge between the two areas, with their very different social structures. And this intention was intensifed by expectation of the imminent end.[12] But the history and sociology of early Christianity cannot be understood from its intentions alone. The objective function of a religious phenomenon is seldom identical with its intention, even though that function is always mediated through the intentions of men and women. We have to look for the objective function, to a far greater extent, in the unintended consequences of religious intentions. The rainmaking ceremony of a native tribe may have the intention of "conjuring up" rain. But it also has an objective function; and it is this to which it owes its firm position in the tribe, in spite of

---

11. Any one-sided restriction of the term "functional" to mean ordering functions would have to be sharply criticized. See R. Dahrendorf, "Struktur und Funktion," in *Pfade aus Utopia* (Munich, 1967), 213–42. For the discussion about integration and conflict theories, see pp. 9–29 of R. Rüschemeyer's introduction to the German translation of T. Parsons, *Essays in Sociological Theory,* rev. ed. (Glencoe, Ill.: Free Press, 1954); German title: *Beiträge zur soziologischen Theorie* (Neuwied, 1964).

12. See, e.g., Mark 13:10.

its frequently manifested failure. That function will rather be to cement the tribe's solidarity, and this is very useful in the face of threatening crises in the food supply—and especially so at times when the ceremony fails. A function, accordingly, has a teleological aspect as well as an intention; but unlike the intention, this teleology cannot be ascribed to any determining subject.

This thesis may also be applied to early Christian eschatology, for example. Its intention was undoubtedly to proclaim the imminent end of the world, when the present world will perish, giving way to a new heaven and a new earth. This intention was quite simply confuted by the march of time. And the problem of "the delay of the parousia" is too clearly articulated in the New Testament for us to be able to rest content with the information that here utopian desires had outrun all the checks of reality. People perceived the reality clearly enough; but for all that, they continued to pass on expectations of the imminent end and continually filled these expectations with new life, most obviously in the Montanism of the second century. Yet there was no crisis.

A phenomenon like this can in my view be satisfactorily explained only if we ask: What was the objective function of this imminent expectation? For that function exerted its influence irrespective of the compromised intention—or, better, at a deeper level than the intention. Anyone who in his imagination continually saw the present world (which meant ancient society) going down to destruction in the mythical flames of fantasy could be helped by such eschatological images to resist the norms and obligations with which society confronted him. Every way of life is bound to a social world, which is often symbolically heightened and interpreted through mythical images.[13] A new way of life can make its way only if the old world is destroyed and deprived of its power through the symbolic acts of mythical fantasy.

In this way the functionalist analysis does, I think, offer fruitful categories for a sociological analysis of early Christianity. Its advantage is not least its ability to integrate phenomenological and reductionist approaches. It is open in both directions, yet differs from both in one respect: phenomenological and reductionist theories of religion often purport to determine the nature, the heart, the truth or the falsity of religion. They know that religion is either "an encounter with the holy" or a simulation of nonreligious social reality. In a functionalist approach,

---

13. For the phenomenon of "symbolic heightening," see W. E. Mühlmann, "Umrisse und Probleme einer Kulturanthropologie," in W. E. Mühlmann and E. W. Müller, *Kulturanthropologie* (Cologne, 1966), 15–49. Attention should also be drawn to G. M. Vernon, "The Symbolic Interactionist Approach to the Sociology of Religion," *IJRS* 2 (1966): 135–55.

on the other hand, it is by no means necessary to identify the social function of a phenomenon with its essence. Admittedly, people find this recognition difficult in an age when social relationships count as the essential thing, or when—in the theological variant of this viewpoint—God is defined as co-humanity (a viewpoint to which some people might prefer a robust agnosticism).

We may apply the word "functional" to whatever contributes to the solution of fundamental tasks within a limited social frame of reference. But a definition of this kind immediately confronts us with three other questions: the question about the limits of social functionality, the question about the frame of reference, and the question about the fundamental tasks.

The choice of a functionalist analysis does not imply the thesis that every phenomenon in society is in some sense or other functional. In the first place, we ask about function only in the things that have become socially effective and have established themselves—just as in the case of an organism we postulate a functionally appropriate structure, if the organism is to be able to go on living. This is initially no more than a postulate—a working hypothesis. It is not an a priori assertion that everything is functional. The postulate claims merely that it is useful to ask about functionality, and perhaps in the process to discover disfunctionality too. (I may mention in passing that I would emphatically refuse to see all historical processes of integration and conflict as objectively functional.)[14]

A second qualification must be made with regard to the frame of reference. There is no such thing as function per se. Function always relates only to a given whole. But in history this "whole" can never be as clearly defined and demarcated as it can in a natural organism.[15] The frame of reference for a sociology of early Christianity is initially the whole of society in the era of the principate. But it is useful now and again to choose a different frame of reference—Jewish-Palestinian society perhaps, or the early Christian congregations. From the point of view of society as a whole, early Christianity, for example, was certainly not an integrating movement. On the contrary: it exposed its members to an intensified conflict with society. But internally, the early Christian groups developed a very considerable integrating force. It is therefore useless to talk about integration without stating what our frame of reference is.

---

14. Carlsson criticized the functionalist approach as nonhistorical; see his "Betrachtungen zum Funktionalismus," 257. This criticism would be justified if one were to see theories as anything more than aids—ways of grasping reality from different aspects.

15. Carlsson also saw this correctly ("Betrachtungen zum Functionalismus," 237ff.).

Finally, a definition of the fundamental tasks at issue is of central importance. In my view, it is plausible to assume that these fundamental tasks are two: to create order and to master conflicts. The first task is to exclude manifest conflicts from particular sectors of central importance; for even the most liberal of societies is dependent on a basic consensus. The second task is to react to conflicts by way of change and adaptation. Complete order could be achieved only through absolute compulsion, while an exclusively antagonistic society would be chaotic and hardly capable of change. Of course continual attempts are made to see social processes one-sidedly, from a single perspective. Then every conflict is interpreted as a threat to the fundamental order, and every ordering structure is presented as a sublime instrument of compulsion within social antagonisms.

Corresponding to these fundamental tasks, we find two distinguishable groups of functionalist theories about religion:[16] integration theories on the one hand, and conflict theories on the other. Moreover, a further differentiation emerges, because in both integration and conflict processes we can distinguish between religion's restrictive function and its creative one. We may therefore conclude that religion has four possible functions. We can briefly indicate these beforehand by way of the following table:

	Integrative function	Antagonistic function
Restrictive function	*Domestication* internalized social compulsion	*Compensation* suppression and illusory solution of conflicts
Creative function	*Personalization* socialization of the natural human condition	*Innovation* actualization of conflict potential

The different sociological theories about religion (which can almost always be reinterpreted functionalistically) can all be fitted somewhere or other into this system of coordinates. The Marxist theory of religion,

---

16. F. Fürstenberg distinguished between an integration and a compensation theory (*Religionssoziologie*, ed. F. Fürstenberg [Neuwied, 1964], 13ff.). But in my view compensation is only one possible function of religion in social conflicts.

for example, especially stressed the compensatory nature of religious phenomena; Émile Durkheim emphasized their compulsive, socially integrative character;[17] and for Peter Berger and Thomas Luckmann they exercise a personalizing function through the establishment of a sacred cosmos.[18] Protestant ethics were used as prime example in the discussion about the innovative function of religious phenomena.[19] But every sociology of religion takes other functional aspects into account as well. The Marxist theory, for example, does not wholly fail to recognize the critical element in religious "protest," which aims at renewal.

1. THE INTEGRATIVE FUNCTION OF RELIGION

Every society is faced with the task of imposing order, over against the notorious readiness of men and women to break away from controls. Up to now this task has never succeeded without compulsion. But neither has it ever succeeded without a degree of assent on the part of those involved. It can hardly be denied that human beings transcend their natural condition only if they are able to internalize the order handed on to them by society. The acceptance of sociocultural values and norms has rightly been termed the human being's "second birth," being seen as an extension of possibilities otherwise doomed to total atrophy, but also as a drastic selection of the many possibilities theoretically open to a newly born individual. Social order is therefore double-faced: its function is both restrictive and creative.

Religion has undoubtedly always played an important part in transmitting, internalizing, and legitimating social order. We already see this from the tendency to project this social order into the cosmos, so as then — in a reverse movement — to legitimate the earthly order from that cosmos.[20] The king with his royal household is first of all heightened into the divine Lord of the universe with his angels, so that, in the

---

17. See E. Durkheim, *The Elementary Forms of the Religious Life,* trans. from French by J. W. Swain (London: Allen & Unwin, 1915; reprint, 1954; Glencoe, Ill.: Free Press, 1947).

18. T. Luckmann, *Das Problem der Religion in der modernen Gesellschaft* (Freiburg, 1963), and *The Invisible Religion* (New York: Macmillan, 1967); P. L. Berger, *The Sacred Canopy: Elements of a Sociological Theory of Religion* (Garden City, N.Y.: Doubleday; London: Faber & Faber, 1969).

19. Max Weber, *The Protestant Ethic and the Spirit of Capitalism,* trans. T. Parsons, foreword by R. H. Tawney (London: Allen & Unwin, 1930; reprint, 1948, etc.; New York: Scribner's, 1958).

20. E. Topitsch analyzes this process in *Vom Ursprung und Ende der Metaphysik* (Vienna, 1958). Mühlmann talks about "cosmological reflection" ("Kulturanthropologie," 34ff.).

reversal, he may then be legitimated as God's representative. In this way the symbolic projections of a religiously interpreted world often (though not always) correspond to the social world. Insofar as this social world is compulsive in character, its religious internalization too is an internalized compulsion. And insofar as it allows human potentialities to develop, this development also takes place through the corresponding world of religious symbols.

A. *The Domesticating Function of Religion*

Social order can never prevail against the antisocial tendencies of human behavior simply by way of outward compulsion.[21] For the people who have the obvious means of compulsion at their disposal are no more free from antisocial tendencies than anyone else. And who is supposed to control them? Moreover, external compulsion does not create any genuine integration which could stand up to collective and individual situations of stress and strain. The social scene may be as quiet as the grave, but behind the deathly silence, latent and dammed-up disintegration is always at work. So every society tries to steer and control its members by way of the unnoticeable, internalized "compulsion" of shared convictions and values—even the people who enjoy positions of power. We ought therefore to see domestication here as socially integrative compulsion. Cognitively, this domestication manifests itself in the legitimizing of social behavior, and especially the legitimizing of the distribution of property, power, and prestige; motivationally, it means that norms and their sanctions are internalized; while emotionally, domestication appears in the reduction of socially undesirable tensions in critical situations, whether these be social or individual.

Did early Christianity exercise domesticizing functions in this sense? The unreserved legitimation of government power that we find in Rom. 13:1ff. certainly points in this direction. But generally speaking, early Christianity dissociated itself firmly from the world, and this comes out even in the context of Romans 13. Anyone who is integrated into this world is lost to Christianity, which awaits a world that is new. Early Christianity is anything but an attempt to legitimize and internalize social orders through religion. In the Roman Empire it was rather the emperor cult of which this might be said. In legal proceedings against Christians, this cult was introduced as the touchstone of their loyalty to the state; and that loyalty was then often refused. After Constantine, and

---

21. On the following passage, see esp. J. M. Yinger, "Die Religion als Integrationsfaktor," in *Religionssoziologie*, ed. F. Fürstenberg, 93–106.

after Christianity had been promoted to state religion, the Christian church did indeed make a considerable contribution toward domesticizing the people living in the absolutist state of late antiquity. But that is another story and would take us beyond the boundaries of early Christianity. Christianity certainly became transformed from a subcultural trend on the fringe of ancient society into the social cement of the absolutist state of late antiquity; and this is undoubtedly the central problem facing every sociological investigation of Christianity in the ancient world. But in a sociology of *early* Christianity, only a partial aspect of this problem concerns us. Here the question is: What was there about the social structure of early Christianity to make this transformation possible? The following hypothesis, for example, is worth examination: it was above all the love patriarchalism of the early congregations which developed patterns of social integration among small groups. These integration patterns were able to stand up to considerable strain and could therefore be adopted later by a changed society.

B. *The Personalizing Function of Religion*

What from one angle is internalized compulsion is from another the socialization of the natural human disposition. The "sacred cosmos" set up by the religions,[22] which is intimately linked with the social world in any given context, is an attempt by men and women to build up a spiritually structured world that is related to human beings and is imbued with meaning—a world without which no human being can "breathe." Cognitively, it makes it possible to order subjective experience and communication with other people, provided that they inhabit the same religiously interpreted world. Motivationally, it gives actions a meaningful purpose, even though the goals may be far off and may require renunciation of the immediate satisfaction of wants and needs. Emotionally, it provides an awareness of a world in which men and women can be at home, in which even limit situations have their place. For in religion it is not merely a matter of reducing socially undesirable anxiety in limit situations. It is equally true that in religion people are made aware of limit situations, and that linguistic, ritual, and practical acts are developed as a way of meeting the challenge these situations present. The internalization of "the sacred cosmos"—like the assumption

---

22. This central characteristic of the traditional religions was worked out especially by M. Eliade; see *The Sacred and the Profane,* trans. from French by W. R. Trask (New York: Harper & Row, 1961), and *Patterns in Comparative Religion,* trans. R. Sheed (London and New York: Sheed & Ward, 1958). T. Luckmann and P. L. Berger have analyzed the social function of this "cosmization" in their work on the sociology of religion.

of every world of significance handed on socially—is a second birth in which human beings transcend their natural condition.

This notion about the sociocultural "second birth" is, of course, reminiscent of the early Christian idea of rebirth. But that idea itself is particularly well suited to bring out the difference between the two concepts. The adoption of Christian norms, symbols, and interpretations which is enacted in baptism is not identical with the general socialization of the human being but is in fact an abandonment of that socialization. In the early Christian faith, rebirth is a third birth, not a second one. If someone was converted to Christianity during its early years, that was a sign that in his or her case general socialization had failed—or at least that was the way outsiders saw the matter (see p. 198 above for Pliny's opinion of the early Christians, in his *Epistulae* 10.96). Correspondingly, the sacred cosmos set up in the symbolic acts of the early Christian congregations was not the cosmos that was socially accepted. Their cosmos was essentially a "new world," whose realization people in the congregations thought they could already discern. Here men and women were not introduced to a symbolic world of significance that corresponded to society as it existed. This was rather the destruction of that sacred cosmos through the symbolic acts of the new "kerygma," which —as we see from the early Christian hymns— proclaimed a human failure as Lord of the universe, with the subjugation of all other powers.

It is characteristic of early Christianity that the new world of symbols which replaced the old one is still relatively open, fragmentary, and mysterious. It is not yet consistently structured through and through—not even in its boldest "constructor," the apostle Paul. To the distress of some theologians, what is missing here is a theology of salvation history embracing history as a whole. What is dominant are the crass alternatives of faith and works, Moses and Christ, the old human being and the new, servitude and freedom. What is presented is not a finished, consistent sacred cosmos, of the kind built up by later theologians, often with an intellectual boldness that one can only admire. What we find here is something different. This is a new symbolic world of significance in the process of development. What we experience is the transition from an old to a new cosmos, whose contours are still in many cases blurred. And we are caught up, not least, in the jubilation of people for whom wisdom begins with themselves and who think nothing whatsoever of the wisdom of "the world" (1 Cor. 1:18ff.). This is not integration into an existing society. Here a new means of human personalization is thrown open, and a new way of life established.

So we see: the integration theories of the sociology of religion, in these two variants, do not provide the instruments for grasping early Christianity analytically. The essential reason is that, in the context of society as a whole, the early Christian faith was in fact a phenomenon of social *dis*integration. It originated in the Palestinian Jesus movement, which was a movement of itinerant preachers, without any settled home, trade, or family. The people who handed on the faith that later separated itself from Judaism and became Christianity were initially people who had left home and possessions. They were outsiders who embodied a socially deviant behavior which, in other variants too, was unusually widespread in the Palestinian society of the time. We need only think of the Zealots, the Sicarii, the messianic claimants, and the Essenes, as well as the people who were simply beggars and brigands. Nor is the progressive consolidation of early Christianity in local congregations identical with social integration, for the early Christian groups were undoubtedly on the fringes of society.

Yet for all that, approaches based on integration theories do have a value, namely for the analysis of small groups. In the early Jesus movement we already find an integrative feature, for both Simon the Zealot and Levi the tax collector were among Jesus' followers, and they belonged to two mutually hostile groups. These two people were integrated into a group of itinerant charismatics on the fringe of society. But afterwards integration patterns developed in "settled" local congregations too (in the Hellenistic ones especially), patterns that promoted the integration of people belonging to different classes. Other "associations" in the ancient world were very much more homogeneous, socially.

2. THE ANTAGONISTIC FUNCTION OF RELIGION

The integration theories maintained in the sociology of religion also see religion's function as the regulation of conflict — the conflict between the individual and society. But here the superior power of society is so obvious that we can hardly talk about a conflict at all, if by conflict we mean the clash of two social forces. Here, in discussing conflict theories of religion, we shall describe only the theoretical approaches which assume that the function of religion has to be sought in economic, political, and cultural conflicts between different groups. In this case too, religion can be seen as either restrictive or creative. But in order to be able to distinguish these two aspects functionally, the conflicts themselves must be open to a functional interpretation. That is to say, they have to be viewed as an instrument of the social change without which no society can survive.[23] Social changes can be slowed up or accelerated according to whether conflicts are suppressed or given external form. Religion can be said to have a restrictive function when it is able to "contain" tensions tending toward change, and a creative function when it gives concrete form to the potential for social conflict.

This distinction is meant functionally. It is not a value judgment. To arrive at a value judgment would mean stressing that the "creative" function of religious phenomena does not by any means have to be viewed in exclusively positive terms. We need only think of the explosive fanaticism that we so often come across in religious history. Conversely, we can perhaps view with some degree of sympathy the resistance of conservative religion in the Maccabean wars to the progressive Hellenistic reform program of people in Jerusalem.

A. *The Compensatory Function of Religion*

If religion has a restrictive function in social conflicts, then it must offer some substitute for the social change that has been prevented. In the Maccabean rebellion, for instance, the swaggeringly heightened sense of election could have been a compensation for frustrated "progress" in civilization and culture. This would mean that there may perhaps be an intimate link between the social and economic backwardness of Jewish Palestine and its immense religious claim.[24] The compensatory function of religious phenomena is shown cognitively in the creation of a counterpicture to social reality (i.e., not in mirrror reflections of the cosmos), motivationally in the redirection of existing impulses toward surrogate objects, and emotionally in the defusing and mitigation of social tensions. Karl Marx provides the classic description of the compensatory character of religious phenomena:[25]

> Religious misery is at one and the same time the expression of true misery and protest against true misery. Religion is the groaning of the oppressed creature, the feeling of a heartless world, and the spirit of a dispirited condition. It is the opium of the people.

---

23. See R. Dahrendorf, "Die Funktionen sozialer Konflikte," in *Pfade aus Utopia*, 263–77.

24. See M. Hengel's investigation *Judaism and Hellenism,* trans. J. Bowden (London: SCM Press; Philadelphia: Fortress Press, 1974). He takes sociological aspects into account as well.

25. K. Marx, "Zur Kritik der Hegelschen Rechtsphilosophie: Einleitung" in *Die Frühschriften,* ed. S. Landshut (Stuttgart, 1964), 208 (*Critique of Hegel's Philosophy of Right,* trans. A. Jolin and J. O'Malley [Cambridge: Cambridge University Press, 1970]).

For a sociology of early Christianity, the Marxist variant of the conflict theory of religion is particularly important, because in Marxism we find analyses of early Christianity which are based not merely on an explicit theory of religion but on a differentiated sociological theory about the ancient world as well. Here we must confine our discussion to only a few points.[26]

The foundation of every Marxist theory of religion is the substructure/superstructure theory. This theory can be treated more or less subtly (or "dialectically," to take the word often used). According to its "dialectical" interpretation, the theory aims to do more than to establish the existence of a dependency between two classes of things, the material and the mental or spiritual. It is far more concerned to interpret both the material *and* the spiritual as human products and to rob them of the sham appearance which suggests to us that they have an existence of their own, independent of anything human beings do or think. This basic thesis asserts that the contradictions in material production recur in the spiritual products of human beings — partly in the form of an illusionary triumph over these contradictions, partly as their mere reproduction. The possibility that the superstructure may have a retroactive effect on the substructure is not in principle denied.

The Problem of the Substructure

The Marxist analysis of early Christianity may be summed up here in M. Robbe's words: "Christianity issued from the contradictions of a highly developed slaveowning society. It grew up in the tension-charged encounter between east and west which took place in the Roman Empire at the beginning of our era."[27] According to the Marxist view, the slaveowning society was contradictory because material goods were produced by slaves and consumed by slaveowners; and although slave labor could be stepped up only to a limited degree (because it was devoid of personal interest), the labor of free men was looked down upon. This inconsistency had two results. It led (1) to the imperialism of the ancient world, in which slave labor was *quantitatively* increased through the enslavement of whole peoples. The tensions between east and west to which Robbe refers are therefore tensions inherent in slaveowning society

---

26. See F. Vittinghoff, "Die Theorie des historischen Materialismus über den antiken 'Sklavenhalterstaat,'" *Saeculum* 11 (1960): 89–131; R. Sannwald, *Marx und die Antike* (Zurich, 1957); N. Brockmeyer, *Arbeitsorganisation und ökonomisches Denken in der Gutswirtschaft des Römischen Reiches* (dissertation, Bochum, 1968), 33–70; B. Stasiewski, "Ursprung und Entfaltung des Christentums in sowjetischer Sicht," *Saeculum* 11 (1960): 157–79.

27. Robbe, *Ursprung des Christentums,* 29.

as system. After the campaigns of conquest had ended, the same inconsistency led (2) to the *qualitative* transformation of slavery. Dependent colonates were now created in which the *colonus* was given a piece of land, so that he acquired an interest in his own labor. These assumptions are undoubtedly worth thinking about. In our present context we should remember two things.

First, the social and economic conflicts of antiquity were seldom fought out by slaves. There were certainly a number of slave revolts, but mainly in the late phase of the Roman republic. In general, "the class struggle was only something for a privileged minority. It was played out between wealthy freemen and poor freemen, whereas the productive mass of the population — the slaves — merely provided the passive substratum for these combatants."[28] Of course we should have to ask whether here it is still possible to talk about a class struggle at all, in the strict sense — a struggle, that is, between the owners of the means of production and the exploited producers. It would be better to talk more cautiously about a socioeconomic struggle over the distribution of material goods, power and prestige, a struggle which characterized antiquity like every other historical era. Here the begetters and sustainers of protest "from below" are often not the lowest class of all. They are more apt to be the groups that are threatened with a decline in the social scale, with a consequent loss of social and cultural identity. The Zealot movement in Jewish Palestine was partly recruited from small-holders who had got into debt (Josephus *Antiquities* 18.8.6).

Second, we should remember that even in this distribution struggle the fronts between different classes were never entirely clear-cut. There were rival parties in the upper classes themselves. Often, one of these parties made common cause with "the lower orders" as a way of eliminating rivals. Things were no different in Palestine. It was the alliance between a section of the priestly aristocracy and the freedom fighters that led to the elimination of "the doves," and to the outbreak of the Jewish War (Josephus *Jewish War* 2.17.2).

If the Marxist approach is formalized into a more general theory about social conflict, this can be a valuable help in analyzing early Christianity; for new movements such as the Jesus movement often spring up in the tensions of social conflict. In Palestine we find the sociopolitical conflict between the different structures of rule (empire, monarchy, and theocracy). In addition there was a socioecological conflict between town and

---

28. K. Marx, *18. Brumaire.* Foreword to the 2nd ed. of 1869 in *Ausgewählte Schriften* I, 9th ed. (Berlin, 1958–9), 223 (Eng. trans. *The Eighteenth Brumaire of L. Bonaparte,* trans. E. and C. Paul [London: Allen & Unwin; New York: International Publishers, 1926]).

country, a socioeconomic conflict between the producers and the profit-making class, and a sociocultural conflict between different groups all claiming to embody "the true Israel." All these conflicts are connected. There is no reason to reduce them to a single dissension. Even less is there any reason to trace the Jesus movement back to these conflicts, in a causal or genetic sense. For very different trends, evoked by entirely opposite attitudes of mind, were all fed by the same social situation in Palestine.

It is even more difficult to make intensified class antitheses responsible in the case of the early Hellenistic congregations. Friedrich Engels assumed that here Christianity was initially a "religion of slaves and freedmen, the poor and those without any rights, peoples under the yoke of Rome, or peoples who had been dispersed by her."[29] These statements about the social makeup of the early Christian congregations are open to scrutiny. But these congregations were in fact made up of people from different classes. In Antioch we know of Manaen (Menahem), who had been brought up at the Jewish court (Acts 13:1), while in the Corinth congregation we hear of a city treasurer, Erastus (Rom. 16:23). Pliny the Younger (*Epistulae* 10.96) testifies that in Bithynia the Christian superstition had already spread to all classes. It is to the credit of Marxist scholars that they recognize this. A. B. Ranowitsch, for example (clearly picking up what Engels had said earlier), writes: "Christianity was from the beginning a religion of the oppressed—slaves and freedmen, the poor and those without any rights, peoples who had been enslaved or dispersed by Rome." But he then goes on:

> The magnetic field of the new religion also attracted representatives of the exploiting groups among "peoples under the yoke of Rome or dispersed by her." As far as the imperial power was concerned, these groups had practically no more rights than slaves over against their masters. From the very beginning Christianity brought together the most widely varied groups, with different, sometimes even opposing interests.[30]

Here a theory is salvaged through the metaphorical use of the term "slave"; for can we really trace early Christianity back to the antithesis between slaveowners and slaves (and other groups without rights) if the Christian congregations brought together exploiters and exploited?

---

29. See F. Engels, "Zur Geschichte des Urchristenums," in K. Marx and F. Engels, *Über Religion* (Berlin, 1958), 255 (*K. Marx and F. Engels on Religion* [Moscow, 1956]).

30. A. B. Ranowitsch, "Das Urchristentum und seine historische Rolle," in *Aufsätze zur Alten Geschichte* (Berlin, 1961), 135–65; quotation from p. 144.

The Problem of the Superstructure

The analysis of the superstructure is based on Feuerbach's projection theory, according to which religious ideas are wishful thinking, the self-presentations of the human mind. Marx's development of this theory led among other things to two different theoretical assumptions that are not easily reconciled. We shall call these the opium theory and the fetishism theory.

According to the opium theory, religious symbols build up a counter-picture to social reality, the new world overmastering the old. These symbols therefore also have a critical force and can be thrown into the scale *against* social reality. In this sense they embody an elemental protest. But because the instrument of this protest is itself illusion, this is the opium of the people (not opium *for* the people!).

The fetishism theory, on the other hand, stresses the correspondence between the social substructure and religious ideas. In material production, the products seem to lead a life of their own, independent of human activity (this is "the fetishism of material goods"). And in the same way, in "the cloudy region of the religious world" "products of the human brain seem to be endowed with a life of their own; they are independent configurations, which are related to one another and to human beings."[31] The dependence of one's own material product is reflected in the products of religion, the incalculability of the capitalist system, for example, being mirrored in the incalculability of divine predestination, and so forth.

According to the opium theory, therefore, religious symbols behave asymetrically toward their social basis. They contain reflections of what is lacking in social reality. According to the fetishism theory, on the other hand, there is symmetry between religious symbolism and social reality. Religious projections reflect existing dependency. In analyzing the history of early Christianity, Marxism assumes that it underwent a profound transformation in this respect. At the earliest stage, religious symbols offering a counterpicture to reality were dominant. Eschatology was a protest against this present world. The book of Revelation,

---

31. K. Marx, *Das Kapital*, 3rd ed. (Berlin, 1953), 78 (Eng. trans. *Capital*, trans. E. B. Aveling and S. Moore [London: Sonnenschein, 1887; New York: Appleton, 1889; often reprinted]). M. Robbe writes in "Marxismus und Religionsforschung," 174: "The experience of helplessness takes form and acquires independent existence (thus becoming reproducible) in a specific religious feeling. In this feeling its worldly content is transcended and now—absolute form being given to the situation of human helplessness— appears as the "Wholly Other," the "numinous" (at all events, in all its different forms, otherworldly). At the same time in this feeling human beings seek the illusory abolition of what is experienced."

accordingly, counts as the oldest document of the early Christian faith. Later on, the orientation changed:

> When the church was in the process of becoming established, about the middle of the second century, it regrouped and reexamined its position. The expectation of the imminent end of the world was now condemned as heretical. Hate of the world of violence, oppression, and injustice was now replaced by the doctrine of the renunciation of resistance and love of one's enemies.[32]

Here Marxism fails to realize that from the very beginning Christianity combined the two things: opposition to the world—and an unconditional "yes" to every person; eschatology—and faith in creation; heightened standards of behavior—and the forgiveness of sins; and so on.

Every conflict theory about religion is indebted to Marxism for important stimuli.[33] But it is an error to think that every conflict theory is bound to be Marxist. This ought to be made clear terminologically too. Instead of talking about the class struggle we should rather speak about a conflict over distribution. Instead of discussing the contradictions of a "slaveowning society," we should consider the contradictions and conflicts in the society of the ancient world generally, and instead of projections we should talk about "symbolic action." Provided these modifications are made, it is surely a heuristically valuable assumption to say that in its symbolic acts early Christianity articulated social conflicts and tried to master them. But whether these symbolic acts have a merely compensatory character is questionable.

B. *The Innovatory Function of Religion*

In situations of social tension religion can also help to actualize social conflicts and to develop new solutions.[34] What tremendous social energy was unleashed by Muhammad and Luther, for example! This was not merely a matter of "containing" energy by providing compensatory surrogates. These energies were actually triggered off in the first place. They were no doubt already latent, but they were certainly not defused by the religious impulses. The prophetic aspect especially of the biblical religions—Judaism, Islam and Christianity—cannot, in my view, be

---

32. Ranowitsch, "Urchristentum," 150.

33. See R. Dahrendorf, "Karl Marx und die Theorie des sozialen Wandels," in *Pfade aus Utopia*, 277–93; D. Lockwood, "Soziale Integration und Systemintegration," in *Theorien des Sozialen Wandels*, ed. W. Zapf (Cologne, 1969), 124–37.

34. On the following passage, see esp. J. M. Yinger, "Toward a Theory of Religion and Social Change," *IJRS* 7 (1971): 7–30.

comprehended through the theoretical approaches to religion we have looked at up to now.[35] And this means that early Christianity is equally inaccessible by way of this approach; for early Christianity was a prophetic movement through and through.

Prophets have visions, ecstasies, and inspirations which other people find it hard to enter into. Here everything seems irrational. And it may initially appear to be a hopeless task to try to understand their appearance functionally. Yet this is possible, if we remind ourselves that it is of vital importance for every society to develop new solutions — but that in strongly traditional societies, with religious legitimations, whatever is new must be religiously legitimated too. Anyone who wants to make what is new obligatory has to be authorized by God. The Israelite prophets of doom were undoubtedly "functional." By fitting the fall of the Israelite kingdom into the symbolically interpreted world, they made it possible for Judaism to survive in exile, creating a profounder identity for the Jewish people. In their revelations, visions, and ecstasies, the religions are in this sense feeling their way toward fresh paths, alternatives, new forms of living, new interpretations of the meaning of life. What comes into being in the process will always initially be viewed as erroneous. Most of it has no lasting effect.[36] Some of it may later on prove to be the "solution" to a problem. As we know, the prophets of doom were first of all completely isolated. And although the vision of love, reconciliation, and grace offered by the Jesus movement was certainly born out of the crisis-torn society of Jewish Palestine, it was not able to develop there. It found acceptance mainly in the flourishing towns and cities of the Mediterranean world. Here, on the fringes of society, a new way of life matured, an alternative that was accepted by the whole of society — after profound changes both in that society and in Christianity itself.

The innovatory function of religion is manifested cognitively in the development of a new symbolic cosmos which is set over against the cosmos previously accepted, often with an apodictic claim to revelation. This new cosmos shows itself motivationally in the reversal of

---

35. But prophetic movements are found everywhere. See W. E. Mühlmann, *Chiliasmus und Nativismus* (Berlin, 1961); V. Lanternari, *The Religions of the Oppressed*, trans. L. Sergio (London: Macgibbon & Kee, 1963; New York: New American Library, 1965).

36. See J. M. Yinger, "Theory," 29: "Many religious innovations probably very quickly die away without having exerted any considerable effect on the social system. They appear in situations which were not vulnerable to their attack, or were not sufficiently susceptible. It is probably true that charismatic leaders are identified only after their influence has been established. Other people of potentially equal influence disappear and fail to find a place in the field of history, because the time was not ripe for their innovations."

incentives, in the setting of new goals, in a "blueprint" for "the new human being"— in short, in a new motivational structure. Emotionally, it must above all evolve an immunity to the generally keenly felt and harshly inflicted resistance of traditional norms, obligations, and interpretations of life. This immunity is achieved through the development of a sense of martyrdom and election which can stand up to even the greatest strain. We find all these features in early Christianity.

Since religious revival movements are a reaction against a hitherto accepted symbolic world which they often then systematically destroy, they have features that people today like to call "emancipatory." They "unmask" a traditional sacred cosmos, showing it to be an interpretative world constructed by human beings, and in this way they de-alienate the alienation that can be discovered in religious phenomena.[37] The beings previously thought to be gods are disclosed as products of the human mind. On the basis of its prophetic Jewish heritage, early Christianity viewed the gods as at most demons. Precepts now superseded were regarded as "human works" (Matt. 7:1ff.). At least they had no value in themselves: the Sabbath is made for man (Mark 2:27). And yet it is quite wrong to judge early Christianity from merely one side, as a step toward "emancipation." The destruction of an ancient, humanly constructed symbolic world is balanced by the creation of a new one, which is regarded not as a human work but as the ultimate revelation, even if in our eyes it may be no less dependent on the symbolic procedures of human beings than all the other worlds of religious symbol. Anyone who fails to comprehend the splendor of this newly created mythical, interpretative world, and anyone who fails to respect it, understands nothing at all about early Christianity. These new symbolic ideas and acts in all their boldness can no more be reduced to the classification "emancipation" than the Gothic cathedrals, or Luther's doctrine of justification. They do indeed testify to a tremendous yearning to transcend the natural human condition and are therefore signs of a profounder humanity. But what they do not promote is "emancipation," if emancipation means liberation from authorities which cannot be rationally legitimated. The very contrary is closer to the mark. They are bound up with a binding claim to revelation which, from the "emancipatory" viewpoint, would have to be rejected as authoritarian, if we wanted to take both early Christianity and emancipation really seriously. Whether this claim is valid is not under discussion in a functionalist investigation of Christianity. What we have to consider is the social function of that claim. Anyone who destroys a religiously established symbolic

---

37. P. L. Berger has rightly stressed this de-alienating feature in *Sacred Canopy*, 96ff.

cosmos, or restructures it, must do so in the name of a higher warranty. The legitimation of what is new must outdo the legitimation of the accepted authorities. The pagan religions of the Hellenistic world, which early Christianity unmasked as works of the human mind, were relatively tolerant. The opposition to them was fundamentally intolerant. The "emancipatory" element in early Christianity is too intimately linked with its authoritative claim for us to be able to separate the two.

In the context of the sociology of religion, an analysis of early Christianity as an innovatory religious movement ought, in my view, to answer four questions:

1. What contradictions and tensions in Palestinian society led people to search for new "solutions" to religious and social questions? For example: the tension between the different structures of rule promoted the rise of radically theocratic movements; socioeconomic tensions encouraged the growth of socially deviant behavior (brigandage, begging, the itinerant charismatics, and so on); tensions between the town (Jerusalem) and the country led to criticism of the Temple state aristocracy; the rise of groups pressing for more rigorous ethical standards triggered off the countertrend of a more radical proclamation of grace. New impulses spring up in a field of social tension, and it is plausible to assume that they continue to develop where these tensions are particularly strongly felt.

2. What were the innovatory intentions of the different new movements? Social tensions no doubt impel the search for something new, but they do not actually produce the new thing itself. The tensions experienced have to be interpreted, articulated, and legitimated.[38] To take an example: foreign Roman rule was of course a burden on every province. The fact that it had such explosive effects in Palestine particularly can be understood only if we remember the specifically Israelite traditions and intentions which made the dichotomy of a people chosen yet subjugated a compelling problem. There were many possible reactions and new impulses. That these new impulses should initially have been sustained by tiny minorities is quite understandable.

3. Why did some of these impulses prevail while others faded away? To ask this is to ask what determines "selection" in all the competing attempts to find the answers. As we know, the Jesus movement failed in Palestine and spread in the Hellenistic world. But the social reasons

---

38. The significance of religious intentions and legitimations can in my view be very well analyzed on the basis of the "theory of action model" which G. Kehrer has recommended for the analysis of religious aspects of social change; see Kehrer, "Religion und sozialer Wandel," *IJRS* 7 (1971): 31–59.

that contributed to its rise are not identical with the reasons that encouraged its dissemination. For example, it is difficult to link the spread of early Hellenistic Christianity with social tensions. Of course there were tensions everywhere. But compared with other periods, the first and second centuries particularly were actually a time of relative stability in the towns and cities, and there was an astonishingly high level of culture, a level that was not reached again until modern times.[39] In addition, these were years when there was considerable local and social mobility, as well as good transport and communications. Perhaps it was precisely this era of relative peace and widespread communications which favored the spread of Christianity, with its integrative element. At all events it would be worthwhile examining this counter-theory to the favorite "crisis" interpretation of early Christianity.

4. Finally, we ought to consider the way early Christianity adapted to new functional correlations — its change from a charismatic movement to a practicable and institutionally consolidated way of life.

To sum up: a functional analyis provides appropriate theoretical categories for a sociology of early Christianity. In this context, conflict theories would seem to offer a better explanation for many phenomena than integration theories. But the two models complement each other. Christian groups which conflicted with society developed new integrative patterns. A conflict suggests that integration has failed; integration points to conflict that has been surmounted. In the conflict theories themselves, the innovatory function of religious phenomena should engage our attention rather than their compensatory function; and here innovation is not identical with what is today termed "emancipation."

We have confined ourselves in general to an analysis of religious phenomena and have excluded the question about religion's essence and its truth. It would be wrong to equate the social function of anything with its essential nature. To say this is not to fall back on a general precautionary theological proviso, designed to undermine from the outset any unwelcome results of religio-sociological analysis. There are objective reasons for the statement. Almost all human utterances and creations are in some way or other personalizing and domesticating, compensatory and innovatory. These are not specifically religious functions. Religion is a priori no more domesticating and compensatory than any other sector of human life. And if in religion the restrictive aspects largely outweigh the others, that is because the same is true of life in general; innovation and personalization are always less probable than domestication and compensation. Religion is probably "conservative" and

---

39. See N. Brockmeyer, *Sozialgeschichte der Antike* (Stuttgart, 1972), 110.

"progressive" to precisely the same degree as human beings generally. And no doubt religion is also just as inconsistent as human beings. For in religion we find all types of human behavior, from rebellion against the gods to masochistic subjugation to them.

So at the end of a functionalist investigation we are faced all the more inescapably with the question: What is the specifically religious factor in all these religious phenomena?[40] What, at least, is the essence of religion in its historically analyzable form (which does not mean that we can decide how it will develop in the future)? What is "the holy"? How can it be rationally analyzed? We are in fact confronted with the very questions we excluded at the beginning, on the grounds that they were phenomenological and reductionist. They are in no way illegitimate. But it would seem that they cannot be answered by way of sociological analyses.

A CODA

The use of a functionalist approach in some of my essays has given rise to a number of misunderstandings that require clarification. "Functionalism" was first developed in ethnology. That is, it was first used to investigate cultures that seem to be relatively static, since on the one hand they only have an oral history (which does not permit any reliable reconstruction of their prehistory), while on the other they conceive of the future as a repetition of archetypal patterns. In cultures of this kind, the methods of historical sociology cannot be used. For here the subject of the scientific investigation is present function, not past origins, and the dominant method is empirical field research, not the analysis of historical sources. Both these facts led temporally to an estrangement between historical scholarship and sociology.[41]

In my own essays I have chosen, among other things, a "functionalist" way of looking at the social history of early Christianity; but this was from the very beginning an expanded and modified "functionalism." For what we are considering here is not a static society but a fundamental social transformation — the rise of a new religion and its spread throughout the Roman Empire. In order to understand this social transformation, we have to expand functionalism. We no longer merely have to

---

40. See Matthes, "Religionssoziologie," 238: If one analyzes religion with such general categories as personalization and cosmization, it is no longer possible to say logically "why they are actually *religious* phenomena."

41. See the illuminating remarks made by P. Burke in *Sociology and History* (London and Boston: Allen & Unwin, 1980), 21f.

ask: What is the function of this or that social phenomenon in preserving the existing social equilibrium? We have to ask preeminently: What is its function in changing society?

This new question forces us to take up conflict theories, not merely interpreting conflicts as a contribution to the consolidation of the existing social order (perhaps as a way of establishing hierarchies or securing the acceptance of certain standards) but seeing them as a contribution to the transformation of society. So the function of conflicts must be understood not as their contribution to the stabilization of the existing social equilibrium but rather as a search for a new equilibrium, pointing beyond the present social order—pointing, that is, to the society of the future. Conflicts have an innovatory function.

This historical expansion and modification of functionalism is indebted to ideas put forward by the German sociologist Ralf Dahrendorf.[42] He developed them in sharp criticism of American structure functionalism and was unmistakably inspired in so doing by Marxist ideas. But this is a Marxism that has been deprived of its utopian content. As in Marxism, conflicts are regarded as the driving power of social change, which continually takes place and is always necessary; but here — other than in Marxism—this change is not conceived of as ending in a classless society, free of conflict. Conflicts have an innovatory function: they do not serve to stabilize systems. Since Darhrendorf is less well known outside Germany, let me stress that in the present essay I have deliberately adopted his criticism of classic functionalism. This makes it possible for me to take up Marxist ideas in a non-Marxist paradigm. But it has not been clear to every reader of my work that in this way I have essentially modified the functionalist analysis. This has escaped even J. H. Elliott, though I should like to draw explicit attention to his instructive criticism of my theoretical approach.[43] I can agree in principle with many of his ideas, but I cannot see how far they have a bearing on the variant of "functionalism" that I am maintaining here.

But I have also used an "expanded functionalism" in the sense that theoretical approaches are deliberately applied as a heuristic instrument, as a way of arriving at historical findings. Theoretical models are

---

42. The following essays have influenced me particularly: R. Dahrendorf, "Die Funktionen sozialer Konflikte," in *Pfade aus Utopia,* 263ff.; "Karl Marx und die Theorie des sozialen Wandels," ibid., 277ff; and the studies gathered together under the heading "Gleichgewicht und Prozess: Wider das statische Vorurteil in der soziologischen Theorie," ibid., 212–313.

43. J. H. Elliott, "Social-Scientific Criticism of the New Testament and its Social World: More on Method and Models," *Semeia* 35 (1986): 1–34.

not an end in themselves. The truths inherent in competing approaches, phenomenological and interpretative as well as Marxist, should *all* be brought into play. They are all perspectives that we cannot do without. In the final study of the present volume I have therefore put into practice the theoretical program put forward here and have attempted to arrive at a sociological theory of early Christianity, in which it is deliberately interpreted from three different perspectives. For it is only through different theoretical perspectives that we can do justice to complex historical phenomena.

9

Some Ideas
about a Sociological Theory
of Early Christianity

———————◆———————

S HALL WE EVER succeed in finding a comprehensive theory
with which to interpret all the sociologically relevant facts about
Christian beginnings? The doubts are understandable. One person
thinks the data too fragmentary; another finds theories about the
sociology of religion too one-sided; a third considers their nontheo-
logical premises suspect; a fourth has doubts about their ethical
implications. Many fat tomes would have to be written in order to do
justice to all the questions. Yet for all that, I should like tentatively in
this short essay to outline a sociological theory about Christian beginnings. It is impossible in this brief space to enter explicitly into all the
objections I have indicated, but implicitly they play their part in the
discussion. What I should like to say is not confined to any particular
approach in the sociology of religion. On the contrary, I have chosen
three different theoretical perspectives, each of which throws new light
on Christianity in its early years. The first perspective is phenomenological; the second is based on the integration theory; and the third
adopts the viewpoint suggested by the theory of conflict.[1] The shift from
the one approach to the other is intended to show that from every
perspective we can discover something that is true, but that no approach
taken by itself is enough to provide an appropriate theory about the
social history of early Christianity. The whole is an attempt, on the way

---

1. I am well aware that there are many more possible approaches in the sociology
of religion; for the German-speaking area alone, see *Religion in den Gegenwartsströmungen
der deutschen Soziologie,* ed. K. F. Daiber and T. Luckmann (Munich, 1983).

to a more comprehensive theory. And it is as an attempt that I should like it to be judged.

1. AN INTERPRETATION OF EARLY CHRISTIANITY
FROM THE VIEWPOINT
OF A PHENOMENOLOGICAL SOCIOLOGY OF RELIGION

According to its own way of understanding itself, religion is a response to the experience of "the holy." The relation to a "Wholly Other" is inherent in the religious phenomenon itself. A phenomenological sociology of religion respects this self-interpretation. It dispenses with an all-embracing sociological theory of religion.[2] But it does see an intimate link between religion and social behavior in two respects; for both "the experience of the holy" and the "response" to that experience are socially mediated.

Experiences of the holy are *interpreted* experiences. The interpretative patterns derive from the traditions of the particular group to which we belong, or which we have joined. Religiously speaking, reality is open to many interpretations. Every "interpreted world" is a limited selection of many possible ways of interpreting the holy. Consequently, religious interpretations become plausible only if they are jointly "inhabited" — that is to say, only if they are rooted in an interpretative community, in which certainty is mutually conferred and defection from the collectively interpreted world is jointly resisted; for such defection is a constant threat.

Religion is a community of interpretation and action. It is a response to the experience of the holy. And this response is given by way of shared social and ethical behavior — that is, through patterns of conduct and institutions which acquire their binding character from a specific experience of the holy, and which are developed and handed on in the conviction that this is a way of responding appropriately to the holy as call.

A phenomenological or hermeneutical (i.e., *verstehende*) sociology of religion will present early Christianity first of all as an interpretative community with shared fundamental convictions. These fundamental convictions are collective patterns of interpretation in which the early

---

2. A sociology of religion inspired by phenomenology has in my view found its most convincing expression in P. L. Berger, *The Sacred Canopy: Elements of a Sociological Theory of Religion* (Garden City, N.Y.: Doubleday; London: Faber & Faber, 1969).

Christian experience of the holy is expressed and made communicable.[3] Many of them are derived from Judaism and were to a great extent made accessible to non-Jews too by way of the Christian proclamation. One of these convictions was the central axiom of creation: Jews and Christians taught that the existence and structure of the world should be seen as the expression of a sovereign divine will. For them the world was contingent, the outcome of a *creatio ex nihilo* — a creation out of nothing, which was given new effect in the resurrection of the dead. Ultimately speaking, what corresponds to this world is not reason (which seeks for necessary and unalterable structures in the world) but a will which — since it is the image and echo of the divine will — like that divine will itself, has a new world as lodestone.[4]

In what follows I should like to outline six basic axioms shared by the interpretative community of the early Christians. We discover these axioms in different texts, in different themes, and in different intellectual trends in early Christianity.

1. The personal charismatic axiom: that is, the conviction that God can be experienced by human beings. His spirit (or his "charisma") is present in persons: in the prophets and the history of the people of Israel, in Jesus himself, and in Christians who are possessed by his spirit. The central personal charismatic relationship to which all others are related is the relationship to Jesus. Through him God's message is perceived in a form that can never be superseded.[5]

2. The eschatological axiom: the personal charismatic relationship to Jesus is unique because with him a new world begins. Christians are living in a transition from the old world to the new — in the tension between that which is *already* present and that which has *not yet* been fulfilled. The world is not going to remain as it is now.

3. The conversion axiom: human behavior is not fixed once and for all. It is open to radical reorientation. The encounter with Jesus leads people to leave behind old patterns of behavior and to turn to new ways of living. The breach between the old life and the new

---

3. The following ideas about some (relatively formal) basic convictions in the Christian religion are much influenced by D. Ritschl, "Die Erfahrung der Wahrheit: Die Steuerung von Denken und Handeln durch implizite Axiome," in *Konzepte* (Munich, 1986), 147–66.

4. On the indissoluble connection between the biblical belief in creation and the idea of will as an independent dimension of human behavior, see A. Dihle, *Die Vorstellung vom Willen in der Antike* (Göttingen, 1985).

5. On the concept "personal charisma" as distinct from "the charisma of office," see W. Schluchter, "Max Webers Analyse des antiken Christentums," in *Max Webers Sicht des antiken Christentums,* ed. W. Schluchter (Frankfurt, 1985), 11–71.

can be so profound that it can be interpreted as dying with Christ and living with him.

4. The axiom about the kerygma of suffering: there can be a hidden message in suffering, whether it be the requirement to eliminate suffering, or whether it be the charge to witness through the endurance of suffering (to the point of martyrdom) — to witness to something that cannot be denied by anything in the world. In the light of this axiom, the suffering of Christ is interpreted as a message about liberation from sin and death.

5. The integration axiom: anyone who is possessed by the early Christian experience of the holy is in duty bound to behave so that the frontiers between "insiders" and "outsiders" lose their absolute force. This behavior may mean bringing home "the lost," or it may mean receiving into the community people who have previously been "far off." Even enemies must be loved. The person of Jesus is seen in the light of this axiom: Jesus seeks the lost and integrates in himself both divided humanity and hostile powers.

6. The change-of-position axiom: just as the early Christian experience of the holy relativized the dividing line between insiders and outsiders, it also deprived of its absolute force the hierarchical order between people at the top and people below. The first should be ready to assume the position of the last. Christ is the model for this mode of behavior: he humbled himself so as to be exalted above all powers.

These six basic axioms certainly do not cover all the principles held by the early Christian interpretative community. Nor would I dispute the breadth of variation in which these fundamental convictions are historically manifested. On the contrary, the very way the axioms are woven into different contexts and themes shows that a few formal basic patterns of experience and behavior existed in most early Christian groups. They represented a vertical structure of shared thinking and experience which could be reflected in different surface patterns. The interpretative axioms form an implicit canon in the early Christian world of conviction. They define the religious perspective that was shared by Christians and in which they lived. At the center of this perspective is the figure of Jesus.

But early Christianity was not merely an interpretative community. It was a community in action as well, a community which had developed patterns of behavior corresponding to the shared basic axioms, and which had a particular sociological character or impress. This may provisionally be described by saying that early Christianity was a personally charismatic conversion movement, which alienated its members from the existing social world in order to integrate them into a new one. The early Christian experience of the holy was therefore at once disintegrative and integrative in its social consequences. It had a potential for both innovation and conflict, which led to estrangement from the world in which people had previously lived; but it also possessed a power of diffusion and integration, which continually captivated new people.

Let me now go on to develop this summary description of early Christianity a little further.

A. *The Basic Personal Charismatic Structure of Early Christianity*

The personal charismatic relationship to Jesus is the key to an understanding of the early Christian faith, both sociologically and theologically.[6] In Jesus' proclamation and his fate, Christians recognize the presence of a power outside everyday life. This power is freely acknowledged — that is, without the use of any compulsion or force — although it cannot draw on accepted authorities, neither on Scripture and tradition nor on convincing arguments or established institutions. The charismatic authority of the figure of Jesus is shown by the fact that this authority is experienced quite directly as helpful and saving. Only at a secondary stage is its claim conveyed with the help of traditional authorities — legitimated by scriptural evidence, for example, and integrated into a total "philosophical" interpretation of the world.

There are personal charismatic relationships in every religion. In early Christianity they move into the center of a new religion. We find a heightened personal charismatic relationship to Jesus, both soteriologically and eschatologically; for "faith" (which is the theological term for the personal charismatic relationship to Jesus) is in itself already efficacious as a salvific power. Faith is enough to make the holy accessible. Paul can define "faith" as the principle of the new religion and can distinguish Judaism from Christianity on the grounds of a different relationship between faith and works (although it is doubtful whether his definition is just toward Judaism). At the same time, the personal charismatic relationship is eschatologically heightened, for with Jesus a new world begins. By entering into a personal charismatic relationship to him, the believer has entered into this new world.

---

6. This basic structure of early Christianity is analyzed by W. Schluchter, following M. Weber (see n. 5 above); J. H. Schütz, "Charisma and Social Reality in Primitive Christianity," *JR* 54 (1974): 51–70; B. Holmberg, *Paul and Power: The Structure of Authority in the Primitive Church as Reflected in the Pauline Epistles,* CB.NT 11 (Lund, 1978); R. Bendix, "Umbildungen des persönlichen Charismas: Eine Anwendung von Max Webers Charismabegriff auf das Frühchristentum," in *Max Webers Sicht des antiken Christentums,* ed. W. Schluchter, 404–43.

B. *The Potential of the Early Christian Movement*
for Innovation and Conflict

In traditional societies, personal charisma is the essential force leading to social innovation. If the traditional way of living is hallowed by religion and origins, and if every deviation from it can be suspected of being rebellion against God and the gods, only a charismatic can lend legitimacy to renewed patterns of living — someone, that is, who without the support of recognized authorities can make people believe that through him a divine power is acting in a benevolent, helpful way. If the personal charismatic relationship actually becomes the basic structure of a religion, if it leads people to expect that God's spirit can be efficacious in everyone, independent of hard and fast roles, then a general readiness for individually mediated reawakenings can develop.

The innovatory power of early Christianity was now intensified because the personal charismatic relationship to Jesus was closely bound up with two patterns of behavior, both of which exhibit the utmost preparedness for conflict with society and with existing ways of life. These two patterns of behavior are conversion and martyrdom.

Conversion is more than a new orientation (or, better, retro-orientation), which turns back to traditional norms and values. The call to repent, so familiar to us from the history of Israel, becomes necessary when a traditional way of life is abandoned, although its validity remains unquestioned. A genuine alternative is not in view. There can be conversions to something new only if the norms of behavior themselves are included in the process of decision — when, that is, several ways of life compete in one and the same society, and when exclusive claims are made for them. We see the germ of a pluralistic society of this kind for the first time in the Roman-Hellenistic world. Retro-orientation to traditional norms could here be replaced by a re-orientation to new norms. This fresh orientation was linked with an abrupt breach with the world in which people had previously lived.

An existential reorientation of this kind took place in the ancient world only when people joined one of three little subcultures:[7] Judaism, certain philosophical schools, and Christianity. Any Gentile who became a Jew had to condemn what he had previously reverenced. What he had adored as deity now became for him an idol deserving of the deepest contempt. Anyone who was converted to Cynic philosophy had to change his way of life radically and had to abjure values that were socially

---

7. In the following passage I am drawing on A. D. Nock's classic study *Conversion: The Old and the New Religion from Alexander the Great to Augustine of Hippo* (Oxford: Clarendon Press, 1933).

accepted. In the same way, Christianity required a profound transformation of behavior and attitude. This was a "Judaism for non-Jews," a "philosophy for the uneducated." It required neither the observance of many practical rules of conduct, as did Judaism, nor did it make the intellectual claims of philosophy. But what it did do was to oblige people to give fresh bearings to the whole of life. And in this way it made possible that inward consistency of conduct which we otherwise encounter only in Judaism and certain philosophical schools. Through early Christianity, "conversion" became a pattern of behavior that was accessible to a broad section of ordinary, simple people.

The abandonment of traditional forms of living had to stand up to conflict. The discipleship of Jesus included preparedness for martyrdom, that is, renunciation of violence in achieving one's own purposes and a readiness to suffer violence when the world around took objection to the commitment to new values and ways of life. Sociologically, preparedness for martyrdom means independence of society's sanction system. The martyr demonstrates that he cannot be influenced, even by the physical coercion of the world around.

C. *The Power of the Early Christian Movement for Diffusion and Integration*

The personal charismatic relationship is open to everyone. All can be possessed by the spirit, irrespective of their social status. The personal commitment to Jesus which acknowledges him as a charismatic authority is independent of origin, education, and sex. It transcends social frontiers. Paul's proud assertion "Here is neither Jew nor Greek, neither slave nor free, neither male nor female" (Gal. 3:28) expresses the self-understanding of a community whose center was acceptance of a simple, personal charismatic relationship, which lends equal worth to everyone who is possessed by it.

In fact it was astonishingly early that the early Christian movement crossed the great social frontier which Paul rightly puts first: the frontier between Jews and Gentiles. Christianity began as an internal Jewish revival movement, but as early as the forties of the first century it had turned into an intercultural movement that reached out beyond Judaism and appealed to Gentiles too. This transition may perhaps have taken place step by step. According to the way the Acts of the Apostles tells the story, it was first of all Jews who were seized by the new message, a proselyte among them (Acts 6:5); Samaritans followed (8:4ff.); then one of the God-fearing (i.e., a Gentile sympathizer with Judaism, 10:1ff.); finally Gentiles themselves (11:20). Paul developed his theology as a "doctrine of justification" with the purpose of making it possible for Jews and Gentiles to live together in the Christian congregations (Gal. 2:11ff.).[8] In specific situations he gives this primarily integrative doctrine a polemical emphasis. The target can be Christian Judaists, who were once again questioning whether Jews and Gentiles could live together (see Galatians), or it can be Gentile Christians who seemed to be lending an open ear to anti-Jewish arguments (see Romans 9–11; 14–15). The integrative and intercultural character of the new movement continued to be one of its most striking features.

A second fundamental social barrier was the line dividing the classes — the line between the people at the top and people at the bottom of the ladder. In this respect too the early Christian movement went through an astonishing development. It began in up-country Palestine, as a movement of socially uprooted outsiders, but it soon penetrated to the Hellenistic towns and cities of the Mediterranean world. Here it united people belonging to the lower classes and people from the local upper class. In his "theology of poverty" the author of the Lukan double work stresses more than any other writer the "pauperism" of Christian origins. But in his Acts of the Apostles he describes frankly and without embarrassment Christianity's "social advancement."[9] First of all an Italian centurion is won for the Christian faith (Acts 10:1ff.); then the confidant of a Jewish king appears (Menaen/Menahem in Acts 13:1ff.) — even a Roman proconsul "believes" (Acts 13:4, 12). Finally, King Agrippa II himself comes to consider Christianity a serious option: "Almost thou persuadest me to be a Christian" (Acts 26:28 AV). In fact it remained an important structural characteristic of Christianity in its early years that it brought together people from different classes more closely and intensively than any other association and group in the ancient world.[10]

---

8. On the question of the social function of Pauline theology, see R. Heiligenthal, "Soziologische Implikationen der paulinischen Rechtfertigungslehre im Galaterbrief am Beispiel der 'Werke des Gesetzes,'" *Kairos* 26 (1984): 38–53.

9. His account has sociological value even if one does not view it as historical. For it is at all events evidence that at the end of the first century a Christian writer could assume that the picture of a "socially advancing" or "socially advanced" Christianity would seem plausible.

10. In the last twenty years a new consensus has formed, which corrects the "pauperism" picture of an early Christianity exclusively rooted in the lower classes. In this consensus two different stresses can be noted, however: (1) Early Christianity is assigned to the middle classes. The lower classes are viewed as the clientele who were dependent on these relatively higher social groups. (This is the view taken by E. A. Judge, for example, in "The Early Christians as a Scholastic Community," *JRH* 1 [1960]: 4–15.) (2) Early Christianity is viewed as a conglomeration of classes. Many phenomena in early Christian theological and ecclesiastical history are viewed as a response to latent tensions between a minority

The six basic axioms of the community in which the early Christian experience of the holy was socially interpreted and mastered correspond to the three fundamental marks of the early Christian community as an active group. The personal charismatic and eschatological axiom accounts for the supremacy of a simple personal relationship to Jesus, which takes precedence over all other loyalties and obligations; the conversion axiom and the axiom about the kerygma of suffering are behind the potential for innovation and conflict which allowed Christian groups to "break out" of the general social world; while the integration and change-of-position axioms are instrumental in the movement's power to cross barriers, to diffuse and integrate.

The basic axioms of the early Christian interpretative community undoubtedly had the power to create solidarity, since they made a collective interpretation of reality possible. But we can also detect an influence that runs counter to this, for the new communities assimilated the basic axioms of the early Christian faith to their own needs. These axioms were given a new topical and particular application which served to keep the group in question together and gave it stability. We continually discover that fundamental Christian convictions are stressed in such a way that they meet the needs of a specific group.

1. Personal charisma is developed into a charisma of office: charismatic authority was primarily exercised by Jesus himself, and then by all the people who were especially close to him. Personal charismatic authority was based on the relation of discipleship. Paul replaces this by the relation to the congregation: all charismatics must legitimate themselves by contributing to the building up of the congregation. All have a charisma for this purpose, only in different ways (1 Corinthians 12; Romans 12). Later, charismatic authority becomes tied to particular offices, which are filled by way of a formal procedure (through ordination), are legitimated through succession, and are sanctified through the power to administer the sacraments. Only confessors and ascetics for a long time enjoyed an authority parallel to that of the bishop but not bound to any office.

2. The eschatological axiom: the early Christians expected the coming of the new world. Entry into the community was very soon interpreted as entry into this new world. In baptism, Christians have already been raised with Christ (Col. 3:1; Eph. 2:6). Through faith and love for the brethren (i.e., love among members of the congregation) they have passed from death to life (John 5:24; 1 John 3:14).

---

coming from the (local) upper class and the lower classes. This is my own view particularly. W. A. Meeks has rightly drawn attention to this difference; see "The Social Context of Pauline Theology," *Interpretation* 36 (1982): 266–77, esp. 267.

They have already been received into the city of God (Heb. 12:22ff.). Utterances like this are not an expression of a first, elemental enthusiasm. They are secondary adaptations of eschatology to congregational reality: the congregation itself is presentative (or realized) eschatology. To belong to it already in itself means belonging to a new world.

3. The conversion axiom is a further development of the requirement for repentance made in the groups around John the Baptist and Jesus; for repentance was originally a preparation for the coming of the kingdom of God. In Jesus (unlike John) the connection between repentance and baptism is missing. But in early Christianity the two are closely connected. From being an "eschatological sacrament," baptism turned into the church's rite of initiation. According to the earliest of the Pauline epistles, it is in expectation of the eschatological judgment that Christians turn away from idols and commit themselves to the living and true God (1 Thess. 1:9f.). According to 1 Peter, to be born again (1:23) means being incorporated as a living stone into the spiritual house of the church.

4. The axiom about the kerygma of suffering found its most pregnant expression in martyrdom. Here too the development is illuminating. Paul would prefer to escape martyrdom, for the sake of the community (Phil. 1:24). Ignatius of Antioch, in contrast, seeks martyrdom, for the sake of the community. His struggle against heretics and his efforts on behalf of the monarchical episcopate are indissolubly woven into his martyrdom theology. But even earlier, 1 John interprets martyrdom as life laid down for the brethren — that is, for the community of Christ's people (1 John 3:16).

5. The integration axiom shows most clearly the restricting effect of adaptation to current situations. Whereas the Jesus tradition commands love of enemies, early Christianity shows a tendency to confine love to the inner-congregational sphere. Paul already makes a distinction: one should do good to all, but most of all to those who share the faith (Gal. 6:10). The Johannine writings then talk only about mutual love (John 13:34f.; 15:12ff.) and brotherly love (1 John 2:9 and frequently). The tremendous breadth of the love concept is now no more than an indirect echo: God loved the world — not just Christians (John 3:16). When the world hates Christians, this is fraternal hate: it is Cain's hate for Abel (1 John 3:11ff.).

6. The change-of-position axiom was originally meant to apply to all social conditions. But this can now be traced only in a few texts, above all in the Magnificat, in Luke's Gospel (2:46-55), where the text talks unequivocally about a change of position between the

mighty and the dominated, the poor and the rich. But generally speaking, the demand that the person who wishes to be first should be prepared to be last is applied to conditions of authority in the congregation.

In order to avoid misunderstanding, let me stress that parallel to the "updatings" of the fundamental early Christian axioms which were designed to meet congregational situations and needs, there are still others which reach out far beyond the congregation. The fundamental axioms also put their stamp on the mythical and cosmic utterances of early Christianity, for example. But the "updatings" and restrictions prompted by congregational life show that it was not just that the jointly interpreted world influenced the social behavior of Christians; the life of the congregations also had its effect on the interpreted world.

This brief outline of an interpretation of early Christianity from the perspective of a phenomenological or hermeneutical (i.e., *verstehende*) sociology of religion makes no claim to completeness. I wished to do no more than indicate the bare outlines of such an interpretation. Here early Christianity is viewed as an interpretative community and a community of action. The early Christian experience of the holy is socially mediated through a few basic axioms, which serve as the principles for building a new symbolic world, thus making early Christianity as interpretative community possible. This newly interpreted world corresponds to a personal charismatic conversion movement, whose potential for innovation and conflict embraces the breach with the previous world of society, and whose power of diffusion and integration offers its inhabitants a social world that is new. The interpretative community and the community of action are intimately linked. In early Christianity there is a reciprocal influence between the symbolically interpreted world and the social reality in which the inhabitants of that world lived.

2. AN INTERPRETATION OF EARLY CHRISTIANITY IN THE LIGHT OF THE INTEGRATION THEORY

Religion fulfills objective functions which are independent of the subjective intentions of religious people and may even run counter to these intentions.[11] One of the objective functions which every society has to

---

11. A "functionalist" sociology of religion in this sense finds its classic form in E. Durkheim, *The Elementary Forms of the Religious Life*, trans. from French by J. W. Swain (London: Allen & Unwin, 1915; reprint, 1954; Glencoe, Ill.: Free Press, 1947). A more recent attempt at a functionalist interpretation of early Christianity is K. Messelken,

fulfill is to integrate all its members in such a way that they become loyal members of that society. Religion can be viewed as a way of creating and preserving this loyalty.

There is no doubt that early Christianity exercised an integrative function as far as its members were concerned. But all the same, we have to differentiate; for although it offered intensified integration in small congregations, in society as a whole the integration was selective at most. Some of society's religious values were decidedly rejected by the early Christians (for example, the pagan cults and emperor worship); but at the same time shared practical rules of conduct were stressed, so that Christians could actually recommend themselves as models for the fulfillment of civil virtues (see 1 Pet. 2:13-17). An interpretation of early Christianity in the light of the integration theory will have to explain how this intensified integration in small groups could run parallel to selective integration in society as a whole.

We started with a phenomenological approach, beginning with the early Christian experience of the holy, and asked about the social groups that corresponded to this experience. We must now start from society as whole and try to fit early Christianity into its structure. Research is still in a state of flux, but we shall at least make an attempt.

Looking at society as a whole, we shall take our stand on Geza Alföldy's structural model. Like every model, it contains some simplifications, but it nevertheless brings in astonishingly many different aspects.[12]

Alföldy, for example, rightly stresses the clear-cut division between the upper and the lower classes. There was no single group that we could term "middle class," unless we were to count all the people in all the different groups who had a reasonable hope of rising to the class above them. Another characteristic is the gulf between town and country. This was not true for upper-class people, who had possessions in town and country both. But in the lower classes, the contrast between the two milieus led to a considerable difference in ways of life. A third aspect is the breakup of the lower classes into different dependent groups which were bound to the class above them through various different forms of loyalty and were unable to develop a unified class consciousness. In contrast (and fourth), the upper classes were divided into clearly distinguishable *ordines*, though here we have to distinguish between legal

---

"Zur Durchsetzung des Christentums in der Spätantike: Strukturell-funktionale Analyse eines historischen Gegenstandes," *KZSS* 29 (1977): 261–94.

12. G. Alföldy, *Römische Sozialgeschichte*, 3rd ed. (Wiesbaden, 1984), esp. the chapter entitled "Die Gesellschaftsordnung der Prinzipatszeit" (pp. 85–132). The structure diagram is to be found on p. 125 (Eng. trans. *The Social History of Rome*, trans. D. Braund and F. Pollock [London: Croom Helm; Totowa, N.J.: Barnes & Noble Books, 1985]).

status and genuine power. The "knights" (*equites*, or members of the equestrian order) and the senators were the most important source of recruitment for the imperial power elite, which had the administration of the empire in its hands. But not every knight or senator rose to the highest administrative level. Fifth, the imperial upper class must be clearly differentiated from its local equivalent. This latter group was responsible for local government in the cities of the empire and also administered the country districts which were assigned to the cities. Sixth, and finally, we must remember the special position enjoyed by the emperor's personal social clientele. To this belonged not only the *familia Caesaris* but also and above all the army, that being the essential foundation of power in the Roman military monarchy. These groups were bound to the emperor by especially close ties of loyalty and were set apart from the normal social structure. Here even "a nobody" could still be above the rest, for he had the most powerful master behind him.

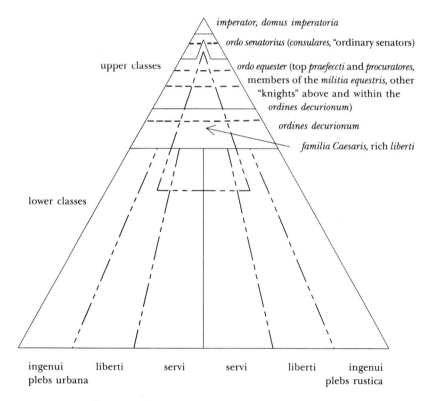

Figure 1: The Structure of Roman Society
according to Geza Alföldy

How do the early Christians fit into in this society? Scholars differ in their individual conclusions, but we can, I think, say three things, on the basis of investigations into the early Christian congregations in Corinth,[13] Rome,[14] and Carthage[15] (these being the congregations for which we have the best sources).

1. Socially, the Christian congregations were deeply rooted in the lower classes. The stereotyped reproach leveled against the first Christians was that they were socially inferior.[16] This was probably based on actual fact, even if the reproach was meant polemically, for it is in line with the way the earliest Christians saw themselves (1 Cor. 1:26ff.). The development of systems for social relief in the early congregations, the continued survival of the theology of poverty, and the slave parenesis can all be most easily explained if we place the early Christians for the most part at the bottom of the social scale.

2. It is also generally agreed that the early Christians were a long way away from the imperial upper class. People belonging to this class are at one in their unfavorable judgments about the new faith. This is true not only of the emperors, such as Nero and Domitian, who inclined toward overweaning, absolutist self-glorification. The same can be said even of such humane members of the upper class as Tacitus, Pliny the Younger, and Suetonius, to whom these emperors were deeply repugnant.[17]

3. We have come to have a more differentiated picture of the way early Christianity made its way into the local upper class. There may have been a few individual Christians among the upper-class families who were really active in local government. Pliny's "every order" (*omnis ordinis, Epistulae* 10.96) must at least include the *ordo decurionum,* or the decurions. But most Christians with a relatively high status were on the periphery of the local upper class, being people who were excluded from the communal offices because they were women, *peregrini,* or *liberti.* However, they nevertheless display certain

---

13. See W. A. Meeks, *The First Urban Christians: The Social World of the Apostle Paul* (New Haven and London: Yale University Press, 1983), as well as my own essays on the congregation in Corinth, *The Social Setting of Pauline Christianity: Essays on Corinth,* trans. J. H. Schütz (Philadelphia: Fortress Press; Edinburgh: T. & T. Clark, 1982).

14. P. Lampe, *Die stadtrömischen Christen in den ersten drei Jahrhunderten,* WUNT 2/18 (Tübingen, 1987).

15. G. Schöllgen, *Ecclesia sordida? Zur Frage der sozialen Schichtung frühchristlicher Gemeinden am Beispiel Karthagos zur Zeit Tertullians, JAC* suppl. vol. 12 (Münster, 1984).

16. J. Vogt, "Der Vorwurf der sozialen Niedrigkeit des frühen Christentum," *Gymnasium* 82 (1975): 401–11.

17. See R. L. Wilken, *The Christians As the Romans Saw Them* (New Haven and London: Yale University Press, 1984).

characteristics which allow us to assign them to the (local) upper class. W. A. Meeks has described these people on the fringe of the local upper class as people with "status inconsistency."[18]

The early Christian congregations were therefore composed of a majority from the lower classes and a minority drawn from people on the outskirts of the local upper class. This second group had considerable influence in the congregations. The decisive point now is that, according to the way they saw themselves, people belonging to the Christian congregations were as much outside the structure of society as a whole as the emperor's own social clientele. For all Christians knew that they were bound to their Master through special (personal charismatic) loyalty. They were his *familia*, his "house," his "soldiers," his "slaves" and "freedmen." These people, then — the emperor's social clientele, and the community of the exalted Lord — were groups with special loyalties who were outside the boundaries of the social structure. But this structural relationship must not be allowed to blur the fundamental difference. The one group was linked with the center of (earthly) power. The other was far removed from that center, but knew itself to be committed to the universal Lord himself. We must accordingly fit the early Christian groups into the structure of Roman society more or less as follows:

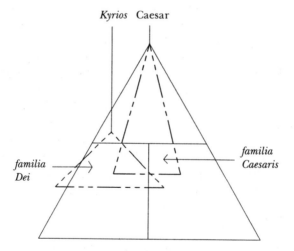

Figure 2: Early Christianity
in the Social Structure of the Ancient World

18. W. A. Meeks has gathered together his ideas about status inconsistency in "The Social Context of Pauline Theology," *Interpretation* 36 (1982): 266–77. The significance of Meeks's important contribution to the social history of early Christianity is that he was the first to construct a comprehensive synthesis, which brings together many themes of sociological research.

If we fit the early Christians into society as a whole in this way, we can arrive in our functionalist analysis at the following working hypothesis.

In its early years, Christianity spread in those social sectors where society came up against the limits of its integrating power.[19] The three most important integrating factors were loyalty to the central authority; a unifying, supraregional upper-class culture in the town and cities; and the local community of the *polis*. At the time of the principate these integrating factors were able to hold together an astonishingly stable society. But even in this society there were small groups who no doubt sensed the need for new forms of integration, but who went their own way. And among these groups were the early Christian congregations.

A. *Early Christianity and Ties of Personal Loyalty as a Factor in Social Integration*

The Roman Empire was not a homogeneous whole. Since it owed its existence to imperialist wars, it had first to grow together into a unity.[20] The principate became the essential integrating factor, for it neutralized the power struggles in the Roman aristocracy which had plunged the republic into a profound crisis. The ancient aristocracy was bound to the emperor through a judicious system that combined some degree of "power sharing" with controls. At the same time the central government succeeded almost everywhere in gaining the support of the local upper classes, whether by founding and conferring privileges on cities with a unified Roman-Hellenistic culture, whether by securing property and wealth through the *pax romana*. Finally, the army was directly bound to the emperor, for it was to the emperor that the officers owed their careers. So it would be true to say that members of the aristocratic, imperial civil service, people in local government, and members of the army all had a chance to experience directly the "positive" results of the principate. In these groups a new, nonregional loyalty grew up that

---

19. Messelken similarly maintains the thesis "that the oppositional spread of Christianity suggests a profound structural weakness in the Roman Empire. To reduce it to a general formula, the problem can be described as the permanently excessive demand made on the Roman-Latin ethic, which was now compelled to hold together an empire which had been gathered together by conquest in favorable circumstances and with the help of a considerable portion of good fortune" ("Strukturell-funktionale Analyse," 266).

20. For this consolidation of the empire, see, as well as G. Alföldy's account (*Social History of Rome*), J. Bleicken, *Verfassungs- und Sozialgeschichte des Römischen Kaiserreiches*, 2 vols., 2nd ed. (Paderborn, 1981).

extended to the whole empire; and the symbolic expression of this loyalty was the emperor cult.[21]

The ordinary country people clung to their ancient local loyalties. But the towns and cities were woven into a supraregional network of communication. It was they that upheld "the empire." Here there could be groups that sensed the need for a new more-than-regional loyalty but that did not find loyalty to the emperor enough — not least because they were not in a position to feel its "beneficial" effects in the same way as the categories mentioned above. We have to look for these groups in the lower urban classes and among people on the outskirts of the local upper class who were not involved in the administration of the towns and cities. But it was in these very groups that Christianity spread, for with its personal charismatic bond with the *kyrios,* it offered a new, overriding, universal loyalty which gave to all men and women a value independent of social status — irrespective, that is, of local origin, ethnic affiliation, and social status.

It is obvious that the bond with the emperor and the bond with the *kyrios* Jesus Christ have some structural similarities. Early Christian Christology used the same titles of sovereignty as the emperor cult: *kyrios,* Son of God, *sōtēr* (savior). In both we encounter a comparable soteriology. "Joyful message" (εὐαγγέλιον) is a technical term in both the early Christian proclamation and in the emperor cult (only in the latter the phrase was "joyful messages," in the plural). The promise of peace is linked with both the emperor and Christ, even if the peace which Christ gives is not the peace which the world gives (John 14:27). The coming of the *kyrios,* like the coming of the *princeps,* is a universal turning point — a turn for the better (see the Priene inscription).[22] Even the ecclesiology shows a structural kinship, with its "sense of empire": just as the emperor is the head who integrates the members of the *imperium romanum* — that is, the provinces — (Curtius 10.9), so the exalted *kyrios* integrates Jews and Gentiles into a worldwide community (Eph. 2:11ff.). These structural analogies do not permit us to make any genealogical derivations tracing Christian convictions back to the emperor cult. They are simply evidence that in the Roman Empire new supraregional loyalties created a related form of expression and could in some sense compete with one another.

---

21. The emperor cult was also sustained by, among others, the "Augustales," associations of rich freedmen devoted to the cult of the emperor. Having now successfully climbed the social tree, they had particularly good cause to identify themselves with the existing order and its guarantors. They are evidence that mobility and a need for supraregional loyalty go together.

22. Reproduced in *Griechische Inschriften,* ed. G. Pfohl (Munich, 1965), no. 118.

But competing claims presuppose that comparable needs and functions are fulfilled.

Our presumption is therefore this: Where a need was felt for some new overriding loyalty, while the binding social and religious power of the principate declined, Christianity had a chance. It offered an alternative integration which remained aloof from the integrating factors dominant in Roman society.

A. *Early Christianity and Supraregional Communication as a Socially Integrating Factor*

The Roman Empire grew together through supraregional communications, supported by a unified administration, a centralized legal system, two generally spoken languages (Latin and Greek), and a network of roads and cities. The local upper classes were gradually romanized or hellenized and shared the same culture. No corresponding centralized culture developed in the humbler classes — with two exceptions: among Jews and among Christians.

The Jewish Diaspora was particularly extensive in the eastern parts of the Roman Empire. It was held together not only by a common faith but by pilgrimages to the Temple, and by the annual Temple tax. The book of Acts presupposes as a matter of course that there was communication between the different regions: Jews in Rome corresponded with Jews in Judea (Acts 28:21); the Jews in Thessalonica knew that there were Christians in other places too (17:6). Christians maintained this supraregional communication network on a new basis. The early Christians saw themselves as the Diaspora of the heavenly *polis* (city, or city-state). Links were forged through constant journeys. Hospitality was highly esteemed (see the Aberkios inscription, which dates from the end of the second century).[23] The letter is a way in which people who are separated can communicate — and the letter became the most important early Christian literary form, apart from the Gospels. Here again, as a community overriding regional boundaries, Christianity was a "Judaism for non-Jews."

The new supraregional community of Christians therefore vied on the one hand with an "ecumenical" upper-class culture — ecumenical in the true sense of the word — inasmuch as it made interregional communication possible for the lower classes too. On the other hand it

---

23. See H. Strathmann and T. Klauser, article "Aberkios" in RAC 1 (1950), cols. 12–18; the inscription is also reproduced there.

was a challenge to the Jewish Diaspora, since it was open to Jews and Gentiles both.

This brings us once again to a sector of Roman society where that society came up against the limits of its integrative power. Impressive though Roman-Hellenistic culture was, it did not bring about the integration of the Jews. On the contrary, a whole series of revolts and wars between Romans and Jews is an obvious sign that as far as Jews were concerned, the *pax romana* was a failure. We need think only of the revolt after Herod's death (4 B.C.E.), the crisis under Caligula, which almost led to war (40 C.E.), and the three great revolts of 66–70, 115–117, and 132–136, which were the only major wars fought within the empire. It is true that there were revolts in every newly conquered province, but this series of wars is quite untypical. A. Heuss is quite right when he writes:

> The peace of the Roman Empire, internally accomplished with positively "ideal" completeness, turned into bloodiest conflict where the Roman state's relations to the Jews were concerned. The Jewish problem is the only real blot on the shining background to the scenery of the imperial era.... Cautious direction was replaced by conflicts of ruthless brutality.[24]

Christianity grew up in the field of tension between Jews and Gentiles — that is to say, at precisely the point where Roman society was convulsed by wars. An early Christian writer proudly maintains that among Christians the traditional enmity between Jews and Gentiles had been overcome (Eph. 2:16), an enmity that he traces back to divisive commandments (2:15). And it is in fact true that early Christianity really can be seen as a new attempt by Judaism at acculturation into its environment. This attempt was characterized by the renunciation of some rules of conduct that cut it off from the world around (especially circumcision and a number of dietary injunctions). This revision of traditional Judaism was justified by an interpretation of the Torah which presented it as a promise that had now been fulfilled: since the coming of Jesus, everyone — through a personal charismatic bond with him — can enter into that relationship to the one and only God which had hitherto been reserved for Jews. This attempt at acculturation too is not an assimilation. On the contrary. Early Christianity, like Judaism, remained a monotheistic heresy in a polytheistic world. This was a "selective acculturation."

As an attempt at acculturation of the Judaism which had been forcibly integrated into the Roman Empire, Christianity was unsuccessful. It

---

24. A. Heuss, *Römische Geschichte,* 3rd ed. (Brunswick, 1971), 387.

spread outside Judaism rather than within it. Yet for all that, structurally it bears the impress of Judaism, for this was a way of life evolved by a subjugated people, in which the many subject nations and groups in the Roman Empire could find themselves. At the center of this world of conviction was faith in the crucified Messiah who, in spite of his execution by the Romans, had risen to be Lord of the universe. What had been excluded from power in this society had here become the subject of hope for a new world. Faith in the crucified *kyrios,* who was above all other lords, offered a new way of life to all the peoples and groups in the Roman Empire who were far removed from the dominating culture of the upper classes.

The alliance between the imperial and the local upper classes created a nonregional, overriding loyalty, oriented toward society as a whole. But we must remember that this alliance was always at the same time an alliance against possible unrest among the lower classes, intended to secure against them the privileges, possessions, and wealth of people higher up the scale. Ideological attempts to cover up these interwoven interests are never completely successful. There were enough groups whose situation found expression in a religion which was remote from the ruling upper class and was yet simultaneously integrated into a new, supraregional community. The parallelism between intensive integration in small groups and selective integration in society as a whole corresponded to this situation. And this parallelism is characteristic of early Christianity.

C. Early Christianity and the Community of the Polis as a Social Integration Factor

The Roman Empire was a general structure overriding many regional structures. It succeeded in linking the central government of a military monarchy with elements of decentralized self-government at local level. The main function of the local upper classes in the towns and cities was to guarantee harmony and order in their particular areas. For Plutarch, this is the sole political function of the cities, which had otherwise lost all their powers (Plutarch *Moralia* 824 c–e). In other words, the cities had above all the task of preventing conflicts—and class conflicts especially.

The *polis,* city or city-state in the classic sense of the term, succeeded in integrating its inhabitants on the basis of equal rights—in principle. It is important to say "in principle," because in actual fact large sections of the population did not have equal rights at all—neither women, nor *peregrini,* nor slaves; and this often meant the greater part of the population. But in the cities of the Roman Empire, the notion of citizens with equal rights became less and less plausible.[25] The differing status of citizens in society as a whole overrode the equal rights of citizens in a city, for a Roman citizen or "knight" was above the rest. On the other hand, the rising prosperity of the cities meant that more and more people made their way into the periphery of the local upper class, without belonging to the old established families at the city's political center.

Early Christianity can be interpreted as a process of adaptation to these changed circumstances. On the one hand it extended equality to everyone in principle. In Gal. 3:28, Paul talks about the equal rights of Jews, slaves, and women. They are all free and belong to the heavenly "city." In naming these people he is picking out precisely the groups who had hitherto been excluded from the notion of equal citizens in a *polis:* Jews in the Hellenistic cities were *peregrini,* while slaves and women suffered equally from discrimination.

On the other hand, the early Christian parenesis takes the de facto inequality into account. The "compassion ethic" was widespread in the Orient, and Christianity carried a variant of this ethic into the sphere of the Hellenistic cities.[26] This compassion ethic proceeds in principle from the factual inequality of human beings. But for that very reason it insists on the obligation of the strong to take special thought for the weak. Hellenistic "philanthropy" was benevolence toward people in the same position and was practiced in expectation of a return. Luke, on the other hand, demands that we do good to those who are far beneath us and that we should renounce the expectation of any reciprocity. He draws a distinct line between this and Hellenistic philanthropy (Luke 14:12ff.). But he modifies the oriental compassion ethic as well. Those who have the lowest place are to take the place of those who are equal. The invitation to "the supper" (which is in itself a social symbol of equal treatment) becomes the token of all good deeds.

Social changes in the *polis* required newer forms of solidarity, superseding the equality notion in its traditional form. This had meant that in public distributions everyone was in principle treated alike, even if needs varied, while anyone who was not a citizen went away empty-handed. The new pattern of solidarity extended the idea of equality

---

25. For the changes in the *polis,* see F. Millar, *Das Römische Reich und seine Nachbarn,* Fischer Weltgeschichte 8 (Frankfurt, 1966), 85–105.

26. H. Bolkestein's book *Wohltätigkeit und Armenpflege im vorchristlichen Altertum* (Utrecht, 1939; reprint, Groningen, 1967) in my view correctly associates the change in social ethics during the period of the Roman principate with a sociological change in the *polis,* even if he does not, as I believe, do full justice to the importance of Judaism and Christianity in bringing about this change, since he sees in them only the spread of a general ancient oriental ethic of compassion.

to everyone and gave the needy and the weak a special claim. Linking up with oriental and Jewish traditions, early Christian groups spread this new "help" ethic in the cities of Roman society.

To sum up: early Christianity, at once rivaling and dissociating itself from the ruling upper classes, offered intensive integration in small groups and selective integration in society as a whole. The dissociation from the ruling upper-class culture especially made possible the development of new forms of social commitment: a personal charismatic bond with the *kyrios*, which surpassed all other loyalties, an ecumenical community (that is, one which transcended cultural limits and local ties), and a new behavior pattern based on human solidarity. Here early Christianity is largely a Judaism that had been made accessible to non-Jews too. It matched up to certain objective tasks which Roman society had to solve: the creation of a supraregional loyalty and the development of new forms of solidarity. And it had an opportunity to spread wherever competing solutions offered by the ruling upper class lost their plausibility.

3. AN INTERPRETATION OF EARLY CHRISTIANITY IN THE LIGHT OF THE CONFLICT THEORY

Every society is marked by conflicts, and not only at the points where they become manifest. On the contrary, it is precisely institutions that seem to us to guarantee the stability of a society which are often "frozen conflicts." The principate originated in the struggle for power between rival aristocratic groups; the institutions of the *polis* grew up out of the class conflict between aristocracy and the common people in the cities. Conflicts, both manifest and latent, show that history is a struggle about the distribution of chances in life—which means the distribution of power, property, and education. All distribution struggles go hand in hand with legitimation struggles, which up to modern times assumed religious forms, although here religion can be both a legitimation of repression and a protest against it.[27]

Who is the determining subject of the distribution struggles in history? This is a matter of dispute. Marxist theories of society are inclined to interpret all conflicts as being ultimately class conflicts. But for a sociological conflict theory, it is sufficient to assume that the available chances in life are scarce, and therefore contested. The agents of this conflict

---

27. The classic form of a sociology of religion based on the conflict theory is the Marxist criticism of religion; see *K. Marx and F. Engels on Religion* (Moscow, 1956).

can be peoples and countries, upper and lower classes; but they can also be rival groups within the same class.

The function of conflicts is disputed too. They can be interpreted in part as a function of the existing society (i.e., as a contribution to the maintainance of that society); for through conflicts a "balance of power" is established, hierarchies and privileges are determined, and common values elicited. At the same time, however, we must always reckon with the fact that within the existing society conflicts are dysfunctional and at best point to a future society in which these conflicts will perhaps prove to be soluble. Some conflicts reveal only a society's deadlocks and inner contradictions—but not its hidden stability.

If we view early Christianity as expression of a legitimation struggle in the conflict for chances in life, we can discover two different "functions" (though it should by now be clear from what we have said that this does not necessarily mean contributing to the stabilization of society as it exists). On the one hand, early Christianity was a "revolution of values" through which groups outside the ruling upper classes acquired chances in life—patterns of behavior and experience—which had not previously been available to them. On the other hand, there are unmistakable signs of repression. An almost violent effort was made to repress any consequences of the new values which would have called in question the ability of the early Christian groups to survive in the society of the time. Paradoxically enough, "revolutionary" and "repressive" tendencies can be found in close proximity to each other; the acquisition of upper-class values (which meant a value revolution) released expectations that were repressed, and often survive only in the form of a utopian hope.[28]

A. *Early Christianity as a Revolution of Values with a Selective Preparedness for Conflict*

We have seen that in competition with the supraregional upper-class culture, early Christianity developed an ecumenical "alternative culture" that appealed to many humble people but could also attract others who were on the outskirts of the upper classes. The very fact of a supraregional community in the lower classes is a "downward transfer of upper-class values"; for otherwise, to live in an supraregional network of relations

---

28. The "millenarian" interpretation of early Christianity has clearly seen this revolution of values in the movement's beginnings and has in my view rightly connected this with a conflict between a native (oriental) culture and the advancing Roman-Hellenistic upper-class culture; see J. G. Gager, *Kingdom and Community: The Social World of Early Christianity* (Englewood Cliffs, N.J.: Prentice-Hall, 1975).

and solidarities was a private preserve of the upper classes. But we can find a comparable "downward transfer" elsewhere too.

In the Jesus tradition, "sovereign" ideals are transferred to ordinary people in some passages: the "peacemeakers" are called blessed (Matt. 5:9). Like the rulers of antiquity, they are to be called "sons of God." In the commandment about loving enemies, the *clementia* of the sovereign is required of everyone—even the people who are persecuted (Matt. 5:44ff.). But above all, in Christianity an ordinary person—a carpenter's son—himself assumes the role of the king to whom all power belongs. Christians are his "household," his "body," his "kingdom." They participate in his power and therefore form a community which is as universally organized as the worldwide power of their ruler.

Property makes accessible ways of behavior that are linked with considerable social prestige. Above all, it permits *liberalitas,* which is shown in endowments and donations for the community of the *polis,* and to which numerous inscriptions testify. Christianity now brings into being a community in which it is not only the rich who have the chance for "open-handedness" of this kind. Here the "open-handedness" of the poor widow (Mark 12:41-44) is more highly esteemed than the liberality of the rich. And it is quite consistent when in early Christianity the appeal to the rich to share their property is put side by side with an appeal that makes an ascetic claim on the labor of ordinary people: the appeal to work in order to have something to give away (cf. Acts 20:34-35; Eph. 4:28; indirectly also 2 Thess. 3:7-13), or even to fast so as to be able to put what has been saved at the disposal of other people (Hermas *Similitudes* 5.3.7; Aristides *Apology* 15.7).

Jesus Sirach belonged to the upper class in Palestine, and he denies wisdom to craftsmen and farmers. Wisdom requires leisure (Ecclus. 39:24ff.). But in the Jesus tradition wisdom's call to learn is extended particularly to "all who labor and are heavy laden" (Matt. 11:28-30). Paul assigns the wisdom of God, which the world does not understand, to the lower classes, who do not count for anything in the world (1 Cor. 1:26ff.). Indeed he makes the point even more strongly: the rulers of this world have not only misjudged this wisdom; they have actually fought against it (1 Cor. 2:6ff.). But in the community of Christians it is available to everyone.

In the distribution struggle about chances for living, the early Christian faith takes up an unambiguous position. We find here the attempt to win power for the powerless, possessions for people who possess nothing, wisdom for the uneducated—even though power, possessions, and education no longer represent what they represent "in the world." They are transformed. But they retain their function in one respect:

power, possessions, and education confer status. It is this assignment of status to all the people who have hitherto taken a back seat in society that is characteristic of early Christianity. In the Jesus tradition the rule of God is positively linked with groups who are socially under-privileged — the poor, the sick, children, and foreigners. The personal charismatic relationship to Jesus confers on everyone a status that is independent of society: Jews, slaves, and women have the same value as everyone else (Gal. 3:28). This assignment of a positive status to everyone in the early Christian proclamation could give ordinary, simple people an "aristocratic" sense of their own value and dignity. They felt themselves to be witnesses of the decisive turn of the age (Matt. 13:16ff.). They saw themselves as "a chosen race, a royal priesthood, a holy nation, God's own people" (1 Pet. 2:9).

Against this background, we may interpret the conflict with the world around in the following way. In withstanding the dissident minority of Christians, Roman society was withstanding the potential elite. A group that was deeply rooted in the lower classes had developed attitudes and values which might be acceptable among a self-confident aristocracy, but which among very ordinary people were bound to be considered ludicrous or outrageous. A closer analysis of this conflict shows that it had three different levels. First, nonconformist patterns of behavior give rise to conflict. Second, they become objectionable when they are exclusively interpreted. But the third factor was the decisive one: the demonstratively confessional decision in favor of a dissident way of life.

The occasion for conflict was provided by specific, deviant patterns of behavior. We find these in three sectors: in religion, in politics, and in the family.[29]

1. Christians (and Jews) refused to participate in the official cults. They stood apart from general religious festivals, neither offering sacrifices nor decorating their houses. They even refused to participate in the emperor's loyalty cult. They rejected occupations that were linked with idolatry, and they avoided eating meat from ritually slaughtered animals.

2. Christians (and Jews) stood aloof from public life. Political offices were problematical for them, since these involved contact with idolatry. For Christians there was the additional reason that govern-ment power was linked with physical force. Christians were not sup-posed to kill — neither, at the highest level, to carry out the *ius gladii*

29. A good survey may be found in W. Schäfke, *Frühchristlicher Widerstand*, *ANRW* II, 23, 1 (Berlin and New York, 1979), 460–723.

nor to inflict death as ordinary soldiers. But for all that, there were Christian soldiers as early as the second century.

3. In family life much was standard behavior among Christians (and Jews) which elsewhere was an ideal. The exposure of babies and abortion were rejected. Marital fidelity was required, heterosexuality enjoined. In addition, Christians rejected divorce, and placed great stress on the control of sexuality. Asceticism as well as monogamy was viewed as a positive way of living.

Yet all these deviant patterns of behavior do not explain the extent of the conflict. One can easily present the first Christians as peaceful, conventionally "well-adjusted citizens"— indeed they themselves considered it important to fulfill the civil virtues in a model way.[30] The decisive thing was the interpretation that Christians gave to their own dissident behavior. It was loyalty to a "heavenly *polis*," of which Christians were citizens, and which in the case of conflict had the right to require the life of its citizens in just the same way as the earthly *polis*. On earth (that is, in existing society) Christians were essentially "strangers," *peregrini*. The tie with their true home was stronger than any other tie. It was this that made compromises so difficult in cases of conflict. It was only when they were given an elitist interpretation that dissident Christian patterns of behavior became objectionable to the world around. But even this does not explain everything.

The problem is that Jews too followed deviant patterns of behavior in religion, politics, and the family. Christians and Jews had much in common. It was no wonder that they came up against the same prejudices, being reproached with atheism, ritual murder, and the donkey cult.[31] But why were Jews more readily accepted than Christians? The answer is obvious. Jews as a dissident minority were following the laws and traditions of their fathers. So in spite of fundamental disagreement with the surrounding world, they were actually endorsing a shared value that the whole of society accepted: faithfulness toward the traditions that had been handed down. It was generally agreed that the gods should be worshiped as they had been worshiped from time immemorial. The Jews only got into difficulties when they won over other people to their way of life. What was objectionable was not being a Jew but conversion to Judaism. Anyone who became a Jew was giving up the religion of his fathers. But among Christians this was not merely the exception. It was an actual principle. One became a Christian not

---

30. This is the impressive way R. M. Grant describes the matter in *Early Christianity and Society* (New York: Harper & Row; London: Collins, 1977).

31. See W. Schäfke, *Widerstand*, 579ff.

through birth but through conversion. Christians became dissidents not because of origin and tradition but because of a personal decision. Christianity was a way of life constituted by decision, a way of life that made an exclusive claim for itself and that appealed for the assent of all. That is why, when Christians were put on trial, the decisive accusation was not the mere fact of being a Christian, or of having been one. That was in itself not punishable. The decisive point was that because of a newly performed act of personal confession a person refused to conform to the religious rite signifying loyalty to the emperor. What was scandalous was dissent on the grounds of a decision. Even favorably disposed Roman officials found this incomprehensible.

B. *Early Christianity as Repressive Adaptation with a Selective Outbidding of the General Consensus*

Selective integration in society as a whole and selective readiness for conflict with that society are two facets of the same thing. Just because of the demonstrative confessional dissent which cut Christianity off from the world around, it sought for this concurrence on the level of practical behavior—at points where neither idolatry nor the shedding of blood was involved. We might talk about an "adaptation" of early Christianity to the world around, but that would be to lay insufficient stress on one decisive feature: the claim to put shared values and rules of conduct into practice in a more exemplary way than the rest of the world. We find a selective outbidding of the general consensus: Christians are not merely good citizens; they are "better" citizens. What is so astonishing is that we can find both an extremity of disagreement and an outbidding of the consensus in one and the same sector. Let me illustrate this from attitudes to the state, to slaves, and to women. We find glaring contradictions here.[32]

Christians withdrew from the state its direct religious legitimation by refusing to conform to the emperor cult; yet at the same time they offered it an unreserved ethical legitimation, as guardian of "the good" (Rom. 13:1ff.). It is true that in Romans 13 Paul names implicit criteria that would make it possible to criticize what the state does: subordination to God, proper regard for "good" and "evil," the bond with the

---

32. A highly illuminating account, in my view, is D. L. Balch, "Hellenization/Acculturation in 1 Peter" in *Perspectives on First Peter,* ed. C. Talbert (Macon, Ga.: Mercer University Press, 1986), 79–101. The repressive features of early Christian attitudes, especially toward slaves and women, are sharply brought out in G. E. M. de Sainte Croix, *The Class Struggle in the Ancient World,* 2nd ed. (London and Ithaca, N.Y.: Cornell University Press, 1981), 103ff., 418ff.

individual conscience. But he does not give these criteria immediate, topical force as standards for a critical judgment. He unreservedly demands obedience, and an inwardly accepted obedience at that, "also for the sake of conscience"— that is to say, out of conviction, not out of a superficial, external conformity. 1 Pet. 2:15 even goes a step further: in their attitude to the state, Christians should be a model for non-Christians and "by doing right put to silence the ignorance of foolish men."

In relation to slaves too we can detect considerable tension. On the one hand, "in Christ" there is no longer any such thing as slavery. Everyone is Christ's freedman or freedwoman. But on the other hand, efforts are made to encourage slaves to fulfill their duties even better than before. Here we find admonitions to assent inwardly to a slave's duties, especially in passages where masters are at the same time exhorted to be considerate toward their slaves (Col. 3:22ff.; Eph. 6:5ff.; *Didache* 4.11; *Barnabas* 19.7; Ignatius *Polycarp* 4.3)—above all, that is, when the relation between Christian masters and their (Christian) slaves is under consideration. When the subject under discussion is slaves in general— or, even more, slaves in non-Christian homes—the admonition to fulfill the duties enjoined and to put up with injustice is more subdued in tone (1 Tim. 6:1; Titus 2:9f.). 1 Pet. 2:18ff. definitely calls unfair treatment injustice but consoles the people concerned by saying that this injustice ought to be borne in the discipleship of Jesus—just as the whole community of his people has to put up with injustice (3:13ff.). The reason why these obvious efforts are made to encourage slaves to fulfill their duties comes out in 1 Tim. 6:1: God's name and (Christian) teaching must not be brought into disrepute. A movement that made slaves rebellious would have had no chance. But even a movement that gave slaves much greater scope in their congregations than many other groups enjoyed in society[33] could all too easily be suspected of shaking the pillars of a social order for which life without slaves was inconceivable.

We meet a comparable contradiction when we look at the role of women in early Christianity. Women are not merely declared equal in principle (Gal. 3:28). There are also still many traces in the early Christian texts showing that in Christianity's beginnings they had an importance that must not be underestimated. Monogamy, the prohibition of

---

33. F. Laub has rightly stressed the offer of a genuinely experienceable "community" as the positive contribution made by Christianity toward improving the situation of the slaves (*Die Begegnung des frühen Christentums mit der antiken Sklaverei*, SBS 107 [Stuttgart, 1982]).

divorce, and the ascetic control of sexuality were all to women's advantage. And yet with its exhortations about the subordination of women, early Christianity goes even beyond the average patriarchal consensus. There were other groups — for example, the Isis religion or Judaism — in which women had more scope than they had in the early Christian congregations.[34]

It is at the very points where early Christianity had a tense relationship to the world around that we find — to some extent as compensation — a tendency to outbid the consensus. Both nonconformity and consensus were selective. They affected different aspects. They were not mutually contradictory. Both enabled early Christianity to set itself apart from the surrounding world. When Christians maintained alternative values and rules of conduct, this dissent took the form of a confessional contradiction that even went so far as readiness for martyrdom. Where rules of conduct and values were shared with the world around, the difference took the form of an outbidding of the consensus. Christians were not merely citizens like everyone else; they were "better citizens." They were not merely slaves, but "better slaves," not simply married women and homemakers, but "better married women and homemakers." Both the readiness for dissent and the outbidding of the consensus have something elitist about them. Other people had to be excelled, both in the contradiction of general values and in the realization of these values. This had its price, for in outbidding the consensus with the world around, hopes and expectations that were alive in early Christianity were repressed — hopes and expectations that can still be traced in the early Christian texts in spite of their repression, so that they continually had a subversive effect.

We can now sum up our analysis of early Christianity from the viewpoint of the conflict theory. Early Christianity is closely woven into the conflict between the upper and lower classes. This conflict was only sometimes manifested in martyrdoms and persecutions, but it was always present. Every Christian ran the risk of being denounced to the authorities. The sociological aspect of this conflict is to be found in the fact that early Christianity was deeply rooted in the lower classes, yet at the same time claimed for itself a modified form of upper-class values and attitudes. Here the surrounding world was confronted with an "aristocratic attitude from below" which, as the expression of a personal decision, had a provocative effect. In this divergent minority the world around was fighting the potential elite. In the congregations themselves,

---

34. See B. J. Brooten, *Women Leaders in the Ancient Synagogue*, Brown Judaic Studies 36 (Chico, Calif.: Scholars Press, 1982).

the manifest dispute with the surrounding world was reproduced in the form of latent conflict; for in order to compensate for and soften disagreement with the world around, the shared consensus was at many points excelled — even at the cost of having to repress hopes and expectations that were justifiable in the light of the congregations' own values.

We have come to the end of our journey. The analyses I have put forward are attempts. They investigate early Christianity from the viewpoint of three approaches offered by the sociology of religion: phenomenologically, as a response to an experience of the holy; from the viewpoint of the integration theory, as a search for new social ties in a changing society; and in the light of the conflict theory, as an expression of social clashes that have never been "solved" in any society up to the present.

The variation in the theoretical approaches is in line with the conviction that theories are always instruments. We use them in order to discover, to describe, to order, and to portray. They are not an end in themselves. If theories make discoveries possible, we must draw on as many theories as possible in order to discover as much as possible. This is true of historical studies in particular. These continually show that there are two sides to everything. To commit ourselves to one particular theory often means seeing only one side.

The three approaches have not been arbitrarily chosen. They are complementary. Religion is a response to a "break-in of the holy." It is the source of social impulses leading to communities of interpretation and action. Christianity too is initially a community which, in its thinking, feeling, and acting, attempts to respond to an overwhelming experience of the holy.

But whether such religious communities have a chance to spread does not depend solely on their religious character. It depends too on whether they fulfill integrative functions in a society as a whole, or in certain sectors of it — whether, that is, they contribute to the task of strengthening social ties and duties between people, the task of giving people a home and an identity, and of protecting them in times of crisis from dropping out of the world they share with the rest of society.

Only in exceptional cases will complete congruence be achieved between religious intentions (with their social implications) and objective religious functions. Invasions of the holy are resistant toward existing societies — indeed they are often opposed to strong social trends. For this very reason they become involved in social conflicts and even themselves become an expression of social tensions, so that historically we can view them as an extension of the distribution struggle for chances in life.

Whereas the phenomenological analysis tries to illuminate the social impulses that are rooted in the early Christian religion, an analysis based on the integration theory tries to make Christianity's chances in Roman society comprehensible. The conflict-theory viewpoint, on the other hand, seeks to bring out Christianity's limitations in the face of social contradictions and inconsistencies. Whether it will ever be possible to integrate these (and other) theoretical approaches in a more comprehensive theory of social evolution may be left as an open question. The goal of our analyses is more modest. The intention was to throw light on a set of historical facts with the help of sociological reflections, and in the process to evoke sensibility for the values and fundamental axioms of the first Christians. These are values that point beyond the framework of past (and present) society. But whether to commit oneself to these values, and how, is a decision that no amount of scientific analysis can ever circumvent.

Index

◆

Ancient Sources

Index

Modern Authors